INTERVIEWING
IN SOCIAL RESEARCH

INTERVIEWING
IN SOCIAL RESEARCH

By

HERBERT H. HYMAN

with

WILLIAM J. COBB

JACOB J. FELDMAN

CLYDE W. HART

CHARLES HERBERT STEMBER

Foreword by

SAMUEL A. STOUFFER

THE UNIVERSITY OF CHICAGO PRESS

CHICAGO & LONDON

A Research Project of the
NATIONAL OPINION RESEARCH CENTER
Clyde W. Hart, *Director*

Library of Congress Catalog Card Number: 54-11209

The University of Chicago Press, Chicago & London
The University of Toronto Press, Toronto 5, Canada

Foreword

What people say as well as what people do are woven into the fabric of history.

In the last three decades there has been a technological revolution in the recording of the spoken opinions of representative samples of entire populations. Historians, so many of whom are humanists with an aversion to tools like statistical devices for sampling or like IBM punched cards for analysis, have been slow, indeed, to recognize the significance for their profession of this technological revolution.

But not so other social scientists, especially in social psychology and sociology. And not so industrial organizations, which have found that systematic sampling of opinion of management and workers, of customers, and of the general public can provide facts indispensable for policy-making.

This technological revolution has depended on many inventions. One class of inventions involves the application of mathematical principles to the selection of a sample which can reproduce the responses of a population, with a small calculable error. Another class of inventions involves the development of scales of measurement. Still another involves a host of new techniques of analysis, facilitated by the miracles performed by new electronic computing machines. A large and cumulative literature of new ideas and criticism is helping to make each of these processes more effective.

More study is needed. But there is one link in this effort, in particular, which thus far has not received as much constructively critical examination as its importance deserves. This link is the human middleman in the normal process of eliciting opinions—the interviewer. In spite of the obvious possibility that bias, conscious or unconscious, of the interviewer might cause serious bias in responses, there has been surprisingly little systematic study of the interviewer and the interviewing process itself. To help fill this gap, the present volume provides a much-needed fund of information.

The major studies which led to this book had their genesis in a combined interest, shortly after World War II, expressed by the National Research Council, on behalf of the natural sciences, and the Social Science Research Council, on behalf of the social sciences. A joint committee of the two councils was established, called the Committee on the

v

Measurement of Opinion, Attitudes, and Consumer Wants. The committee was a diverse body, comprising mathematicians, social scientists, leading practitioners of public opinion research, and representatives of important consumers of applied research—in advertising agencies, industrial establishments, and such associations as the American Standards Association and the American Society for Testing Materials. Among the first problems which this committee examined was the need for a systematic study of the interviewer and the interviewing process. The authors of the present volume were urged to undertake this study, with financial assistance provided through the vision of the Rockefeller Foundation.

The committee takes no credit for and assumes no responsibility for the conclusions of the authors, who were left completely free to publish any findings they chose, without prior review or criticism. As chairman of the committee, however, the writer of this Foreword wishes personally to commend this volume to a wide reading public.

This volume is important both in its substantive findings and in the ways it reaches them. The authors are not "mere technicians." Sophisticated in psychological and sociological theory, they have molded theory into operational propositions and have put these propositions to the test with actual field investigations and experiments.

What they say is not intended to be the last word on the subject. Standing on the shoulders of work previously done, they give us a clearer and wider vision than we have ever had before of the human element in the interviewing process. It is to be hoped that future investigators, standing in turn on the shoulders of the present authors, can, in the years ahead, extend the vista further.

For the work of ascertaining the thoughts and wishes of people, their hopes and frustrations, their attitudes and values, is becoming ever more important to the complex world in which we live.

SAMUEL A. STOUFFER

HARVARD UNIVERSITY

Preface

In 1947 the National Opinion Research Center undertook to study systematically the sources of error in research that depends upon interviewing as a method of data collection.* The purposes of the study were (1) to determine and evaluate empirically the factors that may operate within the interview to produce error in the data derived from it and (2) to test the amenability of these factors to methods of control designed to minimize their effects.

In the effort to attain these objectives, the first step was to collect or to construct a complement of hypotheses concerning the nature and mode of operation, under varying circumstances, of error-producing factors. This involved not only a thorough critical search of the speculative and research literature but also an assessment of materials in the files of research agencies and consultation with experienced research persons to discover any hunches that had arisen out of their experience. It involved, further, careful scrutiny and analysis of the interview situation through empirical observation of interviewing under both natural and experimentally contrived conditions and through clinical interviews with experienced interviewers and their respondents.

The hunches and hypotheses resulting from this first phase of the study guided all subsequent phases. A careful search was made of the research literature to discover studies which bore directly or indirectly on any of the hypotheses. The hypotheses were further tested, as circumstances permitted, by setting up quasi-experimental projects in connection with studies made primarily for other purposes, either by NORC or by some other research agency or person. Finally, hypotheses pertaining to error-producing factors that seemed to operate quite generally or with weighty effect were studied more thoroughly and definitively through specially designed experimental studies.

The present volume developed out of this program of research and is basically a report of findings. But it is more than that; it has turned out to be a treatise on interviewing as a method of inquiry in the social sciences, with special attention to sources of error and their control. It

* These studies were commissioned by the Joint Committee of the Social Science Research Council and the National Research Council on the Measurement of Opinion, Attitudes, and Consumer Wants. They were originally projected to occupy a period of two years; as it turned out, they extended over nearly six years.

begins with a documented exposition of the universal dependence of social scientists upon interviewing and an appraisal of the self-consciousness or sophistication of specialists in the various areas of social scientific study with respect to conditions affecting reliability of the method (Chap. I). It then examines, on the basis of previous research, supplemented by qualitative data developed in the course of our own studies, the nature of the interview situation and, against this descriptive background, develops plausible hypotheses about the factors that tend to produce error (Chap. II). The volume then examines successively the operation of these factors in the interviewer (Chap. III), in the respondent (Chap. IV), and in dynamic and variable relationships between interviewer and respondent under the impact of situational factors that are largely external to both of them (Chap. V). Finally, attention is given to the nature and significance of the effects produced by these factors under normal operating conditions (Chap. VI) and to various methods of measuring and reducing these effects (Chap. VII).

Throughout this work the contributions of Mr. Hyman have been pre-eminent. He directed the research and largely planned and wrote this report. But, under his guidance, the entire project has been a genuinely collaborative one. Besides serving as consultant on virtually all phases of the research and handling the statistical analysis and interpretation of results in several specific studies, Mr. Feldman prepared the original draft of Chapter VI. Mr. Stember and Mr. Cobb were also perennial consultants and collaborators on phases of the research, and they jointly prepared the original draft of Chapter IV. In addition, Mr. Stember prepared the original draft of Chapter V, and Mr. Cobb the original draft of Chapter VII.

But many persons besides those listed as author and associate authors made substantial collaborative contributions. Don Cahalan, Gordon Connelly, and Miss Anne Schuetz rendered invaluable assistance in developing the original research plans. Mr. Cahalan also, with the assistance of Hugh Parry, Helen Crossley, and other members of his staff at the University of Denver, had a large hand in planning and carrying out the Denver study of validity and interviewer variance. Paul Sheatsley's specific research contributions are only partially indicated in the text; over and above these, he advised continuously on research planning and on interpretation of research findings and read critically every research report as well as most of the text that follows. Miss Shirley Star and Eli Marks also gave cogent advice and criticism in connection with many of the problems that arose during the course of this work.

Mrs. Ruth Blumenstock Cooperstock deserves special mention here because of her indefatigable work in digesting the research literature on interviewer effect. A special note of appreciation is due also to Mrs. Michael McGarry, Mrs. Nella Siefert, and Mrs. Ada Caplow for their capable assistance in the preparation of the manuscript and in the construction of the Index.

Representatives of a large number of research agencies—academic, governmental, and commercial—not only contributed helpful ideas but also made available collections of data from their files, reshaped their own studies at times to make them serve better some need incident to our research, and occasionally participated jointly with NORC in designing and executing some quasi-experimental study. Especially helpful in this connection and in the critical reading of special research reports, as well as portions of this volume, were Daniel Katz, Herman Witkin, and Lester Guest. We are particularly indebted to Frederick F. Stephan, W. Edwards Deming, Samuel A. Stouffer, and Leland C. DeVinney for their constructive advice and assistance in connection with major aspects of the work. In the early phases of the research, also, we received many helpful suggestions from members of the Committee on the Measurement of Opinion, Attitudes, and Consumer Wants, who gave us on numerous occasions their constructive advice and sympathetic support.

Finally, we wish to acknowledge our indebtedness to the Rockefeller Foundation for its generous support of our research.

Certain precautionary statements made at appropriate points in the following pages are generally applicable to this work and should be constantly borne in mind by the reader. Research inevitably reflects the reality conditions prevailing at the time the research is done. The concepts and methods employed in any study cannot, in most instances, greatly transcend the current state of scientific knowledge and the limited research facilities, including trained personnel, currently available. The research that has been done on sources of error in the interview—our own research as well as that of others—is obviously subject to such limitations. In nearly all studies the subjects used were interviewers who were available in research agencies and in colleges and universities where research training is undertaken. Generalization of our conclusions to researchers of greater maturity and sophistication than these subjects has to be made, therefore, with due and proper caution. It would be dangerous, however, though consoling, for the mature and sophisticated interviewer to assume that he is not equally subject to the operation of the same error-producing factors affecting the varied group of interviewers covered by the studies we are here reporting. As a matter of fact, the available evidence suggests that, while the sophisticated interviewer may be less subject to variable errors of a careless sort, he is probably equally subject to certain serious biasing errors. Moreover, it seems likely that much research will continue to depend upon the co-operation of relatively large numbers of interviewers of substantially the same caliber as those used in previous studies of interviewer effect.

Of course it is not to be assumed that the way to reduce or eliminate error is simply to adapt one's research objectives and methods to what one assumes to be the present level of competence of available interviewers. That kind of accommodation could only freeze performance at its present level and continuously impoverish research. As we attempt to make clear in this report, it seems to us that there are other remedies to be employed, even within the limits imposed by prevailing reality conditions. Many of these remedies pertain more to the researcher himself than to the interviewers upon whom he must depend. Even so, there should be continued and enlightened effort, particularly in large-scale research undertakings, which involve dependence on a corps of field interviewers, to lift the level of interviewer competence.

It should be clearly borne in mind, too, that reduction or elimination of interviewer effect is only one of many considerations which the designer of a survey must take into account in defining his objectives and setting up his procedures. Obviously, one would not wish to impose restraints upon interviewers which would so impair their effectiveness as to make the interviews relatively sterile. One certainly would not forego using a type of question which, though it increased the likelihood of bias, provided the only available means of gauging, even roughly, the dimensions of a certain variable. In this area, as in sampling and all other areas, a doctrinaire attitude is to be avoided. The important considerations are, first, that the researcher make every effort consistent with his larger purposes to secure results that are valid and reliable and, second, that he know what risk of bias he is taking and recognize willingly and clearly the limitations it imposes on his endeavors. There is reason to believe that many aspects of current study design are amenable to improvement in this respect without in any way limiting efficiency in other respects.

CLYDE W. HART

TABLE OF CONTENTS

LIST OF TABLES

CHAPTER I

A Frame of Reference for the Study
of Interviewer Effect

1. THE SETTING OF THE PROBLEM

Interviewing as a method of inquiry is universal in the social sciences. The literature of anthropology is a product of the interviewing of informants. Sociologists have made wide use of the method. The writings of psychiatrists, clinicians, and psychoanalysts about man and society had their beginnings in an interviewing situation—diagnostic and therapeutic interviews with patients. The periodic censuses of the United States and other countries are monuments to the interview method, and the thousands of students making use of these historical archives, whether conscious of it or not, cannot ignore their ultimate dependence on interview data. New applied fields cutting across the classic disciplines—human relations, industrial relations, communications research, area studies—all make use of interview data. Public opinion research, as a common resource of the political scientist, public administrator, social psychologist, and historian is built upon the foundations of interviewing.

It is clear therefore that fundamental inquiry into the problem of interviewing may have wide ramifications and general value far beyond the specific context of survey research within which this study was initiated. Yet the very universality of interviewing as a method and the infinite variety of the procedures subsumed under the term create a difficulty. No single investigation—not even a score of investigations—could bear directly upon all the concrete forms and manifestations which interviewing takes. Inevitably, some of the principles to be developed, some of the quantitative findings that will be generated, and particular procedures to be recommended after examining the weight of our evidence may not be applicable to the interviewing problems of readers in particular fields. Note how contrary to our rules and experience in modern survey research the following prescription for proper social research interviewing is:[1]

The interviewer must have a very good memory. The information has to be obtained in the course of general conversation. . . . Usually the interviewer has to remember all the answers he has obtained and write them out

1

after he has returned to his own place. . . . Usually he has to talk a good deal about general topics, partly to show that he understands the conditions in the region and partly that he is interested in acquiring new knowledge. It will not do for him to make it plain that his interest is to obtain statistical information. . . . It will not do for the interviewer to ask one question after another even when the respondent has shown a willingness to talk. . . . Sometimes several questions worded differently have to be asked in order to obtain one answer, if the first or first few answers are not satisfactory. In such cases these questions . . . must not follow one after another, but other questions or general discussion should intervene in order to take the respondent off guard, or to make him understand exactly what information is wanted . . . In some cases some sort of pressure has to be exercised on the respondent. The pressure must not be so great as to make the respondent feel he is under compulsion to supply information, nor should it be so slight that he may disregard it entirely.

Yet who is to say that there are not particular conditions under which this prescription is appropriate.

The foregoing quotation is from a description by the Chinese representative on the U.N. Statistical Commission of the interviewer's task in collecting information, developed out of the difficulties of initiating statistical inquiries among the Chinese people. Lieu even commends to the interviewer such bizarre behavior, arising out of the requirements of his research situation, as the following: "In the production of polished rice, he must know the quantity that can be obtained from a picul of paddy," and "the interviewer must choose his respondents, which sometimes makes random sampling very difficult."

Inevitably, any empirical research on interviewing method can only sample a fragment of so vast an area; yet we seek findings of some generality. Even if we were to limit the area to that of public opinion interviewing within America, we would still encompass such a diversity of procedures, topics, problems, respondents, and interviewers that a single methodological inquiry would seem to be gravely inadequate. There is one solution that is available. It is that while we operate within a narrow realm in the *concrete* sense we shall focus on *fundamental* processes within the interview that transcend our specific research setting. That is why a survey specialist seeking specific and elaborate prescriptions and remedies will not find them in this report. They might be inappropriate to his own current interviewing problems; they would certainly be obsolete by 1970; and they would have little relevance to the larger social science audience. As Roethlisberger and Dickson state in their discussion of interviewing method:[2]

It is evident that the interviewing of a child, a psychoneurotic, a native of a primitive community, or the normal adult of a civilized community in-

volves different modifications in the way the interview takes place. . . .
There is always the danger for the beginner that he attach a significance to
the rules of performance that they do not have. He tends to treat them as
absolute prescriptions which should never be violated and he tends to mul-
tiply them without end . . . rules for conducting the interview are substituted for understanding.

In order for us to increase our fundamental understanding, we must
inquire, for example, into the social and psychological meaning of an
interview for the two parties involved. We shall explore some of the
cognitive and motivational processes operating within the interviewer.
We shall ask how his behavior is molded by these processes but in turn
modified by the nature of his task. We shall examine some of the reactions of the respondent when he is confronted by an interviewer.
Then, we shall elaborate on the relation of errors in the data to ongoing
processes within the humans who operate in interviewing situations of
various types. By the elaboration of data and theory about such more
general and abstract features of *any* interview, we shall hope to achieve
some degree of generality.

The concrete materials on which this study is based will, of course,
have immediate relevance to the activities of current survey agencies,
and data on the magnitude and control of error will be presented in
detail. Implicit in that presentation is the limitation that the quantitative
findings relate only to the current operations of some public opinion
agencies. But it is our hope that no such limitation will affect the larger
and more theoretical features of this report.

In presenting any detailed research report on one phenomenon, one
naturally excludes from discussion many other phenomena which may
be relevant to the problem. Thus, in concentrating on understanding
interviewer effect, we may run the danger of narrowing our vision too
much. In order that the reader should have what we would regard as
the appropriate perspective for interpreting our ultimate findings, we
shall first discuss some broader matters.

2. THE EVALUATION OF ERROR—QUANTITATIVE EVIDENCE

The present report is in the nature of a dangerous confession. Research workers using the survey method are willingly exposing themselves to criticism by reporting on a most comprehensive study and
demonstration of errors in their findings. This is dangerous, for the
natural reaction may be to damn the method summarily because of its
fallibility. It is therefore of the utmost importance to evaluate the study
and demonstration of error in a proper manner.

Let it be noted that the *demonstration* of error marks an advanced stage of a science. All scientific inquiry is subject to error, and it is far better to be aware of this, to study the sources in an attempt to reduce it, and to estimate the magnitude of such errors in our findings, than to be ignorant of the errors concealed in the data. One must not equate ignorance of error with the lack of error. The lack of demonstration of error in certain fields of inquiry often derives from the nonexistence of methodological research into the problem and merely denotes a less advanced stage of that profession.

We are here studying those errors which occur in survey research as a result of the method of personal interviewing. We shall find many instances of error, which might make the reader regard the interview procedure developed in the survey field as inferior to the interview procedures used in other types of scientific research. Yet in some of these other fields, the errors committed by interviewers may conceivably far exceed those we will demonstrate.

Social anthropology rests in great measure upon information collected through the interviewing of informants. That such interviewing is not free from unreliability is clear from occasional discrepancies between the published reports of different ethnologists who have happened to study the same society.

For example, Murdock's observations of the Tenino of central Oregon differed from earlier reports by other anthropologists.[3] Different anthropologists have offered sharply discrepant accounts of Pueblo culture despite obvious lack of independence in the observations.[4] Other more elaborate instances present themselves. The village of Tepoztlan as described by Lewis is quite different from the same village as it was described earlier by Robert Redfield. In summarizing the differences between the two studies, Lewis remarks: "The impression given by Redfield's study of Tepoztlan is that of a relatively homogeneous, isolated, smoothly functioning, and well-integrated society made up of a contented and well-adjusted people. His picture of the village has a Rousseauian quality which glosses lightly over evidence of violence, disruption, cruelty, disease, suffering and maladjustment. We are told little of poverty, economic problems, or political schisms. Throughout his study we find an emphasis upon the cooperative and unifying factors in Tepoztecan society. Our findings, on the other hand, would emphasize the underlying individualism of Tepoztecan institutions and character, the lack of cooperation, the tensions between villages within the municipio; the schisms within the village and the pervading quality of fear, envy, and distrust in inter-personal relations."[5] Despite their common experience with the same society, Fortune contradicts Margaret Mead's account of the Arapesh:

A theory has been advanced that this social culture "works, selecting one temperament, or a combination of related and congruent types, as desirable, and embodying this choice in every thread of the social fabric." According to this theory the entire Arapesh social culture has selected a maternal temperament, placid and domestic in its implications, both for men and women. The theory has been applied to the cultural analysis of Arapesh warfare, and has led to conclusions that "warfare is practically unknown among the Arapesh—the feeling towards a murderer and that towards a man who kills in battle are not essentially different—abductions of women are not unfriendly acts on the part of the next community." These conclusions we, of course, must reject on the basis of our preceding evidence.[6]

Such reports clearly demonstrate the existence of the problem. Yet one can find no single published methodological inquiry where the reliability of anthropological field-interviewing is *systematically* estimated through the *deliberate* procedure of assigning different field-workers to make parallel studies. More than this, one finds only rarely in specific studies any careful description of the procedures by which the data were obtained, which would permit some inference as to error. Thus Stavrianos examined all articles based on field research appearing in one of the professional anthropological journals over a period of fifteen months. In five of the seven studies evaluated the method used in the collection of data was not even described.[7]

This is not to say that anthropologists are unaware of the problem of interviewer effect or objectivity of data in general. As Lewis points out, restudies of the same community are hindered by practical considerations such as "limited funds for field research, the time pressure of studying tribes who were rapidly becoming extinct, the shortage of field workers."[8] Linton, Radin, and others have also stressed the problem and have suggested specific field procedures to insure scientific data.[9] Mead has alluded very recently to the need for training anthropology students "to form an estimate of their own strengths and weaknesses as observers" and has made some brief suggestions for studies of the conditions affecting errors of observation.[10] Kluckhohn in a monograph devoted to the use of the interview and other personal documents in anthropology repeatedly stresses the importance of the problem and laments the neglect of it in the past. He remarks:

The limited extent to which ethnologists have been articulate about their field techniques is astonishing to scholars in other disciplines. . . . Few interviews are printed and almost none in their entirety. Circumstances are but partially sketched. . . . The role and participation of the observer is little detailed: one is not consistently told . . . how many questions and what questions the interviewer asked, whether notes were taken in the presence of the subject and others . . . somewhat comparable interviews under somewhat standardized conditions are not presented and analyzed. . . . Particularly neglected in the past has been the responsibility of the anthropologist to report upon himself. . . . Anthropologists must realize that the "contradictions" between various personal documents from the same tribe may arise, not from different periods or different degrees of acculturation or from personal idiosyncrasies of the several informants, but from the varying approaches of the investigators.

And he urges the development of experiments on interviewer effect—

The anthropological mode must become more objective both as regards gathering and analyzing data. This will be much facilitated by a number of needful experiments. Anthropology, in general, stands on the threshold of an epoch when the coarseness and crudeness of its work requires the refinement which can only be brought by a partially experimental approach.[11]

Bartlett in the course of an interdisciplinary symposium with anthropologists and other social scientists has similarly stressed the importance of reliability of observation under field conditions and recommended the joint application of a test approach for the prediction of efficiency of observation, and an experimental approach to the factors affecting goodness of observation in complex social situations.[12] However, these suggestions in the literature have not been accompanied by empirical work on the problem. Psychiatrists have also shown a relative lack of inquiry into the quality of the data collected by psychiatric interviewing. Yet, psychiatric diagnosis rests essentially upon interviewing. Kempf remarked thirty years ago:[13]

If each important institution can be induced to give, sealed, to a central committee, its actual working system for classifying cases as dementia praecox, manic-depressive, paranoia, hysteria, and neurasthenia, illustrated by cases, the differences would probably be so varied that the whole system would have to be abandoned because the faithful assumption that symptoms are similarly applied and evaluated throughout psychiatry would be brutally discredited.

That such differences in classificatory systems would in turn lead to interviewer differences is patent, and concrete evidence will be presented later. Here again there is critical awareness of the problem, but too little accompaniment in the way of massive empirical study of error.

There is no intention to disparage the intelligence of scholars in these other disciplines by remarking on this situation. The intention is merely to set the proper framework for the reader in evaluating the data to follow. As a matter of fact, the most plausible explanation of the difference in critical attention to interviewer error would seem to lie not in any greater natural sophistication of the survey researcher, but in the differing social organization of research in the respective sciences. Psychiatrists, anthropologists, and scholars in many other disciplines traditionally work by themselves, whereas the systematic coverage of large populations and the manipulation of masses of data in survey research require the use of many scientists working co-operatively. It is this difference in the circumstances of work which affects the saliency of the problem of interviewer error and the ease of measuring it. Merton brings this interpretation forcefully to our attention in a discussion of the difference between the European scholar in the Sociology of Knowledge and the American researcher in Mass Communications. Of course, the generality of his remarks goes far beyond these two specific fields.[14]

The lone scholar is not constrained by the very structure of his work situation to deal systematically with reliability as a technical problem. It is a remote and unlikely possibility that some other scholar, off at some other place in the academic community, would independently hit upon precisely the same collection of empirical materials, utilizing the same categories, the same criteria for these categories and conducting the same intellectual operations. . . . There is, consequently, very little in the organization of the European's work situation constraining him to deal *systematically* with the tough problem of reliability of observation or reliability of analysis.

By contrast, in survey research men work in a group situation, and as Merton puts it:

With such research organization, the problem of reliability becomes so compelling that it cannot be neglected or scantily regarded. The need for reliability of observation and analysis, which, of course, exists in the field of research at large, becomes the more visible and the more insistent in the miniature confines of the research team. Different researchers at work on the same empirical materials and performing the same operations must presumably reach the same results. . . . Thus, the very structure of the immediate work group with its several and diverse collaborators reinforces the perennial concern of science, including social science, with objectivity; the interpersonal and intergroup reliability of data.

Merton's argument takes on added plausibility when we consider the fact that the few instances where we find an elaborate treatment of interviewer differences in other fields are those where the normal isolation of the individual worker has been altered in the direction of group organization of work. Thus, four of the major studies in psy-

chiatry which we shall report shortly involved many military psychiatrists screening large numbers of troops in the last war. Several of
the *Studies in Clinical Psychology* come from military settings. Under
wartime conditions, the availability of many observations by many
clinicians made salient the problem of variation in diagnosis and provided a natural opportunity to design experiments.

What makes the interview method in all fields singularly exposed to
criticism is the fact that the data collected are so *clearly* derived in an
interpersonal situation. In other methods where the same sort of indeterminacy may actually operate, the visibility of the problem may
not be so marked, and criticisms are unfairly reserved for the interview
method. Thus, experimentation with animals is the basis for much of
our knowledge in physiology and psychology. But when criticism of
such experiments occurs, it is rarely, if ever, on the ground that the
data are in part a product of the peculiar interpersonal relations between animal subject and human experimenter. Such an argument
seems too farfetched. While such sources of indeterminacy are no doubt
small in magnitude, it is not beyond the realm of possibility that "interviewer effects" do occur. Liddell, whose classic research on condition-
ing in animals extended over many years, remarks:

> Another fundamental characteristic of the method is the intimacy which
> develops during training between animal and experimenter. In the course of
> months or years this intimate relationship alters infallibly, first in the direc-
> tion of dependence and solicitation, but later toward avoidance or hostility.
> We believe that this feature of Pavlov's method differentiates the study of
> conditioned reflex action from investigations in essential physiology. In
> chronic physiological experiments of long duration the cooperation of the
> animal must be secured; but, within the *limits which the physiologist im-
> poses upon his thinking, intimacy between animal subject and investigator is
> taken for granted and does not enter into the appraisal of the results of the
> experiment.*[15]

More recently Christie has raised the issue in most general terms of
the neglect by animal experimenters of such "extra-experimental" conditions as the previous experiences of the rats used.[16] (We might well
add to this class of conditions the interpersonal relations.) He argues
and even demonstrates that these factors affect the results observed but
are rarely used as a basis for the selection of the animals or the evaluation of the findings. The indeterminacy is present, but neglected here
because it is not so patent as in the survey interview.[17]

Granted the possibility of interviewer effects on the data in all social
sciences making use of the interview, we might raise the specific issue

as to the actual occurrence and relative magnitude of interviewer effects in the survey and other fields.

While it is impossible to estimate the magnitude of error typical of these fields because of the scarcity of empirical data, it can easily be established from the few studies available that interviewer effects do occur. For example, in psychiatry we have a number of large-scale studies revealing considerable variation in the results obtained by different military psychiatrists.[18]

Thus Star presents data on the frequency of rejection for general psychiatric reasons and the specific psychiatric classification applied for a group of 107,000 recruits screened by different psychiatric examiners during the month of August, 1945, at U.S. Army Induction Centers.[19]

Since the interviewers used were not all of the highest professional training and the brief screening interview was hardly sufficient time for comprehensive examination, the results may overstate the *general* seriousness of the problem of reliability in psychiatric interviewing. Nevertheless, they demonstrate clearly that there is such a problem.

The range in proportion rejected for psychiatric reasons was "from .5% at Camp Beale, California, to 50.6% at Manchester, New Hampshire. . . . Not only was there wide variation in the psychiatric rejection rates, but also there was wide variation in the specific diagnoses given for these psychiatric rejects. While in the nation as a whole, 39.9% of all psychiatric rejects were diagnosed as psychoneurotic, the percentages varied among stations with at least 50 rejects, all the way from 2.7 to 90.2. . . . It might be argued, by way of explaining such enormous variability in diagnosis, that the statistics . . . represent a faithful picture of the actual incidence among the populations drawn into these induction stations. This argument would be easier to support if the stations *within* a given region had somewhat the same rates and if the variability within regions was much less than the variability between regions. But when Pittsburgh had 3 times the proportion of psychiatric rejects of Philadelphia, when Detroit had 3 times the proportion of Chicago, New Orleans 3 times the proportion of Dallas, and Seattle-Portland 3 times the proportion of San Francisco, it is difficult to believe that the standards were the same in all places."[20]

Similar evidence is available in the experiences of the United States Navy in World War II. Hunt and Wittson in discussing sources of error in neuro-psychiatric statistics remark:

A further source of erroneous diagnoses enters with the prevalence of local fashions or biases in diagnostic practice. A specific psychiatrist or local psychiatric unit may be predisposed toward the use of certain diagnostic categories and the neglect of others. Thus the final diagnosis in any particular instance may be a function of the diagnostic prejudices of the particular psychiatrist examining the patient rather than a direct function of the specific symptomatology present. . . . In surveying the relative incidence rate for the various neuropsychiatric disorders in numerous Naval installations, one is struck by variations which appear to be impossible for explanation in terms of a genuine variation in the nature of the samplings involved, and seem plausible only in terms of differing local diagnostic customs. One of the authors has already pointed out differences of 800% in the relative incidence of psychoneuroses in random samplings of medical surveys from various Naval hospitals. Such differences also appear if one examines Naval training station selection figures. If we look at the figures for special order discharges from training stations for the month of April, 1943, we find that only 30% of the discharges from Great Lakes were for constitutional psychopathic state, but 60% of those from Farragut fell in this category. The incidence of psychoneurosis among total discharges at Great Lakes, however, was 24% compared with 10% at Farragut. . . . Another sampling from the training stations (for the month of May, 1945) shows that at this time only 2% of the discharges from Great Lakes were for psychoneuroses, while this diagnosis was given in 60% of the discharges from San Diego. . . . It does not seem that these differences can plausibly be explained wholly in terms of genuine differences in the recruit population sampled. Diagnostic preferences must be operating to distort the real picture.[21]

An elaborate experiment conducted by the British in 1945 yields further evidence on the reliability of psychiatric interviewing.[22] The same 125 army officer candidates were examined by two different War Office Selection Boards composed of highly experienced staff. In the process, a number of different psychiatrists who were members of the selection boards conducted independent interviews lasting from twenty to sixty minutes and appraised both the general suitability of the candidate and his specific standing on fourteen to eighteen carefully defined traits. While quite high agreement was demonstrated between the *pooled* judgments of the two boards, and between certain pairs of examiners, the agreement between psychiatrists was not high. The reliability co-efficient obtained for the appraisal of general suitability was .65, and the median co-efficient for all the traits was only .47.

Another demonstration, based on a large number of observations but only on two interviewers, is available from the psychiatric services of the RAF during World War II.[23] This demonstration was based, however, on a carefully designed experiment, in which each psychiatrist assessed the general predisposition to break down and the occurrence of ten traits on the basis of the three-quarter hour interview he conducted with an equivalent half of a total group of approximately 1350 pilots. Agreement in the *general assessment* of predisposition in the sample was exceedingly high. However, the specific symptoms recorded were quite different for the two psychiatrists. Thus, for example, Psychiatrist I found 23 per cent of the pilots "under training" to show morbid fears or anxiety, while Psychiatrist II found 39 per cent of his interviewees to show such symptoms.

Studies in the civilian setting have been few, and the observations are generally limited in number. But they demonstrate the problem. Ash reports data on the reliability of diagnoses for a series of fifty-two patients examined at a psychiatric clinic connected with a government agency.[24] Independent judgments were made by three psychiatrists, and disagreement by major diagnostic categories occurred in at least one-third of the cases.

In a much larger study, Mehlman reports data on the differences in diagnoses assigned to patients in a state mental hospital.[25] Patients were allocated in an unbiased fashion to one of a series of psychiatrists for diagnosis. Significant differences among psychiatrists were demonstrated. Depending on the specific categories studied, the comparisons are based on from 597 to 1358 patients examined by from nine to sixteen different psychiatrists, making the evidence quite impressive.

Putative evidence of interviewer differences in psychiatric procedures is available from a study by Grayson and Tolman in which a group of thirty-seven clinicians gave their definitions of a series of standard terms in common use.[26] The wide variation in the definitions that different clinicians gave to such common terms as "aggression," "anxiety," "compulsive," and "defense" suggests that there would be considerable unreliability in the application of such terms to actual patients.

Data on invalidity in diagnosis following psychiatric examination, rather than the mere reliability between interviewers, is available from a study by Masserman and Carmichael of one hundred patients in which they found that "during only a year of follow-up study a major revision in the diagnosis had to be made in more than 40% of the patients.[27]

Qualitative evidence of error in psychiatric interviewing is available from one study where the actual content of the interview was electrically transcribed.[28] The authors conclude:

> Even the most proficient note-taker misses critical material. . . . Perhaps more important in the recording of psychiatric interview data is the influence of conscious and unconscious screening in the therapist himself. The incoming sensory material often is neither adequately nor completely re-

corded. The authors found by comparing memories, notes, and actual transcriptions that important material often was omitted. At times recorded interviews elicited responses of startle and surprise, as though the therapist had not previously been in the actual situation and had not previously heard the patient's and his own verbal productions. Omissions, distortions, elaborations, condensations, and other modifications of the data occur, and these all contribute to the difficulty of evaluating what really happened.

Differences between psychiatrists in the *subtle dynamics* of their interviewing behavior, differences that are possibly relevant to the variations in results reported earlier, have been demonstrated through the application of instruments previously developed to describe social interaction processes.[29] Using such instruments, Chapple found significant differences in the degree of "activity" (ratio of talk to silence) of two psychiatrists, each of whom interviewed equivalent samples of 250 patients. Similar differences were found within another sample of 40 men interviewed by two psychiatrists with respect to an index of "tempo," another formal dimension of verbal behavior.[30]

If we turn from psychiatry to the related disciplines of clinical psychology and counseling, we find a similar state of affairs. In counseling, the great concern with the actual nature of the therapeutic procedure has led to a series of studies where an accurate description of the entire content of the interview is available from electrical recordings. Seeman compares the character of the interview technique of the six counselors he used with the techniques of counselors employed in an earlier study by Snyder and demonstrates that the incidence of given types of behavior is strikingly different in two studies.[31]

Covner, by comparing the counselor's written report of interviews with an electrical transcription, demonstrates that there are large and significant omissions of content in the written record, alterations in the time sequence of remarks, and lack of precision in the notes, leading to ambiguity.[32] Such findings were conservatively stated, since the counselor was aware that a transcription was being made and wrote his report immediately following the interview. (Both these factors are absent from normal counseling interviews.)

Presumptive evidence of differences in counseling behavior is available from studies of the attitudes of counselors toward given interviewing practices. Whether these different attitudes carry over into actual behavior is, of course, unknown from such studies. McClelland and Sinaiko, for example, report that among a group of thirteen expert counselors with relatively homogeneous backgrounds there was considerable disagreement on the correctness of twenty-four of the sixty-four specific interviewing practices on which they were queried.[33]

For another evaluation of clinical interviewing involving the application of a standardized procedure, we again turn to the military situation. The work of nine different clinicians who administered approximately five hundred Rorschach tests to soldiers in the course of the Aviation Psychology Program in World War II was compared. All examiners received the same rigorous course and had the same standardized instructions to give to their subjects. While detailed data on other features of the responses are not presented, significant differences were observed in the average number of responses obtained.[34]

In a similar experiment in the civilian setting, a comparison was made of the results obtained by fifteen different examiners administering the Rorschach to a total of 633 veterans who were patients in a clinic.[35] The subjects were presumably assigned to particular examiners merely on the basis of the current work-load, and the assumption is made that initial differences in the type of patient seen by a particular examiner could not account for the findings. The examiners were a fairly homogeneous group, all having been trained in the same methodological approach on the Rorschach test. In the aggregate for all examiners, significant differences in the results were obtained for a large number of the categories used in scoring the responses. The writer notes, however, that some of these differences may be due not to the actual behavior in the interpersonal situation but to the ways in which the scoring system was later applied, since each examiner scored his own protocols.

One final study demonstrates how intractable the problem of interviewer effects can be. Three clinicians working in close co-operation with a given group of children *over a period of seven years* in the California Growth studies rated the presence of certain needs. Although there was considerable agreement in the ratings of *single* needs, there were marked differences in the degree to which each clinician found *sets* of needs co-existing in the subjects.[36]

It is clear that interviewer effect is a fundamental problem faced by all the social sciences which make use of the interview method in the collection of data. It is in no way exclusive to the survey field. But more than this, interviewer effects in all these fields have their parallel in the errors of observation and measurement or interpretation found in other sciences.[37] When we note that there are observer differences in reading chest X-ray films or in interpreting the results of laboratory tests for syphilis or in appraising the malnutrition of children from medical examinations or of physicians taking a brief medical history or in rating the state of repair of telephone poles or in categorizing short segments of observed behavior or in noting the transit of stars in a telescope, we must acknowledge the fact that interviewing is not uniquely vulnerable.[38]

Bertrand Russell's well-known and penetrating comment on animal psychology illustrates the problem:[39]

The manner in which animals learn has been much studied in recent years, with a great deal of patient observation and experimentation. . . . One may say broadly that all the animals that have been carefully observed have behaved so as to confirm the philosophy in which the observer believed before his observation began. Nay, more they have all displayed the national characteristics of the observer. Animals studied by Americans rush about frantically, with an incredible display of hustle and pep, and at last achieve the desired result by chance. Animals observed by Germans sit still and think, and at last evolve the solution out of their inner consciousness.

This brief review suggests that one basic issue is simply the magnitude of errors in the collection of data by different methods of inquiry, efficient ways of estimating their presence in any research, and the safeguards or checks upon such error. Further, it suggests that any fundamental study of interviewer effect in a given field such as survey research may make a larger contribution, since the results have relevance to the improvement of methods in many scientific fields.

3. THE EVALUATION OF ERROR—LARGER CONSIDERATIONS*

The demonstration of error in the interview must not only be weighed against the prevalence of error in other scientific methods for the collection of data. In addition, whatever crudities and disadvantages characterize the method must be weighed in relation to the gains to be derived through its employment. Some crudity may be the price willingly paid in order to obtain essential information. This practical consideration furnishes one appropriate context for the evaluation of our later findings.

Murray states this calculation eloquently in discussing how the scientist should orient his research into personality.[40] His remarks are eminently pertinent to our problem. "If he continues to hold rigidly to the scientific ideal, to cling to the hope that the results of his researches will approach in accuracy and elegance the formulations of the exact disciplines, he is doomed to failure. He will end his days in the congregation of futile men, of whom the greater number, contractedly with-

---

* Much of the material in this section has been presented in a previous publication of the project, "Interviewing as a Scientific Procedure," in D. Lerner and H. D. Lasswell, *The Policy Sciences* (Stanford: Stanford University Press, 1951), pp. 203–16.

drawn from critical issues, measure trifles with sanctimonious precision." And elsewhere in describing his choice of methods, he states: "We tried to design methods appropriate to the variables which we wished to measure; in case of doubt, choosing those that crudely revealed significant things rather than those that precisely revealed insignificant things. Nothing can be more important than an understanding of man's nature, and if the techniques of other sciences do not bring us to it, then so much the worse for them."

The interview, by definition, belongs to a class of methods which yield subjective data—that is, direct descriptions of the world of experience. The interest of many social scientists in the phenomenal world calls for such data, no matter how crude the method of collection may have to be. For example, three of the most prominent emphases in social psychology today—the emphasis on desires, goals, values, and the like by students of personality; the current interest in social perception; and emphasis on the concept of attitude—all imply subjective data. While not unique, the interview method has certain advantages for the collection of such data.

Methods exploiting other personal documents such as diaries, life histories, or letters do yield an elaborate picture of the individual's world, his desires, and his attitudes. They have many advantages.[41] However, these sources are relatively inflexible or inefficient for certain scientific problems. They may not exist for the particular population of individuals we need to study, or they may be available only for some self-selected and possibly biased subsample of that population.[42] In addition, such documents may not contain information on particular significant variables, since they are generally spontaneous in origin. It is true that even total life histories have been commissioned for a particular scientifically selected sample of individuals who were requested to cover given areas in the document, but this calls for an act of cooperation far greater than is required for many problems and greater than can be required in most instances.[43] In addition, the new applied role of the social scientist as an adjunct to policy-making requires continual fact-finding or research as events occur or are anticipated, and the interview method in conjunction with sampling is uniquely adapted to such time pressures.

The self-administered questionnaire method provides subjective reports by the respondent and has the advantages of cheapness because of the reduction of interviewer costs and the possibility of group administration, plus applicability on a systematic sampling basis. However, it has limitations which are not characteristic of the personal interview method. Most obvious is the fact that the interview permits the study of illiterates or near-illiterates for whom the written questionnaire is not applicable, and this may be an important limitation for studies involving the national population. So the Research Branch of the Army, which made the most extensive use of self-administered questionnaires, found it necessary to interview all classes of recruits with less than fourth-grade education.[44]

Secondly, since it is always possible for the respondent to read through the entire questionnaire first, or to edit earlier answers in the light of later questions, the advantages of saliency questions become dubious, and it is difficult to control the contextual effects of other questions upon a given answer.[45] Such effects have been found to be sizable.[46] In the interview situation, it is obvious that later questions can be hidden from the knowledge of the respondent and can have no effect on the results of an earlier question.

Thirdly, a variety of gains result from the fact that the interviewer, while he might be a biasing agent, might conceivably be an insightful, helpful person. Thus he may be able to make ratings of given characteristics of the respondent, he might be able to explain or amplify a given question, he might probe for clarification of an ambiguous answer or elaboration of a cryptic report, or he might be able to persuade the respondent to answer a question that he would otherwise skip. All such advantages involving the insightful and resourceful interviewer are lost in the self-administering situation where the mistakes of the respondent have a quality of finality.

A whole class of supposedly objective methods has been applied to these problems. Inferences can be drawn about the inner world of the individual from one or another item of behavior. For example, the individual's behavior may be observed under relatively natural conditions, the observations being made covertly as in studies involving eavesdropping upon conversations, or merely in an informal and unobtrusive manner as in classic participant observation. Or very molecular aspects of behavior may be measured by specialized instruments, these aspects being regarded as indicators of some intervening variable as illustrated in the use of a physiological index. Or indices of attitude may be abstracted from statistical records of past behavior or from the concrete products of past behavior, as illustrated by the analysis of voting records, expenditures or time budgets, or subscription figures, or as illustrated by content analysis of media. Such methods seek to avoid the errors created by the artificiality or nonspontaneous character of a formal interview, and to free us from dealing with purely verbal materials. All have in common an aversion to the subjective, and a reliance on inference.

While the methods have this advantage, they also have certain limitations not characteristic of the interview. Great ingenuity is required if the investigator is to find appropriate indicators of particular intervening variables, and errors may well arise in the process of making circuitous inferences about attitude from very remote behavioral indicators. Vernon states the limitation well when he remarks: "It is largely owing to the indefiniteness of the behavioral content of traits, attitudes and interests, that verbal methods have been so extensively developed."[47]

How circuitous the inference from behavior can become is easily illustrated by selecting from the literature such bizarre researches as an analysis of subscription figures to the "Nation" as an indicator of radical attitudes, or an analysis of the characterization of unmarried women in a sample of novels as an indicator of popular attitudes toward the role of women, or the measurement of sweat secretion as an indicator of the impact of advertisements.[48]

The informal observation of behavior under natural conditions is generally not a flexible method, in that the environment may simply not provide any avenue for the expression of the behavior which is relevant to the particular problem, and then a really tremendous act of inference is necessitated. To find out a person's thoughts one must sometimes ask him a question! This is axiomatic in the case of studies concerned with the past. For example, one of the most lavish governmental social research projects in recent years involved the study of the reactions of the German and Japanese populations to strategic bombing, but these investigations were not undertaken until after the end of hostilities.[49] It is obvious that the natural setting of the postwar world was not appropriate to observing the reaction to the bombing of three years earlier. Here it was necessary to reconstruct the past either through the memories of the respondent reported in the course of interviewing or through historical records.

Just as research may be oriented to a past situation which was not and cannot now be currently observed, so, too, research may be geared to a future and not yet existent situation. People's wishes, plans, desires, and anticipations about the future may be central. Here again observation at some point in time permits only bare inference as to the perspective on the future, and it is only through personal documents such as the interview that this dimension of man's thought is revealed.

For other problems, it is theoretically possible to use observational methods. If one could wait around indefinitely, the natural environment would ultimately liberate behavior relevant to a given inference. However, practical limitations preclude such lengthy procedures. As Vernon puts it: "Words are actions in miniature. Hence by the use of questions and answers we can obtain information about a vast number of actions in a short space of time, the actual observation and measurement of which would be impracticable."[50]

It should be noted, however, that observational methods were developed in a very efficient and massive form in at least two places and were found adaptable to a host and constant flux of policy problems of an attitudinal sort when handled on a continuing basis. In the United States, for a period of years, the Office of War Information operated what were known as correspondence panels.[51] A nationwide network of correspondent observers reported periodically on the concerns, remarks, attitudes, etc., of people in their communities. To give focus to the reports, these panels received periodic briefings as to what to look for in the way of relevant material. Similarly in England, Mass Observation's national panel of voluntary observers provides a wideflung network of covert observers reporting periodically to headquarters on their observations of behavior, conversation, and the like.

An observational approach to attitudes can sometimes achieve adaptability by placing the subject in a specially contrived experimental or laboratory situation in which the behavior relevant to a given inference would appear. Here one can escape the unpleasantness of dealing with mere words, and one can study many problems not amenable to observation under natural conditions. However, it should be noted that the behavior exhibited here is as much bound by the unstated conventions of the contrived situation or laboratory, and by the explicit instructions which are characteristic of all experiments on humans, as is the verbal report by the nature of the formal interview. Moreover, the ability to obtain the participation of ordinary people as experimental subjects is limited. Consequently, generalizations from such procedures may have an inadequate sampling basis.

It should also be noted that the exponents of observation under natural conditions neglect to realize that the behavior observed in real life is conditioned by a host of *unknown momentary* factors operating in the environment just as the verbal report of an individual is bound by the formal interview situation. In brief, one is always playing some role in relation to some situation—whether the situation be that of the laboratory, the arena of everyday life, or the interview—and the real issue is the kind of situation in which the attitudinal findings are liberated and the ability to relate the findings to that situation.[52]

There are many research problems which merely require data that, by definition, are objective. Consequently, there need be no recourse to interviewing. Even here the interview method has had widespread use because of certain practical advantages. The decennial censuses of the United States deal in great measure with data as objective as the presence of "inside plumbing," and such information could be collected by mere observation of the building. Yet the census enumerates such characteristics by interview. Many other interview surveys for governmental purposes have been conducted on household possessions, the state of repair of given equipment, the job record of the individual, etc. Here again theoretically the information could be collected by observation or by the examination of records. However, the facts may not exist in any set of records, or it may be less expensive and unwieldy to enumerate a whole series of such needed facts in the course of a single interview. In addition, the interview enables one to relate the given datum to other characteristics of that *same individual* which can be measured simultaneously. For example, insurance company records in the aggregate contain objective data on every health insurance policy covering any member of the population, but they do not permit one to analyze such coverage in relation to health needs and experiences, medical expenses, family income, and other significant variables. Similarly, voting records reveal the political behavior of individuals, but the ballot does not have any place for the social and psychological characteristics of the voter. Consequently, beyond a certain gross ecological level, it is impossible to analyze the correlates of such behavior merely by the employment of such sources.

All of this suggests that there is an important function which the interview method performs in the collection of subjective and even objective data which should not be forgotten in drawing conclusions from any findings on error.[53] How well the method performs this function is, of course, a legitimate question. One cannot use the argument of essentiality as an excuse for perpetuating errors and crudities that are *remediable*. If anything, the reduction of error becomes all the more crucial in the instance of a method that is widely used and essential in scientific research.

4. THE EVALUATION OF ERROR—SOME NORMATIVE CONSIDERATIONS

The evaluation of error is fraught with complications. The demonstration of error in social research interviewing should be weighed against the prevalence of error in other fields of interviewing; the appropriate starting point being that we deal with a universal problem.

The damaging effect of error in the interview should further be weighed against the fact that the method provides easy—and possibly unique—access to comprehensive data on realms of experience which are important topics for scientific study. But the complexity is further multiplied! As we seek to apply our specific findings on error to the general betterment of interviewing within social research, we must interpret the nature of error broadly. Otherwise we shall evaluate the problem badly. The very concept of error requires discussion and clarification.

If interviewer error were unitary and easy to determine, there would be no need for such discussion, but this is not the case. Error is of two major types and, in certain instances in social research, very difficult to measure. In social research, the measuring instrument is the interviewer. We use many such instruments for a large-scale survey and our aim is to insure that the instruments are reliable—that the results do not change with the accident of which particular interviewer is employed. In so far as there occurs inter-interviewer variation, different interviewers obtaining variable results when applied to the same or equivalent respondents, our over-all measurements are subject to one type of error, which it would be desirable to estimate or reduce. Moreover, in the usual survey, since interviewers are frequently assigned to different types of respondents, such variation in their behavior reduces our ability to establish functional relations between variables, leading to general laws, since uncontrolled factors present in one interview and absent in another might obscure or distort the relationships.[54]

While variation between interviewers is a very legitimate aspect of error and worthy of attention, it does not exhaust the nature of error in the interview. Whether or not interviewers differ in the results they obtain, there is also the problem of whether any or all of them obtain accurate results, results that approximate some true value.[55]

The twin goals of a reduction of inter-interviewer variation and an increase in the validity of the results must always be kept in mind. While this would seem obvious, there are circumstances that readily lead to the neglect of one component of error, and a consequent false evaluation of the total problem. Much past research into interviewer error in the social survey, and much of our own research, has been limited to inter-interviewer variations because of the relative ease of studying the problem. As indicated in Chapter VI, the number of studies of interviewer effects on validity is negligible. While upon reflection, validity seems so obvious a problem, given these partial data, there is always the danger in practice of making decisions and evaluations purely in terms of the restricted concept of error as being synonymous with inter-interviewer variation. Thus, one might well institute a certain procedure which has been shown to reduce variation among interviewers at the expense of some loss in the validity of the aggregate results. Thus, in later chapters, we discuss the reduction in inter-interviewer variation that accompanies the use of certain types of questions. However, in so far as such questions are inadequate to the revelation of certain attitudes or certain dimensions of attitude, one must balance the gain in reliability against the loss in validity in the answers of given respondents, and one would seek some compromise or optimal solution.

Evaluations oriented purely to the reliability problem also run the danger of conservatism because the standard against which any interviewer's performance is appraised is that of another *current* interviewer, or that of all *current* interviewers. Since our discipline over interviewers is bound to have some small effect, we consequently rule out as a norm any aberrant, radical forms of interviewing that are outside of our current practice. We ultimately approximate to a uniform and smoothly operating staff all engaged in the best current practice, but perhaps far from ideal practice. It is only as we have as a norm a form of interviewing that approximates close to valid results, that we become radical and experimental. It must be the neglect of this latter concept of interviewer error that accounts for the rarity of innovation. Note how bizarre Kinsey's cross-examination approach to the research interview appeared to us in social research or how recent it is that public opinion workers have begun to exploit the procedure of group-interviewing of a number of respondents. Why has no one emphasized the reverse, having the single respondent interviewed by a group of interviewers?[56] The lack of emphasis on the validity aspect of error has led to orthodoxy in procedures.

The problem of gross effects on the validity of results must be brought into context in evaluating our later findings. Our difficulty lies, however, in determining the presence of gross effect or invalidity. Certain surveys are made with the objective of eliciting from the respondents an answer which would describe accurately some factual characteristic, such as age or formal education, or some item of future or past behavior, such as voting in an election or cashing a bond. In such instances, it is easy to define a true value, and theoretically possible to obtain criterion data against which to evaluate interviewer error. However, even in such instances, the *practical* problems of obtaining such criterion data have limited the study of gross effects and led to all sorts of approximations for criteria.

But what of the problem in surveys of an opinion or attitudinal type, surveys, for example, concerned with such matters as the public's general sentiments about Russia or taxation or socialized medicine? Under such conditions, the direct estimation of gross effects is complex, since there is little or no agreement on the nature of "attitude," and consequently a criterion may neither be accepted nor even exist. In so far as the objective of such a survey was specifically defined in terms of some particular social situation within which such opinions would be expressed or acted upon, the problem would logically not be different from that of the factual survey. It is in this direction of greater specification of the situational setting of opinions that one might easily solve some of the problems of validating opinion surveys and also approximate to greater validity of interviewing procedures. One would then aim to simulate within the narrow environment of the interview the very conditions that characterize the larger situation.[57] Unfortunately, it is most rare to find a study which is so precise as to concern itself, for example, with the opinions of Negroes about discrimination, as these would be expressed in a Negro-white social setting or in the context of immediate reactions on specific Army policies in World War II. Generally, opinion surveys concern themselves with the general structure of sentiments in a given area; these sentiments being regarded as *internal* states underlying but different from behavior.[58]

How then shall we decide that our interviewers are obtaining truthful and adequate reports from respondents of their inner feelings? Apart from traditional procedures of accepting the appraisal of some judge as a criterion, we ultimately decide that certain reports are more valid representations of inner states than others, or rather we decide that descriptions given under particular conditions are bound to be more valid. In the end analysis, such decisions are predicated on some model or conception of the nature of attitudes and upon some theorizing as to the nature of the interviewing procedure under which attitudes are best revealed. Such models obviously function as criteria for evaluating the validity component of interviewing error. A moment's reflection convinces us of this fact. Why is rapport almost universally accepted as essential to a good interview, and why is the interviewer who obtains more of it regarded as better? Simply because of the assumption that people talk better in a warm, friendly atmosphere, and the additional assumption that attitudes are somehow complex and hidden and a lot of talking is essential before the attitude is elicited. Why is probing regarded as desirable in attitude research? Because of the conception of attitude as many-faceted, equivocal, subject to qualification and shading and the like, and the conclusion therefrom that a simple initial answer cannot convey the total structure.

Why do we generally regard an interviewer who obtains a great many "don't know" responses as bad? It is because of the simple assumption that people have beliefs about most everything, and the corollary view that the interviewer who does not elicit the answers must be doing something wrong.

With many such specifics, there is no problem. They would be accepted by reasonable people. Probably no one would contest the fact that the interviewer should not provide the answer himself, since the attitude we seek, whatever its real nature, is the property of the respondent. However, as a general problem, we must turn to the critical examination of such models, since they underlie the evaluation of our specific findings and affect the larger question of improvement of interviewing. While we cannot hope to establish the definitive model for attitudes or opinions, we can modify certain extreme past views in the light of reason. More particularly, we can examine whether past theorizing about the interviewing procedures most appropriate for the revelation of attitude, howsoever defined, has been adequate to the *total* problem. It will be evident upon such examination that many suggested interviewing procedures either bear little logical relationship to the validity problem or merely cope with the problem of validity to the neglect of reliability. We gain little if we adopt procedures which maximize the validity of reports from a given respondent at the expense of a great increase in inter-interviewer variation. Reliability must not be sacrificed in social research.

A proper balancing of these desiderata is essential in developing good interviewing procedure in social research. The neglect of the problem of inter-interviewer variation has been especially characteristic of developments of interviewing methodology for research purposes which originally stem from the clinical fields. There, the elements of the model having to do with the uniqueness of the individual case and the depth and complexity of mental processes, plus the traditional orientation to treatment rather than the collection of comparable research data, combine to yield the model procedure of a highly trained and insightful interviewer operating with maximum freedom who explores the respondent's attitudes through depth in a setting of great rapport. For the moment, we shall grant a gain in validity in the reports of some respondents. However, it is obvious that the absence of some form of standardization may well lead to greater inter-interviewer variation, and the neglect of this problem in certain writings makes one question the over-all wisdom of the recommendation.

Occasionally there is also a certain dogmatism about such extreme statements, which makes one pause. They seem too certain of their conception of the phenomenon under study, of the procedure that is best, and too convinced of the skill of the fieldworker. One can adopt the position that freedom gives play for the skilled worker to exercise his judgment and insight and that one should not put a Freud into a straitjacket of specific rules of procedure which would allow him to interview no more skilfully than the most mediocre worker. However, one must also keep in mind that the number of Freuds in our midst is limited, and that there is grave difficulty in determining in advance which particular interviewers should be given freedom to exercise their genius.

Such views may also go too far in emphasizing the requirement of rapport. Interviewers can be encouraged to the point of great chummi- ness with the respondent. While friendliness is fine, and rapport impor- tant, a certain degree of formality may be superior to *maximum* rapport. Where the relationship is too warm and intimate, the respondent may react excessively to the interviewer. The materials in Chapter II illus- trate this danger well.

In addition, while one must also grant that there is complexity in so- cial attitudes, certainly the truth does not always lie in the tortuous, complex, hidden process. One can go too far in postulating such a model in social research. In the deserved popularity of such conceptions, one can vulgarize them. The belief prevails too widely that the richer and deeper and lengthier the remarks of the respondent, the more likely is this to be the genuine picture of the attitude. Interviewers are encour- aged to keep probing and to question the validity of a thin answer. Cer- tainly there is much truth in this point of view, and we may miss the full complexity of a deep, tortuous attitude structure in a given respond- ent by not pursuing the answer far enough. But conversely, we may distort the situation just as much if we forget that there are some people in this world with no hidden depths and only superficial attitudes on certain issues. In such instances, repeated probing may only suggest di- mensions that were never operative in the first place. The interviewer unconsciously "salted the mine," as the confidence man used to do de- liberately!

Murray remarks on the dangers of such extreme views in discussing the proper balancing of emphasis on the manifest and the latent in personality research.[59]

A psycho-analytic case history seldom portrays the patient as an imaginable social animal. Even in describing normal people the psycho-analysts put emphasis upon the aberrant or neurotic features, because these are the things which the practice of their calling has trained them to observe. It is as if in giving an account of the United States a man wrote at length about accidents, epidemics, crime, prostitution, insurgent minorities, radical literary coteries and obscure religious sects and made no mention of established institutions: the President, Congress and the Supreme Court.

Such categoricalness about the model of the phenomenon and the model procedure, as well as an unbalanced emphasis on the validity component of the larger problem, can be illustrated in a quotation from Woodside. In suggesting what is proper interviewing procedure for research inquiries into sexual behavior and fertility problems, she states:

> *As most of us know,* while the itemized questionnaire or the doorstep interview may be adequate to obtain information on such things as—say—individual preference for radio programmes or breakfast foods, these methods are *totally unsuited* where the questions touch on involved personal and emotional reactions, *inevitably* associated with sexual and contraceptive behavior.[60]

The assumptions underlying this specific model are of the general order previously described and can be explicated from other portions of the text. The depth character of the processes is revealed in:

> There is more to it than this, when you are dealing with a subject as emotionally charged as sex. The interviewer needs to know something of people, and to have an awareness of psychological mechanisms such as ambivalence, repression, rationalization, when he encounters them not in the text-book but in the individual. . . . Though one's subject cooperates in all good faith, he or she may be unable to free themselves of the inhibitions arising from their own inner conflicts . . . or escape from giving the approved answers imposed by outer cultural standards.

The emphasis on uniqueness of the respondent, on the requirement of warmth of rapport, and on the skill of the investigator is seen in:

> Always we have to remember that they are not ciphers or anonymous "subjects," but they are human beings, each with individual personality make-up and an individual life situation. If we want them to talk to us, to reveal something more of themselves and their attitudes than appears on census sheets, we have first of all to be sincere ourselves, sincerely interested in them as persons, yet at the same time being alert to their reactions and their interview behavior. . . . We will probably only get the information

we want by allowing and even encouraging our "subject" to talk in what may seem an irrelevant manner about himself. The experienced observer sometimes picks up his most important clues from a chance remark.

As Murray implied, such *extreme* conceptualizations are bound to distort the phenomenon and reduce validity. Kinsey erred similarly, but on a limited aspect of the problem, when he started from the assumption that false reports from his respondents would tend *always* to reduce the correct estimates of sexual behavior, and not to inflate them. He then designed his interviewing methodology in this light, but in this instance, it can even be shown by analysis of his own data that the assumption is unwarranted.[61]

That the phenomenon, attitudes about sex, is *inevitably* associated with involved, emotional reactions and *totally* unsuited to the straightforward, standardized research inquiry seems questionable simply on the axiomatic ground that people differ and there are *some* people somewhere for whom simple questions under standardized conditions would be adequate. Furthermore, the empirical evidence of many past inquiries of a quantitative sort also calls into question such a view. We need only look at sexual inquiries in the United States, Puerto Rico, or England to note that relatively standardized procedures at the least cannot be *totally* unsuited to the problem. Thus Mass Observation in commenting on a survey of sex attitudes in Great Britain remarked that, "In this survey, as was the case with that on birth control, many people stopped at random in the street were eager to talk to perfect strangers who they were not likely to see again."[62]

Similarly, Finger, who conducted an inquiry into sex beliefs and practices among 138 unmarried male students via a standardized questionnaire administered under careful conditions, remarks:

> The nature of the responses at least suggests general lack of inhibition in answering. . . . The reliability figures leave little to be desired, if they can be taken at face value. . . . One is tempted to compare the figures obtained in this study with those resulting from interview studies of other populations. . . . The findings of approximately 93% masturbators checks reasonably well with Ramsey's, Kinsey's, Hamilton's, and Merill's. . . . Ramsey found 30% of 17 year-olds reporting homosexual experience, while the present study reveals 27%. Approximate agreement is found in most of the other comparable items."[63]

In addition, there seems to be an essential illogic about the argument. If emotional reactions are inevitable, does it not follow that the interviewer as well as the respondent *must* have difficulty, and that the lack of standardization might conceivably provide less control over the interviewer's difficulties?

Finally, one must note in the illustration from Woodside that the problem of reliability is completely neglected. Admittedly, she is speaking of the small-scale, qualitative inquiry; nevertheless, there is still some comparability.

It is axiomatic that no model of an extreme nature can be regarded as generally ideal. The nature of attitudes, apart from formal definition of the concept, will vary with the subject matter under study. Some will be affect laden, others not. Some will be deep and tortuous, others superficial. The same attitude will vary in its character in given cultural and sub-cultural settings. The purposes and conditions of social research are so various that we must be flexible in our conception of what is appropriate interviewing methodology. More than this, any model procedure must somehow compromise between the requirements of reliability and validity.

Apart from such logical considerations, one questions the authority of most traditional conceptions of proper interviewing procedure, when one notes the wide variation in the recommendations of different investigators on the same problem. Where there is so much disagreement, one might well be tentative in his views. The lack of consensus can be demonstrated for an earlier era from a study by Cavan.[64] She tabulated the suggestions in the literature of the twenties as to the proper interviewing procedures in gathering life history materials. Some of the results are reproduced below in Table 1, and indicate that past consensus is so poor that such conceptions in totality afford little guidance.

TABLE 1

How to Handle the Interview

(The Conceptions of Thirty-eight Different Investigators)

	No. of Times Mentioned
Control of the interview:	
Provide ample time and appearance of leisure........................	7
Interviewer should control the interview and adapt it to the particular case	6
Explain the purpose of the interview to interviewee...................	5
Make appointment with the interviewee ahead of time...............	1
Keep the interview to the main issue...............................	1
Comfort of interviewee:	
Use informal and natural manner, tact.............................	4
Avoid distractions...	2
Make interview agreeable and entertaining.........................	2
Avoid fatiguing interviewee......................................	1
Put interviewee at ease..	1

No. of Times
Mentioned

Making friendly contact, identifying oneself with the interviewee:

Open the interview with the interviewee's interests, e.g., with adolescents, vocational interest; with mothers, their children, etc. 11

Use the interviewee's language, dialect, slang 6

Refer to some common past experience or relate personal incident similar to one interviewee has related, particularly when interviewee is embarrassed or inhibited 6

Get confidence, rapport 3

Agree with interviewee whenever possible 2

Avoid urging frankness 2

Explain interview as a way of becoming acquainted or to help the interviewee 2

Intimacy needed to obtain complete statement 1

Occasional physical contact, such as touching the arm of the interviewee 1

Do something together, such as having lunch 1

Giving interviewee confidence:

Give interviewee feeling of security, "transference" in psychoanalysis . . . 2

Promise confidential use of material from the interviewee 2

Securing spontaneous response:

Make interview optional 3

Do not grill, coerce, give advice, show authority 7

Avoid antagonizing interviewee 2

Avoid direct questioning 1

Permit interviewee to "pour everything out" 1

Wait until interviewee is ready to talk 1

To secure veracity, avoid leading questions or suggestions 5

To overcome inhibitions:

Use another approach 1

Speak of experiences the interviewee might have had 1

Incentives to induce interviewee to talk:

Flatter interviewee, "his experience is unique," "only the best in his profession are being interviewed," etc. 4

Appeal to pride, vanity, through giving him a part in a research project . . 2

Appeal to interviewee's desire to help others, that his experiences will help others 2

Let interviewee feel he is leading the interview 1

Promise that no punishment will follow the interview 1

Apart from the variability that characterizes the table as a whole, the examination of specific suggestions is revealing. One notes that concrete types of behavior are recommended for the interviewer. Such recommendations are an essential for standardizing the behavior of many interviewers and thereby coping with the problem of inter-interviewer variation. Yet one senses that in specific instances, some of the suggestions are mere "common-sense" opinions, or that they are presented at *too concrete* a level of description. They are too categorical and not befitting the wide variety of situations and phenomena under research study. For example, it is not clear that "occasional physical contact" is necessarily a good means of achieving the larger goal of "friendly relations." It might well be undesirable for circumstances involving a male interviewer with a strange and reserved female respondent! Nor is it clear what ultimate end in terms of data the goal of friendly relations serves and exactly how well it serves that end.

Therefore, while concrete prescriptions serve to standardize procedure, they may suffer from too great specificity in relation to the wide variety of interview problems. Some resolution of this dilemma is required and can be found in providing concrete rules and also in providing some larger framework of principles which allows for altering the rules under given circumstances. Thus, for example, Roethlisberger and Dickson in the course of their classic investigation of industrial workers developed an elaborate interviewing method.[65] They make a significant distinction between *"rules of orientation"* and *"rules for conducting the interview."*

The rules of orientation embody a conception of the nature of attitudes plus a theory of the interview as a social situation affecting the adequate expression of attitude. These rules are intended as a general framework of principles to guide the interviewer's specific behavior. The rules of conduct, by contrast, involve very concrete suggestions for the behavior in which the interviewer should engage to elicit valid information.

By this distinction, Roethlisberger and Dickson are suggesting that the concrete behaviors or performance of the interviewer may well change with given circumstances, and that the real measure of the goodness of a procedure is its appropriateness to some larger objective. They remark:

> The rules of performance should play a secondary role to the rules of orientation. If the interviewer understands what he is doing and is in active touch with the actual situation, he has extreme latitude in what he can do. Whether or not the interviewee faces the light is not of first importance. . . . The rules of performance must address themselves to the situation.

While the general logic of the Roethlisberger approach is impeccable —a set of procedures that are concrete and yet flexible and derived from some larger conception of the phenomenon—here again one senses a slightly disproportionate emphasis in the model of attitude advanced.

While these authors caution against complete disbelief about the manifest remarks of a respondent, they, too, suggest an identity of the deeper with the more genuine. "The interviewer would not have been misled by the manifest content of the statement"; "It is necessary to treat individual responses as symptoms, rather than as realities or facts, of the personal situation which gradually is disclosed as the interview progresses"; "Most omissions that occur in an interview involve not only things about which the speaker does not wish to talk but also things which lie so implicitly in his thinking that they have not yet become conscious discriminations." This excessive emphasis upon the hidden subtleties of attitude leads them to give the interviewer great freedom to exercise his judgment with consequent danger of error.

In developing a model interviewing procedure, one must somehow balance the gains in reduction of inter-interviewer variability that come from standardization against the possible loss of validity due to the inflexibility of the procedures for the range of circumstances, the constraints placed upon the interviewer's insight, and the loss of informality. One can array various approaches in the literature along the continuum of the freedom allowed the interviewer. Depending on the position on this continuum, one notes that the validity component has presumably been maximized through the exercise of great freedom in interviewing, or that the reliability component has been maximized through standardization of procedure. One can also note whether or not *alternative* procedures are developed to treat whichever component has been neglected. Thus, Kinsey made a choice in some degree like that of Woodside.[66] He recognized that an interviewer given freedom to conduct an inquiry in his own way might well use a biased wording or order of questions, or that two interviewers might at least exercise their freedom in different ways and thus make the data noncomparable. He also realized that verbatim recording of the answers was not subject to interviewer bias in *coding*, and that subsequent coding in the office could be more standardized and would permit easy checks of reliability. Nevertheless, the interviewers were given no standard question wording or order of questions, on the grounds that the insightful, highly trained interviewer would find the unique procedure that was most suited to obtain a valid report from the particular respondent. Similarly, by coding in the field situation, the insightful interviewer could take into account minor nuances of gesture, emphasis, and the like and perhaps make a more valid (although less reliable) judgment than the office coder confronting the bare words on a page. Thus Kinsey sought greater validity at the price of a possible loss in reliability.

Yet, there was not complete neglect of the problem of inter-interviewer variation. The lack of procedural standardization was presumably compensated for by the development of long and intensive training of the small crew of interviewers, testing of them in advance of field work to determine the agreement in their coding behavior, and ultimately by the application of empirical tests of agreement in their collected data.

Hamilton's decision, although he was working in the same area of human sexual behavior represents a complete contrast with Woodside's or Kinsey's approach.[67] He recognized not only the possibility that the interviewer might use a biased wording and order of questions, but that even minor changes in inflection from interview to interview would jeopardize the comparability of the data. More than this, he believed that the distance in feet and inches between interviewer and respondent and the position of the respondent vis-à-vis the interviewer could affect the results. Consequently, each question was printed on a little card, and the interviewer merely handed it over to the respondent who was seated in a chair *roped* to the floor at an exact and unchangeable distance from the interviewer. Here we insure comparability, but the interviewer cannot make his full contribution. And it is possible that the extraordinary safeguards of reliability might well operate to make the general situation so bizarre that any gains deriving from an informal chat in a homey atmosphere are also lost.

As one contemplates these contrasted studies, it might appear as if one were driven to the unpleasant choice between interview data that are completely reliable but also completely sterile as contrasted with interview data potentially full of validity but with a high order of unreliability. Actually, the choice is not this difficult. Under certain circumstances, it is possible to have maximally flexible procedures and to approximate some degree of reliability by elaborate training and selection of personnel. Such is the possibility in a study with a small field staff and long operating schedule, as was the case with the Kinsey report. In other instances, where research involves a massive staff, one can adopt reasonable procedures which involve considerable standardization and yet flexibility within a framework of general principles. In public opinion research, ideally one notes such an orientation to the validity and reliability problems. The order of questions and their specific wordings are standardized, but the interviewer is permitted to make certain *innocuous* changes in the procedure to suit the needs of the respondent —such as repeating the question, stressing a word that was not attended to, or introducing the question with some parenthetical remark which might clarify some element of confusion. He is also instructed to probe beyond the initial answer so as to clarify ambiguous answers, to provide an elaboration upon an inadequate report, or to show the reasoning behind the attitude. Training in nondirective, i.e., unbiased, probing is provided for the interviewer, and written instructions in advance of the given survey provide a list of "don't's" and also a uniform interpretation of the questions, objectives, and procedure for the interviewing staff so as to maintain reliability.

In such large-scale social research projects, one can also compensate for the apparent loss in validity, attendant upon the standardized procedure, by alternative instruments. Instead of trusting to the wisdom of the interviewer to probe in the proper place, to be insightful, to sense a distortion, and the like, one can develop *systematic* procedures to deal with these problems. The great mistake of those who advocate the extreme in freedom is to identify the solution of these aspects of attitude measurement *solely* with the interviewer. In social research, interviewing is only one small part of a larger system, which includes research and questionnaire design, pretesting, and analysis. If rapport is desirable to elicit real attitudes, one does not entrust it entirely to the devices of the interviewer. One can standardize the interviewer's behavior and rely on gaining optimum rapport by careful planning of the procedure and the pretesting of the questionnaire to determine empirically whether rapport has been gained. Thus, what might appear to have been lost through the constraint upon the interviewer is regained through *systematic* exploitation of some other feature of the research process. The practice of obtaining interviewer report forms wherein the interviewer comments on the motivation, interest, hostilities, etc., of the respondents gives the analyst the benefit of the interviewer's insights, without their biasing the actual field data to the point where respondent's report and interviewer's insight are inextricably mixed.[68] Here again, what is apparently lost in one phase of the research process is regained in another stage.

The needs to be covert, to dissemble the research purpose, to describe the richness of a complex attitude structure do not have to be entrusted to the whims of the interviewer. Such requirements can be met within the framework of standardized procedure by systematic attack upon them. Projective questions and covert approaches can be adopted *routinely* and solve the problem that the lack of disguise is not conducive to reports of private feeling. Open-ended questions or complex batteries of polling questions can be used systematically by every interviewer and provide insurance that neither validity nor reliability will be sacrificed.

This false location of such problems in the interviewer's realm is illustrated clearly in Roethlisberger and Dickson's account. Their conception of attitudes, as indicated earlier, is that of deeper and complex structures. But they place the full burden of treating this complexity upon the interviewer. They promulgate, as one rule of orientation, that "the interviewer should not treat everything that is said as being at the same psychological level." Let us grant the conception of levels of functioning, but let the analyst treat of this problem systematically, rather than the interviewer. Are there not devices for the analyst to discriminate the conviction from the lightly held attitude, the self-deception from the real? They postulate another rule which suggests that the interviewer should treat the responses as indices with some deeper personal meaning. Does not this admonition apply equally, if not better, to the analyst? Then if one developed systematic research designs to cope with such problems of attitude measurements, one could constrain the interviewer without any loss in validity.

5. THE EVALUATION OF INTERVIEWER ERROR— THE ULTIMATE PERSPECTIVE

Our aim in these introductory sections has been to provide a broad perspective on the problem of interviewer effects. We have suggested that such error needs to be evaluated in relation to other methods and must be balanced against many other considerations. But nowhere have we raised the ultimate consideration that interviewing—good or bad—is only one of the problems requiring methodological consideration in social research. This study concentrates on interviewing and treats it at great length because of its complexity. However, it would be a great mistake if the exclusive focus of this report were to be matched by exclusive attention to problems of interviewing. The problem must come into prominence, but so must other problems of theory and method if we are to make real advances. It was in this spirit that two related projects were commissioned by the Social Science Research Council to parallel ours. Those reports read in conjunction with this provide a far more rounded view of current methodological problems.

CHAPTER II

The Definition of the Interview Situation

1. QUALITATIVE DATA ON THE DEFINITION OF THE INTERVIEW SITUATION

All research into the nature of interviewer effects is guided by some model or image of the interview situation. A particular image of the interview directs us to study certain features as the sources of error; other significant features of the interview may never be examined simply because our image or model fails to recognize them. The adequacy of the model is obviously of great importance. How shall it be derived? If we turn to the explicit or implicit model of an earlier investigator, we have no assurance of wisdom on his part. His model may well have been based on too narrow a conception or a wholly false view of the interview.

Thus, if the influential writing of Simmel or the texts of Park and Burgess and other leading sociologists are our guides, our attention will be directed to one important aspect of the interview; we will see it as a "circular response," in which "there is stimulus and response, with every response becoming a stimulus for another response (and) interviewer and interviewee generally stimulate each other in new ways as the interview proceeds step by step."[1] But such a conception may lead us to neglect noninteractional sources of effect, such as an interviewer's lack of skill in recording quickly or accurately. Or it may cause us to overlook the residues of earlier interactions, such as *persistent* autistic influences on the interviewer's perceptions, or the effects of the sponsorship of the inquiry upon *all* of the respondent's answers, in favor of observing the minor dynamic process of question and answer.

If we turn instead to the classic study by Rice of "Contagious Bias in the Interview,"[2] we are informed by the title and the subsequent interpretation that "this bias was in both cases *communicated*, no doubt unconsciously, to the interviewed, and appeared in their own answers" and by the summary description that "an inquiry . . . disclosed a *transfer* of investigators' individual bias to applicants, and a corresponding distortion in *replies given by the latter* to scheduled questions."[3] Here we are again directed to focus on interviewer effects that operate via the communication of cues to which the respondent is presumed to be alert. Rice's findings are undeniable, but there is no support whatever for his

34

particular explanation of them. The findings reported are perfectly compatible with the notion that the interviewer simply distorted the recording of given answers in accordance with his own prejudice, or that he interpreted ambiguous answers in autistic ways. It is Rice's conception of the nature of an interview that forces his explanation.

Wisdom would dictate that our conception of the interview—fundamental to our entire program of research—be predicated on some sound basis. And when we consider the origin of earlier conceptions of the interview, we realize that they represent essentially a priori views based on some particular social science orientation. They may have little empirical basis; and more, they may not even stand up to logical examination. Thus the Young or Bogardus view conveys the notion of *reciprocity* between respondent and interviewer—hardly an appropriate description of a situation in which one of the parties is often an "aggressor" with a prepared course of action and a definite goal while the other is an unprepared "victim." Rice's view suggests that the respondent is keenly oriented to the mental processes of the interviewer—hardly in accord with the common experience of the survey interviewer, who finds many respondents completely detached or apathetic and answering questions in the most perfunctory way.

Winds of doctrine in social science may well be responsible for enthroning an oversimplified view of the interview, which in turn is the basis for research into interviewer effect and its control, but which sadly neglects many important factors. Thus, perhaps the most influential point of view about interviewer effect in public opinion research has been that the interviewer's *own opinion* or ideology is the most decisive factor. A detailed study of this particular factor is given prominence in a classic work on methodology in public opinion research, and an elegant mathematical proof is accordingly presented that the best solution to the problem of bias is a proper balancing of the *ideological* composition of the field staff.[4] Dedicated to the control of interviewer bias in its election surveys, the American Institute of Public Opinion followed the lead of such studies and attempted to balance the political structure of its staff in its 1948 surveys.[5]

But such a mathematical proof and such an administrative procedure have relevance only on the assumption that the primary source of bias lies in the interviewer's ideology. It may be, for example, that the interviewer's ideology is far less important in producing bias than his *beliefs* about the true sentiments of the population. If this were so, one might have used a 1948 staff which was perfectly balanced ideologically, but which would nevertheless have biased the results because of the widespread belief that Dewey would win in a landslide. A letter from one interviewer after the 1948 election implied this possibility: "The last political poll I did October 25 was overwhelmingly for Truman. I didn't feel entirely satisfied when I sent my work in. I felt that perhaps I hadn't filled my quota properly."

Consideration of such a plausible source of bias—the interviewer's beliefs about the opinions of his respondent—seems to have been wholly neglected in more than a decade of methodological work on the problem. Why, when it is so obvious? Must it not be because we remained blind to the obvious so long as we stuck narrowly to our preconceptions? And these preconceptions about ideological factors operating within the interview possibly received prominence because they were part of a one-sided theoretical emphasis on motivational constructs. We overemphasized the interviewer's motivation to alter the results, the influence of his wishes on his perceptions, and the respondent's motivation to conform to the interviewer's opinions. Cognitive factors in the interviewer *deriving from other sources*, such as his belief about the respondent's true sentiments, were not noticed because such concepts were less prominent in influential bodies of theory. Prevailing theories and conceptions of the interview must be at least temporarily suspended while we go about examining the situation in its true complexity. Lundberg rightly remarks in discussing the Interview Method that "it is not possible here to enter into a detailed consideration of the intricate interstimulation and response which are the structure and content of the interview. The fact is that there are very few scientific data available on the subject, although research in this field lies at the very foundation of sociology."[6] A sound conception of the interview, which in turn would guide future research on interviewer effects into appropriate directions, would seem best achieved through empirical study. Then we might check whether the interview actually conforms to our preconception of it, and broaden our views, where necessary, to accord with reality.

Such an approach has been the starting point for much of our experimental work on interviewer effect. With many fragments of data obtained by a variety of means, we have tried to reconstruct at least a portion of what actually goes on in the survey interview. However, we have been less interested in the *overt* actions within the interview and concerned more with subtle implicit processes going on in the *minds* of interviewer and respondent. We have sought an account of the interview as it appears to the individuals experiencing the situation, on the assumption that it is the way the situation is defined to the respective parties which is most important. There may be significant aspects of the interview which are not readily observed—private experiences which the individuals will not or cannot articulate to us, behavior of which the parties are not aware. These realms unfortunately are inaccessible to our methods, but we shall gain considerable knowledge of the situation. MacLeod has stressed how much phenomenological inquiry revolutionized research on perception.[7] So too, a phenomenology of the interview may radically change research on interviewer effects and even the broader field of survey research.

Toward a description of the interview, we now present the fragmentary beginnings. We shall examine several "case histories"[8] of interview situations and see what leads they can furnish us in our research, what alterations they require in the traditional conceptual scheme. Systematic discussion of principles and presentation of quantitative evidence of their operation will be postponed until Section 2 of this chapter, and in later chapters experimental evidence of the biasing effects of these phenomena will be presented. The reader is referred to Appendix A for a detailed report of the methods used in collecting these data. It is sufficient here to state that, in each case, the interviewer was asked about his (or her) experiences and reactions directly following the interview, and that the respondent's description of the same interview situation was obtained through a special interview conducted a few days later.

Detachment of Respondent and Interviewer from the Social Impact of the Interview

The first case reveals an interview situation in which the interviewer defined the respondent as "*a creep*" toward whom she felt intensely hostile.

The woman interviewer, in describing her feelings about the male respondent, remarks: "I just didn't trust the guy." Later she adds the comment, "He made me creep." When asked what movies she thought the respondent preferred, she suggested "something sadistic." Her image of the respondent was that of an unscrupulous, untrustworthy person, as evidenced by her statement: "When I came to the factual questions and discovered that he was occupying a home in a veteran's housing project it annoyed me because I doubt *very* much that he is a G.I." This general attitude existed not only with respect to his personality, but also with regard to the specific answers he gave. In answer to the question as to whether she felt annoyed or irritated by any of the respondent's opinions, she said: "Yes, nearly all of them with the exception of his statement on why he was a liberal, but even that I mistrusted."

And while all this is going on in the mind of the interviewer, the respondent's image of the interviewer is that of a pleasant, polite, attractive person, and he answers that she was "suitable to my idea of an interviewer." When asked about it, he says "I'd like to know her better" and adds "I wouldn't mind to discuss a few things with her." The respondent even thought the interviewer "liked" him and added very cautiously, "I had such a feeling, I don't know why."

Despite the intense hostility on the part of the interviewer there was none expressed by the respondent. The only suggestion of any disturbing element for the respondent is given in answer to the question, "Did you have the feeling that the interviewer was surprised at any of your answers?" He said, "Yes, she was surprised that I didn't know about the Better Business Control. I hope you don't fire her on this account." Apart from this, there are no overt indications of any effect from the interviewer operating on the respondent. He reports no such influences, and examination of his answers fails to suggest any.

The direct observation of such an interview and some of its peculiarities stimulates us immediately to think in *new* ways about the interview situation and the process mediating interviewer effects. Whether this particular situation is common is beside the point. It is the unusual event that may be the very basis for new theoretical developments.

Here is one example of an interview situation which by all the rules ought to be an extremely poor situation for the collection of valid data. In addition to the intense hostility of the interviewer, she reports that she "was particularly worried and depressed" that day and "in a special hurry to complete the interview" and the interview was conducted in the street. Further, the interviewer was in definite ideological disagreement with the respondent.

The case hardly is in accord with a conception of the interview which sees *both* parties reacting strongly to one another, with the respondent attuned to the ideology of the interviewer, and responsive to it. This respondent is apparently unaware of the interviewer's feelings. Yet, this is not because of any intellectual deficiencies on his part or apathy about politics, since he is a well-educated, middle-class person who says about himself: "I'm highly interested in political questions and I'm fully aware that the relations between this country and Russia is the basis on which my own family could live or die. I'm a Catholic and I firmly believe that what Russia is doing does not have God's blessing." He then expanded upon Soviet-American relations for a while longer.

It is clear that the content of the responses may, *under given conditions,* be completely unaffected by strong undercurrents of hostility and ideological disagreement on the part of an interviewer. And this is paradoxical only in relation to the preconception which sees the interviewer's sentiments being transmitted to a sensitive receiver, which is exactly what this interview situation was not like. The respondent seemed to have as his motive for being interviewed the desire to "sound-off." He had well-formed political opinions and his main interest was in the actual questions. In addition, his ideology seems well supported psychologically, and he therefore feels no insecurity in expressing his own view. Thus, when asked if he was concerned about whether his opinions were like others, he remarked, "Yes, but I feel that I expressed the feelings of the major part of the American public—even in the delicate Negro question." This despite the fact that there was no "delicate Negro question" in the interview. The respondent essentially remained detached from the social features of the interview situation, showed no insight about the other party and thus was not influenced by the undercurrent.

Just as the respondent may be insensitive to the attitudes and feelings of the most vital interviewer, there is also the good possibility that some interviewers are not responsive to the most flagrant behavior of a respondent. Interviewers may well develop a professional attitude toward their work so that they seldom become fully *ego*-involved in the situation. It is only when we conceive of the interview as equivalent to a *natural* conversation, in which both parties initiate or break contact or react to each other for reasons of personal whim or preference, that it seems strange to think of the interviewer as being able to withstand such experiences. The physician reacts to illness differently from the layman. It is part of his day's work. The psychiatrist is accustomed to reports that might horrify the ordinary man. So, too, the professional interviewer may be task-oriented and treat peculiar and annoying respondents as part of the hazards or normal experiences of his job.

Let us turn for additional evidence to a somewhat different type of data. The *mutual* experiences of respondent and interviewer within a *given* interview were one avenue to revealing the phenomenology of the interview situation. Another avenue was the reconstruction of *one side* of the situation—the interviewer's—through long narrative accounts of the *totality* of his experience.[9]

Note the objective way in which another interviewer—G—describes her feelings during what must have been a hair-raising day even for a survey interviewer:

I remember one day when I ran into a woman with a beard—she looked as though she might be a freak in a circus. But when I got in she was terribly cordial and really better informed than the average. And that same day I ran into a household with an idiot child, and the woman just said, "Well, come in," and she explained about the child and we went on with the interview. I was kind of nervous though. I didn't know what he'd do. Every once in a while the child would make sounds I didn't honestly like. And wasn't it interesting—The same day I ran into a couple who were quarreling. But she was perfectly lucid. She'd answer the questions calmly—then turn and resume the personal quarrel with her husband. Once in a while he'd try to answer—but she'd cut him off.

Or take the report of K, another experienced woman interviewer. When asked how she felt when she ran into people who were prejudiced, she replied:

"I'm extremely interested. Prejudice interests me—to see how much of it occurs.". . . When asked if it depressed her, she answered: "It depresses me at times—but I don't need a psychologist—it doesn't get me down. It interests me enough to discuss it with friends—it's a topic of conversation. . . . I frankly think on that, it disturbed me very much when I started. I've done it so long now, I know what to expect. I'm horrified it (people's understanding) is as low as it is, but I must accept it as such, because I can't raise it. It's more to me, on your surveys, a complete and total lack of interest in the questions we ask. . . . But as creatures of habit, after you're accustomed to it, it doesn't hit you in the eye any more. It does momentarily incite you."

While there may well be many interviewers whose *feelings* remain outraged by the behavior of their respondents, it is perfectly possible that they may be able to control their *conduct*. Feelings are one thing —overt conduct another. It is purely an assumption, based on little fact, to conceive of the interviewer's feelings spewing forth in all directions. Let us for the moment accept the testimony of these interviewers at its face value. A highly experienced woman interviewer—KO—describes her strong feelings about some respondents:

We deal with political polls, what people think of national and international events. It concerns every damn person so acutely. The fact that a woman wouldn't be interested in expressing such opinions angers me. It's annoyance with that section of my sex which hold themselves above such things. I recall an interview with a young, very nice woman. The interview went beautifully. Then I got to the question on atomic energy, and she pointed to her small son and said, "How can I pay attention to such things, I have more important things to take care of." My *unspoken* reaction, naturally, was "No matter how well you take care of him, if you don't take care of atomic energy, all your care may be wasted. . . .

Yet she then goes on to say:

Of course I simply smiled—I don't think I showed my reaction. That bothers me—the necessity of remaining sweet as pie all the time—I'm not a blank thing. I'm a person with very strong opinions of my own. I have to make some sort of effort to keep myself out (of the interview). I have schooled myself. When the person expresses an opinion, no matter what it is, I look like I approve. You can't remain blank—that's impossible. . . .

And she implies a kind of fragmentation between conduct and affect:

I get sick over the answers. But the part of me that gets sick and bothered is the socially conscious part. . . . One part of me gets disgusted, but the other wants to find out as a basis of action. Statistics on anti-semitism disturb me—but you've got to start from some point. You need to know what your points are. . . .

She further indicates how a "task orientation" intervenes. Thus, when asked whether *that* part of her rebels while she interviews, she replies:

Yes, but afterwards. While getting the interviews you're also engaged in a lot of drudgery—the basic drudgery of getting the job done. The other part gets lost. Very often people will ask, "What do people say?" I don't know. I can't remember at that moment. . . . The actual opinions don't register from one to the next interview. Only at the end, when I look over all of them, the pattern hits me in the eye. Then I get unhappy.

Another highly experienced male interviewer—MA—reports the same violent affect over the answers of respondents:

There's something gnawing at my faith in democracy. I'm nowhere nearly as sure as when I was in college that the people are fundamentally right. More likely, the people are wrong. . . . I can't say any more, "Give the people their head, and all will be well." People are much too pliable—they will act strongly on issues on which they have only the vaguest understanding. . . . It's all a cause for profound disheartenment.

Yet when asked what he does about this, he again stresses the separation between conduct and affect:

I lay it on the side. I think I'm fairly successful as an objective interviewer in presenting a front of complete impartiality. I've learned not to be surprised or shocked. For example, when I've worked in the South and run into Mississippi farmers who launch into a diatribe about New York Jews[10] . . . What do I do about it? I neither agree nor disagree. If I'm pressed into expressing an opinion, I try to be as vaguely noncommittal on their side as I can. The few times I've worked on surveys with basic social meaning, I've tried to get as accurate and objective a picture as possible of what the person thought. No matter how disagreeable the medicine is, you have to take it. There's no point in attempting to start any attitudinal interplay. It would have an influence on the respondent's opinion. I try as hard as possible not to influence them—I don't really know if I achieve it.

And later he indicates that such affect can find its issue in more radical ways than in the conduct within an interview. Thus, when asked why he continues to be an interviewer in the face of this disheartenment, he replies:

Who says I do!! That's one of the basic reasons I left the field. For a while it was a very serious thing with me. I was profoundly disaffected . . .

I was very upset by it . . . but I was naive . . . I still had hopes. It didn't really become serious till after I had done a great deal of interviewing.

Thus we should, at least provisionally, admit the possibility that some interviewers, despite violent reactions to the ideology of the respondent, may not reveal this in their conduct toward him. Their orientation to the task may intervene to disrupt such feelings. They may be strongly aware of their volatility, but in the light of long experience and admonitions about bias, they may be able to control their conduct toward the respondent.[11] Such control, such temporary fragmentation of the personality of the interviewer, is possibly a function of the degree of intensity of feelings aroused in the interviewer or of his habituation to the experience or of his training. That indignation or disagreement may be communicated and may bias the interview under other conditions is of course not to be denied, but this must be regarded as a function of specialized factors. We are indebted to the writer James Stern for his incidental revelation of his experiences as an intensive interviewer during the U.S. Strategic Bombing Survey of Germany.[12] As an individual with no previous interviewing experience and great sensitivity of feeling, he was not hardened to the following interview:

"It is difficult for me to tell you how I'm getting along under the Occupation. You see"—and promptly like a pricked balloon all the life that was in the meagre dress under the ancient cloche hat seemed to collapse. Only the arms—like a drowning person's arms, as they quickly rise before disappearing for the last time—came up to hold the dropped head while the words gurgled out as from a body saturated in water. "Oh, I'm sorry and ashamed, I really am, but you see, all my men, all I still had to live for, my husband, my boys, my husband's brothers and all their boys—all my men, you see, are killed or missing," then, "killed or missing," she repeated several times like a chant, like a chant that had stamped itself indelibly and forever on her brain from having seen it too often in the newspapers or in the dreaded official telegrams.

And he reports his reactions:

Well, what do you do and say, you damned Gallup poller? You, with your fatuous Fragebogen, its questions about prices and taxes, about wartime domestic problems, the military and political leaders already dead or jailed, about what plans she and her family have for the future, that charming rosy little hell called the future? What do you do and say with all that Galluping nonsense on the table to be answered and across the table the forlorn life with nothing to live for and not the courage to take it because as long as the heart goes on beating life is dear or because someone said long ago that this in the eyes of almighty God is the greatest sin. What do you do and say, you who are no physician or priest or psychoanalyst but a human worm with a full stomach and a wife and home and future and friends next door and a nervous system like a coil of taut and quivering copper wire? What do you do and say?

But that he was not typical is clear—Stern continues:

I once summoned up the courage to ask a tough, square-faced sergeant that, after he'd been knocking what he called "the bull-shit outacrying Krauts." I asked, not because I knew he was a psychologist by profession but because I knew he was a different kind of a worm and I wanted to try and learn a lesson. "What did I say," he said, as though what he said was all there was to be said. "Why, I said, Madam, you better quit that blubbering quick, we gotta long way to go yet and they ain't gonna keep my dinner warm on accounta you, that's what I said, and Jesus, was my dinner cold, no sirree."

That an interviewer such as Stern may flagrantly bias results by the most direct communication of sentiments is clear from his running account of another interview:

"Did I blame the Allies for the airraids? Ha, why naturally, we never once raided America. England? England started them. England."

"England started the airraids," I repeated, dropping the smile now and barely asking the question. "England started the bombing of open cities and villages? England, I suppose, started that before the Germans flattened Guernica in . . ."

"I don't know anything about Guernica . . . and . . ."

"No, of course, you wouldn't."

"I know England started the air warfare against Germany by bombing Freiburg and Karlsruhe in 1940, in May 1940 and . . ."

"And Germany, of course," I said, managing the smile again, "bombed Warsaw and Rotterdam in *1941!* And, of course, Germany never declared war on England . . ."

"Of course not, the English declared war on us."

"Well, well," I said, "That's very interesting, just why did England declare war on Germany?"

"Why? Why, how would I know? (Aus Feindschaft gegen uns) From hatred of us, I suppose."

I let the laugh out and said, "Did you ever listen to the Allied radio?"

"The . . . Never" was spat out like venom striking tin.

"Never?"

"Never, I said."

"Oh, well," I said calmly, smiling, "Oh, well, that explains a lot."[18]

Perhaps we have gone too far in thinking that the danger from the interviewer's strong feelings is that they might be *communicated* to the respondent and affect his replies. Experienced interviewers may be well aware of this. All the primers warn about it. The greater danger might be that such feelings affect the perception or judgment of a given answer or the private decision as to the validity of the answer and cause bias in such areas of the interview as the recording or probing operation. Here there has been little admonition to the interviewer, probably in all likelihood because our basic conception of the interview directs us to the communicational features, and not to these other components.

Let us turn now to another interview, illustrative of different principles. In our first case, "The Creep," despite great hostility on the part of the interviewer, there was no perceptible effect on the respondent. He was detached from the social impact of the interview, because of a firm orientation to the issues involved. In this new situation, we perceive somewhat different processes at work. The particular interviewer manifested no strong feelings about the respondent, but even if she had, it is unlikely that there would have been any biasing influence, because the pattern of behavior of the respondent predisposed against it.

This proprietor of a liquor store in Brooklyn had been interviewed by a female interviewer. Here is the reconstructed pattern. The orientation of the respondent—a self-defined *"tough guy"*—seems to be a compound of cynicism, generalized hostility, and detachment from the social process because of egocentrism.

Here is his orientation to the interview situation as such:

He began the session with some negative comments to the interviewer about public opinion polls. When asked later why he wanted to be interviewed, he said: "I didn't want to be interviewed. Naturally, if she's walking her feet off I'll help her out." But he added: "Not that I saw any point in the interview." This apparent note of sympathy for the interviewer is the only suggestion of any positive response to her as a person.

The cynicism and hostility and complete detachment may be best indicated in his summing up of the experience. He said: "This here interview thing's a bunch of ———. I think it is a backdoor way of getting information for a commercial outfit—A congressman is still going to vote for whoever he wants to."

What about the impact of the experience:

This is best indicated by his answer to the question asked of him several days later, as to whether he remembered the interview pretty well. He replied: "Almost forgotten it" and comments—"I don't know—it was in one ear and out the other—a conversation like any others. I wouldn't be improving my mind any to try and remember." When asked what impressed him most about being interviewed, he replied, "Nothing about it impressed me at all. She came at a time when we were a little busy and I had to answer between customers, on questions I'd have to think six months about."

As to the impact of the interviewer:

In reply to a question as to whether the interviewer created an initial favorable or unfavorable impression, he says: "Neither, no impression" and remarks, "I wasn't concerned. I've seen better looking dames."

With respect to any biasing influences from the interviewer, there is no evidence from examination of the entire protocol that his responses were at all affected. Conceivably, one might argue that the respondent's hostility represents the biasing influence of the interviewer's personality, but it seems entirely as likely that his hostility is diffuse and would have asserted itself with any other interviewer.

There are occasional bits of evidence of an orientation to the interviewer, and a concern about her, but this is mixed with other patterns which predominate. He says that he thought the interviewer "liked" him and that "she seemed to be satisfied that I was giving her the proper answers." But this is contradicted by other blustering remarks to various questions. For example, when asked whether he was concerned if his answers were like most other people's, he replied, "Never thought—I know my opinion is different. It's no news to me." And when asked in what way he thought the interviewer might have found him different from most of the people she talked with, he said, "I don't know these things—I'm not interested in what people think of me." And later he remarked in answer to the explicit question as to whether the interviewer seemed satisfied with his answers, "Yes, she had to be."

While this hostility is operating within the respondent, what is the view of the situation in the mind of the interviewer? The interviewer reported that he expressed "some hostility" when he was first approached and that the main reason he submitted was that he "was being courteous, found it hard to say no." The interviewer's reaction to his initial tirade about surveys was "he let me have it about opinion (surveys) in general. He did this but was very pleasant—so I went ahead and I was glad. He seemed a very decent sort."

In relation to the generally negative attitude of the respondent to the entire situation, the undercurrent of hostility and cynicism and contempt, the interviewer seems to show a strange lack of insight.

A variety of conjectures suggest themselves in relation to this case. It would seem that just as a respondent may be untouched by an undercurrent of activity on the part of an interviewer, so, too, may an interviewer be oblivious to the affect within the respondent. And perhaps it is just as well. Insight under either of these conditions would disrupt rapport even further and perhaps touch off effects that would distort the answers.

It seems suggested also that a respondent with this type of personality and orientation to the interview would be untouched by biasing tendencies on the part of *any* interviewer, assuming they were operating. In addition to the hostility and cynicism, he was detached from the social features of the interview because of egocentricity. Thus to one question in the actual survey: "What do you think of the problems facing the U.S. today, which one comes to your mind first?" he answered, "My own problem," and in reporting about his experiences in the interview, he never mentioned a single question that had been asked, and seemed to show no interest in the original questions.

"Good" Rapport in Relation to the Opinion-Giving Process

The first two cases reported depart from the traditional conception of the way in which the interview situation is structured and from our assumptions as to the process by which bias is mediated. Despite poor rapport and hostility on the part of one of the parties, there was no bias. Let us examine now a case which is the prototype of the good interview situation and observe whether bias operates. The general interpersonal atmosphere of the situation can be quickly conveyed:

The respondent invited the interviewer into her home, offered to take her hat and coat, and even offered her some food, a rather unusual occurrence. The atmosphere seemed very relaxed—the respondent was so folksy, it couldn't have been otherwise. The high point in rapport was typified by the respondent's later remark about the interviewer: "She had a headache and wasn't afraid to ask me for some aspirin. I was glad she felt like she could ask me."

The affection was definitely reciprocated. Both parties reported that they would like to know each other better. The interviewer said of the respondent, she "was so sweet and friendly she had no impulse at all to refuse a chat with a stranger." She also commented about the respondent: "While not mentally stimulating, her innate kindness and optimism is most attractive." The respondent, in describing her initial reaction and motives in being interviewed, said, "Just because she came to the door and seemed like a nice person and had some questions to ask me."

A further bond between them was found in the fact that the interviewer and the two sons of the respondent had attended the same local university, and this acted as a basis for a kind of class solidarity. And there was in fact no marked class disparity or difference in ideology.

The whole interview situation seemed to be in the nature of two women friends having a *"hen party."* There was no note of any dominance in the situation, nor was there any evidence of hostility. Although the respondent definitely saw this as a social situation and reacted strongly to the interviewer, this was not to the exclusion of the survey content. There was a nice balance of interest in both the social situation and the questions. The orientation of the respondent to the interview *per se* was satisfactory. She was matter of fact about it, but nevertheless definitely interested and highly conscientious. Thus:

> She reported a real interest in the questions and felt a great responsibility to answer correctly. She commented on the use of the survey results: "I didn't think it would make much difference—unless they might bring it up in Congress. That's why a person should be very careful about answering so as to give the right one." The interviewer's evaluation is of the same order, "She tried hard to get the real meaning of each question." The respondent's sincere approach is conveyed by her last comment: "I figure somebody has started something to try to better things and I think that's fine."

But this conscientious devotion to answering the questions never reached any dangerous intensity. The situation was not felt to be a test, and there was no terrible need for the respondent to do well. While the respondent was not very knowledgeable, this did not make her feel inadequate:

> The interviewer reported that she "felt her lack of knowledge was common to women, so was not embarrassed," and the respondent said, "I was wishing my husband was here to answer the questions—he knows more about it than I do." This remark did not seem to reflect any feeling of *personal inadequacy*, but would seem more an expression of what she accepted as her culturally defined role. It was all right for women to have inadequate knowledge since this is not their proper domain. There was no sign that the woman interviewer expected any more or resented the respondent on this account.

Yet what mars this ideal picture is the intrusion of an interviewer effect:

> According to the interviewer's remarks there was no bias: "She asked me what I thought of sending food to Russia. I did not reveal my opinion." But while the respondent said, "She didn't *try* to change my opinion,"[14] she also said: "Once in a while I asked her how she felt and we seemed to agree on our ways of feeling." She also reported that the interviewer agreed with her opinions, as indicated by "just her way of talking. Now it may be that she didn't but she didn't let on that she didn't."

Let us speculate about this case. Here was a situation which by the traditional view of proper interviewing had all the desirable elements —no marked disparity in group membership, excellent rapport, no hostility or sharp divergence in ideology, considerable social interaction, willingness of the respondent to assume her role and the requirements of the survey seriously yet no special insecurity about her opinions, no explicit communication of biasing tendencies, and insightful handling by the interviewer. What then is wrong with it? It was too good! The identification with the interviewer was too great; the rapport was too much and the respondent seems to have been biased in the direction of compatibility with the interviewer's sentiments. However, this case is only paradoxical in relation to our preconceptions about the proper interview conditions for the revelation of attitudes. We have oversimplified the picture. We have assumed that great rapport and friendship patterns and a lot of social interaction are *requirements* for good interviewing, without ever observing the precise operation of those factors upon the behavior of a respondent. Carried away by the emphasis on rapport, we have perhaps vulgarized the concept and have mistaken "love" for rapport. And interviewers may have followed suit, and striven for great chumminess with their respondents. A certain degree of businesslike formality, of social detachment, may be preferable.[15] When rapport transcends a certain point, the relationship may be too intimate, and the respondent may be eager to defer to the interviewer's sentiments. This would seem especially the case when the respondent has little real involvement in the task. When he is not particularly interested in the issues or has no strong views of his own, he may not mind or even prefer to take over the coloration of a very friendly interviewer. Perhaps, where the issues are of such a character as to create real task involvement, there is a counterbalance to the deleterious effects of excessive rapport.[16]

MA—a highly trained interviewer, in describing his experiences, clarifies the problem very nicely:

> A neighbor gets a friendly hello. It may make the opening easier, but the respondent may be less truthful to the neighbor. There are two factors involved. The interview may be friendly but invalid, or less friendly but more valid. Even in city interviewing, if I get too friendly, they may want to make an adaptation to me . . . When there's too much friendship, when the interview is too cozy, they may conform. . . . If the barrier is too high you get false answers. If the barrier is all the way down, you also get a false answer—there's too much identification with you, too much courtesy.

Interviewer effects deriving from an excessive orientation to the interviewer seem also to be related to another factor besides the ease with which high rapport is obtained. In describing their views about, and their experiences in, interviewing situations, different interviewers varied in their reports of respondent orientation to the social features of the situation. This seemed in no way related to impressionistic estimates of their ability to obtain optimum rapport. For example, here are the facts according to K—a highly experienced woman interviewer:

When asked if respondents were interested in her or the questions, she replied, "It's pretty equally divided. There's a great interest in you—in what you're doing, what it's all about. . . . There's also a great deal of sympathy offered an interviewer for having a very tough job." When asked if the respondents were interested in her personally, she answered: "Yes, unfortunately. (They ask) do you make a lot of money at this? Do you like to do it?" When asked if they ogled her or examined her clothes she replied: "Not too much, but you expect a certain amount of it." When the question was put as to whether she felt they were interested in her opinions, she replied: "Very definitely! They ask me mine, before they give theirs— *only too often.*[17]. . . They also ask after giving their answer—'Am I right,' 'Do you agree with me?' "

Note the difference in the report of MA, a highly experienced male interviewer:

When asked whether the respondent's focus of interest was on him personally or on the questions, he replied: "They're interested in all those things in varying degrees. I don't think there's nearly as much interest in me as in what it's about. . . . The focus of interest, I think, is very rarely on the interviewer—on me as such. I never feel self-conscious, or been made to feel self-conscious. I'm not aware of personal scrutiny after the first minute or so. Beyond that point there's not too much curiosity." When the matter was pursued, and he was asked what types of respondents evinced an interest in him, he was vague: "It's hard to give an accurate answer, I should say, and it's almost always momentary. (It occurs) at the beginning of the interview. It occurs when I'm not native to the area where I'm working."

Or take the report of M—a highly trained male interviewer with at least equal ability in making rapport who works in the same city with K:

When asked if respondents look to him for guidance, he replied, "You mean do they say 'what do you think'. . . It doesn't happen often. I'd say *only with one per cent* of the cases,[18] one per cent or less." He does remark later in another context, "Oftentimes when you've finished the questions, the person will say, 'Well, how did I do—did I answer about the way most everybody else did?' " But when the matter was pursued by the question as to whether this reaction was characteristic of special situations, he was not very certain: "I would say that it's the people of the more intelligent sector who ask that. *I seem to feel* that it's more apt to be men than women."[18] To the question as to whether this reaction varied with the subject matter of the survey, he replied: "I can't give anything on that. Wait a minute—You see some surveys—it sticks in my mind that some surveys ask what people think more than others do. But that doesn't make sense, since they're all opinion surveys. I guess I haven't anything sensible to say."

The tentative guesses to be made from these protocols about the factor within the interviewer responsible for this difference in the orientation of the respondent is that it lies, in part, in a kind of *intrusiveness* of the interviewer, a tendency to want to enter deeply into the respondent's affairs, which naturally increases the orientation of the respondent in the direction of the interviewer. In part, it may also derive from an emphasis in the interviewer upon the prestige-value of possessing opinions and other things. Perhaps this latter concern increases the feelings of respondents that they must voice opinions, even when they have none, and they may try to absorb them from the interviewer.

Note the continual thread running through K's report about her experiences as an interviewer. Among her early remarks, prior to any inquiries about it, she comments:

"If your second question was about Russia or Japan, or Greece or Turkey, they'd fold up (terminate the interview). They were afraid to show their ignorance." Then later on, she says, "Then also the question's asked—'Did I say the right thing?' You get a lot of that. They take it as an IQ." And again later, she reports: "Others, I believe give an opinion that means exactly nothing to them . . . and they're ashamed to say 'I don't know' despite the fact that it's quite all right." And later on with respect to a discussion of probing in the interviews, she says: "You can't be too persistent . . . otherwise there'll be too much embarrassment, and they'll discontinue the interview. People have a great deal of ego as far as the lack of opinion or knowledge on a subject. They don't like even before a stranger to show they don't have an opinion on it. You frequently find they'll become arrogant—or assume a disinterested attitude."

She does at another point in the interview mention this contradictory note: "If they really don't know and say so, that's all right—that's part of your job. My reaction is just as satisfactory as if it's fluent. I've had people tell me after a 'don't know' answer, so that you're convinced of their sincerity, that 'I'm going to learn about these things. . . .' That's satisfactory because you're completely convinced that you've had a genuinely good interview, even though most of the answers are 'don't knows.' "

Now, while it is certainly true that many interviewers report encountering this reaction of shame when a respondent appears ignorant, and it must occur in reality, the pervasiveness of this theme in K's experience must have something to do with her own particular behavior. For example: in the report of M on his experiences—a lengthy 17,000 word account, there is hardly a mention of the problem. Perhaps K liberates this atmosphere in her interviews because of the prestige-value of opinions in her own mind.[19]

Note also, in the two reports, the difference in the personalities of the two interviewers and the gratifications they obtain from the experience. K remarks:

"I'm a very friendly soul. I never go anywhere without someone speaking to me. I enjoy it. . . . If I had to go out and get me a job, I'd try to get into personnel work. I like to speak to people—hear their ideas—analyze the different types. . . . I'm just genuinely interested in human nature—human beings—their behavior—what makes them think as they do.

"When you live in ———, you travel in a certain sphere, and they bore me to tears after a while. There's a certain sameness and this is a perfect interlude. My husband says, 'You sure know some screwballs.' That's right! You can't take the same thing for a steady diet. There's something interesting in an intelligent screwball. . . . I can give you a concrete example. I met a kid, 20 years old, . . . a cultured smart boy. He was working as a bank clerk, but he was giving it up. He was going to learn to be an embalmer—it intrigues me why this kid was going to be an embalmer and I found out. I don't want to listen to these same damn people with the same ideas all the time. I would never meet a kid like that socially—or if I did, it would be a rarity."[20]

But M describes his gratification in interviewing differently. He says about himself:

"Every fresh person encountered is a new experience, I say this as though I was a person terribly interested in people, but I'm not. I don't know what the answer is. I'm fond of people, but also strangely capable of getting along without them." When asked at another point what was gratifying in the interview, he replied: "I think that's epitomized in the hosiery survey where, good God! asking 3000 women a stupid question like that would be the most routinized inquiry. In that case, I'm a theoretical enough guy so that I became terribly interested in what the pattern of stocking buying was." At another point, he remarks: "Apropos of that, I'm not very much interested in people—though I'm conscious that isn't altogether faithful to the truth. I just can't tell you about myself. I haven't the bubbling interest in people that many an extrovert has. I seem to enjoy people most when I come to, what we might call, intellectual grips with them."

Note also how this interviewer has either no intense desire to intrude himself too deeply into the respondent, or at least is highly guarded against this tendency:

In recounting a certain interview, he remarks: "She was a little embarrassed to have me come upon her in what seemed to be almost her living quarters. But at such a moment, I think I probably have a quality of disarming simplicity—at any rate I try to convey to the person . . . a sense of my complete unawareness of surroundings. . . ." Later on, he expands on this theme: "I realize that if I'd been interested in anything other than getting their attitudes, I would have also been less objective. . . . No one whom I've interviewed has ever been aware of my eyes wandering to their surroundings of their home."

Similarly, MA shows no strong interest in the respondent or tendency to be intrusive, and he guards against the dangers. Thus at one point he says:

"One thing I have found with the Jewish group—whenever I've come into a Jewish household, and come into contact with something familiar, and identified myself as Jewish—I've invariably noticed extreme and strong reactions. You get snatched up. It's so obvious that there's a strong chance of coloration of the response that it's something I'm wary about. I try to keep that out of the interview till the interview is over." And while this interviewer does describe a very strong interest in his respondents, this interest is of a very *specialized* sort. Thus when asked if he was interested in the respondent himself, he replied: "Yes, but how interested can you be. I'm interested in his attitudes and combinations of attitudes. The average middle class city home bores me."

This third case history of an interview and related material from the interviewers again suggest some modification of the usual view. Some degree of sociability on the part of the interviewer is obviously needed. Some degree of rapport is obviously called for. But there needs to be some clarification of dimensions and types of rapport and of desirable forms of sociability. Sociability that is predicated on intrusiveness may increase the orientation of the respondent to the interviewer, to the point where bias is more likely.

Modification of our usual preconceptions ultimately leading to better theory was one product of the case study of the interview situation. Established concepts were re-examined and a more refined view of their relevance to the interview was obtained. This, in turn, led to systematic empirical work on interviewer effect, which will be reported in later chapters.

In addition, in conjecturing on the diverse phenomena already reported from the case materials, we were led to recognize the larger significance of concepts previously neglected. The recognition of these concepts, in turn, sensitized us to new phenomena implicit in the case studies, and led to further theorizing.

Role Prescriptions and Interviewer Role Conceptions
in Relation to Interviewer Effects

Again we shall temporarily defer any elaborate discussion and listen to M's remark in the course of recounting his experiences. Prior to this point in the narrative account, he had dwelt on the tensions and alternation of elation and depression that occurred during his field work. He had then been asked whether such affect interfered with his actual work. He remarked:

"You'd suppose that the tension would influence the character of the work done by an interviewer. I mean specifically the way the interview itself is carried through. But I am inclined to feel that once started on Question 1, the interviewer falls promptly again into a rather set way. I don't mean that he interviews like a machine, though perhaps I do mean this. He is doing a routine, and from the moment of initiation till he's through, he's pretty largely controlled by the more automatic mental processes. . . . You see, when you're interviewing a person you're rather an automaton—you're back in your routine, and you're caught up in it. *You aren't an independent person, a free agent.*[21] You're not that till you've left the presence of the person, and embarked on the wide sea of searching for the potential next person."

In part, M is merely repeating what we have already reported in the other interviewers—he reports what we have labeled a "task-orientation" or a "fragmentation" between conduct and feeling, but he emphasizes as the explanation something generally neglected, when he says he is not *"independent,"* not *"free"* when he interviews. It is *prescribed* that he behave in certain ways simply because he is an interviewer, and it is this prescription of the "interviewer's role" which intervenes between his conduct and his own private feelings or ideology, between the stimulation from the respondent and his more natural reaction.

Upon consideration, it is quite obvious to anyone that all survey agencies define in a formal way what is the proper behavior of the interviewer, and the case studies were not required in order for us to know this. However, the case studies do stress that such roles are accepted, and this has been too often neglected in the attention we have given to the *"natural"* processes within the interviewer which presumably operate to cause bias.

Yet the maintenance of the prescribed role is not always easy. The intensive interviews indicate that at times conflict is felt between the requirements as set down by the agency and what the interviewer feels is a legitimate deviation required to meet certain problems. Bias then occurs not out of ignorance, but because the interviewer decides he *has to* flout the rule. Thus, M, the very interviewer quoted above as accepting the prescribed role, remarks on a hidden crime while conducting an interview with a foreign person:

"I felt qualified to paraphrase with strictest faithfulness to the sense. I realize that this is *indefensible* so will make no attempt to defend it.[22] Yet, I feel in doing as I did that I performed conscientiously as an interviewer in a public opinion survey."

The pressures of given situations in causing deviations from the accepted role is also demonstrated in the remarks of KO in discussing the unpleasant respondents she periodically encounters. She was asked how the unpleasantness affected her:

When the respondent lets you in on sufferance, you feel a sort of obligation to get the interview over as quickly as possible—with the least bother to the respondent. You have a sense of pressure—it's pretty unconscious. On the other hand when you're received cordially, you have a more leisurely feeling—you're not afraid to keep repeating the question if you have the slightest suspicion that the respondent doesn't understand. You probe more completely.

The impact of a variety of situational pressures on the interviewer's normally accepted role is seen most clearly in another type of phenomenological data collected. For reasons to be described later, the interviewer listened to an electric transcription of a completed interview, was asked to imagine himself in the actual situation, and was given the task of recording the answers on the appropriate questionnaire. He was also asked to report any thoughts or reactions he experienced while doing the task.[23] Pieces of B's narrative show the difficulties he faces in maintaining his prescribed role.

After Question 1:

"I feel this is one of those interviews where I'll have to record quickly and copy it over."
"I hope he'll stick to the questions. I'll probably get very bored and that may interfere with my *proper* interviewing technique with him."[24]

After Question 6:

The interviewer didn't have to continue probing. . . . He feels he has answered it and you don't. Rather than ask him again and antagonize him (the third time you ask it, it is really dangerous because he's liable to get very annoyed) I would have coded it.

After Question 8A:

I started to get that helpless feeling. He did not answer the question and I was forcing the answer out of him. You have to force him, but as you force him, he reacts by feeling more strongly.

After the very lengthy Question 11:

These long ones give me trouble. Since it's such a long question, I wonder if their answer relates to the question as a whole and I have to quickly read it over again.

After the very lengthy answer to Question 17:

I feel irritated. I have no room—[25] I have to write all over the place. How can you write verbatim if there's no place to write verbatim. I get very irritated. I don't feel I can get it down this way (verbatim). If I have to start interpreting what's important, what's relevant and what's irrelevant, I do it in terms of what I think. Here there is no time to determine it in objective fashion. Here you have to come to a decision in terms of your own likes and dislikes. I get doubtful. Am I writing down the things which really are important? I may not be objective in that I'm picking out certain things and leaving out others.

The case studies thus not only reveal the importance of the role *prescribed* for the interviewer by the agency in inhibiting natural biasing tendencies; they also reveal the importance of situational pressures in shattering the normal role with consequent bias. And what is suggested is that as such a role is shattered, the interviewer is forced into certain types of biasing behavior as a "task aid," as a means of coping with the problem.

Beyond this, they reveal the importance of *idiosyncratic* definitions of the role of the interviewer in producing bias. While the role is *prescribed by the agency* and usually maintained by various enforcement measures or by the interviewer's sheer acceptance of it on the basis of knowledge of the agency's demands, there may well be conflict with other definitions of the role proceeding from a variety of sources. For example, the interviewer may have views as to what other interviewers or his immediate field supervisor or particular respondents regard as proper interviewing behavior. While we have no evidence as to such direct *social* influences on the definition of the role, we do have considerable evidence that the definition may often proceed from certain *beliefs* the interviewer has as to the nature of attitudes, the nature of respondent behavior, or the quality of the survey procedures, although there is the possibility that they may also provide *gratification* for various needs.

Note the recurrent report by F of a certain kind of probing behavior while interviewing and the reasons for this behavior:

I'm not satisfied with a "yes-no" answer. I probe into it to make sure they understand the question. I often get "no"; it's not really a "no" answer—it may be a "yes" answer. Frequently, the answer is due to misunderstanding—lack of knowledge. I probe just a bit even though the interview doesn't call for probing on "yes" and "no" answers. . . .

The issue was later pursued by asking her why she probed beyond the "Yes" and "No":

The "Yeses" are all shades, some "Yeses" are close to "Noes." You read a sentence to the respondent—he's only catching the essential words—it's difficult to know what he considers essential—you'll never know his interpretation. So, I probe.

And she continues:

On Survey 152, on Question 1 (Can Russia be trusted?), you usually get what he'd *like* to see—that Russia *should* be trustworthy.[26] That's not the question—when I get such a "Yes" answer, and then probe, I may get that it's impossible (to trust her)—the "Yes" may change to "No." Also on the question on whether they expect a war, you also get wish fulfillment at first. If you're going through it quickly, you may not uncover his real opinion on the given question.

She was then asked how she knew that the question was misunderstood:

I read the questionnaire before I get started. I could readily see that the question was colored by political factors. Respondents will frequently become excited—you'll get a lot of wish fulfillment. On the whole I probe wherever possible. It isn't a matter of selecting certain questions in advance to probe on. I see in the course of the probing and interviewing the difficulty—the specifications give you a lead on that.

She reiterates the basic point:

I usually try to veer away from "don't know" answers. I probe especially hard. I usually feel the "don't know" is a cover up for inadequate information. I want to know why they say "don't know"—is it because of disinterest, inadequate information? Sometimes you get an automatic routine interview and not the true picture. . . . It's not that the person really doesn't know—people may have attitudes.

And later she remarks:

They're apathetic—they're fulfilling their obligation. They get through the questions quickly—they don't listen and it's easiest to say "DK." The minute you accept the "DK" it makes it easier for them to continue. . . . You take a question like the expectation of war. A large proportion will have a feeling about whether a war is coming. When I get a "DK" to that, I probe.

F's definition of her role in the interview, of the behavior that is most desirable, includes probing extensively, even where the instructions do not require it. It is interesting to note that, in relation to the traditional view of ideological sources of bias, the interview results she might conceivably obtain would appear paradoxical. With respect to one of the very examples she discusses, the question on whether Russia can be trusted, it is amusing that while she *herself* thinks Russia can be trusted (her general ideology might be loosely labeled pro-Russian), she would not be prone to accept a "pro-Russian" answer from a respondent because of her belief that respondents often answer in terms of their wishes, and that the interviewer should probe to clarify the issue. Such peculiar behavior can only be understood by acknowledging the operation of certain role definitions which intervene between the interviewer's own political sentiments and his behavior.

Now, whether F's tendency to probe is really desirable is not at issue. It might well be that probing yields more valid pictures of respondent attitudes, and this question will be discussed elsewhere.

What is clear is that the differing roles that interviewers define for themselves with respect to probing, rapport building, recording, etc., will account in part for differences in the results they obtain.[27] It is also clear that there could be fruitful inquiry into the interviewer's *general* view of his job to determine the variability in the definitions given by interviewers. The interviewer has to engage in a *variety* of behaviors during an interview and while the role may be prescribed in certain respects, there may well even be aspects of his performance for which no definitions at all have been established by the agency, and other aspects where the prescription is ambiguous. Where there is no comprehensive standardized definition in the first place, it is only natural for interviewers to vary. Thus MA remarks:

> I think more emphasis should be given in non-directive interviewing to setting up the levels to which the study director wants the material to be explored. There is a tremendous lack of consistency in this business of different levels of probing. Many good interviews are wasted on that account. It would be a very good job if they determined at the planning stage just how far the probing should go—just how much can be handled in the analysis.

Here certainly there is opportunity by training or field instructions attached to the survey to standardize these definitions or to provide new ones.

In addition to clarifying existing theories of the interview and of interviewer effect, the phenomenological studies had even more radical implications for theory and research on interviewer effects. It not only led to a more complex view of the processes we had been concerned with earlier, but also brought to our attention features of the interview situation we had not previously been aware of. In the discussion of idiosyncratic roles as a source of effect, we noted that often the reason a given interviewer assumed a certain role was because of given beliefs as to the nature of attitudes. F believes that the initial answers are superficial, that the truth lies deeper, and therefore probes. The cognitive world of the interviewer thus assumes importance. Let us turn to a striking demonstration of this:

Bias-producing cognitive factors within the interviewer.[28]—Again, let us defer any discussion of principles, and insert ourselves into the experiences of interviewers. Listen to this theme running through the narrative account by G:

> She spontaneously remarks in the beginning of her account: "The average woman thinks only of her job, or if she's a professional woman, of her profession. I just don't think the average woman has as much social consciousness as the average man." Later when asked if she can ever tell how a respondent will answer, she remarks: "Yes, you can pretty much tell. From the way they start off—right with the first question (you can tell) whether they're going to be a 'don't know' respondent." And then she continues, "Yes, usually you know the garrulous type right from the first." And when probed about predicting attitudes, she remarks: "No, I can't tell too well how they'll stand—except that if you look about the household, or at certain types of men, you can tell they're staunch Republicans."

Or take this report from another interviewer, N, clearly a somewhat mixed picture, but suggestive of certain cognitive dimensions operating within the interview situation:

> When asked if she could make guesses about the attitudes of respondents, she replied: "I often get fooled. On Russian questions I perhaps unconsciously make such guesses. But if I do that I'm likely to write down what *I* think. Therefore I try not to." But when the issue is pursued by asking her whether there were any characteristic types of respondents, she says: "Once they start talking, I can predict what they'll say—by an attitude you see they have, unless you don't have continuity in the questionnaire. I could just about tell which people would say they hadn't heard of the Marshall Plan—lower income housewives. Very rarely you get a lower income housewife who is well aware of things—they don't have the time." And when asked what attitudes housewives exhibited, she said: "On a series of questions about approving sending food to Europe, if she'd said earlier that she didn't know about the Marshall Plan, she will be one who wants to take care of her own family and no one else." When the matter was pursued by asking her what *constellations* of attitudes they exhibited, she replied: "Ignorant, narrow, uninformed. They remind me that they're people who could be easily led. Their thinking is superficial and on the surface. I always hope that a variety of questions will make them feel that they need more understanding—will stimulate them."

Such reports from interviewers were vivid demonstrations that special beliefs and perceptions about the respondent might operate upon the interviewer to produce expectations about how his respondents will answer questions. These expectations might well be a potent source of bias if they were to guide the interviewer at various choice points and affect his decisions on probing, recording, classification of answers, etc. This suggestion from the phenomenological data was elaborated into a detailed theory about the types of such beliefs and corollary expectations, and the biasing effects that might follow. The empirical research generated from such findings will be reported in Chapter III.

Attitude-structure expectations.—Certain of these expectations seem to be predicated on the belief that the attitudes of any respondent are unified, are bound together in some organized structure. Consequently, the interviewer would expect the respondent to answer later questions in a manner consistent with the early answers. As N remarked, "Once they start talking, I can predict what they'll say." This particular phenomenon might be labeled an "attitude-structure expectation," and it would seem that interviewers, like most other human beings, would be prone to it. Thus, Ichheiser has stressed the frequency of this belief, the "tendency to overestimate the unity of personality," in accounting for misunderstandings between people.[29] He also suggests that the operation of such a belief might well influence the behavior not only of the perceiver but also of the other person, in our case, the respondent. He suggests that there is a "tendency of other people, whether consciously or unconsciously, to anticipate and to adjust their behavior in some degree to the expectations and images we hold in our minds about their personalities."

Many psychologists have stressed the universal tendency of humans to organize and make meaningful their perceptions.[30] For example, Bartlett talked of an "effort after meaning"[31] and Asch showed experimentally how fundamental it is to develop an organized, unified impression of others from only discrete bits of information.[32] Upon presenting subjects with only half-a-dozen adjectives characterizing some unknown person and asking them to give their impression of the person, he *always* obtained an organized picture. He reports:

> When a task of this kind is given, a normal adult is capable of responding to the instruction by forming a unified impression. Though he hears a sequence of discrete terms, his resulting impression is not discrete. In some manner he shapes the separate qualities into a single, consistent view. *All subjects* in the following experiments, of whom there were *over a thousand*, fulfilled the task in the manner described.[33]

That such expectations might well persist even in the face of contradictory reports from a respondent during the interview is also supported by extensive psychological literature on the influence of an initial perceptual organization on subsequent perceptions.[34] One of Asch's experiments demonstrates this process in a way most relevant to our discussion of interviewer effect.

Two lists of adjectives characterizing some unknown person were identical in content, but the order of the words in the second list was reversed. And the picture of the person reported by his subjects varied with the order. This could only mean that the perception was dependent not on the mere content but on the initial impression. Asch remarks: "When the subject hears the first term, a broad uncrystallized but directed impression is born. The next characteristic comes not as a separate item, but is related to the established direction."[35]

Direct evidence of this very sort is available from a phenomenological account given by an interviewer—B—as he listened to an electric transcription of a synthetic interview, which pictured a rather bigoted respondent but contained occasional answers that were inconsistent with the totality of attitudes. His running account of his feelings shows the immediate formation of a picture of the respondent and the dynamics by which the expectation was maintained despite contradictory answers. After hearing the answer to Question 1, he spontaneously reported:

I do have some impressions. The respondent seems very doubtful about giving his opinion—a little suspicious. I don't have too much respect for this particular respondent. My immediate impression is that he's one of those types of individuals who thinks in very personal terms.

After Question 2, he remarks:

I was right—immediately he's going off on tangents. He's not really interested in the survey—he's interested in getting rid of any personal feelings he has. I feel he's an old geezer. . . .

After Question 2A:

Everything he says revolves around himself and is increasing my dislike of this respondent. . . . I feel hypocritical that I have to encourage him even though I don't like him.

After Question 3:

That whole thing just confirms my opinion. My dislike grows. . . . I already know what this guy is like. I just have to get it down. I feel he's hypocritical—he doesn't give a damn about the rest of the Americans, he's just covering up. He just cares about himself—it's guys like him who cause all the trouble.

At Question 7, the answer on the record was contradictory of the previous answers. However, the interviewer, instead of changing his belief, maintained his original impression and rationalized the contradiction:

He's still wary about giving his *real* opinions. He started to *backtrack*. It gives me a nice insight into his character.

At Question 8:

I feel foolish. I know the handwriting on the wall. I know what this guy is going to say. He just doesn't know anything about these things. I feel what's the use of asking these people these questions. It isn't much use asking them—after a while I can guess the answers. This guy just doesn't approve of anything outside the United States and doesn't know anything outside of the U.S.

After Question 11, to which the respondent gave a long and mixed answer:

It occurred to me that I didn't have to listen actively to his remarks. I would know what he would say. Wait a minute. I coded the wrong response. . . . I almost guessed that answer in terms of what opinion I've formed of the person.

After Question 13, which asked whether the respondent had heard anything about a current issue:

I was just thinking as he said that, "you're a damn liar.". . . I'm sure he's covering up—he's trying not to show his ignorance. I was amused—he hasn't heard a damn thing about it.

Then I think, "well, what validity has this question got?" He says he's heard of it. I have to put it down that way, then I wonder how valid this survey is. Is my impression of what he's heard better than his own impression of it? Halfway through I have the impression I know what his answers are and the way he answered this helped me confirm my judgment. I've no way of testing it, of asking him—"Are you sure you've heard of it?" I just feel skeptical about the response; I really feel the correct answer is "no," but not to appear dumb he would answer "yes." I could almost have predicted this answer. He wouldn't admit his ignorance.

After Question 15:

I could almost have predicted this answer to some extent. He wouldn't admit his ignorance. I feel that's true—I can write down his answers fairly well, yet I'm not allowed to; I'm limited by interviewing procedure; I'm a little sore about interviewing procedure, I feel he's justified when he says, "I've answered that already." It's true, I do know what he's thinking.

Role expectations.—The phenomenological data also suggest another type of belief operating upon the interviewer in setting up expectations about the answers of the respondent. We might conceive of role expectations to denote the tendencies of interviewers to believe that certain attitudes or behaviors occur in individuals of given group memberships, and therefore to expect answers of a certain sort from particular persons.[36] Some of these beliefs might well occur because of traditional role prescriptions characteristic of all societies as illustrated in G's remark: "I just don't think the average woman has as much social consciousness as the average man." Some role expectations might well be posited on the basis of an oversimplified belief, a stereotype about some ethnic group. In either case, at the initial moment of interaction in the interview, the respondent might be pigeon-holed on the basis of some membership cue, and the structure of his attitudes would be expected to correspond with that role.

One of the case studies of a particular interview situation shows clearly the development of a role expectation, in a somewhat stereotypic interviewer, and is suggestive of the actual biasing effects on the results. MM, a middle-class, middle-aged white female interviewer in the course of her work interviewed a working-class Negro girl of twenty-three. The respondent had completed high school and was now married to a fireman in a commercial laundry. They resided in Chicago in a furnished apartment for which they paid $9.00 a week in rent. Within this situation of obvious class and racial disparity, a role expectation quickly developed. It is interesting to note that the questionnaire opened with a traditional saliency question on "the biggest problem facing the U.S.," to which the respondent replied, "There are a lot of places in the U.S. where there is segregation of the Negro. That's a problem for the U.S." It might well be that accidental factors, such as an *initial* response being "racially oriented," would contribute to the speed with which an interviewer would organize the experience in terms of the well-institutionalized roles of social groups. We shall return in Chapter V to the significance of such "situational determinants" of interviewer effect. It is clear nevertheless that the interviewer quickly organized the experience around the theme of the Negro respondent!

When asked what impressed her *most* about the interview, she replied: "The shabbiness of the building, the low IQ of the respondent." In response to a question, as to the activity the respondent was engaged in, MM in a gratuitous attempt to paraphrase Negro speech, noted, "just a settin'." She returns to the concept of "low intelligence" in a number of places in her report. Thus, in answer to the question as to whether the respondent was embarrassed by any of the questions, MM remarks: "Because of her low IQ she felt embarrassed by most of the questions." And in a number of other places, she remarks that the respondent "felt inadequate," and "felt she could not answer the questions." The interviewer structured the situation so much in this way that she felt it necessary on the original interview blank, after the respondent commented on an information question, "That one's slipped my remembrance," to make the parenthetical note, "colored girl, 23 years old." When asked later to rate the level of information of the respondent, the entry "not at all" informed was checked, and when asked to guess what sort of movies the respondent would prefer, MM writes, "some light musical comedy or story."

There is suggestive evidence that this role expectation did operate to affect the behavior of the interviewer.

While one cannot deny the possibility that this respondent truly had little information and few attitudes, the magnitude of the ignorance seems exceptionally great. On three out of four questions on recent major political events, the respondent was recorded as "DK." In six instances on opinion questions, she was recorded as "DK." Free-answer comments were sparse throughout the ballot. That this seems spurious is suggested by the contrasting pattern of response recorded by a second interviewer who obtained the reactions of the respondent to the experience of being interviewed. The re-interviewer obtained very full answers. In addition, while the respondent did tell the re-interviewer periodically that "she didn't know very much," she also remarked that she found most of the questions "very interesting." And as long as six days after the interview, she remembered the contents in sufficient detail to report with respect to a question on the occupation of Germany that it was difficult and that the interviewer had named "3 or 4 countries that had troops stationed in Europe. She said if all the others pulled out, should U.S. troops stay there." Certainly to remember this rather remote political question so faithfully seems to contradict the overwhelming pattern of ignorance and lack of opinion that the first interviewer recorded. It seems very likely that the initial interviewer did not pursue the issues very much and may have accepted inadequate answers because of the general view of the respondent as unintelligent.

All this would be perfectly natural in the interviewer as a human being. Psychologists have stressed the prevalence of stereotypes in a population and the persistence of these over time, and this might be the prepared framework for role expectations in the interviewer.[37] But even the many interviewers without ethnic stereotypes might have role expectations. Psychologists might conceive of the role-expectational process as an illustration of the more fundamental law that perception of a part is determined by the properties of the whole in which it is contained. Thus Krech and Crutchfield in an application of this principle to the perception of individuals state, ". . . when an individual is apprehended as a member of a group, the perception of each of those characteristics of the individual which correspond to the characteristics of the group is affected by his group membership."[38] Sociologists argue for a fundamental character to such expectations, in seeing regularities of behavior corresponding to group memberships, and expectancies about the behavior of persons in given positions or groups, as part of social reality, almost as a precondition for society.[39] The interviewer as a member of society has some framework of role expectancies built into him.

An experimental demonstration of the way in which role expectations arise out of racial stereotypes and the regularities of social life is available in the work of E. L. and R. E. Horowitz.[40] The experiment by analogy shows how such expectations could create errors in the perception of an interviewer. The fact that the demonstration is based on young children underscores the fundamentalness of such processes.

White children from the first to the tenth grade living in a community in a "Border State," which was characterized by highly institutionalized patterns of segregation, were shown pictures for very brief exposure times. After seeing a library scene containing only four white boys reading, the children were asked, "What is the colored man in the corner doing?" There was an increasing tendency with age for the children to report the nonexistent Negro as engaged in some menial activity. There was a similar increase in the tendency of the children to answer the question, "Who is cleaning up the grounds?", asked with respect to a picture containing nothing but a building and grounds, by saying that it was a Negro. On a third picture of a beach pavilion with tables, the children were asked, "What is the colored girl doing at the table at the right?" There is a regular decline with age in the report by the children that the Negro girl is engaged in nonmenial activity.

Such demonstrations show by analogy that a strong belief about the role that a given group will assume may well influence the cognitive or perceptual processes of an interviewer.

Probability expectations.—The demonstration of expectations led to theorizing about a third type of belief operative within the interviewer which might set up expectations about the answers to be obtained. The expectations mentioned thus far develop during an actual interview, on the basis of early answers or group membership characteristics of the respondent. However, *prior* to any such cues in the given interview, interviewers might well have less differentiated and less rigid, but nevertheless real, expectations about the attitude of *any* respondent on the basis of some belief about the prevailing sentiments in the population on prominent issues. This phenomenon might well be labelled a probability expectation to denote its statistical content and also its tentativeness in relation to subsequent specific expectations developing within the given interview.[41] Unfortunately, no example of this process is available in the qualitative materials on the phenomenology of the interview. The concept developed too late to be explored by these means.

However, statistical data, bearing on this, will be reported shortly, and from other published sources, there are suggestions at least that such beliefs about the distribution of sentiments have psychological reality. Clark, for example, asked students in a course in public opinion research to predict the percentage results to certain questions. While there was great variability in the predictions made in the class, all students essayed a prediction. Moreover, with respect to such institutionalized attitudes as social distance toward Negroes, there was considerable uniformity in the predictions. Thus two-thirds of the students predicted that less than 25 per cent of the population would answer "Yes" to the question, "Would you be willing to have a Negro family in your own social and economic class move in next door to you?"; and over half the students predicted that less than 25 per cent would assent to club membership for a Negro.[42] Similarly, in the course of an actual field study of the biasing effects of probability expectations on survey results, Wyatt and Campbell asked 223 student interviewers to make predictions of the percentage distribution of replies to various poll questions.[43] Such predictions were proffered, and in the case of such a public issue as political party affiliation in May, 1948, in Columbus, Ohio, over one-third of the field staff predicted that the Republicans would receive at least 60 per cent of the major-party vote.

Another demonstration of such expectations is available as a by-product of one of the experiments cited in Chapter III. The NORC national field staff was asked to estimate which answer would be the majority position with respect to the question, "In general, do you feel the United States is now spending too much on our program for European recovery, about the right amount, or not enough?", with the following results:

	Percentage of Field Staff
"Too much" would be majority position	37
"Right amount" would be majority position	63
"Not enough" would be majority position	—
	100

Such expectations operating upon the interviewer, whatever their specific cognitive content may be, would seem to be obvious sources of error, but it is interesting to note that cognitive factors of this type, underlying the objective interviewing situation, had never been examined in prior methodological research on the survey interview. We had been preoccupied with the ideological factors within the interviewer, with his motivation to influence the results, and had neglected his perception and beliefs (or construed his beliefs as simply mirroring his motivations). We had been concerned with what he communicated of his point of view to the respondent, and not with the way he saw the respondent. This omission must derive from our historic emphasis on the immediate communicational aspects of the interview, and our theoretical leanings toward motivational determinants. Because we never entered upon any direct examination of the interview situation, we could not correct our view. Out of this emphasis upon the communicational process in the interview, we saw the interviewer as asking questions and recording answers, in the process of which he perhaps communicated information, and we neglected the many judgments he made in the process. By contrast, in all research on "evaluational interviewing," where the interviewer assesses a candidate for some purpose, methodological attention has been focused on judgments and the cognitive processes underlying them, which might lead to error. There we find a classic literature on "halo effect" in judgments, and on the influence of stereotypes in judging applicants, stressed in relation to interviewing of this type.[44]

It is interesting to note that the one published investigation we have found which emphasizes the *centrality* of cognitive processes in the interview is by Oldfield.[45] And this investigation was based in part on the direct observation of appraisal interviews and inquiries among interviewers. The main theoretical influence apparent was Bartlett's, whose classic contribution was to the study of cognitive processes. Oldfield also emphasizes that interviewers obtain an immediate impression of a subject, and he expands on the biasing potentialities of such impressions:

> It is characteristic of the first impression that it may be stable and persistent in a degree which often appears to be out of keeping with the length and nature of that part of the encounter which gave rise to it. It may remain, sometimes in a recognizably compulsive form, when further evidence regarding the candidate thoroughly belies it. To such an extent is this sometimes the case that the interviewer may be constrained to make the most vigorous conscious efforts to discount it. (p. 103)

Detection and control of biasing expectational processes.—The phenomenological interviews are also suggestive of the possibility that certain interviewers may be less prone to such expectation effects. For example, MA reports very little of it, and in his case this seems to be a function of his system of generalized beliefs. He does not accept easily the notion of consistency or unity of attitude, and he does not seem stereotypic. Thus, in the context of a remark he made about the prejudiced attitudes he encountered, he was asked whether such attitudes were more characteristic of certain groups, to which he replied:

"Yes, I'll say this—you find it more in certain parts of the country. But you find it in every area, in every class, in Brooklyn or Atlanta. Oh, it's true that in Atlanta it's very rare to find a radical." The matter was pursued by asking him if he could tell in advance which people would be like that, and he said: "Rarely. You get used to being surprised. You never can tell. If you knew what people would say in advance, you'd be out of business. I've never been able to tell in advance. Dress, features, manner, income is never an indication of attitude. Sometimes you can make a generalization, but you have to be careful. . . . If you're talking on a political issue and you come into a solidly Republican section, you will find conformity, but you always find exceptions."

In a later discussion of the gratifications he derives from interviewing he reports:

"I get continuing gratification from the simple realization that people are different from one another. I've run into such peculiar combinations of attitudes. When you find apparently varying sets of opinions within the same individual, it's apt to jar you enough to realize once more that you never can tell. I find it a continuing wonderful thing. You don't run into groups or patterns. It may be true in some basic attitudes that large groups are influenced by the same things, but in many other attitudes, you find inconsistencies."

In the unrelated context of a discussion of how he knows when an answer is invalid, he states: "I don't know unless it's the tone of voice or the manner. If it's a long and overlapping type of questionnaire, you can detect outright inconsistencies. But the most honest individual in the world gives conflicting answers unless he's an extremely well-integrated person and has all his attitudes thought out."

And M, in discussing his behavior and experiences, suggests that a strong task orientation, an attention to the required detail, prevents his forming such expectations. It is suggestive also that M was the interviewer with relatively little intrusiveness or social orientation toward the respondent, and perhaps this prevents him from synthesizing impressions. Thus, in the context of a discussion of his probing behavior, when asked whether certain types of probes were more effective for given types of people, he replied:

"All I can say is I haven't discriminated. I can't contribute anything on that. It takes a person of different mentality than mine. In general, I can say this of interviewing, I don't generalize consciously about the reactions. If you were to ask me at the end of a survey how most people answered I couldn't tell you. I couldn't discriminate, for example, that younger women answered such and such a way. When I'm with a person, you're pretty absorbed in getting what they say. I'm a *tabula rasa.* I don't give a damn. I'm not thinking. I'm just a recording machine. It helps me in my objectiveness."

Granted that we find in our later experiments that expectations are potent sources of bias, the qualitative material on individual differences among interviewers in their susceptibility to expectations will lead to an important area of research. If there are such biasing tendencies, varying among interviewers and related to given factors, it may be possible to detect them by a variety of means and select interviewers who would be less susceptible. While such a testing approach goes far beyond the present project, existing psychological theory gives some guidance in a search for the nonsusceptible interviewer. The voluminous studies on stereotypes about ethnic groups might provide clues that would differentiate interviewers less prone to role expectations. With respect to attitude structure expectations, literature from experimental work on perception is most useful. Thus, in Thurstone's factorial analysis of perception,[46] one of the radical factors inferred was that of "speed and strength of closure," certainly akin to the attitude-structure expectation phenomenon, and many writers have talked of such polar approaches to perceiving the world as the synthetic vs. the analytic type, the former somewhat akin to the pure attitude-structure prone interviewer.[47]

More recently Frenkel-Brunswik[48] has argued that "intolerance of ambiguity," the inability to accept the existence of conflicting or contradictory or complex elements in some object and to be flexible in perception, is a *highly general* formal characteristic of the individual, rooted in the personality. Those who are intolerant of ambiguity would obviously be prone to attitude-structure expectations as interviewers, and if this truly is a pervasive characteristic of the individual, it could be more easily located. We might well find certain simple perceptual tests of this general tendency.[49]

2. QUANTITATIVE DATA ON THE DEFINITION OF THE INTERVIEW SITUATION

The case study material was rich in suggestions of new ways of looking at the interview situation and led toward fruitful theory about the mechanisms underlying bias, the barriers to bias, and the correlates of bias. These theoretical insights were ultimately tested by a variety of experimental means, the results of which are reported in later chapters.

The reader may have felt that some of the phenomena described were exotic—existed only in occasional deviant or exceptional interviewers and respondents or in the few we selected for presentation.

Moreover, even if such theory about the correlates of bias is verified experimentally, this would provide no evidence on the *generality* of the process. The experiment would simply prove the precise operation of such factors on bias but could not establish the generality of such effects in the usual survey. Therefore, it would be desirable to have some notion of the usualness or unusualness of these processes in the interviewer and respondent.

In this section we present data on the frequency among interviewers and respondents of some of the phenomena already reported. In some instances, cross-tabulation of the reported phenomena also provides some preliminary test of a theory about the biasing effects of such phenomena.

General Detachment of Respondents from the Opinion-Giving Process

The evidence from some of the case history material was that past writers may have overemphasized the intensity of the experience for the respondent of being interviewed on many current public opinion surveys. The material suggested that a respondent may be so *non*-involved in the opinion-giving process that he is not concerned about giving the "right answer" or pleasing the interviewer or anyone else. This would not preclude other kinds of bias, e.g., the biasing effects of expectations on the interviewer's handling of the data, but it would reduce the sensitivity of the respondent to the interviewer's opinion, and the communication of cues about the interviewer's attitudes.

It may appear perverse to argue that such a phenomenon is a good thing. It is not a good thing from the point of view of long-term public support of the *institutions* of interviewing, survey research, and democratic decision-making, or from the point of view of the seriousness of the sentiments expressed in surveys. It is not a good thing in terms of the value-systems of human beings. It may even point to the larger fact that we are studying the wrong problems at times. Certainly there are many problems about which respondents must be intense, and perhaps we have neglected these for the study of the very kinds of issues that do not concern people. But it may well be a good thing from the narrow point of view of the reduction of certain types of interviewer effects in current surveys. Some quantitative evidence that this is truly a widespread phenomenon, somewhat uninfluenced by transient events, is available.

Thus, Sheatsley reports data on the attitude of respondents toward the polls and to the experience of being interviewed, as revealed in a special questionnaire administered by NORC to a national sample of Americans.[50] While he shows clearly that there is little in the way of *strong* criticism or hostility to public opinion polls among those who consent to being interviewed,[51] he also shows that the general reaction of a considerable portion of the public might be loosely described as "lukewarm." Thus, while two-thirds of the public expressed the view that polls are a "good thing for the country," 18 per cent of the sample said public opinion polls don't make any difference one way or the other, and 10 per cent had no opinion at all about the polls. And among the favorable individuals, there was little clarity in the reasons for their sentiments. Ten per cent of the favorable respondents could proffer no reason at all why they regarded polls as a good thing, and 35 per cent could only remark that "they show how people feel" or "it's nice to know what people think." And those who were not favorable essentially revealed a pattern of indifference, as indicated in the main reasons they gave for their sentiments—"Politicians, leaders pay no attention to them" or "They're just opinions, don't settle anything." While three-quarters of the public reported that they would be favorable to being interviewed again, most of those expressed no enthusiasm; 54 per cent merely saying that they had "no objections." This sample was also asked if they had ever been approached for an interview on a previous survey. And among those who reported a previous experience, certainly the most "favorable" group to the process, since they have *doubly* consented to be interviewed, 38 per cent described their reaction to the previous experience as "no criticism, but no special enthusiasm."

These data had been collected in 1947, and comparable data were again collected on a national sample in 1948, shortly after the widely publicized failure of the polls to predict Truman's victory. While Sheatsley clearly shows that this event did reduce support for the institution of polls, from our point of view he also shows that "lukewarmness" is a *characteristic* pattern. Thus, while the proportion of the public who expressed the view that polls are "a good thing" dropped from 66 per cent to 47 per cent, those who frankly said polls are a "bad thing" rose only to 6 per cent, and the major increase was in the indifference category. Certainly one might have expected that the public would show widespread hostility or derision following such a failure, but by and large this did not occur. People don't get that excited about the institution!

In 1950, the reactions of a national sample to an NORC survey were again ascertained.[52] So that respondents would feel easier in reporting their genuine feelings, a written questionnaire was handed to the respondent at the end of the interview, completed by him, and returned to the interviewer in a specially prepared sealed envelope. One question asked whether the respondent thought that obtaining people's opinions in public opinion surveys was useful. While this general procedure and the particular question wording were different from Sheatsley's, the data support the view that "lukewarmness" is a stable and widespread pattern. While 60 per cent felt it was very useful to obtain people's opinions, 10 per cent said it was of little or no use, and the remaining 30 per cent said it was "somewhat useful." These results run quite parallel to Sheatsley's 1947 findings.

The re-interviews with respondents, used as a basis for constructing the case histories previously reported, also provide some meager evidence on the frequency of detachment among respondents. While this sample contained only fifty cases in selected cities, it is noteworthy that about one-quarter of them said either that the questions were of no interest at all to them, or that only some questions were interesting. With respect to the point made previously, that respondents may not feel any embarrassment about their particular opinions or lack of opinions, the re-interview procedure is unique in affording some quantitative statement of the magnitude of such equanimity. A battery of questions in the re-interview related to this problem, and an overall reading of the entire protocol was used as the basis for rating the respondent's attitude toward his own answers. Over half of the respondents were rated as "not self-conscious" about their opinions, this despite the fact that many had given *uninformed answers* or *no answer at all* in the original survey.

By way of documentation of this latter point, among fifteen respondents who were at best able to answer correctly only one of three simple information measures, dealing respectively with Acheson's appointment as Secretary of State, a nationwide address by President Truman, and the Dutch-Indonesian conflict,[53] eight of them were rated by their interviewers as "satisfied with their answers," and five of them reported that they "understood all the questions."

Detachment of the Respondent from the Social Aspects
of the Interview

The case material suggested that, because of the lack of strong rapport, sheer apathy, egocentrism, violent hostility, or cynicism, the respondent may remain rather detached from the interview experience. Thus he may not have too much interaction with the interviewer and this would reduce the operation of one kind of bias. Some evidence on the frequency of such detachment from the interviewer is available from a mail questionnaire administered to the nationwide staff of interviewers of the National Opinion Research Center.[54] If we can regard the interviewers as accurate informants about their respondents, and certainly in this area there would be no conscious reason for them to report in a biased way, they suggest that respondents are not very interested. The question asked of them, and the marginal results are reported in Table 2.

TABLE 2

ORIENTATION OF RESPONDENTS TO THE INTERVIEWER AS REVEALED IN
THE REPORTS OF THE NATIONAL NORC FIELD STAFF

"In general, thinking of most of the respondents you interview, would you say they are very interested in you yourself—your opinions, your work, your background, your family—or are they only mildly interested in you yourself, or don't they take any personal interest in you at all?"

	Percentage of Total Field Staff
Most respondents very interested in interviewer	17
Most respondents mildly interested	63
Most respondents show no interest at all	20
	100
	N = 150

Additional evidence on the indifference of respondents to the social aspects of the situation is available from the re-interview study reported earlier in this chapter. In their replies to a direct question as to whether they liked the interviewer, twenty-one of the fifty respondents said they "had no feeling about him at all"—they neither liked him nor disliked him.

The self-administered questionnaire given to the national sample of respondents in 1950 to determine their reaction to the interview experience also provides data on the detachment of respondents from the interviewer. Respondents were asked whether they thought the interviewer had any opinions, and if so, whether his opinions were the same as, or different from, their own. Over three-quarters of the answers were that the interviewer "didn't seem to have any opinions of his own." One interviewer even reported the bizarre reaction of a number of his respondents who, after reading this question on the form, asked him if he was supposed to have opinions and if he had neglected to tell what his opinions were. In part, this finding reflects the general ability of interviewers to conceal their own opinions from the respondent, but it also must reflect to some extent the detachment of respondents—since one would expect that respondents who are keenly concerned about these matters would sense the existence of opinions in the interviewers. Even where the respondents were aware of the existence of interviewer opinions by and large, they showed little insight into the actual nature of these opinions. This is not to say that this aware group may not be oriented to what they *conceive* to be the interviewer's opinion, but simply that they have not sensed his real opinion, or that the interviewer has masked his real opinion. This can be demonstrated by cross-tabulating their answers as to whether the interviewer's opinions were the same as, or different from, their own against objective evidence as to the disparity between interviewer and respondent opinion. Since the interviewers had completed the same questionnaire as was administered to the respondents in the survey, it was possible to sort out two groups, those respondents interviewed by interviewers who actually agreed with them on a general question on the survey, and those where the interviewers disagreed. The evidence is presented in Table 3.

TABLE 3

RESPONDENT BELIEFS ABOUT INTERVIEWER OPINIONS AS
RELATED TO THE OBJECTIVE DISPARITY IN OPINIONS

PER CENT REPLYING INTERVIEWERS HAD:	AMONG RESPONDENTS WHO WERE INTERVIEWED BY INTERVIEWERS WITH OPINIONS THAT WERE ACTUALLY:	
	Same	Different
Same opinion............	19%	23%
Different opinion.........	2	1
No opinion..............	79	76
	100%	100%
	N = 472	N = 446

It is clear that there is no relationship between the actual disparity in opinions and the perception of disparity. It is interesting also to note that among the small group who sense the existence of interviewer opinions, there is overwhelming belief that the interviewer is not in disagreement.

Detachment of Interviewers from the Situation

The case material reported earlier suggests that past theorists may have overestimated the intensity of the motivation of the interviewer to influence the respondent, or the intensity of his reaction to the sentiments expressed by the respondent. Interviewers may well be highly involved in their *job* and very concerned with the *issues* studied, but this interest is not focused on the specific interplay with a given respondent. Quantitative support for this revision of theory is available from the results of the mail questionnaire administered to the nationwide field staff.

Thus with respect to a question asking the interviewers to rate for a variety of purposes the importance of public opinion surveys, the purposes emphasized by about two-thirds of them were "institutional," service to scientists, or service to the democratic process, and not the value of the interview to the respondent. It is true, however, that one-third of the total staff stated that the use of polls "to educate the people who are interviewed" is a "most important" function. But over half of the staff felt that it was not the interviewer's responsibility to educate an uninformed respondent, even when the respondent desired to continue the discussion *after* the formal interview was terminated, and 80 percent of the staff felt it was not their responsibility to enlighten a prejudiced respondent, even if he wished to continue the discussion *after* the interview. Two-thirds reported that they do not feel privately irritated by a respondent's opinions. That the general orientation of the interviewer might be described as a *"Task Involvement,"* and not a "social orientation" to the respondent or an affect-laden experience, is also clear from other data. A majority report that they only occasionally or hardly ever would enjoy staying on to chat with their respondents. Only a tiny minority report that they have frequently made friends with a respondent. About half of the staff reports that there were no particular questions on past surveys which they would have preferred *not* to ask—despite the fact that NORC's past surveys have covered questions ranging from personal financial matters to experience with mental illness and questions about sex.

With respect to the question as to whether they would object to asking certain *hypothetical* questions of respondents, most interviewers report that they would not strongly object to inquiries into the most sacred areas. They seem to regard the interviewing process as a job—no matter what the content. Thus only tiny minorities report that they would strongly object to asking the respondent, "Has anyone in your family been in a mental hospital?" or "Do you think masturbation can cause mental illness?" and only about one-quarter report strong objections to the bizarre question, "Have you provided for the Salvation Army in your will?"

In this connection, it is most interesting to note that interviewers occasionally reported as their chief failing the fact of their social *"over-involvement"* in the interview situation. They were asked early in the mail questionnaire the open question, "What would you say are your chief failings as an interviewer?" Certainly nothing in the literature of interviewing would have suggested that this would be regarded as a failing—if anything the notion of high social involvement would have appeared to be an approved trait. Yet, 10 per cent of the interviewers spontaneously report that their chief failing is "over-involvement." They say: "I'm too sympathetic," "I like people too much," "Too many people open up to me about personal problems," "A disinclination to keep the respondent precisely to the subject."

And *none* of them suggests that his failing lies in his *lack* of social involvement. It must be that interviewers have learned the wisdom of being somewhat detached as a basis for carrying on their work efficiently and as a preventive against bias. But this wisdom from experience has been neglected in the prevailing body of theory about interviewer effect.

Further evidence of an inferential sort on the detachment of interviewers is available from the questionnaire administered to all interviewers. Certain questions were intended as indicators of personality traits. Among these was a question specially designed to measure the general "sociality" of the interviewer. As in all personality inventories, such measures take on clearest meaning in relation to statistical norms. In this instance norms were constructed by administering the same questions to a national sample of respondents. In Table 4 are presented

TABLE 4

SOCIALITY OF NORC STAFF AS COMPARED WITH COLLEGE EDUCATED WOMEN IN A NATIONAL SAMPLE

"In dealing with problems of intimate concern to you, do you prefer to talk them over with other people, or do you prefer to keep them to yourself?"

	Percentage of Interviewer Population	Percentage of "Norm" Group in National Sample
Talk with others.......	38	69
Keep to self..........	62	31
	100	100
	N = 151	N = 90

the distribution of answers among the interviewers as compared with the answers for the college educated women in the national sample,[55] the population group most like interviewers in general characteristics.

The mere examination of marginals, in which it is noted that two-thirds of the interviewers are not "sociable," suggests that our traditional views have been in error. However, in relation to the norms, it is dramatically demonstrated that interviewers are not as sociable as their counterparts in the population. This would suggest that their involvement in the social setting of the interview would not be as great as it was presumed to be in past theorizing.[56]

Occurrence of expectational processes.—A variety of measures from the mail questionnaire suggest that such processes are frequent in occurrence, although not characteristic of a majority. Thus, as a measure of "role expectations," interviewers were asked, "How often do you feel you can size up the respondent and predict most of his answers in advance?" A little over one-third of the staff reported that they could do this half the time or better. However, when followed by an open question asked of everyone as to the cues used in building up role expectations, only a small minority flatly answered that it was impossible to predict the answer. Admittedly this question is loaded in the direction of increasing the estimate, but the very high figure is nevertheless striking. The detailed cues used in such expectational processes are reported in Table 5.

Further evidence of the operation of expectational processes was

TABLE 5

FACTORS ENABLING INTERVIEWERS TO PREDICT RESPONDENTS' ANSWERS

"What sort of things about the respondent help you predict his answers?"

	Percentage of All Interviewers*
Role factors	
Economic level: class, occupation, home, neighborhood	54
Nationality, religion, ethnic group	6
Age	11
Sex	4
Attitude-structure factors	
Education, intelligence, interest in subject	17
Co-operativeness: initial response to interviewer	16
Answers to first few questions	11
Respondent's attitude toward the interview situation	10
Personality factors in respondent	10
Miscellaneous	4
Impossible to predict	13
Don't try to predict, don't know	17
	N = 151

* Percentages total more than 100 because of multiple answers.

furnished by interviewers in connection with an experiment on coding in which interviewers were asked to code answers under two conditions: first, with the answers to a given question isolated from the totality of answers to the questionnaire and, secondly, with these answers imbedded in the total context of answers.[57] In conjunction with the experiment, interviewers were asked what elements in the normal field situation aided them in classifying difficult or ambiguous answers into a precoded category. About one-third of the interviewers reported the use of contextual aids of a stereotypic sort, such aids being almost pure examples of expectations predicated on the general characteristics of the respondent. For example, one interviewer remarks: "If he is an ignorant person, I judge his answer on the fact that he doesn't really know what the question means and I often put 'don't know' for this type person."

Another source of evidence on the frequency of expectational processes is available from a question asked in Elmira in the 1948 Election study. Respondents were asked to estimate how given population groups would be likely to vote. Since the interviewers filled out questionnaires also, the answers to this question provide an estimate of role expectations. The interviewers completed these questionnaires prior to the first wave of interviewing in June. Consequently, the estimates of role expectations revealed in the tables below are conservatively stated, since the interviewer is predicating his judgment prior to the campaign and prior to the choice of presidential candidates. It is logical that such beliefs would be even stronger at later dates closer to election day. In Table 6 below, selected data are presented on the frequency with which interviewers expect a number of population groups to vote in some systematic direction. Also presented is the frequency with which interviewers checked the alternatives: "don't know" how the given group will vote, or the group "will not vote as a bloc." This latter statistic gives an estimate of the *rejection* of role expectations.

It is clear that over half the field staff had a role expectation of a *uniform* sort for each of the four population groups presented, and that only about one-quarter of the staff rejected expectations of this type.

Analysis of the Elmira data on role expectations supports the suggestion of an expectation-prone interviewer. If we intercorrelate the interviewer's report of, or the rejection of, role expectations for each of the four population groups, we can determine the consistency of interviewer proneness. High consistency would strengthen the notion that there is some stable pattern within the interviewer making him prone to such processes. The six correlations range in value from .38 to .87 with a median value of .59 suggesting a fairly strong tendency for the interviewer either to reject consistently the notion that the voting of these groups can be predicted or to expect them to vote in some particular fashion.[58]

TABLE 6

INTERVIEWERS' BELIEFS AS TO VOTING BEHAVIOR OF VARIOUS GROUPS
IN POPULATION*

	Percentage of Interviewers Believing That
Rich people will vote predominantly Republican.........	76
Factory workers will vote predominantly Democratic......	55
Farmers will vote predominantly Republican.............	55
Poor people will vote predominantly Democratic.........	58
	N = 33

Belief That Following Groups Will Not Vote as Bloc or Don't Know How Groups Will Vote:	Percentage of Interviewers
Rich people......................................	21
Factory workers.................................	27
Farmers..	24
Poor people....................................	27
	N = 33

* These data were made available through the courtesy of the 1948 Political Study of Elmira.

In the discussion of the case material on expectational processes, it was noted that even among the small number of interviewers studied there was a variation in the proneness to such tendencies. Certain conjectures were advanced, based on the material and on a larger body of theory as to the types of interviewers who would be prone to such processes. The mail questionnaire affords some more reliable evidence on personality factors correlated with such expectational processes. Certain questions were asked which might be used as diagnostic indicators of stereotypic traits.

Four measures from the F-Scale of the Berkeley Study of Authoritarianism which had been found empirically to correlate with stereotypy were asked of the interviewers.[59] These asked the interviewer whether he agreed with statements on the inevitability of war, the desirability of a strict leader, the desirability of severe punishment for sex criminals, and the strict rejection of pre-marital sex relations. The answers to these questions were pooled into an index, those disagreeing with three or more of the items being classified as "non-stereotypic."

Cross-tabulation of this index against the questions designed to measure expectational effects provides some evidence. The data are presented below.

TABLE 7

The Relation of Stereotypic Personality to Expectational Processes in the Interview

	Can Predict the Respondents' Answers Half the Time or More	Answers Generally Split Along Class Lines	
Stereotypic.........	44%	44%	N = 63
Non-stereotypic.....	30	37	N = 88

Social orientation of respondents as a function of the personality of the interviewers.—The case material was suggestive of the fact that certain kinds of interviewers, labeled "intrusive," are likely to increase the sensitivity of the respondent to the social aspects of the situation. More quantitative evidence in support of this suggestion is available from cross-tabulation of replies to the mail questionnaire. Certain measures were designed to reveal the social orientation of the interviewer and these can be tabulated against the measure of the frequency with which interviewers reported that respondents were keenly oriented to them. These data are presented below:

TABLE 8

The Relation of Measures of Interviewer Intrusiveness to Respondent Being Socially Oriented to the Interviewer

	Per Cent Who Report That Respondents Are Very Interested in Them Personally	N
Among interviewers who very often feel like staying and chatting..	28%	72
Only occasionally feel like staying and chatting.............	10	59
Hardly ever feel like staying and chatting..................	—	20
Among interviewers who feel some responsibility to educate uninformed respondents.............................	24%	67
Don't feel responsibility to educate uninformed respondents....	13	83
Among interviewers who feel they should enlighten a prejudiced respondent.................................	30%	30
Don't feel they should enlighten a prejudiced respondent.......	14	120

Variations in roles assumed by interviewers as a function of cognitions.—Some evidence that interviewers differ in their views of their proper function in the interview is available from the mail questionnaire administered to the current NORC staff. The open question referred to in the foregoing, on their chief failings as an interviewer, yields some evidence on the degree to which they regard probing as desirable or important. While the answers cover a wide range of behaviors, it is interesting that the two most frequent failings reported referred to contrasted functions within the interview, "not probing well or enough" vs. "general carelessness or difficulties in writing." Those who referred to each of these areas to the exclusion of the other numbered 21 per cent and 23 per cent respectively.

A specific question was also asked as to the preference for handling surveys that contained mainly open questions requiring probing, rather than surveys containing mainly pre-coded questions. The split is almost even, with 55 per cent preferring the pre-coded type of survey.

That this latter variation in orientation to the job is partly a function of beliefs about the nature of attitude can be inferred from the reasons interviewers gave for their preferences for pre-coded questions vs. free-answer questions which involve probing. No matter what the preference, the predominant reason given reflected some belief as to the nature of attitudes. Thus, among those interviewers who preferred pre-coded questions, 25 per cent gave as their reason, "respondents aren't articulate enough, don't make answers consistent, can't back up their opinions." Among those who preferred free-answer questions, 35 per cent claimed that "this comes closer to what people really think and it gets at people's real feelings" and an additional 18 per cent gave the clearly related reason, "the respondent feels freer and gets a better chance to express himself." These figures give a conservative indication of the cognitive basis for preference for a given interviewing role, since some of the other categories of reasons did contain answers bordering on beliefs about the nature of attitudes. However, since these categories were less clear, they have not been lumped with the above.

3. THE VALUE OF A PHENOMENOLOGY OF THE INTERVIEW

A Framework for the Evaluation of Quantitative
Data on Interviewer Effects

Let us imagine what this study would be like if Chapter II had not been written. In Chapter III, devoted to sources of effect within the interviewer, we shall see that the most strenuous experimental study failed to reveal any "ideological bias" in the sense of systematic distortions of respondent attitudes in the direction of interviewer opinions, *operating uniformly over all classes of situations.* In Chapter VI, on the magnitude of effects in usual survey operations, we shall see that careful large-scale field experiments revealed negligible differences in the results obtained by different interviewers on a variety of questions. Confronted with such findings, one might have rejected the evidence on the grounds of technical flaws or evaluated it as "unusual" or "atypical," since the evidence seems so contrary to past research and to our traditional views of interviewer effect. Any research project is bound to be limited in size, and the reader can always reserve his judgment and assume that another experiment will reverse the verdict. But the juxtaposition of these necessarily limited quantitative studies with the qualitative materials on the nature of the interview situation should give one some confidence in accepting these findings and, in addition, make plausible and understandable what might otherwise appear a bizarre, unexplainable finding. Here is one obvious function of Chapter II. We can begin to understand the experimental findings that will be reported and evaluate them properly.

Depending on the plausibility of major experimental findings in relation to our view of interviewer effects, we might, as just indicated, have accepted or rejected the findings. But buried under these main findings —for example, the general unimportance of ideological bias—was the possibility of specialized interviewer effects occurring under certain conditions. But under what conditions? Here the qualitative materials give guidance. They hint at the special circumstances that hinder or facilitate the operation of biasing tendencies. And, in some instances, the direction in which they lead analysis is exactly contrary to the path we might have taken. Thus, for example, if we had sought for ideological effects that were differentially great in particular subgroups of respondents, we might normally have expected to find these effects located in the apathetic, the uninformed, the uneducated, for such individuals would have less conviction and would presumably be more suggestible. But the qualitative materials show that apathy is one of the very safeguards against the interviewer's opinion being communicated, and that ideological bias may occur essentially as a task aid when the situation causes difficulty in performing given assigned functions. And the apathetic do not create such difficulties, since their opinions and lack of opinions are unequivocal.

Such evidence led to a more refined hypothesis, which, when tested, yielded positive evidence of a curvilinear relation between respondent apathy and bias, that is, both apathetic and highly involved respondents seemed to be less affected than the "somewhat involved" group.[60]

Another example of the development of more sophisticated models of the operation of ideological effects is presented in Chapter III, where we sought the differential occurrence of ideological effects among interviewers who anticipated difficulties in handling certain questions—a lead which came from the discussion of situational factors and the disruption of roles.

Similarly, Chapter V, on the influence of situational factors in interviewer effect, grows out of the evidence that the interviewer is usually predisposed *not* to bias the data, and that a variety of pressures *disrupt* the normal pattern and invoke the biasing tendencies. Chapters III and V now incorporate a series of experiments into the influence of such factors.

But these chapters by no means exhaust the respective areas of research into expectational and situational factors in interviewer effect. Nor does this total manuscript exhaust the problem. Further tests are called for. With respect to such future research, a host of new hypotheses can be generated from the qualitative materials.

Finally, apart from the relevance of these qualitative materials for research into interviewer effect, there is a relevance of the findings to the general operations of public opinion agencies. We now acknowledge that attitudes are not independent of the circumstances within which they are liberated. We shall be better able to interpret the meanings of our voluminous findings on American public opinion in the light of knowing a little better what the situation is like in which respondents voice these sentiments. We generally have little but the recorded words from which to draw our inferences. The case materials in Chapter II give us some feel for the relation of respondents toward the social world about which they are so continually questioned, and toward the interview situation in which they voice their sentiments.

CHAPTER III

Sources of Effect Deriving from the Interviewer

1. THE NATURE OF EXPECTATIONAL PROCESSES

The phenomenological data in the previous chapter showed clearly that interviewers frequently have certain beliefs about their respondents which produce expectations as to the answers that should be elicited to the questions in the survey. While the *existence* of what we have called role expectations, attitude-structure expectations, and probability expectations was supported by considerable qualitative material, only suggestive evidence was presented that such expectations *actually affect* the behavior of interviewers in such a manner as to alter survey results. Moreover, no evidence was presented that any alterations in the results deriving from such expectations would lead to less validity in measurement. The possibility might be entertained that the interviewer's expectations have a foundation in truth and consequently enhance validity. Therefore, it now remains for us to present convincing experimental evidence on actual expectational effects and their contribution to error.

In so doing, we should not be too hard on the interviewer or make him bear *exclusive* responsibility for such behavior. Role and attitude-structure expectations among interviewers may merely reflect larger scientific emphasis upon determinism, since these expectations build upon a concept of *regularity* in behavior. Kluckhohn brings this interpretation to our attention in the course of a discussion of life-history materials in Anthropology.[1] He suggests that factors of an accidental or idiosyncratic sort are usually neglected in explaining social or cultural or personal dynamics and sees this as part of a larger tendency in traditional Western Science to abhor "chance." He remarks:

That endless idiosyncratic variations can and do occur in the life of each human being hardly requires—in principle—extensive documentation. All sorts of things happen which could not have been predicted on the basis of knowledge of human biology or of the cultural, social, or impersonal environments. Even casual social contacts of brief duration . . . often seem crucial in determining whether one's life proceeds along one or another of various possible courses.

Kluckhohn then emphasizes that the belief in regularities can blind one to the significance of such accidental factors and uses words almost identical with our description of role-expectation effects:

The analyst who wants to really comprehend the total personality of the informant or revelant must "get behind" the various masks, temporarily

83

stripping off (but not forgetting) the layer which is the totality of responses expected of the subject (for example, as old man . . . as grandfather, etc.).

In addition, such expectations, since they are expressive of tendencies to organization of perception, are fundamental psychological processes. Since they often involve the ordering of people by certain categories, they are in the very nature of society. Much evidence in support of this view has already been presented in Chapter II; Oldfield in commenting on the expectations he observed in his interviewers similarly stresses this larger context. He remarks:

Lastly, we have to consider briefly certain special aspects of the construction of the homunculus (representation—image of candidate). It would, I think, be incorrect to suppose that this process occurs of itself *ab initio*. We all possess certain generalized frames of reference in regard to which other people are assessed, and it is fairly plain that to a greater or less extent these are involved not only in making judgments about the completed homunculus but also in its construction. That is to say, there exist for each individual ready-made skeletons upon which the homunculi are built, and into which the impressions of their human counterparts are fitted. This process represents our tendency to assimilate people to types. It has the advantage of reducing the time required for the building of the homunculus. But if the number of such standard skeletons is severely limited, this also possesses certain obvious disadvantages.[2]

Prior to the presentation of the evidence, however, it is important to clarify a theory of such effects. Such theory will guide us in interpreting our experimental findings and will provide more comprehensive understanding of the total problem than our necessarily limited quantitative evidence.

That expectations of some order, no matter what their specific content, do exist among interviewers seems unquestionable. That their biasing effects on the data would be unconstrained is questionable.

In survey research, the specific interviewing procedures prescribed for the interviewer tend to check the arbitrary exercise of his expectations. For example, the "rules of the game" require mechanical recording or coding of what has been said and the exact adherence to question order and wording. For example, the rule to record the respondent's words verbatim and to code a reply in the answer box that most nearly corresponds to the actual words reduces the biases arising even when the interviewer holds contrary expectations.

That such legislation over the interviewer is not merely on the books, but actually exercises *some* control, is clear from the material presented in Chapter II, where it was shown that an interviewer may strongly sense the conflict between his expectations and what the agency requires of him. However, it is also clear that such rules would *not preclude* the operation of expectations. Reference to the Chapter II materials again reveals that under conditions of stress, or difficulty in the interview situation, the rules may be consciously flouted. Moreover, only brief thought is needed to realize that the interview situation is not *that* rigid. There are various choices left to the interviewer. He can continue to probe, or he can accept the answer already given. He can ask the next question, or he may assume that he already knows the answer and that the question is therefore redundant.[3] In addition, the interviewer must apply his judgment in coding an equivocal answer into one of a limited number of prepared answer boxes, and even the most rigid rule to record answers "verbatim" allows the interviewer to omit irrelevancies without defining what an irrelevancy is. At all these points of choice, the interviewer may well let his expectations be his guide.

The interview situation might be characterized then as one with some control over the interviewer's expectations. Within these controls, however, there is still some realm of freedom, and the controls may be ignored under particular conditions of stress.

Thus, we would anticipate that expectation effects would be moderate in magnitude over the general run of data, but might reach extreme magnitude in the particular instances where both situational difficulty and freedom of choice were great.

An additional complexity in the operation of such expectations upon survey data ought to be considered. Whether the basic expectation is an attitude-structure expectation predicated upon the early answers or a role expectation predicated upon an initial judgment of the respondent's group membership, it might actually be contradicted by evidence in the course of the rest of the interview. Humans are not so simple and consistent! Such contradictions might shatter an original expectation. Conceivably the interviewer might then abandon all such tendencies and treat each response segmentally. While this is not beyond possibility, what appears to be much more likely is that such contradictions, if noted, would produce some reorganization of the initial expectation, or an alternative expectation which would then govern the interviewer's subsequent behavior. This at least would attenuate *constant* errors over a large battery of questions spread throughout an interview, although it would not reduce the *total* occurrence of errors arising from expectational processes per se. The tendency for reorganization rather than complete fragmentation of all expectations would seem supported by the extensive literature previously cited on the primacy of organization in perception. Incidentally, such processes, it will be seen, make it difficult for us to measure the *full* extent of expectational effects by quantitative laboratory experiments, since a particular instance of biasing behavior on the part of the interviewer may not correspond with a basic expectation that we have *experimentally created* or measured, and would therefore be regarded as negative evidence. Yet, this behavior may well represent an error related to a more subtle or idiosyncratic expectation, emerging in the course of the experiment, which we are not aware of. Consequently, much experimental data will give a conservative picture of the total biasing consequences of expectational processes, and it would only be through extensive phenomenological data that one could evaluate the full effects of expectations. That such perceptual reorganizations occur in the course of interviewing, each one in turn producing expectational effects on the data, is clear from the findings of a study where the total interview process was brought under observation through covert electrical recording of the interview.[4] The study will be reported in detail in Chapter V. From the examination of the transcription and the returned schedule, it was possible to score the occurrence of "biasing" errors on questions of prejudice toward Negroes and Jews. These were errors which led to a spurious measurement of the respondent's real attitude, through distorting the *direction* of the attitude toward the more or less favorable end of the dimension. The analysts noted that, while such errors did occur, the direction of the effect was *not* consistent over the series of related questions. After examining the recording for the interplay between interviewer and respondent, they remark: "As far as direction of biasing behavior was concerned, the interviewer very often took his cue from the respondent, and then in turn exerted some influence upon the respondent, *in a sort of spiralling process.*"[5]

They also remark: "We were not able to develop a measure of bias based on the material in the recorded interviews which clearly revealed the operation of any of the *interviewer's own* prejudices.[5]

In other words, the interviewer exerted some biasing effect on the measurement of prejudiced attitudes, but this did not stem from his own ideology nor from a rigid initial expectation. The behavior seemed clearly governed by an attitude-structure expectation, but one which emerged and developed in relation to the sentiments progressively expressed in the course of the interview.

Such considerations of the reorganization of expectational processes in relation to the play of experiences upon the interviewer emphasize again the role of situational determinants of interviewer effects, which will be treated fully in Chapter V.

While some reorganization of expectations is likely to occur, it is also quite likely that initial expectations can at times be rigid and maintained in the face of contradictory experience. While the ratio of rigid expectational effects to fluid or reorganized expectational effects cannot be exactly specified, no doubt both phenomena operate in some degree.

For example, the occurrence of both types of expectational processes and, incidentally, their strong influence upon interviewer behavior can be noted in Oldfield's study of the personnel interview.[6] His report shows vividly the existence of initial expectations:

> As to the forms which the first impression may take, my inquiries among interviewers have indicated, as might have been expected, that these are varied . . . We may distinguish the following. . . . an immediate feeling of like or dislike and connected with this, a tendency for the formation of spontaneous judgments of a quasi-ethical character regarding the candidate's personality. . . . Judgments of a predictive character relating to the candidate's future either in general or in a restricted sphere. Such judgments are of the form "he will never get on in the world," or "she will make a good shorthand typist.". . . Lastly, but from the standpoint of the conduct of the interview perhaps of the greatest importance, is a sense of knowing how to deal with the candidate,—of perceiving the proper attitude to adopt towards him.

But later on, he implies that such expectations also emerged in the course of interviewing and may go through reorganization:

> Another important feature of the conscious processes is the tendency for more or less clearly formulated judgments about the candidate to emerge. Every now and then the process of observation is broken into, and a judgment is either deliberately made or involuntarily alters consciousness. The emergence of these judgments often appears to arise from the crystallization of an attitude toward the candidate. What has been vaguely felt about the candidate may become more or less explicitly formulated. Now it is, I believe, the constant play of such attitudes which are intrinsically judgmental in character, that determines the interviewer's conduct of the conversation; and it is in this sense that observation and a growing apprehension of the candidate regulate the steps the interviewer takes."[7]

Yet the problem is not so indeterminate as it would appear, for the respective strength of rigid initial expectations vs. "fluid" expectations can be specified to some extent, as well as the determinants of these strengths.

The *overriding* influence of the initial expectation cannot be denied. The evidence provides ample support for this view. The phenomenological data of Chapter II suggests how compelling in character initial expectations are. Asch's study, previously cited, shows the influence of an initial impression in organizing subsequent fragmentary information about a person. A study by Kelley confirms Asch's basic finding. Here the conditions had greater similitude to the real-life interview situation, since the findings were obtained for subjects observing a real other person rather than for subjects reacting to a mere list of adjectives attributed to a person.[8]

Prior expectations were established by instructions in fifty-five male students that a person who would come to teach them in class had a certain characteristic. The expectation that the "teacher" was "rather cold" or "very warm" was randomly applied among the students who were required to write a free essay-type characterization after they had observed the "teacher" and to rate him on a series of traits. It was found, as with Asch, that the initial trait, in this instance warm vs. cold, organized and affected the general judgment and reaction to the other person and even affected the students' *behavior*. For example, students attributed more good qualities to the teacher when the prior expectation of "warm" was provided.

Another extension of Asch's basic work, but one with almost direct relevance to role expectations, was conducted by Haire and Grunes.[9] The basic finding shows the strength of an initial expectation in the face of contradictory information. A list of adjectives containing the word "intelligent" was presented to students at the University of California. As with Asch, the subjects were asked to describe the individual who was characterized by the items listed. What makes the experiment peculiarly relevant to role expectation is that the students were instructed that the individual in question was a *"workingman."* The findings demonstrated that fragmentary items are reacted to in an organized fashion, in that, as with Asch's subjects, the students were able to give a coherent description. More important to the present discussion was the fact that the initial instructions that this was a "workingman" operated to prevent the incorporation of the quality of "intelligence" into the description, since these students had a clear and well-organized picture of a "worker" into which intelligence did not fit.

While the detailed findings will be cited later, about 60 per cent of the students in some manner distorted the characteristic "intelligence" in their descriptions. An extreme instance of this phenomenon was the remark of a student that "intelligence was not notable even though it is stated."

A much larger literature gives general support to the influence of an initial expectation upon subsequent behavior. While studies showing the influence of an initial expectation upon subsequent perception of *another person* are few in number, a much larger literature gives support

to the general influences of initial expectations upon subsequent judgment of various discrete *stimuli*. The studies are too voluminous to be
cited, but the effect of imputing some authorship of a given type in altering the meaning and consequent evaluation of a text as in "prestige
suggestion" experiments, and the effect of some initial uni-directional
context in altering later judgments, have all been well established.[10]

One such set of experiments may be cited for their dramatic demonstration of the way in which initial stimulation somehow established an
expectation which altered subsequent auditory perception. These are
chosen for their parallelism to the experience of conversation in an interview. Twenty-five years ago, Marbe reported a number of studies
conducted by his assistant, Schorn.[11] In these studies, the expectation
was produced partly by experimental instructions and partly by the
initial direction intrinsic in the material, as in the later experiments by
Asch. In one of these experiments, twenty subjects were read a list of
eight verbs in very quick tempo, and by instructions the set was established that these would all express movement. The fifth verb in the sequence however was "sehen" (see). When the subjects were asked to
reproduce the words, seven did not mention *sehen*, and an additional
seven substituted "gehen." In another experiment of parallel design, the
twenty subjects were instructed that the words would be expressive of
grief or fear. The word that was out of context was "beten" (to pray).
It was omitted by seven of the twenty subjects, and five others substituted "beben" (to shiver). In a third parallel experiment, the set was established that the words would all relate to a mental process. The word
"senken" (to sink) was out of context and was omitted by half of the
subjects. An additional five subjects substituted "denken" (to think).
In a final experiment, Schorn read a short political text over a loud-
speaker (Haustelephon) to nineteen subjects. The subjects had been
told that the text was taken from a "Socialist" newspaper. In reproduc-
ing the passage, three of the subjects substituted for the sentence, "Wir
lassen die Monarchie" (We permit the Monarchy), "Wir hassen die
Monarchie" (We hate the Monarchy). In addition, a large number of
sentences were reproduced which had not been contained in the original
text but which were harmonious with the pattern of Social Democracy.

While none of these studies approximate the *flux of experiences* over
the longer duration of a live interview with consequent greater opportunity for reorganization of perception, they do show that a discrete
aspect of experience is altered by the initial expectation. They all give
support to the hypothesis that subsequent experiences, even if contradictory, will be assimilated into the framework of the initial expecta-

tion. In the place of the experimentally created expectations, we merely substitute the natural ones in the minds of our interviewers.[12]

Such experimental findings on the potency of the initial expectations take on plausibility when one notes the variety of dynamic processes which the interviewer has at his disposal in resolving apparent contradictions. Some of these were revealed in the phenomenological accounts presented earlier. For example, Interviewer "B" was aware of the contradictions in the reports of the simulated respondent but *rationalized* the contradiction as being not the genuine attitude of the respondent. Haire and Grunes, in a refined analysis of their data, report a number of dynamisms by which the initial organization is protected from the contradiction.[13] Thus five out of the total forty-three subjects had no difficulty in *denying* the reality of the trait "intelligent" in the workingman. For example, one subject remarked "he is intelligent but not too much so since he works in a factory."[14] A much more frequent defense involved the incorporation of the item "intelligent" with a weakening of its significance by the process of *encapsulating* it in the description in such manner that its full meaning was distorted.

We may well consider certain other features of such expectational processes which would reduce the biasing influence of expectations early in the interview. While early expectations would have considerable effect on subsequent data in the interview, and emerging or reorganized expectations would bias the end portions of the interview data, we should expect some *degree of specificity* in the expectations, which would attenuate any *global* effects on the *entire* interview. While interviewers generally would expect a certain structure of congruent attitudes or a pattern of attitudes correlative with some group membership, it is unlikely that they would predict on this basis the answer to *every one* of the questions. While Ichheiser comments on the "tendency to overestimate the *unity* of personality,"[15] we may conjecture that most humans do not see others as operating with a *Weltanschauung*—a totally unified body of sentiments. While system and order would be expected, it would probably be of the nature of several subsystems of attitudes, each expected to be orderly but separate. Similarly, interviewers might expect a man to have a certain series of attitudes which differed from a woman's attitudes, but they would probably not regard such role determination as encompassing every realm of attitude.

Therefore, an initial expectation would generally bias the interviewer's behavior with respect to three or four subsequent questions which he believed to be relevant or related to the initially expected structure and not bias the rest of the questions.[16]

The experiment by Kelley, cited earlier, illustrates this specificity. Detailed data show that the prior expectation of a "warm" or "cold" person did not affect the ratings of *all* the characteristics of the teacher. The effects were differential depending on the degree to which the warm-cold variable was regarded as relevant to the characteristics rated. Kelley is suggesting that the forces deriving from an initial expectation are constrained in their effects on subsequent data by a kind of logic of relevance.[17]

Other detailed findings by Kelley suggest that prepared role expectations or probability expectations *prior* to the onset of the interview would be attenuated to some extent in given interviews by the evidence that a particular respondent does not fit the prepared categories. Presumably this finding would not bear upon the influence of attitude-structure expectations which, by definition, emerge only following contact with the given respondent. Several different accomplices were used as the "teacher" who appeared before the classes. The influence of the expectation "warm-cold" was not uniform in magnitude for all such "teachers." Kelley is again suggesting some limitations upon the effect of certain early expectations upon subsequent interview data.

Just as tentative expectations *prior* to the onset of the interview might be dissipated with certain respondents who do not fit the mold, so, too, there is the possibility that given respondents might accentuate the operation of an expectation because of their characteristics. A given respondent might either appear to typify a certain role and thus accentuate role expectations, or might be regarded as having comprehensively organized attitudes, and thus accentuate the operation of attitude-structure expectations. A suggestive demonstration of this latter possibility is available in the study by Frenkel-Brunswik, cited in Chapter I.[18] As previously indicated, three judges following prolonged observation, rated groups of boys and girls on the strength of nine particular drives—e.g., drive for autonomy (a striving for independence and freedom), drive for aggression, etc. It was noted earlier that Brunswik analyzed the agreement between judges in the ratings assigned on the *specific* drives. What concerns us here is the refined analysis Brunswik made of the tendency of the judges to find *patterns of drives* co-existing in the children. By intercorrelating the ratings, she could determine, for example, whether judges regarded children who had a strong need for autonomy as having little need for "social ties." While these intercorrelations, of course, are partly determined by the fact that there are truly interrelations between various motivational processes, it will be seen shortly that the single ratings and the relations between ratings reflect the biases of the individual judges. Consequently, the intercorrelations implicitly bear upon the problem of attitude-structure expectations, since they establish what contents are regarded by the judge as forming a common structure.

Brunswik noted the rather interesting finding among *all* the judges that their ratings of the drives were more highly intercorrelated for the female subjects than for the male.[19] While it is not beyond possibility that the organization of drives is less specific in women, there seems to be no real evidence in support of this. It seems more likely that the judges were simply inclined to the *belief* that the structure of motives in women is more comprehensively organized. For Frenkel-Brunswik's judges, who incidentally were women, the old saying that "woman is fickle" may not be accepted. By extension, it is suggested that interviewers might be more prone to exercise an attitude-structure expectation when interviewing one type of respondent rather than another, on the basis of strong beliefs as to the relative consistency or unity of given kinds of people.

Such phenomena as the facts that expectations will generally not subsume all the possible contents covered by the total questionnaire and that prior expectations will not be applied routinely to all the respondents tend to reduce the massiveness of the bias produced. The bias would be maximal only for those interviewers whose expectations tend to be *comprehensive* in scope and *rigid* or persistent in the face of the contradictory appearance and remarks of respondents. That there are variations among interviewers in these respects is supported by the qualitative data presented in Chapter II and the statistical data therein presented showing the distribution of expectations among the current NORC field staff. We are not concerned here with the problem of the determinants of such individual differences or their relevance to the control of error through selection methods. These matters will be dealt with elsewhere. What is clear is that there is some reduction of the serious biasing effects, since not all our interviewers have extreme tendencies. Some minority of them even seem free of expectations about their respondents.[20] Others seem to show strong expectations, but among these, the expectations may not be comprehensive in scope. However, that there would remain some small number of individuals who would have beliefs calculated to produce expectancies over a wide range of characteristics is suggested by another finding of Frenkel-Brunswik's. She intercorrelated the nine sets of drive-ratings assigned the subjects for each of her three judges separately. Apart from any question of variation in the relationship between a *particular* pair of drives, she noted that the judges varied strikingly in the *formal* tendency to regard *any* possible pairs among the nine drives as falling into the same clusters. Thus, out of seventy-two opportunities to find pairs of drives exhibiting a common pattern,[21] Judge "H" found twenty-five such instances, whereas Judge "F" found only seventeen and Judge "G" only twelve. In other words, judges or raters or interviewers seem to vary in the mere tendency to expect narrow or comprehensively organized structures, and with some, there is a considerable approximation toward a belief in a simple unitary structure.

One demonstration of such a belief in the unity of a subject's behavior, and in this instance its pervasiveness, is available in a study by Elkin.[22] A life-history document was circulated to thirty-nine judges, who were asked to make certain interpretations of the case. The judges represented such a diversity of backgrounds as psychiatry, anthropology, social work, sociology, and psychology, as well as the laity. Within the academic disciplines, there was further variety, since the psychologists included both experimentalists and clinicians, and the sociologists both theorists and "objective researchers." While differences of interpretation occurred in practically every area, there was consensus on the one point that the subject had developed *gradually and consistently.* The judges, in other words, did not acknowledge incongruity.

Another consideration of importance with respect to the biasing consequences of such expectations is their *contents.* An entire staff of interviewers might conceivably entertain expectations, but the *specific attitude* that was regarded as the accompaniment of lower-class status or the accompaniment of an initial attitude of atheism or the majority position in the population might *vary* from interviewer to interviewer. By contrast, all interviewers might *agree* as to the attitudes that accompany a given class position.

The bearing of these respective distributions of the contents of interviewer expectations on survey results (their biasing effects) is difficult to schematize. Ultimately, one would have to explore such questions as whether uni-variate and/or bi-variate characteristics are more affected by expectations of homogeneous or heterogeneous contents. It is clear that this question of the distribution of the contents of expectations over a staff is of great importance.

Incidentally, it should be noted that variations in the contents of expectations among interviewers make it difficult to gauge the full biasing effects of expectations in purely quantitative laboratory experiments. For example, if a given initial expectation is created experimentally and we observe the interviewer's behavior on a simulated question or answer, it may appear to us that the attitude recorded is not congruent with the expectation. However, for that interviewer the attitude elicited might be a legitimate part of the over-all structure. Thus, ability to obtain an apparently inconsistent answer might logically not deny our theory, and the finding would be only a pseudo-negative one.

While laboratory experiments of the usual design may be insensitive to *variations* in the contents of expectations among interviewers, natural-like field experiments to measure expectational effects are likely to be insensitive to *universally* held expectations. In the field study, the usual procedure would be to compare the results for interviewers interviewing equivalent groups, and to correlate these variations in results with some measure of expectational tendencies obtained for each interviewer. It will usually not be possible to measure the effect of a universally held expectation, because one cannot gauge a change in the survey result (the dependent variable) except by the standard of another interviewer's work. (In the laboratory experiment, since one, by definition, has a criterion of what the answer ought to be, one can measure change whether it is differential or universal.) Thus, it is likely that either type of experiment will understate the *total* effects of expectational processes, the extent of this understatement being a function of the relative proportion of expectations with universal or differential contents. Such methodological considerations again emphasize the importance of inquiry into the contents of expectations, and their distribution.

That peculiar idiosyncratic definitions of the contents of given structures of behavior occur is beyond doubt. From one item of behavior, the most varied expectations or inferences can be drawn as to its meaning or correlates or what structure accompanies it. In the RAF study previously cited, on reliability of assessment of pilots, the two psychiatrists prepared introspective reports of their methods. Examination of these reports indicated the operation of attitude-structure expectations as a guide to the diagnostic process. The writers conclude that the:

> two observers . . . have been guided in making their assessments by certain combinations of the traits listed, and that they have been so guided without being fully aware of the process. These combinations of traits seem to have provided the observers with an indicator in selecting what is significant from a very large number of variable factors. That such indicators form the basis of the clinical method of diagnosis is evident in the definition of syndromes in terms of objective phenomena.[23]

The detailed analysis of the intercorrelations between single traits attributed to the pilots by each of the two psychiatrists shows that there are differences in the way the traits are combined into constellations or in the contents regarded as forming a common structure. The two psychiatrists, working with equivalent samples, obtained different degrees of co-existence for various combinations of traits. For example, apart from the fact that they differed in the frequency with which they observed anxiety or phobias, they differed in the correlative symptoms noted. This is shown below in Table 9 which is constructed from data presented in the original report.[24]

TABLE 9

DIFFERENCES BETWEEN INTERVIEWERS IN THE CONTENTS OF AN ATTITUDE-
STRUCTURE EXPECTATION AS REVEALED BY THE INTERRELATIONS OBTAINED
FOR PSYCHIATRIC SYMPTOMS

SYMPTOM	AMONG PILOTS UNDER TRAINING DIAGNOSED AS HAVING PHOBIAS PROPORTION SHOWING GIVEN OTHER SYMPTOMS FOR*	
	Psychiatrist 1	Psychiatrist 2
Anxiety..........................	14%	54%
Mild obsessional tendencies.............	6	31
Obsessional personality................	2	2
Anxiety *and* obsessional temperament.....	5	2

* The bases for the percentages were 66 for Psychiatrist 1 and 122 for Psychiatrist 2.

In the study by Frenkel-Brunswik already alluded to, a series of findings increase our knowledge of individual differences in the contents of attitude-structure expectations.[25] As already indicated, she intercorrelated the ratings, given the children on every pair among the nine drives, separately for each judge, to see what patterns or combinations existed. She found frequently, for one judge, sizeable negative intercorrelations for a given pair of drives, indicating that this judge regarded the two drives as incompatible. For a second judge, the correlation for the same pair of drives was often positive, indicating that this second judge regarded those two drives as highly related and compatible.

In other words, judges disagreed markedly as to whether a child who was high in one respect was also high or low in another respect. For example, in fourteen instances the sign of the intercorrelation between pairs of drives was reversed between Judges "F" and "G" out of a total of seventy-two possible comparisons. This suggests that there are marked individual or interviewer differences in the components that are regarded as contained within a given structure, or that the meaning of a given entity, in terms of what larger structure it belongs to, shows marked interviewer variation.

Brunswik, by inspecting the differences among judges in the interrelationships between drives, also notes that disagreement was located mainly in certain drives. Thus, there was great variation among the judges in the degree to which they regarded the drive "autonomy" as compatible with other drives, but there was marked agreement on the entities that accompany the presence of "aggression." Thus, there appear to be for certain phenomena, constant or universal attitude-structure expectations, perhaps legitimate, whereas for other phenomena the expectations as to what components belong to the structure are not so clearly defined and may even be idiosyncratic from interviewer to interviewer.

The material in Chapter II suggests that the contents of expectations would tend to be uniform when they involve highly institutionalized patterns or regularities, or at least highly institutionalized beliefs. Thus, we cited as relevant to role-expectational processes, the frequency of belief among interviewers in the 1948 Elmira study that given economic groups would vote for a certain party. It was noted for each of the four economic groups studied that a *majority* of the interviewers predicted that the group would vote in a certain direction. For the group, "rich people" the value was a maximum, with 76 per cent of the staff believing that rich would vote Republican.[26] This suggests that with respect to very well-established and prominent phenomena, the expectations would approximate to uniform contents.

One demonstration of uniformity in the content of expectations in an institutionalized area is available in the work of the Census Bureau in labor-force measurement.[27] The demonstration, incidentally, reveals the significance of role expectations in causing error in factual as well as in opinion surveys. Accumulated experience with the Monthly Report on the Labor Force up to about 1945 had revealed that these surveys were failing to classify a considerable number of people as employed or in the labor force who should have been so classified according to definitions prescribed in the studies. The magnitude of underenumeration of workers in the MRLF prior to 1942 was of such order that a change in the procedure increased the estimate of employment by about one million, this increase coming mainly from people formerly classified as students or *housewives*. Another experiment revealed that about one and one-half million people engaged in unpaid farm work, each of whom contributed a substantial amount (nineteen or more hours) of work per week, had been previously recorded in the MRLF as nonworkers. Similar errors were found to have been prevalent in the classification of people in the 1940 Census. The errors were of such considerable magnitude that it was estimated on the basis of experimental work that approximately one million *women* were classified in the decennial census as engaged in their own home housework who were actually doing a substantial amount of unpaid work in agriculture. In discussing these errors, Ducoff and Hagood remark that one explanation may be that:

there is always a possibility that an enumerator will not ask specified questions if he believes them unnecessary or inapplicable. It is quite possible that a woman interrupted from her housework by an enumerator might automatically be classified as "engaged in own home housework" without being asked if she were at work on a job that week. . . . It seems likely that in many cases either the enumerator or respondent assumed that the proper classification for a married woman who kept house was "engaged in own home housework" regardless of whether she was employed full or part time. Similar mis-classifications of persons who were working and also attending school undoubtedly occurred.

While the concept is never explicitly employed in these discussions, it is clear that a "sex-linked" role expectation was clearly involved as a source of error. The magnitude of the effects on the data, as cited in the foregoing, suggests the inference that role expectations about the non-working status of women must have been rather *widely spread* through the field staff. Each enumerator interviews a very small proportion of the total sample; it therefore seems unquestionable that the expectation must have been characteristic of a considerable proportion of the enumerators in order to bias estimates by a million or more. Again it is suggested that expectancies having to do with highly stable or institutional features of the society will approximate most to uniformity in content.

However, even in such realms, *thorough* uniformity is not to be expected. For example, the data, to be discussed shortly, from our field experiment on role-expectation effects provide inferential evidence that interviewers differed markedly in their beliefs as to the patterns of shopping behavior of men and women. Certainly, no realm could be much more institutionalized than that of the roles of the sexes in the economy of the household. Yet, through the idiosyncrasies of the experiences of our interviewers, they even differed in this respect.

Another instance of objectively well-defined structures which still permitted some play for expectations with idiosyncratic contents is available in an experiment, to be cited shortly, on the biasing effects of attitude-structure expectations. As will be explained, interviewers heard two simulated interviews, one picturing an "isolationist" respondent, the other picturing an "interventionist" respondent. Both of these characterizations were vivid, fairly extreme in content, and highly consistent with the exception of occasional responses. Given the fund of experience with this well-known typology, and the sharpness of the two illustrations of it, one would expect thorough uniformity in the perception of the respondents. While this was the finding in general, one notes that a small number of deviant interviewers were so perverse in their beliefs that they appraised the isolationist attitude structure as interventionist. The detailed data are presented in Table 10 below.[28]

TABLE 10

Variations in (Interviewers') Appraisals of Two Respondents

APPRAISED AS:	PERCENTAGE OF INTERVIEWERS	
	Isolationist Characterization	Interventionist Characterization
Strongly interventionist.............	1	52
Interventionist.....................	1	40
Neither or "Don't know"............	11	8
Isolationist........................	58	—
Strongly isolationist................	29	—
	100 (N = 114)	100 (N = 114)

As previously noted, errors arising from attitude-structure expectations or role expectations will affect the values of bi-variate characteristics—i.e., relations between different characteristics—by inflating or obscuring the true value. Since much opinion research concerns itself with refined cross-tabulations or with problems of an explanatory nature rather than with marginals or problems of sheer description, errors arising from expectational processes assume great significance.

A final theoretical issue with respect to the nature of such expectation effects is the proper evaluation of them. We may well demonstrate that such expectations exist, and that they affect the *answers* recorded for the respondents. Whether these alterations of the answers reduce the *accuracy* of survey *measurements* is another and much more fundamental question, since there is no assurance that what the respondent says in the first place is true.

The thesis could easily be advanced that such expectations on the part of the sensitive interviewer lead him closer to the truth than the mere verbal report of the respondent, and that they should be permitted to operate freely. An influential body of opinion would argue that an individual's attitudes are organized, and that the structure apprehended might represent the truth rather than the discrete report. Such opinion might further claim that the respondent engages in self-deception or deliberate deception or that he gives a casual answer rather than his conviction or that the discrete report only takes on meaning in the light of its setting with other opinions. This view would regard as perversity the acceptance of the respondent's report as valid instead of the report as interpreted by the sensitive observer.

Even if one were to grant this view, evidence has been presented that interviewers *vary* in the tendencies to expectations as such and in the contents they ascribe to given structures. Consequently, while one or another interviewer may apprehend the truth, the operation of such expectations over the entire field staff will reduce the reliability of various results. However, it is our thesis that such expectations blind the given interviewer to the full complexities and realities of the attitudes he is supposed to elicit and record, and therefore, reduce the validity of the results. Empirical data to be presented below will provide some support for the argument, but logical considerations provide strong support for the view that the operation of such expectations is not the best means of increasing validity of survey data.

One might well admit that the answers of respondents in surveys might be invalid, yet urge that measures taken to assess and improve their validity be introduced on a *systematic* basis, by checks introduced analytically or by instituting new modes of questioning, interviewing, and the like. If the interviewer is left to his own devices to check upon the validity of the results, there is no way of distinguishing original data from interpreted data, and checks and corrections might be duplicated. Given the present assumption of public opinion research, namely, that the recorded answer is a faithful account of what the respondent said, rather than an interpretation, the danger of allowing such expectations to distort the respondent's remarks lies not alone in the errors perpetrated, but in the fact that we do not know which is interpretation and which is verbal report.

2. EXPERIMENTATION ON EXPECTATION EFFECTS

To test whether or not there actually was an observable error arising from attitude-structure expectations, a modified form of laboratory experiment was used.[29] By means of phonograph transcriptions, a group of subjects heard two typical, yet markedly contrasting, respondents functioning in a situation as closely resembling an interview as would be consistent with experimental design.

After these respondents had given what were judged to be enough replies to establish their general sentiments clearly (and thus permit subjects to form attitude-structure expectations), test responses were inserted at intervals in the course of the interviews. These test responses took the form either of lukewarm or equivocal responses that were the same in both interviews or of responses that were inconsistent with the attitude structure of the respondent. From the way subjects recorded or coded the discrete but equivalent responses they heard in the two interviews, it could be determined whether or not the two sets of attitude-structure expectations had an effect upon the results.

The experiment utilized a questionnaire of the type frequently used in opinion surveys. The questionnaire contained a majority of pre-code–type questions, but also a few free-answer questions. With this questionnaire as a guide, two dummy interview scripts were written. From these, phonograph transcriptions were made with a professional actor and an NORC staff member playing the roles of respondent and interviewer respectively.[30] The respondent heard on the first transcription was an isolationist, provincial, and prejudiced respondent. The respondent heard on the second transcription was a thoughtful, well-read interventionist. These two types were chosen because of the striking contrasts which it was possible to portray, because question and answer material for such characters was readily available, and because the types were so familiar to most interviewers, as well as laymen, that they would have verisimilitude.

One other reason for the choice of these two types was prominent. Limited funds prohibited testing out the types and empirically determining for the experimental subjects what specific attitudes did not fit with the over-all type and, when necessary, dubbing new material into the record. In the absence of such ideal circumstances, types had to be chosen for which a "good guess" could be made as to the discrete attitudes that would be regarded as contributing to or as inconsistent with the over-all picture. It was assumed that not too much error would occur in identifying *our* conception of the isolationist or interventionist with the *interviewer's* conception of these types. In so far as our conception was wrong, the script would not contribute to the over-all picture intended, and the findings would not be a crucial test of the hypothesis. More than this, as previously suggested, what was regarded as an inconsistent item by *us* might on occasion have been accepted by the subject as a legitimate content of the over-all structure of attitudes. In such instances, accuracy in recording a so-called inconsistent answer would *logically* not have denied the hypothesis at all, but the finding would *appear* to be negative evidence. The comments of several subjects definitely suggest that their accurate recording of an "inconsistent" answer merely represented the fact that they regarded this answer as consistent with the whole, and in this sense the findings to be presented are a conservative test of the hypothesis that recording would be biased in the direction of the expectation.

The characterizations of the two respondents might be regarded as rather extreme, but this was necessary to insure that the interviewers perceived the character as intended, otherwise negative results would have been indeterminate. They might have meant either that no biases arose from such perceptual processes or that the experiment provided no test, since no expectations had been established. In order for the experiment to lend itself to an unequivocal interpretation, it was necessary to magnify the pictures presented. While this might accentuate the magnitude of the biases observed as compared with normal national cross-sections which do include some humans so vague in outline as to have no character whatsoever, the reality of these extreme types is well known to all in public opinion research. Moreover, as is clear from the ratings the experimental subjects gave to the respondents, presented earlier, the intended characterization was even missed on occasion, and in this sense the over-all results are again *conservative*.

It is obvious that the effect of expectations would be especially noticeable, if at all, in the subjects' handling of lukewarm or equivocal replies. For, on the one hand, it is evident that if a response were consistent with attitude-structure expectations there could be no observable expectations effect, since expectations would tend to reinforce the reliability of the interviewer's coding of the reply. Again, if a response were markedly inconsistent with attitude-structure expectations, the chances are that the interviewer's image of the respondent's attitude structure would itself have to be revised, and the expectations along with it. But if the response were lukewarm, it might wave no such red flag, and expectations might have full charge in guiding perception. Therefore, reliance was placed mainly on lukewarm or equivocal responses in testing the hypothesis, although inconsistent responses were likewise employed for this purpose.

The experimental subjects who listened to the transcriptions had in front of them copies of the questionnaires corresponding to the interview. They were instructed to write down or code the answers as they listened. So that errors in recording were not due to the artifact of lack of time, the intervals between question and answer approximated the usual speed of delivery of a respondent. While the time interval was not controlled exactly and did lead to a few complaints about being hurried, the influence of such a factor upon the results can be questioned on the basis of empirical data, presented in the original article, on the lack of any relation of clerical errors to expectation effects. The mechanical quality of the transcriptions was good, so that inaudibility of the answers could scarcely have been significant in accounting for error. Data collected from the subjects as to difficulties in reception show that these were negligible.

So that errors could not be due to lack of practice in handling the mechanics of interviewing on this survey or to unfamiliarity with the rules for handling given questions, the experimental subjects filled out one questionnaire ahead of time, recording their own opinions. In addition to the practice this task afforded, it provided a measure of the subjects' own ideology, so that the influence of this variable on the results could be evaluated jointly with the influence of expectations. At the time the subjects recorded their own opinions, they were given written specifications on the purposes of the survey and the procedure for handling given kinds of answers. A final briefing period was held at the time of the experimental sessions. Just before the transcriptions were played, the subjects were given last-minute instructions—a quick review of the specifications and particular instructions for the sessions themselves, including a request that they try to imagine that this was an actual interview. The subjects were assembled in small groups over a number of different sessions. The order of presentation of the two transcriptions was rotated from session to session so that the influence of temporal factors of fatigue or practice was equally operative upon the results of each of the two interviews for all subjects taken together, and cannot account for the differences in recording of answers.

After each transcription was played, subjects were given time to fill out a so-called "field rating" of the dummy respondent—actually an appraisal of relevant characteristics of the respondent, his extent of interventionism or isolationism, his interest in and level of information about international affairs. This enabled us to determine whether the subject had actually perceived the over-all characterization intended. In addition, subjects were given a form on which to report their personal characteristics and their comments about the experiment—whether they were able to hear each response, whether they maintained the same impressions of the respondents throughout each interview (to determine whether some of the deviant test responses had caused a re-formation of attitude-structure expectations).

Some 117 subjects participated in the experimental sessions. They included regular public opinion poll interviewers from various co-operating agencies, university graduate and undergraduate students.[31] About a third had no previous professional interviewing experience, although they had had related course work in the social sciences. Half had up to one year of professional interviewing, and the remainder had experience longer than a year.

The experimental procedure described in the foregoing should have provided a crucial test of the influence of attitude-structure expectations upon the results. The hypothesis would seem to be proven if the equivalent answers inserted into the two transcriptions were coded differently, depending upon the context within which they were imbedded. However, such a finding might be open to one other explanation. Conceivably the different coding of apparently equivalent answers could be due to uncontrolled factors associated with the way in which the crucial answers were *spoken* by the actor respondent. For example, one answer might have been delivered more emphatically or knowingly than the other. Furthermore, the answers on both records were not word-for-word duplicates, although they were the same in substance. The variation in the results might be attributed to such factors, intrinsic to the answer, rather than to the expectation process operating upon psychologically equivalent answers. To investigate this possibility, the test responses were taken out of context and placed in random order in a series of other typical answers to the questions. The series was then presented to a group of judges in both oral (soundscriber discs) and written form. The judges were asked to code these responses, following the same instructions that had been given to the experimental subjects. The tallies from the judging sessions served to tell what the coding pattern for the test items would be if they were presented out of the expectation context, and they thus served as a guide against which to compare results from the experimental sessions. Those test responses which were not coded according to the design by the judges were eliminated from further analysis.

For two of the questions, there was no doubt whatsoever that the recorded responses were identical in content. These were Questions 7 and 15E on the questionnaire. Both of these were pre-coded questions requiring the interviewer to circle the code on the questionnaire that seemed most nearly to fit the respondent's attitude.

Question 7 was phrased as follows: "In general, do you think that the United States is now spending too much on our program for European recovery, about the right amount, or not enough?" Code categories corresponding to the alternatives were provided. In response to this question, the isolationist said: "All I know is that it's costing us taxpayers an awful lot of money. But I suppose you got to feed those starving people and I guess you can't do it for less. Still a lot of that money is just going down the drain. Them people ain't working over there. They don't appreciate it."

In response to the same question the interventionist replied: "Well, there's no question but that the economic recovery program is costing this country a good deal of money. Still, I presume we must help Western Europe get back on its feet, and I suppose it can't be done for less. Nevertheless there has been a certain amount of mismanagement and waste."

The judges, in the light of specifications which instructed the interviewer to ignore any criticisms of the *manner* in which the money was being spent, coded both responses as "about right amount." The experimental subjects, however, hearing these responses in their contexts, displayed a strikingly different pattern of recording, as Table 11 indicates. Hearing the isolationist's reply, 53 per cent of the subjects coded "too much," while 20 per cent coded "about right amount." On the other hand, hearing the interventionist's reply, 9 per cent of the same group of subjects coded "too much," and 75 per cent "about right amount."

It is interesting here to follow the thinking of one of the interviewer-subjects, who reported his thoughts during a phenomenological session. In speaking of the isolationist's response, this subject said, "Well, he has given two answers which I would ask him to clarify. In one case he said 'Too much,' and in another case, 'About right amount' . . . I get the feeling that this individual really means 'Too much,' but I would put it with reservations . . . He has said both, but I think I'll put 'Too much' for this individual."

The second crucial question mentioned above, 15E, was one of a series of questions about level of interest in foreign and domestic affairs. It was phrased as follows: "How much interest do you take in our policy toward Spain—a good deal of interest, some interest, or practically none?" To this the isolationist replied, "It's the way I told you—I don't follow the papers much these days, but I guess you could put me down as taking a little bit of interest in that." The interventionist responded with, "Compared with the other areas you've mentioned, I guess I'd regard myself as having only a little bit of interest in that."

The judges, following specifications, coded both replies as "some." As Table 11 indicates, there were 20 per cent of the subjects who coded "None" for the isolationist, and only one per cent who coded the interventionist's reply this way.

The differences in the coding of the replies to these questions, then, must be attributed to the operation of the two expectation patterns. Especially under the condition of equivocal or lukewarm responses—the effect of attitude-structure expectations is to influence survey findings. The particular nature of these effects on the results are clearly of two types. First, the marginal distribution on a particular question is distorted. Second, the intercorrelations between attitudes are affected, since

TABLE 11

The Influence of Expectations on the Coding of Substantially Identical Responses to Two Questions
(in per cent)

	CLASSIFICATION GIVEN BY SUBJECTS TO:	
	Isolationist Respondent	Interventionist Respondent
Question 7. Amount spent by U.S. on program for European recovery		
Too much........................	53	9
About right amount................	20	75
Not enough......................	—	1
Don't know and other..............	27	15
	100	100
Question 15E. Amount of interest in policy toward Spain		
Some..........................	76	99
None..........................	20	1
Don't know.....................	4	—
	100	100
Number of cases................	117	117

these intercorrelations are the very essence of the attitude-structure expectation process. Thus, estimates predicated on marginals, and dynamic interpretations based on relations between attitudes, would both be impaired by these effects.

Empirical data collected in conjunction with this experiment provide some evidence on the fundamental problem posed earlier as to the effect of such expectations on the *validity* of survey results.

Thirty-nine of the experimental subjects acted as interviewers in a survey of community attitudes in Denver in 1949.[32] In the case of this survey, since checks on the accuracy of the report on a series of questions were available in the form of official records on each respondent, it is possible to compute a measure of the validity of the results each interviewer obtained. Since the interviewers received assignments which were equivalent, any differences in validity can be assigned to the interviewer. The systematic relation between the validity of the reports obtained by different interviewers in this survey, and their tendency to introduce expectation effects in the experiment, will provide some answer to the larger issue of the good or bad consequences of such expectations. In Table 12 these findings are presented in the form of

TABLE 12

THE RELATION OF EXPECTATION-EFFECT TENDENCIES TO THE VALIDITY OF REPORTS OBTAINED IN THE COURSE OF A FIELD SURVEY

	Prone to Expectation Effects (n = 22)	Not Prone to Expectation Effects (n = 17)
Report of vote in 1948 presidential election Interviewers with		
the least invalidity.................................	8	5
moderate invalidity................................	3	9
the most invalidity.................................	11	3
Report of automobile ownership Interviewers with		
the least invalidity.................................	7	6
moderate invalidity................................	7	4
the most invalidity.................................	8	7
Report of personal contribution to Community Chest Interviewers with		
the least invalidity.................................	5	9
moderate invalidity................................	7	6
the most invalidity.................................	10	2

frequencies. Proneness to expectation effects was measured by the tendency to distort the handling of Question 7 in the experiment, and the relative validity of the interviewer's results was measured by classifying all interviewers into one of three categories defined by the relative magnitude of the invalidities obtained.

In three instances, those experimental subjects who were expectation-prone were more likely to fall into the category of interviewers who obtained relatively less valid results. The data reveal this fact by inspection, and Chi-squared tests for the three items reveal P-values of .02, .85, and .05 respectively. When these values are pooled to get an aggregate test, the difference is significant at the .05 level. One might argue that the invalid results derived not so much from expectation tendencies but from other factors correlated with expectation effects. For example, from evidence presented in the original report of this study, it was noted that those interviewers who are prone to expectation effect differ in experience and skill at clerical tasks, although the differences are not statistically significant. Conceivably, the difference in performance of the two groups might derive from such uncontrolled factors. While the number of cases was small, the relationship between expectation effects and invalidity of results was re-examined, controlling first for length of experience and then for clerical skill. In both refined tests, the relationship persists although it is reduced in magnitude. In this case, at least the expectation process seems to produce blindness rather than insight.

A second experiment was devised to determine the biasing effects of attitude-structure expectations. Like the previous experiment, this one was limited to the test of the hypothesis that such expectations, emerging in relation to a constellation of early attitudes, can affect results purely through the *classification* of answers on pre-coded questions However, it goes beyond the first experiment in specifying some of the conditions under which expectations operate.

Sixty interviewers, members of the current NORC field staff, were sent a sheet containing twenty-five discrete answers to the following question: "In general, do you feel the United States is now spending too much on our program for European recovery, about the right amount or not enough?"

It should be noted that this question was identical with one of the two experimental questions used in the Smith-Hyman study. The interviewers were asked to classify each of the answers in terms of the following code:

> Too much 1
> Right amount 2
> Not enough 3
> Don't know 4
> Not codeable X

From the tabulation of the codes assigned, eight specific answers out of the twenty-five were selected so as to provide a range of items varying in certain respects. Items were chosen which illustrated the following conditions:

1. Responses where the interviewers tended to split close to 50–50.

2. Responses where the main break was between 1 and 2 in the code as well as 2 and 3, so that both types of ambiguities would be represented in the experiment.

3. Responses which were coded "not codeable" with high frequency.

4. Two "control" items—where all interviewers classified the items the same way.

For each of the six experimental items, two "contexts" were then constructed. These consisted of interview schedules containing eleven questions and fabricated responses to each, of which the experimental question with each of the eight responses constituted the sixth question on the ballot. The responses to the nonexperimental questions were designed to produce in the interviewer's mind a picture of a respondent whose general attitudes were in presumed conformity with the preceding code categories—that is—respondents whose answer to the experimental question might be "too much," "about right," or "not enough." In all, fourteen different contexts were constructed—two each for the six experimental responses and one each for the control responses. If the split between interviewers was—let us say—between "too much" and "about right," then one each of these contexts were constructed for that particular response.

The questionnaires were then filled in, containing a fabricated context plus the appropriate experimental item imbedded in the proper place.

A quota of such simulated ballots was then distributed to each interviewer after a sufficient lapse of time to reduce memory. He received the answers in a *context* opposed *to his previous code.* Thus, if an interviewer had coded response No. 6 as "about right" and the main split for that response was between "about right" and "too much," he received the answer in a "too much" context.

Among that group of interviewers who had previously declared the item "not codeable," the concept of a context opposing the original code in direction is meaningless. Hence, within this group, contexts of two different directions were alternately applied. All the interviewers were asked to code the entire set of answers on each of the ballots.

The ostensible nature of the assignment was a routine survey that NORC had conducted, in which we were trying out interviewers as coders in place of the normal office staff. To reduce suspicion, different handwritings had been used, so that no interviewer would receive more than two ballots with the same writing. Otherwise, given the knowledge of the small field assignments in the usual survey, an interviewer might become suspicious.

As contrasted with the earlier experiment, the cues creating the attitude-structure expectations were purely the *written* contents, rather than the combination of content plus all the vocal skills at the disposal of a professional actor trying to create a vivid characterization. In this sense, minimal expectations should have been operative. However, the experiment was pretested on a group of office coders, and where the context we had initially constructed was too weak to produce effects, the context was revised in the direction of a clearer picture, so as to strengthen the likelihood that interviewer expectations would emerge.

As in the first experiment, the measure of expectation effects in the aggregate was that the codes assigned to the experimental items when they were imbedded in particular contexts shift markedly from the original codes assigned the items when they were presented discretely. To measure the *differential* effects of expectations as related to given variables, the magnitude of shift in coding will be presented for items varying in certain respects.

These shifts were evaluated in terms of their direction. Where a shift occurred from a code involving a definite opinion to the code "don't know," the assumption was made that this shift was a "half-shift," since the "don't know" category was regarded as halfway point between the two poles of the attitudinal dimension involved. Similarly, where a shift occurred from an original "don't know" code to a definite opinion, this was regarded as a half-shift, since the distance traversed on the dimension was only half the distance between poles. The assumption seems reasonable, since the category "don't know" was applied *exclusively* for a respondent whose attitude was definitely regarded as equivocal. Where the interviewer himself was equivocal about an apparently definite opinion, he presumably used the category "not codeable."

While these assumptions seem reasonable, such half-shifts are separated in the presentation of the results, so that the reader can evaluate the findings independent of these possibly indeterminate data or can make any assumption he wishes about the "don't know" codes.

In Table 13 below, the results are presented for each of the eight items. It is clear that interviewers in large number shifted their classification in the direction of the presumed context. It is, of course, possible that such shifting of judgment is to some extent sheer unreliability, i.e., a coder given the task of coding the *discrete* item a second time might shift his judgment even in the absence of context. Unfortunately, control measurements of shifting for the repetition of the original *discrete* items were not possible. However, that such shifts were not due to mere capriciousness is indicated by the results for control items. On these items, 89 per cent and 100 per cent of the interviewers coded the items the same as they had previously, despite context. Incidentally, this finding demonstrates that the effect of expectations created by context will be minimal for unequivocal responses.

In addition, comparisons of the amount and direction of shifting among experimental items varying in certain respects indicate that shift in the direction of context is correlative with a number of interrelated factors. This again suggests that such shifts are systematic rather than mere instances of unreliability of coding. For example, it will be noted from the table that the effect of the expectation is greater when the original response is ambiguous. Ambiguity was measured by the degree to which the sixty interviewers disagreed on their original coding of the discrete item. If, among those interviewers assigning a definite code, there were an equal number coding the item in two different ways, the response in question was regarded as maximally ambiguous.

TABLE 13

THE EFFECT OF ATTITUDE-STRUCTURE EXPECTATIONS ON CODING AS REVEALED BY THE MAGNITUDE OF SHIFTING WHEN THE RESPONSE IS IMBEDDED IN AN EXPERIMENTAL CONTEXT

Experimental item	ORIGINAL SPLIT (PER CENT) EXCLUDING RESPONSES "NON-CODEABLE"	PERCENTAGE SHOWING SHIFTS IN THE DIRECTION OF CONTEXT EXCLUDING RESPONSE "NON-CODEABLE"		
		Full Shifts	Half Shifts	Total
1........................	44–56	34	16	50
2........................	39–61	39	16	55
3........................	29–71	15	29	44
4........................	28–72	23	4	27
5........................	21–79	21	32	53
6........................	0–100	0	22	22
Control item				
1........................	0–100	8	3	11
2........................	0–100	0	0	0

This finding on the relation between ambiguity and shifting supports the suggestion made in Chapter II and elaborated in Chapter V that expectational and other biasing processes are often invoked as task aids when the situation is difficult for the interviewer.

That such expectations function to reduce task difficulty in coding is also clear from the fact that the equivocal answers when given in a context are more likely to be assigned some definite code.[33] This can be shown by comparing the proportion of instances for the total of 344 experimental responses given the staff as a whole where the interviewers classified the item as non-codeable under the two conditions.

In the absence of any context, 34 per cent of all the responses were classified as not codeable, whereas in the presence of context only 25 per cent of the same responses were classified as not codeable. However, this 9 per cent reduction in non-codeability for all responses in the *aggregate* does not adequately represent the full effects of context. While some items that had been previously regarded as non-codeable became codeable under conditions of context, other items that were previously codeable seemed to produce a conflict situation for the interviewer when they were placed in a context.

Instead of coding such items, the interviewer sometimes classified a previously coded item as now non-codeable. Such changes implicitly reveal the influence of expectations created by the context, but were not included in the earlier table as "shifts." The complete pattern of changes between codeable and non-codeable categories is presented in Table 14 below.

TABLE 14

THE INFLUENCE OF CONTEXT AS RELATED TO PREVIOUS CODE-ABILITY
(in per cent)

PER CENT CLASSIFIED IN VARIOUS WAYS IN THE PRESENCE OF CONTEXT	AMONG RESPONSES INITIALLY REGARDED AS	
	Non-codeable	Codeable
Non-codeable...............	41	26
Codeable...................	59	74
Number of respondents........	116	258

Certain other findings on the interaction of specific variables in creating effects will be presented below.

Thus far, we have presented two experimental analogies to the biasing operation of attitude-structure expectations on survey results. These have the advantage of specifying most precisely the nature of such expectational effects. As indicated earlier, we can even examine expectations that are *constant* over the entire staff, since we have a criterion of the correct response. Also, by virtue of the control of the design, we can locate the exact aspect of performance through which any such effects operate. However, a limitation accompanies all such procedures. The very nature of the experiments involved the *creation* of such expectations and some element of artificiality. In the more natural field-setting, the respondent's answers may not be so well structured, and a host of uncontrolled situational factors operate.[34]

Moreover, both experiments presented relate to the narrow realm of attitude-structure expectations as they influence only the *recording component* of total interviewer performance. We therefore turn to a field study of role expectations as these affect survey results. In the field study, it is impossible to isolate the locus of the effects, since all components of interviewer performance are inextricably involved. As well, for reasons previously mentioned, it is impossible to measure the effect of universally held expectations. However, what losses we sustain are compensated for by a more typical estimate of such processes under natural field conditions.

This field experiment is described in detail in Chapter VI. It was conducted in Cleveland and was one of two large-scale field surveys designed experimentally so as to permit the measurement of variations in results obtained from equivalent samples by different interviewers. The samples were of households rather than individuals, and in 90 per cent of the instances, the housewife acted as the respondent. On two omnibus questions, certain results for the different interviewers differed so markedly that one could not attribute the differences to mere sampling fluctuations. The first question dealt with whether or not the respondent purchased a series of nine commodities or services, and, if so, whether the purchase had been made in the neighborhood, and the second question was a repetition of the inquiry for the main earner or other major member of the household. Because of the nature of the sample, the first question almost invariably involved an inquiry into a woman's behavior, and the second question an inquiry into a man's behavior. The results are presented below in Table 15.

TABLE 15

SIGNIFICANCE OF DIFFERENCE OBTAINED BY INTERVIEWERS WITH EQUIVALENT ASSIGN-
MENTS ON QUESTIONS RELATING TO PURCHASING BEHAVIOR

CHARACTERISTIC TESTED	AGGREGATED RESULTS FOR 10 PAIRS OF INTERVIEWERS		P-VALUE
	Chi-Squared	DF	
"The last time you shopped for _____, did you get them downtown or in neighborhood stores?"			
Gasoline	30.75	10	.001
Auto repairs	43.21	10	.0001
"Now I'd like to know about the main earner (main shopper) of the household. The last time he (she) wanted any of the following things, did he (she) get them downtown or in some neighborhood area?"			
Clothing	24.01	10	.01
Housefurnishings	38.04	10	.0001

Since the actual test made on these items essentially involved comparisons of the attribute "no purchase" plus "don't remember the purchase" vs. purchase for the different interviewers,[35] the finding shows that there is unusually great variation in the frequency with which pairs of interviewers obtain an answer indicating a woman making the purchase of an unusual item, such as gasoline or auto-repairs, or a man making a purchase of an *unusual* item. It is interesting that the item which is least sex-linked, clothing, shows the smallest difference of the four (clothing is much more likely to be bought by both members of a family), and that other items in the list for which there is no prevailing division of labor between the sexes, buying drugs, patronizing the dentist or movies, etc., show no significant differences.

The very special pattern of these findings suggests that differential role expectations among our interviewers as to the buying behavior of men and women affected the replies they obtained. Out of forty-five questions tested for interviewer differences, these four plus one other question were the only ones on which significant findings occurred, and the three of the five showing the greatest effects were items where the report of purchase of a given commodity by a man or woman would represent unusual behavior.

That the effects are not due to the mere *content* of the questions or items is clear from the fact that the identical question when asked in the context of the behavior of the other sex does not yield a significant difference. For example, housefurnishings, when asked in relation to the female *respondent*, yields an aggregated Chi-squared of 11.631 which is nonsignificant, but when asked about the spouse is highly significant. The difference between the two Chi-squareds when tested by an *F*-test is significant at the .05 level. Similarly, when auto repairs was asked of the male spouse, the Chi-squared was 12.643 or nonsignificant, and the difference between the two Chi-squareds as revealed by an *F*-test is significant. In other words, the identical question, covering the same commodity, only becomes subject to interviewer effect when the referent of the question is a person of a particular sex.

One might raise the query as to why no differences were observed on the question of automobile repairs when the referent was a man, or on housefurnishings when the referent was a woman. Certainly such items are probably regarded as the exclusive purchasing assignments of the respective sexes. Such questions are obviously linked to role expectations. The answer lies in the feature of field experiments to which we previously referred. There might well have been expectations that such items were bought exclusively by men or women, which might well have inflated the frequency of reports of purchase of these items for the given sex over the entire sample. But since these were very likely to be characteristic of both interviewers who were compared, they would not be revealed. For example, it is hard to believe that any interviewer would think that a woman did *not* buy housefurnishings, or that a man who owned a car did *not* buy gasoline. However, with respect to items that are unusual purchases for a given sex, it is likely that fairly often one but not the other of the interviewers would assume that a number of women purchased gasoline, or that a number of men purchased housefurnishings.

That interviewer effects operated on these questions in the Cleveland study is beyond question. The explanation given in terms of role expectations seems plausible, but no real proof has yet been presented. In contrast with the laboratory-like experiments presented earlier, we did not experimentally create any expectations among our interviewers under controlled conditions to which we can point. We merely observed their behavior in the natural setting and *inferred* the operation of certain expectations from the peculiar contents of the findings on certain questions.

However, if it can be demonstrated by refined analysis that these results vary in an orderly way among interviewers differing in role-expectational tendencies, the inference would seem well supported. A series of such analyses are available, all providing support for the inference. Certain selected ones are presented below. It should be noted with respect to these analyses that it was impossible to find enough instances of contrasting characteristics *within* the pairs of interviewers who had equivalent assignments.

Consequently, it was necessary to lump together the results of all interviewers with a given characteristic regardless of the blocks from which they had obtained their interviews. Thus, if the observed differences are interpreted in the light of random variation resulting from *simple* random sampling, it is possible that some seemingly significant differences may merely be due to chance, i.e., due to true differences between the samples of respondents assigned to the contrasted interviewers. These errors of interpretation result from the underestimate of the potential extent of variation between aggregates of clusters of respondents. Also, since we are here relating various interviewer characteristics to differences in the obtained interview results, it is necessary to take account of the variation in results between interviewers with the same characteristic(s). The assumption of *simple* random sampling might lead us to attribute certain fortuitous observed differences to variation in a certain interviewer variable when in reality that interviewer variable is not generally related to that type of difference at all. However, in a culturally homogeneous area like that studied,[36] there is no reason to assume an especially great spatial serial correlation of sexual purchasing roles, so perhaps the assumption of simple random sampling used in our significance tests is not completely unfounded. We have no reason to assume that there is a correlation of any sort between the interviewers' and respondents' characteristics, and we can consider the respondents of interviewers with different characteristics to be reasonably equivalent. We do, of course, underestimate the sampling variance between these two groups but probably not enough to invalidate comparisons completely.

Moreover, in all the analyses that follow, the data are presented purely for subgroups of respondents of common characteristics, thus ruling out certain sources of sampling variation as the explanation. For example, all the data are presented purely for female respondents. In addition, the interviewers who are contrasted are matched in certain respects, thus strengthening the likelihood that the differences observed are due to the independent variable specified.

That the variations in results are related to expectations about sex-roles is first supported by the fact that "unusual" purchases are more frequently reported by interviewers who *themselves* come from households where the sex-roles are unusual. This is shown below for women interviewers who had reported in an interviewer's questionnaire on the purchasing behavior in their own households.

TABLE 16

The Relation of Reports of Purchasing-Behavior That Violate the Usual Sex-Role to Sex-Roles in Interviewer's Own Household

	Among Female Respondents, Percentage of Husbands Reported as Purchasing Housefurnishings	
		N
For interviewers whose own husbands purchase housefurnishings...............................	60	67
For interviewers whose own husbands do not purchase housefurnishings............................	45	307
	Among Female Respondents, Percentage Reporting Getting Autos Repaired	
		N
For female interviewers who had had autos repaired......	46	328
For female interviewers who had not had autos repaired...	38	117

116   *Interviewing in Social Research*

The expectation about the behavior of the respondents and their spouses would thus seem in part to be predicated upon the real but idiosyncratic experiences of the interviewer. However, it has also been argued in Chapter II, and is supported by a body of theory, that such categorizing of respondents' answers in terms of gross group memberships would be related to general tendencies to be stereotypic. We find that this is the case. Interviewers were asked if there were certain types of people they would object to interviewing. A small group stated that they were unwilling to interview Negroes, and this response was taken as an index of stereotyping. In Table 17 below it can be seen that these interviewers are less likely to obtain reports of behavior that violate the usual sex-role.

TABLE 17

The Relation of Reports of Purchasing-Behavior That Violate the Usual Sex-Role to Interviewers' Stereotypical Tendencies

Among Professional Female Interviewers Who:	Among Female Respondents, Percentage of Husbands Reported as Purchasing House-Furnishings		Percentage of Female Respondents Who Reported Obtaining Auto Repairs	
Refuse to interview Negroes.......	43	N = 69	33	N = 83
Are willing to interview Negroes...	46	N = 182	45	N = 40

The theory was advanced earlier that such expectational processes are likely to be invoked in the presence of difficulty, and that they then function as aids in the resolution of the interviewer's task. This theory can be supported in the analysis of the Cleveland study. About half of the interviewers reacted negatively to these questions and indicated that they were among the "least interesting to respondents" or the "most difficult to understand" or the "hardest to answer." Among this group, the frequency with which unusual purchases were reported was less. It is suggested that, in the presence of difficulty, interviewers are more likely to record an answer on the basis of expectation rather than cope with the full difficulty of questioning or probing in a difficult area.[37] The data are presented in Table 18 below.

Situational factors may enhance the operation of expectations not only by creating task difficulties but also by providing clues which facilitate or oppose the normal expectations. An earlier question in an interlocking battery of questions may so-to-speak be a tip-off for the interviewer that he can regard a respondent as performing or not performing a certain role. Questionnaires that have a highly organized character serve exceedingly well for research design purposes but may have this unanticipated consequence for interviewer effect. In the Cleveland survey, such a situation seemed to be present. Prior to the question on auto-repair purchases, the respondent had been asked what mode of transportation was used to do the food shopping. If the respondent did not mention an auto, the probe was asked, "Is there a car available for food shopping?" It can be noted from Table 19 below that the expectational effects on "auto repairs" are related to the characteristic reported by the respondent on the earlier question. Thus, for example, stereo-

TABLE 18

The Relation of Reports of Purchasing-Behavior That Violate the Usual Sex-Role to Situational Pressures

| | Percentage Among Female Interviewers Whose Reaction to the Question Was | | | |
	Negative	N	Not negative	N
Percentage of female respondents having autos repaired....................	37	197	50	248
Percentage of husbands purchasing house-furnishings........................	40	161	53	213

typic interviewers who obtain few reports of auto repairs from female respondents are constrained to obtain increased reports of auto repairs if the respondent had previously indicated that she had or used an auto. It can also be noted from the table that even when we control the characteristics of the respondent by reference to the earlier question the stereotypic interviewers are least likely to obtain deviant reports.

The predictive power of the theory that the Cleveland findings are a product of role-expectational tendencies activated by task difficulty is shown in Table 20. Among interviewers where the two factors combine there is a *minimal* report of unusual behavior.

Thus far, we have described several experimental studies which demonstrate the biasing effects of role or attitude-structure expectations on survey results. We earlier alluded to a third type of expectational process, the "probability expectation," and turn now to some empirical data suggestive of such expectational effects. The data to be presented are from a variety of sources and only fragmentary partly because the phenomenon was not explored early enough to be fully incorporated into experimental phases of the project and partly because this type of expectation is clearly of secondary importance and therefore not as worthy of high research priority.

It should be anticipated that probability expectations will be difficult to demonstrate. For interviewers to expect a particular distribution of attitudes in a sample requires that the object of the attitudes, the issue involved, be exceedingly well known. On ephemeral issues, which con-

TABLE 19

THE RELATION OF EXPECTATIONAL EFFECTS TO SITUATIONAL FACTORS OF QUESTIONNAIRE ORDER

	AMONG FEMALE RESPONDENTS WHO GENERALLY USED AUTO TO SHOP FOR FOOD—PERCENTAGE REPORTING HAVING AUTO REPAIRED	
	Per Cent	N
Professional interviewers *not* willing to interview Negroes..................................	62	37
Professional interviewers willing to interview Negroes..................................	68	97
Nonprofessional interviewers (all willing to interview Negroes).................................	66	56

	AMONG FEMALE RESPONDENTS WHO DID NOT GENERALLY USE AUTO TO SHOP FOR FOOD BUT WHO DID HAVE A CAR AVAILABLE FOR FOOD SHOPPING —PERCENTAGE REPORTING HAVING AUTO REPAIRED	
	Per Cent	N
Professional interviewers *not* willing to interview Negroes..................................	13	15
Professional interviewers willing to interview Negroes..................................	50	38
Nonprofessional interviewers (all willing to interview Negroes).................................	65	34

	AMONG FEMALE RESPONDENTS WHO DID NOT HAVE AN AUTO AVAILABLE FOR FOOD SHOPPING—PERCENTAGE REPORTING HAVING AUTO REPAIRED	
	Per Cent	N
Professional interviewers *not* willing to interview Negroes..................................	6	31
Professional interviewers willing to interview Negroes..................................	13	75
Nonprofessional interviewers (all willing to interview Negroes).................................	18	57

stitute a considerable part of the contents of public opinion surveys, there would be little basis in experience or public discussion for interviewers to build up such expectations. Of course, on issues that are central in the culture, for example, approval of polygamy or private enterprise, or on transient but prominent matters, such as Truman's strength in 1948, we would expect strong probability expectations—but such issues are not encountered too frequently in social research. More than this, we would anticipate that such expectations would be most elusive in their operations. They are *tentative* in relation to more differentiated subsequent expectations established as a result of inter-

TABLE 20

THE COMBINED EFFECTS OF ROLE EXPECTATIONS AND SITUATIONAL DIFFICULTY ON REPORTS OF PURCHASING-BEHAVIOR

	AMONG FEMALE RESPONDENTS, PERCENTAGE OF MALES REPORTED AS PURCHASING HOUSEFURNISHINGS	
	Per Cent	N
Among Female Interviewers		
Who did not react negatively, and whose own husbands purchase housefurnishings	70	47
Who did not react negatively, and whose husbands do *not* purchase housefurnishings	48	166
Who did react negatively, and whose own husbands purchase housefurnishings	35	20
Who did react negatively and whose husbands do *not* purchase housefurnishings	40	141

	AMONG FEMALE RESPONDENTS, PERCENTAGE REPORTING HAVING HAD AUTO REPAIRS	
Among Female Interviewers	Per Cent	N
Who did not react negatively, and who had auto repaired	56	166
Who did not react negatively, and who had *not* had auto repaired	40	82
Who reacted negatively to question, and who had had auto repaired	38	162
Who reacted negatively to question, and who had *not* had auto repaired	34	35

action with particular respondents. While the interviewer might expect that six out of ten respondents would vote a certain way, this expectation holds for the general run of results over the sample and is not necessarily maintained for *a particular respondent* he confronts. The behavior of a particular respondent might conform to the more differentiated expectation about a given subgroup or about a person with a given type of attitude-structure. Consequently, probability expectations would be more fluid and elusive and would often not correlate with particular *subsets* of results obtained by interviewers. The extreme of this would occur under conditions in public opinion research where an interviewer interviews a *particular homogeneous cluster*, rather than a sample of the total universe. In such instances, the interviewer might well regard his probability expectations as irrelevant to his *entire* assignment.

Where probability expectations are strong, and yet in conflict with more differentiated expectations for particular respondents, we could conjecture about a model that might operate in the interviewer. Presumably he would surrender his probability expectations *up to a certain point* in his assignment because they seem less appropriate and valid than his more pointed and specialized expectations. But then in so far as he felt that the total body of results should conform in some degree to his probability expectations, he might *then* feel that he has accumulated too few results of a certain type. He might then do violence to the subsequent individual respondents and even reject the more individualized expectation about any case. Thus, where several interviewers have *common* probability expectations about a well-known matter, one might even find if they interviewed the same individuals that they arrive at the same set of marginal results, despite the fact that they disagree on many individuals, since these can be ordered in any conceivable way so long as the final accounting is correct.

If this argument is cogent, it would seem that the most *insidious* types of interviewer effect might occur just in this realm. Marginal results could be highly uniform over interviewers and subject to no unreliability, and a false sense of security would prevail. But the real meaning of the finding might lie in universal expectational effects plus gross inaccuracies at the level of subsets of results or results for any respondent.

This model seems to conform to a common finding in panel studies when sets of interview data collected by *different* interviewers from the same respondents are examined. It is often noted that there is unusual agreement in the *marginal* distributions obtained by the two interviewers, but considerable disagreement in the cells of the table, i.e., in the classification given the *individual respondents* by the two interviewers. The interpretation usually given to the finding is that the error originates out of some process that is random in character and therefore that the net result of the system of compensating errors is an unbiased set of marginals. Therefore, the evaluation is commonly made that marginal totals are accurate, but that one should be cautious about the accuracy of measurement at the level of the individual. This interpretation of such findings and the evaluation of them certainly is appropriate generally. To invoke the operation of probability expectations and consequently to evaluate the marginals as biased seems unwarranted in most instances. While probability expectations must be widespread, it would be rare that different interviewers would share expectations with the *same content*. Moreover, this very phenomenon of common marginal findings, despite internal differences in the cells, occurs in repeated measurements obtained from *self-administered* questionnaires. Here the phenomenon is obviously a function of sheer unreliability and by definition has nothing to do with an interviewer. However, the alternative explanation that apparently reliable marginal findings may represent the effect of common probability expectations might well be considered in the *special* instance of studies involving questions where there is a well-established prevailing view. A set of data suggestive of this phenomenon is available from the methodological work done in connection with the psychiatric assessment of RAF personnel alluded to in Chapter I.[38] Through a detailed card index, a record was available on all members of air crews who had been referred to a RAF neuropsychiatrist by a station medical officer. This record contained the opinions of the psychiatrist plus certain factual data. Tabulation revealed that 541 of the approximate 5000 total cases were found to have been seen by more than one of the thirty-seven staff specialists. Analysis of the reports filed on the same individuals by two different psychiatrists provided general data on the reliability of assessment, and material in the specific form to bear on our model of probability expectations. In examining these materials, the reader should not regard the level of reliability as typical, since the fact that two or more diagnostic opinions were solicited suggests that these were unusually difficult cases. Moreover, the mere fact that the man was referred by the station medical officer for any opinion at all suggests that the case was more than an ordinary case. However, the fact that this was a clearly defined abnormal population makes it peculiarly appropriate for our purposes, since the psychiatrists would be more likely to have well-structured and common expectations. Compensating for the difficulty in diagnosis, one can, also, indicate one factor that would increase the reliability. The two observers did not work completely independently; the second psychiatrist frequently had a partial statement of the first psychiatrist's general opinion available to him. However, this information should have worked mainly to increase the agreement in judgment of the *individual* cases, rather than to affect the similarity of marginal distributions, our major concern in this discussion.

Table 21, reproduced from the original report, shows that the agreement in the marginal distributions for major diagnostic categories is *remarkably* high, despite the fact that the two psychiatrists differ in the specific diagnosis given to 19 per cent of the individual cases.[39]

Interviewing in Social Research

Several other characteristics besides the general diagnosis were analyzed and reveal this same phenomenon of great agreement in marginal totals despite considerable differences in opinion on the individual cases. For example, in assigning the cause of the disorder to flying duties or in rating the degree to which the individual had experienced stress as a re-

TABLE 21

REACTION TYPES: THE NUMBER OF CASES DIAGNOSED SIMILARLY OR DISSIMILARLY BY TWO DIFFERENT PSYCHIATRISTS AMONG RAF AIR CREWS

DIAGNOSIS OF SECOND PSYCHIATRIST	DIAGNOSIS OF FIRST PSYCHIATRIST										
	Anxiety state	Depression	Elation	Hysteria	Fatigue	Obsessional	Organic-acute	Organic-chronic	Schizophrenia	Lack of Confidence	TOTAL
Anxiety state....	346	13	0	12	3	1	0	0	1	13	389
Depression......	14	34	0	3	0	0	0	0	0	0	51
Elation.........	0	0	0	0	0	0	0	0	0	0	0
Hysteria........	17	1	0	32	0	0	0	0	0	1	51
Fatigue syndrome	5	0	0	0	10	0	0	0	0	0	15
Obsessional.....	2	1	0	0	0	4	0	0	0	0	7
Organic-acute....	0	0	0	0	0	0	0	0	0	0	0
Organic-chronic..	0	0	0	0	0	0	0	0	0	0	0
Schizophrenia....	0	0	0	0	0	0	0	0	0	0	0
Lack of confidence	13	1	0	2	0	0	0	0	0	12	28
Total.......	397	50	0	49	13	5	0	0	1	26	541

sult of flying, the detailed tables presented are of the same order. In such a situation, where there is a specialized and clearly defined population, abnormals, plus considerable past experience of rates or incidences or features in that population, one would expect probability expectations to be especially operative. They might well lead the interviewer or judge or clinician to confirm again the findings of the past, and, in this sense, constitute an example of what Merton has referred to as the "self-fulfilling prophecy," "a *false* definition of the situation evoking a new behavior which makes the originally false conception come *true*. The specious validity of the self-fulfilling prophecy perpetuates a reign of error."[40]

The earliest methodological research into the biasing effects of probability expectations in social research was an experiment conducted by Stanton and Baker.[41] While the concept was never explicitly used, it is clear, upon reflection, that this was an inquiry purely into probability expectational processes, experimentally created in a laboratory-setting. Five professional interviewers with at least one year of field-work experience were hired and instructed that they would query a group of two hundred students presumably to test their memory. The students had previously been shown a series of geometrical symbols, and the interviewers were required to present each such symbol again in conjunction with a new one and to determine the respondent's ability to recognize the correct one. Probability expectations were covertly created by giving each interviewer a "key" attached to his questionnaire, which presumably indicated which symbol had actually been shown the respondents originally. The materials were so arranged that the interviewer was compelled to look at the key each time in order to note the response. In point of fact, the keys combined both true and false information, but it was verified experimentally that the interviewers believed in the accuracy of the key.

It is clear that this procedure was likely to create in the interviewer some expectation as to the frequency of "yes" and "no" answers that would be encountered for each symbol in the series. The effect of this expectation in biasing the results was determined by comparing the per cent of actually correct answers obtained in the sample when the interviewers believed that the symbol had been previously seen vs. the per cent obtained when the interviewers believed the figure had not been previously seen. The results were significantly different depending on the expectation created.[42]

The analogy of the task in this experiment to measurement of exposure to various kinds of media in market research surveys is obvious, and suggests that probability expectations might well be significant in this area. One specific example of this very fact is presented in Chapter V, where it is shown that interviewers, using "confusion controls" in measuring magazine exposure, obtained different reports as their knowledge of the fake items increased.[43]

A study conducted by Wyatt and Campbell provides specific data on the biasing effects of probability expectations in opinion surveys.[44] A survey on sentiments about the 1948 presidential election was conducted in Columbus, Ohio, in May, 1948, by 223 student interviewers from the university. Each interviewer was assigned a specific geographical cluster, in which he was to obtain interviews with twelve respondents selected on a quota-control basis. The results obtained were analyzed in relation to a number of potential biasing factors, among which were the probability expectations of the interviewers. These were determined by having each student estimate, in advance of his work, the percentage distribution of answers to five of the questions. These concerned degree of interest in the campaign, whether the respondent talked about the campaign with others, the media affecting his thinking on the campaign, whether the respondent had a favorite candidate (but not which one), and his general party preference. While it appears as if the *general area* of sentiments studied, political sentiment in the 1948 election would lend itself to the growth of expectations, the *specific* questions examined do not seem to be ones where knowledge would be precise enough to lead to strong expectations, with the possible exception of the party preferred.

(For this latter issue, expectations were fairly pervasive as indicated by the result cited in Chapter II.) Moreover, the clustering of assignments would suggest, as previously indicated, that the probability expectation for the entire population of Columbus might not be a potent source of bias, since the more differentiated expectation relevant to the subgroup, e.g., "people in a poor neighborhood," "people in the Negro area of town," would be likely to take precedence in guiding the interviewer.

For these reasons, the study provides only a weak test of the effects of probability expectations. However, in possible opposition to these considerations, a factor that might enhance the operation of bias in the results is the generally poor quality of the field staff and their lack of motivation. Most of the students had no previous experience and worked without pay on the survey as part of a course requirement. That the quality of their performance was not too high is suggested by the fact that only the 1,155 returns from 100 of the 223 interviewers were used for the methodological study. The majority of interviewers were excluded either because they did not complete their full assignment or had falsified interviews. However, it is conceivable that the screening out of the worse group does leave in the analysis only a superior, relatively conscientious, and relatively unbiased group of interviewers.

The results for interviewers varying in their expectations were compared and tested for significance.[45] The summary results for the five questions are presented in Table 22 below. In the column labeled "direction," a plus sign indicates that the results were biased in the direction of the respective expectations of the contrasted group of interviewers.

Only one of the questions revealed a significant effect of probability expectations. However, from inspection of the results, it appears to us that the individual tests understate the significance of the effects. Taken collectively, the results are highly suggestive in that four of the five questions yielded results in the direction of the interviewer's expectations, with confidence levels below .20. In addition, the tests understate the effects since they were two-tail tests, indicating the probability of obtaining a difference of that magnitude *in either direction.* The likelihood of obtaining a difference of that magnitude, but in one specific direction, by accident of sampling is obviously much less and seems more appropriate for evaluating the hypothesis that interviewers obtain results *in accordance with* their expectation.

TABLE 22

THE BIASING EFFECTS OF PROBABILITY EXPECTATIONS IN THE WYATT-CAMPBELL STUDY

Question	P-Value Level of Confidence	Direction of Differences
2—General interest in the campaign	.12	+
9—Talk about election with others	.02	+
10—Media affecting respondents thinking	.19	+
14—Favorite candidate	.20	—
Ballot—National party affiliation	.15	+

Using these same data, and making the assumption that the five questions constitute independent tests of the hypothesis, we can combine the probabilities into a joint probability. In combining these separate tests, we neglected one-tail of the distribution, partly for the reason mentioned in the foregoing, and partly because the results on Question 14 were in a direction contrary to the hypothesis, whereas, for the other questions, the results go in the hypothesized direction. Deriving the probabilities for the single-tail test, and combining them, yields a joint value significant at the .01 level. The assumption of independence required in this combined test must be qualified in that Questions 2 and 9 are so similar in content that they might be highly intercorrelated. However, even omitting Question 2 which originally provided much support for the hypothesis, the combined test on the remaining questions still reaches the 2 per cent level of confidence. The results, therefore, support the general theory as to the influence of probability expectations on issues of fairly prominent character.

One other demonstration suggestive of the biasing influence of probability expectations is available from the field experiment conducted in Denver. The data are presented in detail in Chapters V and VI, and in the original account of the study, so we will merely summarize the finding.[46] Significant differences in the results that interviewers obtained from equivalent samples were demonstrated for certain open-ended questions. One of these questions involved the report of reasons for satisfaction with the neighborhood in which the respondent lived, and differences were found in the frequency with which "kind of neighbors" was given as the primary reason.

Prior to the survey, interviewers had reported their own rating of the *importance* of "neighbors" in deciding upon the neighborhood. This rating can be taken as a *crude* indicator of probability expectations. While the interviewers were not asked to specify the exact distribution of answers in the various reason categories, it seems reasonable that those interviewers who rated this reason as "very important" are expressing the belief that this is likely to be the focus for the attitude about the neighborhood. The results for interviewers contrasted with respect to the belief that neighbors are important differ in the direction of the hypothesis, although they do not reach the usual level of significance.

A limited test of the hypothesis that probability expectations are tentative and would be surrendered in the face of more differentiated expectations was available from the study, described earlier, on bias in coding due to attitude-structure expectations, experimentally created by imbedding items within false contexts. The interviewers who coded the responses had previously estimated which answer category would be the majority position in the population.[47] To test whether differing probability expectations are effective when in conflict with an attitude-structure expectation, we examined for a number of items the amount of shift in coding due to context for interviewers contrasted in their expectation as to the majority answer to the question. In other words, for one group of interviewers, the attitude-structure expectation was consonant with their probability expectation, and for the other group the two expectations were opposed. The differences were nonsignificant, suggesting that probability expectations are only weak and tentative in relation to expectations predicated on more specific cues in the particular interview. This result, of course, must be qualified in the light of the fact that the contexts were perhaps more extreme and well structured than might be the case in some normal interview situations.

A considerable body of evidence has been presented that expectations of various types do exert a biasing influence on survey results. This confirms the theory developed in Chapter II on the basis of qualitative material that cognitive factors, hitherto neglected, are of great importance in understanding interviewer effects. However, in Chapter II, such a theory was also contrasted with the more traditional view that bias arises in public opinion research through the communication to the respondent of the interviewer's own ideology, or through the interviewer's motivation to influence the results in conformity with his own ideology. It might be argued that some of the evidence presented implicitly supports the traditional theory about ideological determinants of bias, in so far as expectation and ideology are not independent. It is well known that perception is determined in part by such functional factors as needs and attitudes, and one might therefore construe these expectational effects as simply the vehicle or carrier of the interviewer's ideology. This view, of course, has little applicability to expectational effects in "factual" surveys. One would be hard put to think of an interviewer's own opinion or ideology being activated on questions having to do with the possession of certain equipment or the employment status of the respondent or the store in which a purchase was made, except in the very remote instance where such factual data may have some evidential value in the resolution of controversy. With respect to such matters, it is perfectly plausible that an interviewer may entertain expectations about the answers, but it is unlikely that he is motivated by his opinions to affect the results in some particular direction. This consideration points to a fact not previously emphasized that expectational processes have more general applicability or subsumptive power in explaining interviewer effects in social research than ideological factors.

If the ideology were really primary, it would make considerable difference in the inferences we would draw from such experimental research and might change our whole approach to the control of these effects. We will shortly present a body of evidence from experimental tests of the effect of the interviewer's own ideology on survey results. If these findings are negative, despite the fact that the findings on expectation were positive, it would suggest that ideological factors do not lie behind the expectational processes. Otherwise, they should also manifest their effects directly on the end results. We will also present evidence below on the relative strengths of expectational and ideological effects, under conditions where each is held constant in the comparisons, thus providing further proof as to whether expectational effects are merely derivatives of ideological factors. However, prior to the presentation of such data, there is evidence that these two classes of factors are far from highly correlated in classical studies of the relation between attitude or desire and belief about, or prediction of, some unknown such as a future event or the attitude of a group. Thus, in Cronbach's study the correlation between the subject's feeling that a certain event was desirable and his belief that it would probably come to pass averaged only .41. In Wallen's study on relations between the individual's attitude and his estimate of the proportion of a group holding a certain attitude, the co-efficients ranged only from .39 to .56, and in a parallel study by

Travers, the co-efficients ranged from .02 to .98 with a median value of .42.[48] Additional evidence directly relevant to the correlation between probability expectations and interviewer's ideology is available from a study by Clark. Students in a course in public opinion estimated the percentage distribution that would be obtained in answer to a series of questions. In a preliminary study, they were also asked to record their own opinions. The relationship between personal opinion and probability expectation was only moderate.[49] The Wyatt and Campbell study also computed the relationship between interviewer's own opinion and probability expectation for each of the five experimental questions. The value ranged from .13 to .27.[50] Thus, the relation between interviewer ideology and expectations, as inferred from these empirical studies, would seem moderate at best. This is not to deny that, *in general*, cognitive processes are affected by motivational factors. We have too much experimental evidence in support of the general finding. Also certain projective tests, particularly error-choice tests in which an individual's attitudes affect his guesses on questions of "knowledge," imply a relation between expectation and attitude.[51] However, the evidence cited first seems more specific to the interviewer population, the survey situation, and the type of expectations generated within an interview.

3. EXPERIMENTATION ON IDEOLOGICAL PROCESSES

We have thus far demonstrated the significance of certain beliefs within the interviewer that create expectations, which in turn bias survey data. Since these beliefs are virtually independent of the interviewer's own ideology, such biasing effects can therefore not derive indirectly from ideological processes. However, as noted in the foregoing, the classical view of interviewer effect in public opinion research is that the interviewer's own opinions are a major biasing factor—operating upon the data either through the communication of the opinion to the respondent who then alters his response, or through the interviewer's distorting of the questioning or recording, so as to obtain results in conformity with his own opinions. The phenomenological materials presented in Chapter II already cast doubt on the plausibility of this theory. Respondents appear to be insulated from such communications for reasons of apathy, egocentrism, and the like. Interviewers seem to be task-oriented rather than straining for particular answers. Nevertheless, the prevalence of this theory, plus past research purporting to prove the significance of interviewer ideology, required that we investigate the problem directly. Therefore, a whole series of quantitative tests were conducted; all of these essentially yielded negative findings on the *simple* hypothesis that survey results are generally biased through various processes in the direction of the interviewer's own opinions. Within these same tests, certain findings, however, provide clarification and show that the hypothesis *under specialized conditions* has some merit. However, the *generality* of the theory can be strongly questioned. The evidence will be presented in summary form, since much of it is presented in detail elsewhere. The contradiction with past studies is resolved in Chapter VI, where careful methodological analysis of the designs used in past inquiries into ideological factors reveals certain inadequacies which may have produced spurious findings.

As in the case of expectational effects, the influence of the interviewer's own opinion can be studied in the laboratory-setting under conditions simulating the real interview. Such experiments have elements of artificiality but also have the virtue of precision of measurement and control of extraneous factors. In one such experiment, Guest and Nuckols had student interviewers listen to transcriptions of three simulated interviews concerned with labor-management sentiments.[52] The three respondents gave prearranged answers, one predominantly pro-management, one predominantly pro-labor, and one essentially neutral in sentiment. By scoring the errors the students made in recording the interviews, one could determine whether the effects were systematically in the direction of falsifying the general sentiments of the respondent. In addition, the students' own ideologies had been previously determined by an attitude test, and the direction of their recording errors could be correlated with the results of this test. The greatest proportion of errors made were "neutral" in that they did not systematically distort the direction of the simulated respondent's sentiments. Moreover, the remaining biasing errors did not correlate with the interviewer's own attitude. The fact that a considerable portion of the biasing errors were in the direction of enhancement or exaggeration of the simulated respondent's general sentiments, and yet not correlated with the interviewer's own opinions, suggests that the errors frequently arose through a process of assimilating doubtful answers to the attitude-structure of the respondent. The major instance where biasing errors operated to reverse the direction of the sentiments expressed by the respondents was in one of the three interviews on free-answer questions.

Guest and Nuckols' major findings on ideological bias are negative. Interviewers engaged in the simple recording of relatively unequivocal answers make a variety of mistakes, but do not seem motivated to any flagrant biases in the direction of their own opinions. The specialized findings in this study on variations in type of error for given types of questions and recording tasks are treated in Chapter V under the discussion of situational determinants.

A second laboratory experiment of similar design was conducted by Fisher, and provides evidence on ideological bias in the recording of free-answer questions.[53] Student interviewers asked a limited number of questions which were answered by Fisher, playing the part of the respondent. The interviewer, it should be noted, asked each of the questions *a series of times* and obtained each time a different, but long and tortuous, answer which was to be recorded verbatim. The task therefore had some of the elements of a repetitive training exercise, rather than the variety characteristic of a real interview. The total answer to each question was composed of elements, each of which expressed a favorable or unfavorable sentiment on a given issue. By scoring the recorded questionnaires in terms of the distortions and omissions of given elements, Fisher could determine whether the errors were predominantly in one direction. By correlating the direction of such distortions with the interviewer's own opinions, Fisher could test the general hypothesis.

His general results support the hypothesis that interviewers selectively record answers in the direction of their own ideology. However, this finding is limited to the recording of very long and complex free-answers in the context of an unusual interview involving the repetitive asking of the same question. This suggests that the hypothesis has validity only in rather specialized situations where the interviewer is confronted with serious difficulties or where the task is of such a nature that motivation detrimental to performance develops.

This suggested limitation upon the operation of ideological bias was confirmed in a field experiment on the influence of ideological factors on the classification of equivocal answers. The experiment is discussed in detail in Chapter V.[54] In summary, the design involved the analysis of the results obtained by interviewers of contrasting opinions operating successively in two situations. In the first situation, a question form was used which was likely to increase the number of highly equivocal answers, whereas in the second situation, the question form used reduced the difficulty in classifying the answers. The results indicated that ideological bias occurs only in the situation where ambiguity of response creates difficulty for the interviewer in completing his task.

Other large-scale field experiments conducted in the course of our studies show no evidence of the *general operation* of ideological bias. In the major experiment in Cleveland, where role-expectational effects were demonstrated with ten pairs of interviewers, each pair receiving equivalent assignments, no differences in results could be demonstrated for any of the opinion questions, many of these relating to issues of a relatively controversial nature. In the Denver field experiment, where five teams of nine interviewers received equivalent assignments, a large number of tests were made and the differences in results were not found to relate in any simple way to the interviewer's own opinions.[55] Other analyses made on data collected under natural field conditions confirm this general negative finding as to the influence of ideological factors. Of course, many surveys deal with innocuous opinions where one would not expect interviewers to have any intensity of feeling or any strong need to distort the results, and the negative results might be regarded as an artifact of the sampling of issues used on these tests. Yet, if one inspects the wide coverage in the Denver and Cleveland questionnaires, and the opinion contents of the laboratory experiments, this interpretation does not seem warranted. Moreover, such a view, even if accepted, would seriously limit the generality of the hypothesis, since a great deal of public opinion research does in fact relate to transient issues or to issues which, as Chapter II reveals, are peripheral in the eyes of respondents.

A considerable number of tests of the hypothesis were made on survey data collected in the Elmira Panel Study, conducted on the 1948 presidential election, and yield negative evidence.[56] One of these will be reported in detail, since it relates to an issue regarded as peculiarly prone to ideological bias. Certainly, the issue of voting preference for a presidential candidate is normally regarded as a fairly intense issue for survey research. Yet completely negative findings were demonstrated. Between the first and second waves of interviewing in Elmira approximately 22 per cent of the respondents we analyzed shifted their preference in some degree. These shifts can be classified in terms of whether or not the shift is in the direction of increasing support for the Republican or the Democratic candidate. In so far as interviewers were motivated to bias the results in the direction of their own political ideology, we would expect these shifts to vary depending on what types of interviewers had been involved in the successive waves. Thus, for example, if the same respondent were first interviewed by a Republican, and then by a Democratic interviewer, we would expect him to be likely to shift in the Democratic direction. In Table 23 below, the amount and direction of shifting are shown for four different groups of respondents, varying in the kinds of interviewers who conducted the successive interviews. One notes first of all that the *magnitude* of shift in preference is the same whether or not the second interviewer was different from the first interviewer in ideology. One further notes for those respondents where the

132   *Interviewing in Social Research*

second interviewer had a different ideology from the first, that the *direction* of shift in the respondent is unrelated to the type of change in interviewer ideology.

TABLE 23

Shift in Presidential Preference in Elmira as Related to the Ideologies of the Interviewers Used on Successive Waves
(in per cent)

| Percentage of Respondents Who | Among Respondents in Elmira Whose Successive Interviews Were Conducted by | | | |
	Republicans Both Waves	Republicans First, Democrats Second	Democrats First, Republicans Second	Democrats Both Waves
Did not shift.............	78	79	77	75
Shifted toward Republican*.	11	11	11	9
Shifted toward Democratic*.	11	10	12	16
	100	100	100	100
	N = 149	N = 187	N = 56	N = 69

* A shift toward Republican was scored for any of the following patterns: from Democrat to Republican; from Democrat to "Don't know," from "Don't know" to Republican. A shift toward Democrat was scored for any of the following patterns: from Republican to Democrat, from Republican to "Don't know," from "Don't know" to Democrat.

All this evidence is not to suggest that the interviewer's own ideology *never* influences the results he obtains. It merely demonstrates that the hypothesis has little merit for the run of conditions characterizing public opinion research in general. For example, it does have merit under specialized conditions, such as those where the situation confronting the interviewer creates difficulty. The appropriate direction for future research into interviewer ideology as a biasing agent is toward greater complexity—toward specification of these conditions. The theorizing behind such specification can come easily out of the kind of analysis made in Chapter II of the nature of the experience involved in an interview.

This approach to the study of ideological bias can be illustrated by one model, developed in connection with our studies, in which ideological factors are hypothesized as operating basically under rather peculiar circumstances.[57] We argue no great merit for the variables in this particular model, but the formal nature of the approach seems to us the appropriate one. We start with the view that the interviewer may distort the results in the direction of his own opinion *only* in the situation where some difficulty is felt. Yet since our phenomenological data suggest that ideology does not seem to work through the process of *com-*

municating the opinion to the respondent, it would probably operate basically through cognitive processes whereby the interviewer appraises the respondent in some biased way. Presumably, the mechanism of projection would be at work, and the interviewer would see the respondent as having an ideology something like his own. Yet, our phenomenological data suggest that the interviewer organizes his behavior in a more objective manner and that his expectations arise in other ways. Projection would be constrained to some extent by such factors. Thus, for ideology to work via the mechanism of projection, the projection would have to contain some logic, some relevance. We therefore theorized that the expectation about the respondent would be a projected one, mirroring the interviewer's own ideology, only where the respondent was of the same sex as the interviewer, and where the content of the issue has some sex-linkage.[58] In other words, the *vehicle* for ideological bias is an expectation; the *precipitating* factor is situational difficulty; and the *specialized circumstance* is that the projected expectation has some apparent relevance such as being appropriate to the sex of the respondent and the content of the question.

Suggestive data in support of this model are available from the Denver field experiment for a question on personal involvement in voting in a presidential election. Such a question is "sex-role" linked, since women generally are less involved in politics. This lesser involvement is even true for the women in the interviewing staff used: In Table 24 below, results obtained on this question are presented only for the fifteen out of the forty-five interviewers who anticipated they would meet objections in asking the question. The interviewers are further classified by sex and by the degree of involvement they themselves have in presidential elections. For each interviewer in these groups, the answers of respondents of the *same* sex were tabulated and given a numerical weight, and the Mean Score for all respondents of that interviewer was computed. This score expresses the degree of involvement that interviewer obtained from respondents of the same sex. Actually in the Table, the *deviation* of this Mean from the Mean for all respondents of that sex in that entire sector of Denver is presented. Where the value is large and positive, this signifies that the interviewer obtained results showing much greater involvement than really characterizes *equivalent* respondents in the survey; where the value is large and negative, it indicates that the results obtained show much less involvement than characterizes *equivalent* respondents in the survey. It will be noted that the direction of the bias follows the interviewer's own degree of involvement.

The data presented thus far only give suggestive support to the model. To strengthen the theory, it would be necessary to demonstrate that among these *same* interviewers, the data for respondents of the *other* sex do not conform to the pattern, and to demonstrate for other inter-

TABLE 24

IDEOLOGICAL BIAS AS LIMITED BY SITUATIONAL DIFFICULTY
AND PROJECTION TO LIKE-SEXED RESPONDENTS
(Deviation in degree of involvement in presidential politics from
Mean Value for equivalent respondents expressed only for those
respondents who are the same sex as the interviewer)

AMONG INTERVIEWERS ANTICIPATING OBJECTION WHO ARE			
FEMALE INTERVIEWERS		MALE INTERVIEWERS	
Interviewer Attaches Great Deal Importance	Interviewer Attaches Less Importance	Interviewer Attaches Great Deal Importance	Interviewer Attaches Less Importance
.15	−.47	−.29	−.26
.42	−.46	.45	.05
	−.17	.57	.23
	−.03	.73	
	.11		
	.25		
.29	−.13	.37	.01

viewers who anticipated *no* difficulty that the data for either sex-group follow no pattern. The materials are too elaborate to present, but in general they support the model.

4. THE RELATIVE SIGNIFICANCE OF EXPECTATIONS AND
IDEOLOGY AS BIASING FACTORS

The general findings presented thus far on the importance of expectational processes and the insignificance of ideological processes can be shown very neatly in some studies where the two factors have been studied *simultaneously*. The contrasting of findings on these respective factors when the findings are not predicated on the *same* set of conditions involves a considerable element of arbitrariness. The respective findings may have been predicated on interviewing staffs differing in competence, on surveys varying in difficulty of execution, on samples varying in suggestibility, and the like. By analyzing these two sources of bias simultaneously, we control such extraneous factors in the comparison. Incidentally, we can often examine each process controlling the other and establish their relative importance as *primary* factors. At times, we can also see what the total additive biasing effects of both factors are.

A number of such analyses are presented below, varying in the elegance of their design. One limitation inherent in such analyses is that the particular survey-setting may not be equally fertile ground for the operation of expectations and ideology. Thus, for example, a factual survey would provide nominally equivalent conditions for studying both sets of biasing factors, but it is obvious that the handicap is really on the side of proving expectational effects, since *one* would not expect the interviewer to have any ideology about the factual characteristics to be enumerated.

In the Wyatt-Campbell study, the relative importance of the two sets of factors was studied simultaneously.[59] The results obtained by the staff of student interviewers from the one sample for the five experimental questions were analyzed both for expectational and ideological bias.

The data showing the significant effect of probability expectations were reported earlier. We will not present the statistical findings on ideological effects, since they are available in the original paper, but on none of the five questions tested was there any significant difference in the results for interviewers of contrasting ideology. However, the qualification mentioned earlier applies to this comparison. While everything is identical in the two sets of tests, it is hard to conceive of the five questions as particularly amenable to ideological influences. Three of the questions are quasi-factual—whether the respondent talks to others about the campaign, whether given media affect his political thinking, and whether he has any candidate as a favorite. It is difficult to conceive of an interviewer's own opinion on such questions influencing the results.

In the two experiments on attitude-structure expectations described earlier, we have more meaningful simultaneous tests of the relative significance of these two sets of factors as biasing agencies. Both experiments dealt with opinion areas, equally susceptible to expectational and ideological influences. They are, however, laboratory studies with a certain degree of artificiality. In the Smith-Hyman study, the interviewer's own opinions had been previously measured. Consequently, one could determine variations in the recording of any answer for interviewers contrasted in ideology and compare this ideological effect with the influence of the attitude-structure expectation created by context. In Table 25 below, results for the experimental question on approval of U.S. spending abroad are presented in such form that the relative importance of these two sources of bias can be evaluated.

It is clear that the independent effect of the interviewer's ideology when the effect of expectations is controlled is negligible. This can be seen by comparing the results which interviewers with contrasting opinions assign to the same respondent. The change in results at most is 17 per cent.[60] On the other hand, the independent effect of expectations when ideology is held constant is great. This can be shown by

TABLE 25

The Relative Influence of Opinion Versus Expectation on Coding of Respondent's Answer to Question 7

	Subjects Who Code the Answer Correctly into "Right Amount"	
	Percentage	Number of Cases
For the Isolationist Respondent		
Interviewers who feel U.S. is spending too much money ...	19	31
Interviewers who feel U.S. is spending the right amount ...	20	60
For the Interventionist Respondent		
Interviewers who feel U.S. is spending too much money ...	61	31
Interviewers who feel U.S. is spending the right amount ...	78	60

comparing the way interviewers of a given opinion code the replies of the two different respondents. In each of the two comparisons the effect is to change the results by 40 to 50 percentage points. The relative importance of these two factors would, of course, vary from survey to survey depending on the intensity of the interviewer's ideology and the vividness of the attitude-structure of the respondent. In this instance, at least, the expectation effects are much more powerful.

Another simultaneous test of the effect of ideology and expectation was made in the course of the experiment where the effect of attitude-structure expectations on coding was studied by imbedding responses in artificial contexts. The interviewer's ideology was determined by obtaining his own answer to the same question prior to the coding assignment. In so far as ideology had an effect, we would expect interviewers, contrasted in opinion, to differ in the way they coded the identical item when it was imbedded in a given context. By virtue of the design of the experiment, one of the groups of interviewers had an opinion which was in conflict with the expectation created by the context, and the other group had an ideology which agreed with the context. The measure of the effect of ideology when it interacted with a given expectation was to see whether or not the amount of shifting due to context was significantly reduced when the interviewer's ideology operated in opposition to the expectation. The summary results for the three experimental items studied are presented below in Table 26. None of the individual tests is significant, and the aggregate test is also nonsignificant. Ideology has no effect on the coding of these responses, in the presence of an expectation created by context. Again,

TABLE 26

THE EFFECT OF IDEOLOGY WHEN OPERATING IN OPPOSITION TO
ATTITUDE-STRUCTURE EXPECTATIONS AS MEASURED BY AMOUNT OF
SHIFT IN CODING FOR INTERVIEWERS CONTRASTED IN OPINIONS

Experimental Item	Chi-Squared Value for Difference in Shifting Between Two Groups of Interviewers*	Degrees of Freedom	*P*-Value
21	1.22	1	.20–.30
06	.04	1	.80–.90
01	.33	1	.70–.80
Aggregate test	1.59	3	.66

* The two groups are interviewers whose ideology was opposed to context and interviewers whose ideology was in agreement with context.

the result must be qualified in the light of the fact that the context was consistent and powerful and probably created a strong expectation as to the attitude-structure in which the response was contained. Nevertheless, this test confirms the general findings of the large series of analyses made that ideological bias is only of secondary significance as compared with expectational processes.

CHAPTER IV

Respondent Reaction in the Interview Situation

Thus far, we have concentrated on research into the distorting effects on interview data of processes operating within the interviewer. We have seen how the interviewer enters the situation with certain attitudes and beliefs, which operate to affect his perception of the respondent, his judgment of the response, and other relevant aspects of his behavior. But this is only one side of a complex interaction. The respondent as well as the interviewer must entertain beliefs and attitudes which serve to affect the response he makes and which are—in part, at least—a product of the personal interview procedure. This chapter is devoted to a theoretical formulation of the processes underlying such reactional effects and to illustrative empirical demonstrations. A number of the studies cited are from the earlier literature but are reconsidered in the light of a new conceptual framework.

Certain respondent reactions are independent of anything the *particular* interviewer might do, and are merely a function of the interpersonal nature of the interview situation. They are the result of the involvement of the respondent in the interview situation. It is clear that a high degree of respondent involvement is a considered goal of survey agencies, for, by and large, the greater the involvement of the respondent in the situation, the greater his motivation and interest in the task at hand. However, what seems to be crucial from the standpoint of bias is not the *degree* of involvement, but the *nature* of that involvement. The involvement of any respondent in an interview situation may be broken down into two major components—"*task* involvement" (i.e., the involvement with the questions and answers) and what we will call "social involvement" (i.e., involvement with the interviewer as a personality). While rapport may be a function of the degree of *total* involvement, validity may be conceived as increasing with *task* involvement rather than with the *total* involvement. To the extent that a respondent's reaction derives from social or interpersonal involvement, we may expect it to result in bias, since, under such conditions, the response will be primarily a function of the relation between the respondent and the interviewer, instead of a response to the task.

Under what conditions is the social component of involvement increased? First of all, it is obvious that if we remove the "interviewer" from the physical environment, we decrease the possibility of respondent involvement with him as a personality. The case for self-administered questionnaires rests in part on this argument. It is frequently held that there can be no "interviewer effect" if there is no interviewer.

Examination of this view, however, raises certain questions. If we think of interviewer effect as occurring in two different ways, one being that of actual errors introduced by the interviewer in asking questions or recording the answers, and the other being reactive effect upon the respondent of the visible presence of the interviewer, we shall be better able to evaluate this view. True, the self-administered questionnaire, by definition, excludes the former error; but the belief that the physical absence of an interviewer excludes a reactive effect upon the respondent is mistaken.

We do know that subjects filling out questionnaires take account of the prospective readers of their replies.[1] Thus, qualitative data support the notion that there may be present an interviewer effect, even when there is no interviewer. Moreover, the very absence of an interviewer may act as a biasing factor. For in some respects the interviewer might act as a check on tendencies among respondents to distort data in some way that will serve ego-needs.

Although it is clear that self-administered studies often contain some bias arising from social involvement, it may be stated as an initial principle that the social component of involvement will be increased as the interviewer looms larger in the psychological field of the respondent. Obviously, we may expect that the respondent will be more sensitized to the "interviewer" when the latter is physically present.

Assuming that in most cases the social component of involvement will be larger in the presence of the interviewer, let us compare data from studies conducted by personal interview with those conducted by self-administration. Whatever systematic bias may be operating as a result of the greater interaction in the personal interview should be revealed by such comparisons.

1. SYSTEMATIC EFFECTS OF PERSONAL INTERACTION

A number of studies comparing results of personal interview with results from self-administration are available. By comparing the *marginals*, we can assess the systematic effects of the presence of the interviewer, irrespective of specific effects generated by the characteristics of a given interviewer-respondent relationship.

In two studies, reported by Ellis, of the love relationships of female college students, answers from personal interviews of sixty-nine students were compared with those obtained by questionnaires filled out by the same students a year later.[2] The sixty questions were divided into three groups of twenty each, according to the degree to which "the ego would be involved" in answering the question; the judgment as to ego-involvement being made by a group of psychologists. Among the twenty most ego-involving questions, significant differences between interview and questionnaire results at the 5 per cent level were obtained on six of the items; on the two groups of less and least ego-involving items, three out of twenty and one out of twenty differences, respectively, were significant. For example, on the question "How much did you love your mother during childhood?", the distribution of responses was as follows:

	Interview	Questionnaire
Very dearly............	37	25
A good deal............	17	27
Pretty much............	14	10
Not too much...........	1	7
Not at all.............	0	0
	N = 69	N = 69

In general, the subjects exhibited less favorable (that is, less acceptable in our society) response patterns on the questionnaire than in the interview (fifty-five of the sixty items). The questionnaire produced more extreme admissions of traits which have unfavorable connotations in our society, such as jealousy, sadism, masochism, aggressiveness, and strong sexuality, and fewer extreme admissions of traits which have favorable connotations, such as forgiveness, happiness, sensitivity to beauty, and kindness. Also, the questionnaire elicited more extreme admissions of traits connoting intense and "perhaps foolhardy" love. These were not confined to a few of the subjects interviewed. Of the sixty-nine subjects, fifty-three gave on the whole less favorable questionnaire than interview responses, eight about the same, and only eight more favorable responses on the most ego-involving items, and the distribution on the other items was very similar.

Ellis concluded that in investigations of love and marital relationships among college students, the questionnaire technique may produce more self-revelatory data than the interview method. Similar findings were obtained in a later test with uncategorized responses.

Since the interviewer in the Ellis study was a male, the findings conceivably could be accounted for by the sex difference between interviewer and respondent. However, Ellis refers to a study by Pointer, which yielded similar findings, even when the interviewer was a female. Pointer concluded that "the questionnaire is more reliable on the basis of the larger number of admissions of sex practices among the (questionnaire) group."

The design of the Ellis study was such as to render the results open to serious question. Since the questionnaires were unfortunately administered a year after the personal interviews, it is impossible to be sure that differences are due to the method of inquiry. During the particular time of life when the students were being questioned, willingness to express attitudes on the subject of love relations might conceivably be undergoing fairly rapid change in the direction of greater freedom of expression and greater willingness to admit conventionally unacceptable traits. Then too, the experience of the individuals during that year might well have been such as to alter attitudes themselves. For these reasons, the data collected by Ellis, while suggestive, remain inconclusive.[3]

Evidence tending to confirm Ellis' general findings is yielded by a study conducted by the Survey Research Center of the University of Michigan.[4] Anonymous questionnaires, group administered, covering the attitudinal area of satisfaction with job and supervisor were obtained from workers in a utility company. Personal interviews with 328 of these respondents were conducted at a later date, using two questions that were similar to the original wordings in the questionnaire, but not identical. For reasons of the research design, these interviews were conducted only with those respondents who had exhibited on the questionnaire extremely high or extremely low morale. In so far as such respondents might differ in the intensity of their feelings or their outspokenness, the generalizability of the results to all workers must be qualified. It should also be noted that the lapse of time between the two sets of measurements was approximately two months, creating the possibility that any differences might reflect the systematic effect of real changes in the work situation.

Comparison of the results revealed a general tendency among the workers to report less dissatisfaction in the personal interview. Most interesting is a refined analysis which showed that the change in procedure had a differentially greater effect on "blue-collar" workers than on "white-collar" workers. These differential effects support the notion that the anonymity of the self-administered questionnaire permits greater expression of unsanctioned attitudes, since the blue-collar workers in general were found to be less satisfied with their work.

Another study affording a comparison between the personal interview and the self-administered mail questionnaire was conducted for *Time* magazine by Lazarsfeld and Franzen.[5] A mail questionnaire was sent to 3,000 *Time* subscribers and 1,052 were returned. Several weeks later, 1,387 of the original group of 3,000 were interviewed with the same questionnaire. Of those, 505 interviews were conducted with persons who had also replied by mail. For this group, both a completed interview and a mail questionnaire were available, enabling the results to be compared. The survey items covered a wide range of personal and family characteristics.

Differences between the interview and mail answers were found to be significant at the 5 per cent level for eighteen of the sixty-six items covered. These items may be classified into four groups following the interpretations placed on the differences by the authors:

1. A higher degree of education, heavier correspondence, and more time spent in magazine reading were reported in the personal interviews. The authors' interpretation is that "the answers obtained by mail are more qualified than the answers given to an interviewer." In the case of magazine-reading time, they say "It is reasonable that the interview answer represents an outside guess while the mail answer is more carefully weighed."

2. For total family income, price of refrigerator, price of washing machine, values in the upper brackets were reported more often in the mail questionnaire. The interpretation made here is that activity in the higher extremes is more readily admitted in the mail questionnaire.

3. Questions on "unusual types of activity." These include writing to newspapers, holding offices in clubs, etc. All these were more frequently given in the mail questionnaire. The authors' interpretation is that "in general, the unusual type of activity is more freely divulged in the mail response than in the interview."

4. Number of magazines read. The number was much greater when reported by mail than when reported by personal interview. The authors say, "Probably the reason is that the mail query offers more time for consideration."

The report concludes that "answers obtained through a mail questionnaire are appreciably more informative and therefore more satisfactory than answers obtained by an interviewer. On many questions that involve a degree of activity, the mail answers are more qualified. On subjects dealing with buying power, mail questionnaires overcame a reluctance that is apparent in interview responses to reveal activity in the upper extremes, . . . and fewer people refused information on income." Further, "These findings substantiate several claims that are usually made for mail answers: (*a*) bias that comes from the respondents' desire to impress or conceal from the interviewer is eliminated;

(*b*) answers to personal questions are more frequently given in an anonymous mail reply; (*c*) a mail reply is filled out in leisure and thus produces a more thoughtful answer."

These conclusions, however, depend on the interpretation of the authors. In every case they explain differences in favor of the mail questionnaire, by classifying the contents of the questions in various ways, after the fact. When more activity is reported by mail, the authors attribute this to "more time for consideration" or "activity in higher extremes more readily admitted by mail" or "unusual activity more freely divulged by mail"; but when more activity is reported from the interview, they say that the answers by mail are more qualified or that respondent's desire to impress the interviewer is eliminated. The alternative interpretation could be made that the presence of the interviewer acts as a check on the veracity of the answers, in that it may make the respondents give a more conservative answer, that is, one that will not seem inconsistent with the circumstances known to the interviewer.

Parenthetically, it should be remembered that we are dealing here with those persons who *replied* by mail questionnaire. Although the interpretation that "answers to personal questions are more frequently given in an anonymous mail reply" may be correct for those who *do* reply by mail, there are many more people who do not reply at *all* by mail. The minority who do take the trouble to answer by mail could scarcely be expected to leave many questions unanswered. Thus, while the study may provide additional evidence on the known fact that people will not answer all personal questions in an interview, it does not support the conclusion that the mail questionnaire can be generally substituted for interviewing, since the majority do not reply at *all* by mail.

Although the data collected by Lazarsfeld and Franzen do not seem by themselves to prove the conclusions of the authors, evidence available from our study of the pressures operating in the interview situation lends support to the general notion that respondents are frequently unwilling to reveal certain kinds of information in a personal interview.

A similar comparison of mail questionnaire and interview was made by John F. Maloney, Research Director of *Reader's Digest*, with results quite different from those found by Lazarsfeld and Franzen.[6] In April, May, June, and July of 1948, the Norwegian Gallup Poll conducted a special test on readers' preference for particular articles in the Norwegian edition of the *Reader's Digest*.

Information on a random half of the sample households was obtained by personal interview, on the other half by a card left for the respondent to mail. The results showed no clear-cut differences in the order of preference for the various articles between the two methods. Over the four-month period, the Spearman rank correlation coefficients ranged from .78 to .84. Further, there were no significant differences in preference for "serious" vs. "light" articles.[7]

A recent study by the Census Bureau compares the results obtained by interview and "self-enumeration."[8] Under the latter method, a schedule is left to be filled out by the respondent and is picked up at a later date.

The study was based on the October, 1948, pretest of census procedures. In selected areas the two parallel procedures were used: interview and self-enumeration. Enumerator assignments were allocated to the two procedures by a random process.

In order to determine the relative accuracy of the two procedures, a re-interview was made of a substantial proportion of the households, employing a more detailed inquiry about selected topics. Whenever the original entry differed from the answer obtained on the check interview, the respondent was asked to explain the discrepancy. In this "quality check," the interviewers were professional personnel from the Washington office, so it may be reasonable to assume that the re-interview information is somewhat more accurate than the original data.

In general, the results of the comparison were inconclusive. However, the check did indicate a possible superiority of the self-enumeration procedure in reducing the tendency to round off responses—i.e., the tendency to over-report highest school grade completed as eighth grade, twelfth grade, etc., or the tendency to over-report age at the convenient rounding-off points of forty, sixty-five, etc. Under the self-enumeration procedure, the respondent has a chance to check back or to look at records.

In the case of education, the quality check resulted in changes for those reporting eighth grade, twelfth grade, and college completed by interview of 19 per cent, 12 per cent, and 32 per cent respectively, while the corresponding changes for the self-enumeration procedure were 17 per cent, 6 per cent, and one per cent respectively. However, these data are based on only twenty-two interview cases and eighteen self-enumeration cases. Similarly, the check changed by one year or more 20 per cent of the individuals reported by interview as forty years old and 24 per cent of those reported as sixty-five years old, while the corresponding percentages for self-enumeration were seventeen and twenty-two. Again the percentages are based on relatively few cases (between twenty-three and forty-nine), and the differences are not statistically significant.

On the other hand, there is more reliable evidence from the pretest that the interview may be *less* subject to error in the case of characteristics or items which require any complexity of definition. One such characteristic is the per cent of the population in the labor force, particularly the report on whether the individual worked last week. We quote: "Work is defined to include all work for pay or profit and work in the operation of the farm, business or profession of another member of the family and to exclude housework and other work around the home."

It is frequently difficult to get the respondent to understand the idea of including unpaid work on a family farm or in a family member's business or profession. In the October pretest, the ratios of persons reported in the original enumeration as "working last week" to persons reported in the quality check were:

	Male	Female
Direct-enumeration procedure	.97	.92
Self-enumeration procedure	.99	.81

For males the difference in the (net) errors of the two procedures is very small. There is, however, a substantial difference in the net errors for females, and the undercount (relative to the quality check results) is larger for the self-enumeration procedure. These results are consistent with our hypothesis (that direct enumeration would be more accurate in this case), since a large proportion of the persons originally reported as not working were unpaid family workers, and this category is, in general, more important for women than for men (and also more likely to be overlooked for women than for men).

Wedell and Smith report a comparison of self-administered questionnaires with personal interview data for a sample of industrial employees queried on satisfaction with the company, aspects of the job, pay, and the foreman.[9] The interview data yielded more favorable worker attitudes, but the findings varied among the six questions tested and among the six interviewers used. This finding agrees with that of Metzner and Mann cited earlier.[10] The general implication of these two studies is that the expression of attitudes critical of the company may be a delicate situation for the worker. Given the personal interaction of an interview, the respondent may feel less anonymous and therefore less free to report such attitudes.

From the foregoing data, it would seem that reactional effects are often facilitated by the presence of the interviewer, yet, the contradictory findings indicate that such effects may, in certain situations, be insignificant. In other situations, while effects are evident, they are by no means uniform in direction.

An experimental comparison of telephone vs. face-to-face interviews by Larsen bears on our earlier suggestion that one effect of the personal interaction of the normal interview may be to reduce prestige-motivated exaggeration by the respondent.[11] While the telephone interview differs in important respects from the self-administered questionnaire, it approximates it in the sense of keeping the felt presence of the interviewer and interaction between him and the respondent to a minimum. In this sense, the findings have relevance to our analysis.

Fairly comparable samples of individuals were queried by the two methods of interview about their behavior following the dropping of civil defense leaflets by aircraft over Salt Lake City. The leaflet was in the form of a postcard addressed to the authorities, and it encouraged the respondent to answer certain questions and to return the postcard by mail. In both samples, the proportion claiming that they had returned the postcard was identical, but comparison with the actual returns validated 80 per cent of the face-to-face and only 16 per cent of the telephone-mailing claims. Further, among the telephone respondents who reported exposure to the leaflet, 50 per cent could not report even one of the three things it told them to do, compared with 35 per cent of the face-to-face respondents. Similarly, 41 per cent of the telephone sample who reported exposure could not identify the officials who had signed the leaflet, whereas only 32 per cent of the face-to-face respondents could not identify the signers. Other differences in knowledge were in the same direction. The claims made on certain other questions also seem less credible for the telephone sample. They report more frequently that they passed on the leaflets, told other people the message, and inquired about the test drop. All of these differences in the direction of inflated answers to questions of a prestigious nature were so-to-speak inhibited in the presence of the interviewer.

It is possible for *systematic* bias to arise from societal circumstances which commonly cause respondents to structure their perception of *any* interviewer in conformity with some preconception, without regard to the particular interviewer's actual characteristics. Such tendencies toward a uniform structuring of perceptions, if pervasive, can affect results in a systematic fashion, i.e., the entire body of data secured may be distorted in a particular direction.

In a study of the effect of sponsorship, Crespi pointed out that data secured under the sponsorship of a fictitious German Opinion Institute probably contained a measure of invalidity due simply to the fact that sizable numbers of respondents feared that the interviewer might be an informer.[12] That such perceptions are by no means unique or limited to stringent cultural climates is revealed in data secured by NORC during the period 1948–52, reported below.

In 1948, because of the Wallace candidacy, NORC sent a questionnaire to its interviewers inquiring about the freedom with which respondents were answering political questions. Although the findings were in no way alarming, the number of spontaneous mentions of such respondent fears by interviewers during the following year led NORC to repeat the questionnaire in 1950 and again in 1952. The number of spontaneous comments on this theme that were received from interviewers, as well as their geographical spread, indicates that the phenomenon was not limited to an isolated interviewer here and there nor to particular localities or types of respondents, and that, in so far as respondent perception of the interviewer would affect data, such effects would be diffused throughout the survey. Illustrative comments are presented below:

From a rural area outside Houston, Texas:

The survey was harder because of everyone being alerted in Houston against giving information to anyone asking any questions . . . respondents just wouldn't talk or answer if they could help it. I believe as long as the situation is as it is, it will be hard to get true opinions on any national affairs. I never had so many refusals.

From San Diego, California:

One respondent, her husband piped up and said, "She's trying to find out if you are a Communist.". . . One man refused to be interviewed, said he wouldn't answer any questions on account of his job. . . . A woman phoned me (and asked me) if I had sent in "those papers," I said, "No." She said her husband said I was probably a Communist and they would check upon him where he works.

From a rural area outside Cincinnati, Ohio:

One woman seriously thought I was a "Commie spy."

From Ogden, Utah:

I have had several people ask me lately if I was a Communist and I don't like it. It's hard to explain to an uneducated person just what you are doing when their suspicions are aroused.

From a rural area outside Youngstown, Ohio:

Some respondents wouldn't answer until I told them I had no Communist leanings. . . .

From New York City:

A good many people refused to answer because they were afraid I was representing a Communist agency, and thought they would become involved in a disagreeable situation.

The statistical comparisons of the 1948, 1950, and 1952 results of the questionnaire sent to interviewers point up the kind of systematic bias

TABLE 27

TRENDS IN INTERVIEWERS' REPORTS OF RESPONDENT FEAR AND SUSPICION*

QUESTION	CATEGORY	PERCENTAGE OF INTERVIEWERS		
		1948	1950	1952
		(N = 93)	(N = 89)	(N = 97)
"Did any of your respondents on this survey seem afraid to *answer* any of the questions?".........	Yes No	41 59 —— 100	41 59 —— 100	41 59 —— 100
(If "Yes") "About how often did this happen?"................	Less than 1 in 10† 1 in 10 to 1 in 5 1 in 3 to 1 in 4 More than 1 in 3	36 33 20 11 100	14 53 8 25 100	19 52 10 19 100
"Did anyone refuse to continue with the interview after he once started it and heard some of the questions?"...................	Yes No	13 87 —— 100	31 69 —— 100	33 67 —— 100
(If "Yes") "About how often did this happen?"................	Less than 1 in 10† 1 in 10 or more	67 33 100	51 49 100	52 48 100
"Did anyone doubt your statement of the sponsorship and purpose of the survey or suspect that the survey was being done for some hidden purpose?"......	Yes No	18 82 100	34 66 100	23 77 100

* The interviewer groups are not identical, since there were some changes in the staff during the period.
† Per cents on these questions are proportion of affirmative group rather than of total group.

which can develop during a period of public fear and desire for conformity.

In general, the data indicate that from 1948 to 1952 respondent fear and suspicion of interviewers had increased to a measurable degree and that interviewers frequently labored under the handicap of respondent fear and distrust. Although the increase in this phenomenon occurred largely during the period 1948–50, the frequency of reported fear showed no decrease in the second time-period, seemingly leveling off at the 1950 frequencies. Parenthetically, it may be observed that the number of interviewers who report suspicions as such shows no increase, but the frequency of its occurrence among their respondents is much higher in the second and third inquiries. This may mean that because of some personal characteristic certain interviewers are more subject to this type of structuring than others, but the extensiveness of reports of fear and suspicion indicate that many interviewers face this situation.[13]

Reactional effects of the type discussed thus far are those which arise from the nature of the personal interview situation itself. Therefore, such *systematic* effects are, for the most part, independent of the *personal* characteristics of the interviewer and are expressions of perceptual, cognitive, and motivational processes common to most respondents in a personal interview situation. True, fears that an interviewer might be a Communist agent or an F.B.I. man might operate partially as a function of a given interviewer's characteristics, but the data cited in the foregoing indicate that a pervasive suspicion exists which is independent of the appearance or manner of particular interviewers.

2. DIFFERENTIAL EFFECTS OF PERSONAL INTERACTION

In addition to such systematic effects deriving from the interpersonal relationship, it should be clear that *differential* reactional effects are also a source of bias. Each interview situation has a unique interpersonal quality. No two interviewers can establish an identical relationship with a respondent, nor are any two respondents likely to react in exactly the same manner to a given interviewer. Where little interaction is present, we can assume that the interviewer does not occupy a large or well-structured portion of the psychological field of the respondent, and thus, we might expect to find little evidence of reactional bias. Respondent lack of social involvement in the situation precludes the presence of reactional effect.

Two of the cases described in Chapter II illustrate the relation between involvement and bias. In the case of "The Creep," we find an interviewer with potentially strong biasing tendencies, but a respondent with a high degree of involvement focused almost entirely on the *task* itself. His social involvement with the interviewer is almost nil. Consequently, we find little evidence of bias, although the *total* involvement may be presumed to be high.

In another case, "The Tough Guy," we also find little evidence of bias, but here there seems to be neither task *nor* social involvement. In conformity with our theory, these two cases graphically bear out the hypothesis that reactional effects are a function of *social* involvement rather than *total* involvement. In "The Creep," task involvement was high and social involvement low, and little reactional bias was present, while in the "Tough Guy" we find both types of involvement low and likewise little evidence of bias.

In contrast to these cases, in "The Hen Party," a high degree of respondent involvement of both types existed. The respondent seemed most interested in the questions and also in a close psychological relation with the interviewer. In this situation of "high rapport," however, we find evidence of reactional bias. Despite the extent of the task involvement, the social involvement of the respondent was of such degree that reactional bias was clearly evident.

These cases indicate the wide range of variation that can exist between interview situations and the extent to which the nature and degree of reactional effects are a product of the interpersonal relationship between interviewer and respondent.

3. SYSTEMATIC EFFECTS OF GROUP MEMBERSHIP DISPARITIES BETWEEN
INTERVIEWERS AND RESPONDENTS

In addition to the systematic effects noted earlier, there is putative evidence that the relatively homogeneous character of most interviewing staffs also induces systematic reactional effects among respondents. It should be apparent that, quite apart from transient cultural conditions which bring about general respondent reactions of fear, there exist other conditions which are likely to produce a stable, well-structured perception of interviewers among many respondents. Since interviewers are a fairly homogeneous group, it seems logical to assume that they will be perceived (and reacted to) in accordance with their homogeneous characteristics. A study conducted by Sheatsley as part of this project presents convincing evidence of the special character of the interviewer population. Table 28 below summarizes some of the main findings concerning the demographic characteristics of several interviewing staffs.[14]

From the data in Table 28, we have calculated that 74 per cent of the interviewers on the current staffs of Gallup, Roper, NORC, Bennett, and BAE taken together are women. Seventy-eight per cent have had at least some college education, and about 98 per cent are white. As Sheatsley has said, ". . . the composition of most national field staffs has dangerous implications for survey bias arising out of the interviewing situation. We have a condition in which the great bulk of market and opinion research interviewing today is conducted by women talking to men, by college graduates talking to the uneducated, by upper-middle-class individuals talking to those of low socio-economic status, by younger people talking to the increasingly larger old-age groups, by white persons talking to Negroes and by city dwellers talking to rural folk."[15]

Of course, the mere fact that interviewers are a homogeneous group is not *proof* that they are perceived in this way by respondents. After all, interviewers are trained to be at ease with people of all strata, and it is probably true that to some extent they are able to overcome class, age, sex, and other barriers to a greater degree than untrained persons of the same background. However, it is doubtful that these can be completely overcome by the majority of public opinion interviewers. The psychological literature on expression makes it clear that subjects can do better than chance in judging the characteristics of individuals even from isolated expressive cues—cues such as judging personality from merely hearing the voice over a public address system[16] or judging occupation from photographs.[17]

Even if respondents may not always judge group membership correctly, there is abundant evidence that subjects use visual and auditory cues in judging group membership. The literature on stereotyping presents overwhelming evidence of a tendency among human beings to make guesses about the group membership of perceived individuals and to behave in conformity with such stereotyped judgments. A recent study by Gertrude Abramson establishes the fact that even such a widely used accessory as eyeglasses may operate in subjects' judgments of ethnic group membership.[18] If subjects can make correct judgments with only isolated cues at their disposal, it is obvious that with the multiplicity of cues in the face-to-face relationship of a personal interview the probability of correct judgment will be greatly magnified.

It seems, therefore, extremely unlikely that even well-trained inter-

TABLE 28
Composition of National Field Staffs

	Percentage NORC Total Group	Percentage NORC Current Staff	Percentage Gallup Staff	Percentage Roper Staff	Percentage Bennett Group	Percentage BAE Staff	Percentage Total Adult Population
N =	(1161)	(200)	(1198)	(277)	(695)*	(69)	
Men	15	12	40	3	14	55	49
Living in small towns and rural areas	13(a)	21(a)	19(b)	5(b)	..(b)	4(a)	32(b)
Aged under 30	32	20	21	11	13	43	23
30–39	36	38	27	24	29	42	21
40–49	23	32	28	43	38	12	21
50–up	9	10	24	22	20	3	35
Negro	4	7	..†	4	..†	6	9
Total college graduates	44	47	48	38	54	90	5
Total with any college education	80	81	77	70	78	100	13
Never attended college	20	19	23	30	22	..	87
Automobile in the family	70	73	..†	..†	68	..†	56(d)
Identify as Republicans	29	..†	45	..†	..†	..†	32(c)
Identify as Democrats	52	..†	38	..†	..†	..†	48
Identify as political independents	11	..†	12	..†	..†	..†	20
Minor parties or not stated	8	..†	5	..†	..†	..†	..

* Returns from mail questionnaire sent to 2,000.
† Data not available.
‡ Less than ⅓ of 1%.
(a) Towns under 10,000 or rural.
(b) Towns under 2,500 or rural.
(c) Gallup Poll release October 19, 1949.
(d) 1949 Survey of Consumer Finances (Federal Reserve Board), Part VI.

viewers can so change their personality that respondents would be unable to identify their group membership. Obviously, sex, age, and color cannot be disguised, and, as far as these characteristics alone are concerned, the interviewer group is fairly homogeneous.

Of course, to some extent the effects of group membership disparity are somewhat mitigated by selective assignment—for example, the very few Negroes on interviewing staffs are usually assigned Negro respondents. Hyman, however, in discussing the possibility of errors in the 1948 poll results arising from differences in group membership of interviewer and respondent, cites the fact that most of the Negro respondents in the Crossley and Roper polls were interviewed by whites, and that about three-fourths of both the Roper and Crossley interviewing staffs had had some college education.[19] "No one can be sure that the composition of the interviewing staffs produces error in the pre-election polls, but it is plausible that lower-class respondents and Negro respondents may have spoken less truthfully on this account. Also, the long term predominance of upper-class interviewers may be a reason why the polls have shown a Republican bias."

While it is likely that a systematic effect among respondents is created by the well-structured image most interviewers present, effects would not be uniform in magnitude or direction on all surveys. A possible greater effect of group membership disparities in election prediction than in other types of survey work has been suggested by Gosnell and DeGrazia, who point out that voting in an election is an *impersonal* situation, while the situation in which the anticipated behavior is measured is an *interpersonal* one.[20] In Chapter V, we shall explore the extent to which effects deriving from group membership disparities are a function of situational factors.

4. DIFFERENTIAL EFFECTS OF GROUP MEMBERSHIP DISPARITIES BETWEEN INTERVIEWERS AND RESPONDENTS

Even assuming, however, that structured perceptions do exist, it seems clear that bias does not necessarily result unless the characteristics of the interviewer are of such an order as would be likely to induce specialized *affective* reactions in the respondent. It has usually been felt that where the interviewer and respondent are sharply contrasted in their group membership characteristics there is likely to be an affective reaction with unfavorable consequences, and that where they are similar in characteristics the opposite consequently will occur. In the past, it has been hypothesized that the specific nature of the affect that presumably varies with the group membership and presumably accounts for the validity of results is the feeling of mutual warmth and sociability, usually characterized by the term "rapport." Thus it has been held that a disparity prevents the achievement of high rapport and in turn results in invalidity, and that a similarity permits high rapport and in turn yields valid results.[21] This theory needs considerable qualification. While there is evidence of reactional effects where group membership disparities are great, this should not be construed as resulting necessarily from lack of rapport. Our evidence indicates that the relationship between rapport and group membership is not of such a simple nature.

In order to test the theory that similarity of group membership necessarily produces greater rapport, tabulations were made of reciprocal ratings of reactions to the interview secured from interviewers and respondents in a nationwide study. In this project, which was part of a larger study of the interview situation conducted by Marshall Brown in conjunction with NORC, respondents were handed "rating sheets" by interviewers at the conclusion of the interview, in which they were asked a number of questions about the interview and their reactions to it. The interview itself dealt with issues of current political policy. At the option of the respondent, the rating forms could be mailed into the NORC office in a self-addressed envelope or returned to the interviewer, sealed or unsealed. In turn, interviewers recorded on a questionnaire their ratings of respondent "honesty and frankness" and also the degree to which they themselves "enjoyed the interview." The rating scale used for enjoyment of the interview was identical on both respondent and interviewer forms.

Assuming that rapport was highest where both interviewer *and* respondent enjoyed the interview, tabulations were then made of the degree to which this variable was a function of respondent-interviewer group membership similarity. The results are presented in Table 29 for the three group membership characteristics tested.

If the assumption is warranted that ratings by respondent and interviewer of the extent to which they enjoyed the interview are a measure of rapport in the interview situation, it seems clear from the table below that rapport bears no necessary relation to group similarity. While among respondents of male interviewers there *is* evident such a relation, the same cannot be said of respondents of female interviewers. Here rapport seems to be equally high with both male and female respondents. Likewise, if we examine the respondents of both the socio-economically high and low interviewer groups, we find that rapport seems to be lowest in interviews with low socio-economic groups, regardless of whether they are interviewed by high or low interviewers.[22] For the two youngest groups of interviewers, rapport seems to be greatest in their interviews with middle-group respondents, while among older

TABLE 29

THE RELATION OF GROUP MEMBERSHIP SIMILARITY TO INTERVIEWER-RESPONDENT RAPPORT

RESPONDENT-INTERVIEWER COMBINATION	PROPORTION OF COMBINATIONS WHERE ENJOYMENT OF INTERVIEW WAS RATED				
	By Interviewer By Respondent	Low Low	Low High	High Low	High High
	Number	Percentage			
Sex					
Male interviewers					
Male respondents........	98	28	27	14	31
Female respondents......	91	43	23	16	18
Female interviewers					
Male respondents........	476	26	23	17	34
Female respondents......	512	29	24	14	33
Socio-Economic Status					
A and B interviewers					
A and B respondents......	77	29	16	23	32
C respondents...........	221	28	17	18	37
D respondents...........	114	39	27	12	22
C and D interviewers					
A and B respondents......	92	19	20	24	37
C respondents...........	378	24	26	17	33
D respondents...........	179	36	32	8	24
Age					
Interviewers under 30					
Respondents under 30....	55	42	31	4	23
Respondents 30–39......	47	32	22	10	36
Respondents 40 and over..	90	39	32	5	24
Interviewers 30–39					
Respondents under 30....	31	39	16	22	23
Respondents 30–39......	33	27	27	15	31
Respondents 40 and over..	78	28	31	14	27
Interviewers 40 and over					
Respondents under 30....	167	23	27	16	34
Respondents 30–39......	224	30	17	22	31
Respondents 40 and over..	431	24	23	17	36

interviewers the age of the respondent seems to have little effect on rapport.

One might argue that whether the *interviewer* enjoyed the interview is immaterial, and that the rapport measure should only be based on respondent ratings of enjoyment. If we approach the problem with this criterion and examine the sum of the percentages in the second and fourth columns in the table (which measure respondent enjoyment alone), we find that group similarity is related to rapport only in the case of male interviewers. All other combinations fail to reveal any direct relationship.

It is entirely plausible, however, that at particular levels of interviewer competence, group similarity may produce greater rapport. Where interviewers are less competent or less experienced, it seems likely that group membership similarities might substantially assist the interviewer in maintaining rapport.[23] This explanation is suggested by the preceding table; by and large, NORC's women interviewers are more competent and more experienced than the men interviewers, and the older interviewers are at least more experienced than the younger ones.[24] For women and older interviewers, as may be noted in the foregoing, the group membership character of their respondents seems to make little difference in ratings of enjoyment, either when measured separately for respondents or when both ratings are compounded.

Granted that rapport is not a simple function of group membership similarity, as has been previously accepted, the theory can also be qualified with respect to the principle that validity necessarily increases with an increase in similarity. The interviewer's rating of respondent "frankness and honesty," alluded to earlier, may be used as an inferential measure of response validity. While, of course, we have no basis for assuming that the interviewers' reports have any absolute validity, it seems reasonable to assume that whatever invalidity they contain is randomly distributed among respondent subgroups. The tabulation of these interviewer reports in their relation to group membership similarity is presented in Table 30.

If we compare the results in Table 30 with those in Table 29, we find a high correspondence. Again, it is only among male interviewers that group membership similarity is a factor in validity ratings. Also, as in the previous table, we find the lower socio-economic groups rated as less honest among both groups of interviewers. Age differences are small and inconclusive.

While there is no evidence here of any relationship of validity to group membership similarity, it would seem, from the preceding tables taken together, that there is a direct relationship between validity and rapport.[25] However, neither of these variables has any general relation to the similarity or difference in the group membership character of respondents and interviewers. Even among specific groups, it may well be a factor other than group membership similarity (e.g., the experience

TABLE 30

THE RELATION OF RESPONDENT FRANKNESS AND HONESTY TO SIMILARITY OF INTERVIEWER-RESPONDENT GROUP MEMBERSHIP

Respondent-Interviewer Combination*	Percentage of Interviewers Rating Respondents as "completely frank and honest"
Sex	
Male interviewers	
Male respondents	68
Female respondents	56
Female interviewers	
Male respondents	79
Female respondents	79
Socio-Economic Status	
A and B interviewers	
A and B respondents	90
C respondents	82
D respondents	66
C and D interviewers	
A and B respondents	88
C respondents	78
D respondents	68
Age	
Interviewers under 30	
Respondents under 30	68
Respondents 30–39	69
Respondents 40 and over	68
Interviewers 30–39	
Respondents under 30	68
Respondents 30–39	66
Respondents 40 and over	74
Interviewers 40 and over	
Respondents under 30	75
Respondents 30–39	80
Respondents 40 and over	81

* For the number of cases in each combination see Table 29.

of the interviewer) that enables him to secure good rapport and high validity in the interview situation.

One further bit of evidence from the same study bears out the thesis that the quality of the data collected is related to rapport in the interview. In this instance, a direct measure of response reliability may be used as the criterion of quality. In the study just described, one question asked earlier in the interview was repeated in written form at the end of the respondent rating sheet, which (it will be recalled) the respondent filled out after the conclusion of the interview. It was possible to isolate the respondents who changed their answer the second time the question was asked, and to compare the characteristics of the reliable and unreliable groups.[26] Here it was found that reliable respondents, when asked to select from among the list of phrases the one that best described the interview, were more likely than unreliable respondents to report that the interview was "like a friendly discussion."

It would seem, then, that rapport and group membership similarity must be viewed as separate operating factors within an interview situation. True, in many situations the two factors coincide, and there is some evidence that under defined conditions similarity may be one of the factors that induce rapport. But that there is no organic or necessary relation between these factors seems established from the data previously presented. It must be that particular other types of affect occurring in specialized instances of disparity are the explanatory principle for the observed effects of group membership disparities. In certain such instances, pressures generated as a result of emotions of fear, distrust, or misunderstanding operate. And because the deviant or minority individual is likely to have a different opinion in the first place, these fears will operate to alter his opinion in the direction of conformity. That this seems more tenable than the notion of rapport as an explanation is also clear from the statistical findings to be presented in the next section. If the factor of rapport were explanatory, results should show a diffuse effect over many questions. This is clearly not the case. The group membership disparities locate their effects only on specific questions—ones where fear and distrust would operate to control the answer given.

In the next pages, we present evidence of differential effects arising from group membership differences between interviewers and respondents. In many of the studies cited, there is no clear proof that the effects noted are not due to processes operating within the interviewers (such as noted in Chapter III). However, the consistency of effects, as well as the fact that they occur on questions in which respondent reactions would be hypothesized by logic, lends support to our belief that the data to follow do, in fact, represent effects arising primarily from processes within the respondent rather than within the interviewer. It is possible, however, that both types of processes occurred.

Effects arising from differences in color.—We have clear evidence that the presumed impersonality of the interview situation does not overcome the reluctance of Negroes to express their opinions freely to whites. In a study conducted by NORC in 1942 in Memphis, a sample of 1000 Negroes were interviewed with approximately 500 cases handled by Negro interviewers and 500 by whites.[27] The two samples were equivalent—that is, the assignments were randomized as between white and Negro interviewers. The survey questions dealt with opinions and attitudes about the war, but there were also a number of questions of a factual nature. Table 31, below, shows that white interviewers obtained substantially different results from the Negro interviewers on most of the individual questions. On almost all the opinion and attitude questions, the white interviewers obtained significantly higher proportions of what might be called by some people "proper" or "acceptable" answers. Negroes were more reluctant to express to the white interviewers their resentments over discrimination by employers or labor unions, in the army, and in public places; to express any sort of belief in the good intentions or even possibility of victory of Japan or Germany; to reveal to white interviewers sympathy for the CIO (possibly out of fear that the white interviewer might think them too radical). Even on some of the factual questions such as auto ownership, reading of Negro newspapers, and CIO membership, apparently some Negroes reported differently to white interviewers than to Negro interviewers. It must be remembered that the survey was carried out in a southern city where fear of the dominant whites is greatest.

TABLE 31

CLASSIFICATION OF QUESTIONS ASKED OF NEGRO RESPONDENTS BY THE DEGREE OF
SIGNIFICANCE OF DIFFERENCE IN ANSWERS TO NEGRO AND WHITE INTERVIEWERS IN
MEMPHIS, TENNESSEE (1942)

QUESTION	CATEGORY TESTED	PERCENTAGE OF NEGROES GIVING ANSWER INDICATED TO:	
		Negro Interviewers	White Interviewers
Difference Between Responses to Negro and White Interviewers Significant at *001. Level*			
		N = about 500	N = about 500
Is enough being done in your neighborhood to protect the people in case of air raid?	Yes	21	40
Do you think this country will win the war?	Yes	59	79
If we win, do you think the Negroes will be treated better, worse, or the same?	Better	34	44
Would Negroes be treated better or worse if Japan conquered the U.S.A.?	Worse	25	45
Would Negroes be treated better or worse if Germany conquered the U.S.A.?	Worse	45	60
Is the army fair to Negroes now?	No	35	11
Is the navy fair to Negroes now?	No	23	11
Have Negroes, *right now*, as good a chance as whites to get defense jobs?	Yes	39	52
Who is most to blame for this? (Asked of those answering "No" above)	Government	8	2
Are labor unions fair or unfair to Negroes?	Fair	30	47
Is it important to concentrate on winning the war or on democracy at home?	Winning the war	39	62
Who would a Negro go to to get his rights?	(White people?)	16	6
	(Police?)	2	15
	(Law courts?)	3	12
	(Nobody?)	26	13

TABLE 31 (Continued)

Question	Category Tested	Percentage of Negroes Giving Answer Indicated to:	
		Negro Interviewers	White Interviewers
What Negro newspaper do you usually read?.....................	None	35	51
Who do you think should lead Negro troops?........................	Negro officers	43	22

Differences Between Responses to Negro and White Interviewers Not Significant at .001 Level but Significan at .01 Level

Do you think Negroes are better off or worse off than before the war (in what way)?......................	Less economic discrimination	21	28
Which do Negroes feel worst about now?.........................	(Housing?) (Discrimination in public places?)	8 8	14 4
Does anyone in your family own an automobile?......................	Yes	20	13

Differences Between Responses to Negro and White Interviewers Not Significant at *01. Level*

About how much longer do you think the war will last?.................	Less than one year.	28	33
Do you think Negroes are better off or worse off than before the war?.....	Better off	38	42
Which do Negroes feel worst about now?...........................	(Job discrimination?) (Wages?)	33 43	28 46
Have Negroes *right now* just as good a chance as whites to get defense jobs (Who is most to blame for this?).....	(Managers?)* (Labor unions?)*	21 7	15 4
Which is fairer (to Negroes) CIO or AF of L?......................	CIO*	36	29
Where do you get most of your news about the war?..................	Talking to people*	13	9
What radio station do you usually listen to?......................	WREC*	52	44
What was the highest grade you completed at school?.................	High school or better*	19	14

* Difference significant at .05 level.

Additional evidence on the effect of color is available in the work of the War Department Research Group. Stouffer reports the following findings from a comparison of responses of Negro troops to Negro vs. white interviewers:[28]

TABLE 32

RESPONSES BY NEGRO ENLISTED MEN FROM AGCT CLASS IV IN INTERVIEWS BY NEGROES AS COMPARED WITH INTERVIEWS BY WHITES

Kind of Response	Excess in Percentage of This Kind of Response Elicited by Negro Interviewers as Compared with White Interviewers
Indicating racial protest.	plus 21
Indicating low personal commitment	plus 14
Indicating lack of enthusiasm for war aims	plus 8
Indicating pessimism about postwar conditions	plus 21
Indicating unfair treatment in the army	plus 16
Indicating lack of high regard for officers and "noncoms".	plus 2
Indicating relatively low personal esprit or job satisfaction in the army.	plus 8

Effects arising from differences in ethnic group.—Differences of religion, creed, or nationality between interviewer and respondent may also produce distortion of results. We have several studies which give evidence that non-Jewish people with anti-Semitic prejudices will express these more readily to gentile than to Jewish interviewers. In a 1943 NORC survey, this question was asked: "Do you think that Jewish people in the United States have too much influence in the business world, not enough influence, or about the amount of influence they should have?"

All interviewers in New York City received equivalent assignments on this study so that a valid comparison of the answers given Jewish and gentile interviewers can be made as in the table below.

TABLE 33

COMPARISON OF ANSWERS OF NON-JEWISH RESPONDENTS TO JEWISH AND GENTILE INTERVIEWERS

	Too Much Influence	Not Enough Influence	Amount They Should Have	Don't Know	N
Percentage of Gentiles interviewed by Gentiles	50	2	38	10	139
Percentage of Gentiles interviewed by Jews	22	8	58	12	88

A Chi-squared test indicates that differences as large as those shown would have occurred by chance less than one per cent of the time.

Although these figures show striking differences in the responses of Gentiles when interviewed by Gentiles rather than by Jews, this finding is somewhat inconclusive because quota-sampling was used on this survey and thus the effects might have resulted, in part at least, from interviewer selection of respondents to fill his quotas. If, for example, Jewish interviewers selected within their quotas gentile respondents who are more friendly to Jews, the effects noted could have taken place.

The well-controlled studies of Robinson and Rohde present evidence of the effect of group membership disparity on respondent reaction and enable us to test the theory advanced earlier concerning the relation of structuring of the interviewer image to reactional effects.[29] Four interviewer groups were used in these experiments: (*a*) Jewish appearing; (*b*) non-Jewish appearing; (*c*) Jewish appearing who introduced themselves with Jewish names; and (*d*) non-Jewish appearing who introduced themselves with non-Jewish names.

In this study we cannot, of course, *know* what the perceptions of the respondents actually were, but the difference between the interviewer groups tested appear to be differences in the degree to which the interviewer was perceived as a member of the particular ethnic group. Our theory would hold that as the likelihood of an organized perception of the interviewer as a member of the ethnic group increases we will find

TABLE 34

THE EFFECT ON RESPONDENT REPLIES OF PERCEPTUAL STRUCTURING OF THE INTERVIEWER AS A DEFINED ETHNIC GROUP MEMBER*

Respondents Interviewed by Interviewers Who Were:	"Do you think there are too many Jews holding government-offices and jobs?"	"Do you think the Jews have too much power?"
	Percentage "Yes"	Percentage "Yes"
Jewish appearing with Jewish name....	11.7	5.8
Jewish appearing.................	15.4	15.6
Non-Jewish appearing.............	21.2	24.3
Non-Jewish appearing with non-Jewish name......................	19.5	21.4

* The number of interviewers and respondents was not reported.

increased effects. The samples assigned to the four interviewer groups seemed to be equivalent in all major respects, so differences secured must be due to differences in the reaction of respondents to the four interviewer groups. In Table 34 above the over-all data from the study are presented for the two questions which constituted the original experiment.

It will be noted, first of all, that the frequency of anti-Semitic responses on both questions is greatest where the interviewer does not appear to be Jewish.[30] As the Jewish identification increases, we find a decrease in the frequency of anti-Semitic responses, so that where an interviewer *both* "looks Jewish" and uses a Jewish name we get the lowest frequency. The order of regression is identical for both questions, and the relation between the degree of structuring and respondent reaction seems clearly established.

Effects arising from differences in sex.—Some highly suggestive evidence that respondents tend in some cases to tailor their opinions in a manner to conform to the opinions or tastes of the sex of the interviewer is furnished by two sets of data. The first of these comes from the "story tests" on movies conducted by the Audience Research Institute in 1940.[31] This technique consists of handing cards to test subjects on which is written a summary in about fifty words of a projected movie story. The subject is asked to indicate whether or not he would like to see the picture. The analysts, surmising that respondents' feelings about new movies on which they have very little information (only a three- or four-line description is given the respondent) are generally so mild that many things might operate to influence their choice, decided to do a study on whether sex of interviewer alone affects decisions to any great extent. They suggest, for example, that when a man has movie tastes which are fairly indefinite he is likely to say that he favors a movie which he believes might appeal to the members of the interviewer's own sex group. Table 35 below presents detailed results of the analysis.

The effect of the interviewer's sex can be tested by comparing the differences between men and women respondents when interviewed by their own sex with the differences between men and women respondents when interviewed by members of the opposite sex. Take as an example the picture, "They Knew What They Wanted." For male respondents interviewed by males, the per cent favorable was ten as against eighteen per cent for female respondents interviewed by females—a difference of eight per cent. But both males interviewed by women and females interviewed by men showed the same percentage favorable—14 per cent. In other words, sex differences among the respondents were small when interviewed by the opposite sex, large when interviewed by their own sex.

In eleven of the twelve tests, the results for male and female respondents interviewed by the opposite sex were closer to each other than for male and female respondents interviewed by their own sex, so that the male interviewer apparently tended to influence female respondents to give more typically male responses and similarly female interviewers tended to influence male respondents to give the more typically female responses.

TABLE 35

RESULTS OF STORY TESTS BY SEX OF INTERVIEWER AS RELATED TO SEX OF RESPONDENT

| NAME OF PICTURE | PERCENTAGE FAVORABLE TO PICTURE | | | | PERCENTAGE DIFFERENCES BETWEEN MEN AND WOMEN RESPONDENTS | |
| | Male Respondents | | Female Respondents | | | |
	Interviewed by Men	Interviewed by Women	Interviewed by Men	Interviewed by Women	Interviewed by Own Sex	Interviewed by Opposite Sex
General Lee of Virginia . . .	45	38	30	34	11	8
Guardian of the Forest	24	25	21	14	10	4
They Can't Do This to Me.	21	24	27	28	7	3
Two Weeks with Pay	10	13	22	24	14	9
They Knew What They Wanted	10	14	14	18	8	0
Lawrence of Arabia	27	32	28	18	9	4
Helen and Warren	5	11	17	19	14	6
The Great McGinty	24	23	13	12	12	10
Lucky	22	17	10	9	13	7
Lucky Partners	11	18	20	24	13	2
Mr. and Mrs. (Test 1)	16	14	26	29	13	12
Mr. and Mrs. (Test 2)	20	19	31	32	12	12

From the binomial distribution, the probability of eleven results in the same direction out of twelve instances, where each instance has a probability of one-half, is only about three in 1000, so that sampling fluctuations do not account for these results.

An NORC sample survey of 1000 respondents in Baltimore in 1947 provides further evidence of the effect of interviewer-respondent sex difference.[32] Two questions were asked dealing with opinions on sexual behavior, and it was thought that they would provide a crucial instance in which disparities in sex would affect the results. (At least six of the interviewers reported to the office that these questions had caused them considerable embarrassment, strengthening the belief that they might be subject to interviewer effects.) The two questions were in the form of statements which were read to the respondent, who was then asked to register his agreement or disagreement: "Prison is too good for sex criminals; they should be publicly whipped or worse." "No decent man can respect a woman who has sex relations before marriage."

The sample was broken into four groups depending on the sex of the respondent and interviewer, and comparisons of the results obtained in these four groups were made.

TABLE 36

THE EFFECT OF SEX DIFFERENCES ON RESPONSES TO SEX-RELATED QUESTIONS

SEX CRIMINAL QUESTION

GROUP	Percentage Agree	Percentage Disagree	Percentage Can't Decide	Number of Cases
Men interviewed by men...........	44	48	8	87
Men by women....................	39	58	3	233
Women by women.................	49	47	4	358
Women by men...................	61	28	11	141

PRE-MARITAL SEX QUESTION

	Percentage Agree	Percentage Disagree	Percentage Can't Decide	Number of Cases
Men by men.....................	37	57	6	87
Men by women..................	36	60	4	234
Women by women...............	50	44	6	357
Women by men.................	58	38	4	139

Chi-squared tests were made to determine the significance of the difference between the obtained distributions of results for respondents of a given sex when the sex of the interviewer was varied. Only one test was significant at the one per cent level. This was in the case of women respondents on the "sex criminal question." All three other differences were not significant. However, the number of cases is too small to show up anything but very large differences, and mere inspection of the table reveals consistencies which are suggestive of certain effects. It is noteworthy that the *women* respondents in the case of both questions expressed the harsher or more puritanical (or perhaps merely more conservative) attitude to both male and female interviewers than did the male respondents. On the other hand, both women and men respondents expressed this attitude more frequently to *men* than to women interviewers.

These results were derived from a random sample of households clustered by blocks, so that any interviewer effects could not have arisen from *selection* of particular respondents by different interviewers. It is true that the assignments of interviewers were not matched, but empirical data on the population characteristics of the samples interviewed by men vs. women show no great differences.

Further light on effects of sex disparities comes from a war-time social survey on attitudes toward a campaign against VD conducted for the Ministry of Health of Great Britain. The survey included 1080 male and 1507 female respondents. All the interviewers were women. Fourteen per cent of the male respondents were characterized by the (female) interviewers as "embarrassed, shy, nervous," as against only 8 per cent of the females. On the other hand, many more of the women were described as difficult, having a "supercilious" attitude toward the inquiry—10 per cent as against only 4 per cent of the men. While such results do not prove interviewer effect, they do suggest that in "delicate" matters of this kind there may be interaction effects when sex of interviewer and respondent are different.[33]

Effects arising from differences in class.—It has been noted earlier that most interviewers are members of the white-collar middle class, while respondents may be drawn from all classes. To find out how class differences between interviewers and respondents influence respondent reaction, we turn to a classic study of this problem reported by Katz.[34] The study was carried out in a low-income area of Pittsburgh. Eleven industrial workers were especially hired and trained as experimental interviewers. Nine middle-class interviewers were used as a control group, five of the regular interviewers on the AIPO staff, the other four inexperienced middle-class trainees.

The opinions reported by the working-class interviewers were consistently more radical than those reported by the middle-class interviewers, particularly on labor issues and particularly for the union members interviewed by the two groups. For example, 59 per cent of the union members interviewed by middle-class interviewers were reported as favoring a ban on sit-down strikes, compared with only 44 per cent of union members interviewed by the industrial workers. Katz summarizes his main conclusions thus:

1. Middle-class interviewers, such as the public opinion polls employ, find a greater incidence of conservative attitudes among the lower-income groups than do interviewers recruited from the working class.

2. The more liberal and radical findings of working-class interviewers are more pronounced on labor issues.

3. The difference (between working- and middle-class interviewers) increases when union members or their relatives are interviewed.

4. Working-class interviewers find more support for isolationist sentiments among lower-income groups than do white-collar interviewers.

5. The difference in the findings may be partly a function of experience in interviewing. But Katz points out that, although experienced

Gallup interviewers were closer to working-class interviewers in results than were inexperienced white-collar interviewers, their findings still differ significantly from working-class interviewers.

Katz suggests that this phenomenon may account for the well-known tendency of the polls to under-predict the Democratic vote and suggests employing more working-class interviewers or better training of white-collar interviewers. He also makes the important point that the bias, if real, should be large in some cases, negligible in others, depending on the subject matter.

Conceivably the difference in results may be due to differences in the ideology or expectations of the two groups of interviewers, rather than to the reactions of the respondents. The opinions of the interviewers themselves were obtained; they revealed that the working-class interviewers were more radical and isolationist than the middle-class interviewers. However, Katz attributes the differences to "better rapport" obtained by the working-class interviewers, suggesting that they were more easily able to get at the true attitudes, because the working-class respondents, especially those with strong pro-labor views, would talk more freely to members of their own class. As evidence of the greater validity of responses obtained by working-class interviewers, he cites the fact that they report more verbatim comments, and that the results they obtain correspond most closely to those secured by experienced interviewers.

Effects arising from differences in residence.—Data to compare the validity of responses obtained by strangers or nonlocal interviewers with those obtained by local interviewers are almost nonexistent. One apparent advantage in favor of the stranger interviewer lies in his anonymity, reinforcing the impersonality of the interview situation, and providing reassurance to the respondent that his answers will not be bruited about the neighborhood. For example, one of the technical criticisms of Kinsey's interviewing method referred to his procedure of building up patterns of intimacy with the potential respondent prior to the actual interview.[35] The psychoanalyst is the repository of our most sacred thoughts partly because he is a "stranger." The sociologists have built an elaborate theory supporting this notion.[36] Except in times of war and spy hysteria, when he might be regarded suspiciously, the stranger interviewer has the advantage. An example of the latter type of situation is furnished by a 1943 OWI survey dealing with security of information.[37]

The survey was made in the cultural setting of a small town during the war, and during the worst period of spy scares. Five local interview-

ers, all women who were widely acquainted, and five nonlocal interviewers were employed in this survey. The interviewing was preceded
by the distribution of a pamphlet giving information on security measures to some, but not all, of the respondents. Two questions yielded responses of doubtful frankness: "Do you think that you yourself know
anything connected with the war which should not be repeated?"
"Have you ever heard people talking about things connected with the
war which should not be repeated?"

The local interviewers got higher proportions of "yes" answers to
both questions than the nonlocal. While the differences are not significant according to the usual tests, they are in the same direction for both
questions, and for subgroups differing in exposure to the pamphlet.

TABLE 37

REACTION OF RESPONDENTS TO LOCAL AND NONLOCAL INTERVIEWERS

Class of Respondents	Percentage Who Knew Things Which Should Not Be Repeated	Percentage Who Heard Things Not Repeatable
Exposed to the pamphlet, interviewed by local inter-viewers......................................	30	49
Exposed to the pamphlet, interviewed by nonlocal inter-viewers......................................	23	40
Not exposed to pamphlet, interviewed by local inter-viewers......................................	17	52
Not exposed to pamphlet, interviewed by nonlocal inter-viewers......................................	13	45

In other words, for all subclassifications, there were more people who
said that they knew things which should not be repeated, or who had
heard others talking of such things, among those interviewed by local
interviewers than among those interviewed by stranger interviewers,
indicating an apparently greater feeling of trust toward the local interviewer.

Relation of group membership effects to cultural norms.—In our earlier discussion of the differential effects arising from the different group
memberships of interviewers, it was pointed out that interviewer characteristics must bring about some *affective* reaction in the respondent in
order to be evidenced in the data. Clearly, both the magnitude and the
direction of such reactions is dependent in part on the social norms of
the cultural milieu.[38]

The effects noted in the Memphis study of differential response of
Negroes to Negro and white interviewers occurred presumably because

the atmosphere in which the study was conducted gave to Negro-white relationships their strongly affective character.

This hypothesis is supported by the comparison of the data secured in Memphis, with a replication conducted in New York City. Because of the difference in the cultural norms surrounding Negro-white relationships in New York, one would expect that the reactions of Negro respondents to the group membership of the interviewer would be less strongly manifested in the data. We will not repeat for New York City the detailed data given for Memphis, but instead we present in Table 38 below a comparison of differences between results obtained by white and Negro interviewers in the two cities, showing how many questions yielded differences at each level of significance. The comparison is based on the eighteen opinion questions and the three questions of a factual nature which were common to both surveys.

TABLE 38

COMPARISON BETWEEN MEMPHIS AND NEW YORK CITY OF DIFFERENCES IN ANSWERS
OF NEGRO RESPONDENTS AS REPORTED BY WHITE AND NEGRO INTERVIEWERS

SIGNIFICANCE OF DIFFERENCE BETWEEN ANSWERS GIVEN TO WHITE AND ANSWERS GIVEN TO NEGRO INTERVIEWERS	FREQUENCY OF QUESTIONS ON WHICH DIFFERENCES BETWEEN ANSWERS REPORTED BY WHITE AND NEGRO INTERVIEWERS WOULD OCCUR BY CHANCE WITH THIS PROBABILITY	
	Memphis	New York
Significant at .1 per cent level	12	3
Significant at 1 per cent level	2	5
Significant at 5 per cent level	4	3
Not significant	3	10

When we compare the individual T-value or standardized differences, that is, each difference divided by its standard error, we find eighteen questions on which the standardized differences are higher in Memphis than in New York, and only two for which the differences were lower. The probability of obtaining eighteen or more higher differences out of twenty-one is about one in 10,000. Thus there is scarcely any doubt that Memphis Negroes are more reluctant to talk freely to white interviewers than are New York Negroes.

CHAPTER V

Situational Determinants of Interviewer Effect

1. NATURE OF SITUATIONAL DETERMINANTS

In previous chapters, we have examined certain basic psychological processes in interviewer and respondent which may become manifest within the interview in such fashion as to cause distortion in the data. The interviewer brings to the situation human propensities of an intellectual, perceptual or cognitive, and motivational order which may reduce his accuracy as a measuring instrument. The respondent's reactions to the questions occur within the context of social relations with the interviewer in accordance with natural human tendencies to perceive and interact with others.

But this cannot be the whole story. These basic processes are mere tendencies which conceivably could remain latent. They are limited by environmental conditions—in this case the special environment of the interview. The arousal of the sources of bias must obviously be dependent upon features of the interview situation. Consequently, in this chapter, we shall develop the foundations of a general theory of the situational determination of interviewer effects and present some experimental evidence on specific situational determinants.

We shall construe the concept of situational determinants in the broadest sense. Thus, it includes the contents and formal types of questions, the procedures established for the interview, the physical setting, the mode of recording, the accidental distractions, the temporary state of the parties, and the like.

That the conditions of the interview may be such as to increase the occurrence of interviewer effects, or, by contrast, to reduce the biasing operation of cognitive and motivational and intellectual processes can be demonstrated in a variety of ways. Mere reflection supports the theory. Conceivably, if we were to give interviewers complete freedom to interview whomever they pleased, ask any questions they wished, in any form, make whatever comments they chose, and record the answers in any fashion they preferred, we would expect interviewer effects to be maximally operative, simply because we allowed the variability among interviewers in intellect, cognition, and motivation to manifest itself without restraint. The interview situation in this instance would be unsuitable for the collection of reliable data. Or if we were to insist that all interviewers refrain from taking notes within the interview and record the answers at a later time from memory, we might introduce bias into every interview, because motivational or autistic factors might affect the memory processes of every interviewer.

The establishment of standardized interview procedures attests the importance of situational determinants of interviewer effects, whether these effects are regarded as varied among interviewers or common to an entire field staff. The precepts given the interviewer in the course of training, or as instructions attached to a particular survey, are so designed as to produce a particular uniform role, or pattern of interview ing behavior, and so to reduce variability among interviewers as well as any undesirable behavior originally characteristic of all interviewers. But such role prescriptions are not always effective and, even when they are, situational determinants of interviewer effect can be of importance. The qualitative evidence presented in Chapter II demonstrates dramatically how pressures generated by the situation force the breakdown of the prescribed role.

2. TESTS OF THE OPERATION OF THE TOTAL COMPLEX OF SITUATIONAL DETERMINANTS

Quantitative evidence can be presented to demonstrate that interviewer effects are mediated by the situation. If the occurrence of effects did derive from a particular enduring set of propensities in the interviewer, independent of the specific situational field in which that interviewer is operating, one would expect interviewers to manifest their effects completely consistently over a variety of circumstances. If, however, effects over a variety of situations are thoroughly inconsistent, one must conclude either that only temporary internal processes are involved, or that the persistent biasing tendencies are activated essentially by situational determinants. In-between the limits of consistency vs. inconsistency of behavior across situations, one obtains an expression of the relative contributions of enduring personal and situational determinants to actual interviewer effects.

Five such demonstrations of degree of consistency of the same interviewers observed repeatedly in different situations are available and are presented below. These demonstrations have in common the property that the specific changes in the situational field from observation to observation are not susceptible to precise analysis. To isolate the effect of a specific single situational determinant calls for the type of experimental approach to be presented in Section 4 of this chapter. These demonstrations, however, have the unique virtue of revealing the effect of the *total complex* of situational determinants under *natural operating* conditions. They are presented in what appears to be an approximate order of increasing similarity of situations.

Our first demonstration is not ideal for experimental purposes because of certain limitations to be noted subsequently. However, it represents the problem concretely and dramatically and contains some new implications for our theory. It reveals the degree of stability of behavior of each of ten interviewers asking the same question on public trust of Russia on eleven surveys conducted between January, 1944, and April, 1945.[1]

While the samples of respondents as between interviewers varied, each interviewer was assigned for each of his eleven surveys a sample from the same community and with identical quota-control characteristics. The results obtained each time contain some component of bias due to the particular set of propensities within each interviewer. Whatever that component of bias be, it should be consistently manifested in the actual results obtained if situational determinants are unimportant. Situational determinants would be revealed by marked changes in the results. This is particularly the case, since the attitude measured was relatively stable over this period of time as indicated by the aggregate trend data for the national sample. Trust of Russia during this fifteen-month period only varied over a maximum range from 43 per cent of the sample to 56 per cent. Four of the surveys obtained values which were within two percentage points of one another, and another four were within three percentage points of each other. Consequently, apart from minor sampling fluctuations, we should regard unstable findings as reflections of situational factors.

The detailed data are presented in Table 39 below. A simple expression of the general level of consistency of interviewer performance for the ten interviewers in the aggregate is provided by ranking the interviewers for each survey in terms of the proportion of their samples who trusted Russia. By correlating the rankings over pairs of surveys, one observes whether an interviewer maintains his relative position within the group of interviewers. The median value for all possible pairs of rankings is .60, indicating that there is some intra-individual stability, but that situational determinants of some undefined sort have intruded themselves into the picture.[2] While the question was identical and the samples were the same, the interviewer had opportunity to change in many respects over the extended period of time.[3] Therefore, the demonstration cautions us against viewing the interviewer as a fixed biasing entity.

The wide variation in stability of results for the different interviewers suggests that the interaction of situational and personal factors which determines interviewer effect is in turn a function of some other personal determinant within the interviewer. There may well be some more basic psychological process differentiating humans who are sensitized to changing situational fields from other humans who are less responsive to external events.

While we have no tests or evidence bearing explicitly on this aspect of our theory, recent experimental research in perception gives strong support to such a typology. Witkin has recently demonstrated that there is considerable consistency in the way in which the individual responds to a series of perceptual tasks.[4] These tasks were so constructed that they yielded a measure of the degree to which the person used his own internal postural experiences rather than aspects of the external visual field in the process of perception. Witkin found that some individuals are markedly "field dependent," or oriented to the external aspects of the situation, whereas other individuals tend consistently to be "independent of the field," and that there is another group of individuals who are persistently unstable with respect to their sensitivity to the field. He remarks: "It is quite clear that a tendency to rely mainly on the visual framework or to remain independent of the field through awareness of bodily experiences represents a fairly general characteristic of individual orientation."

TABLE 39

THE INTRA-INDIVIDUAL CONSISTENCY OF INTERVIEWER BEHAVIOR OVER A SERIES OF TREND MEASUREMENTS OF THE SAME OPINION ON EQUIVALENT SAMPLES

| | PERCENTAGE OF EACH INTERVIEWER'S SAMPLE REPORTING TRUST OF RUSSIA | | | | | | | | | |
| | Interviewers | | | | | | | | | |
	1	2	3	4	5	6	7	8	9	10
First survey	30	75	55	55	80	53	82	80	50	68
Second	25	60	60	45	75	43	65	40	53	30
Third	25	65	40	45	60	33	100	60	47	45
Fourth	45	42	58	40	45	13	95	65	0	40
Fifth	65	40	48	50	60	40	100	85	40	55
Sixth	20	60	48	65	90	73	100	85	73	65
Seventh	60	35	25	25	65	21	100	45	33	45
Eighth	45	35	40	55	60	33	100	70	67	50
Ninth	40	36	48	30	55	22	94	53	40	45
Tenth	30	50	55	45	65	60	95	57	43	20
Eleventh	40	45	40	50	55	40	100	76	40	50
Usual size of sample	20	20	20	20	20	15	20	20	15	20

Other demonstrations are available to show the inconsistency of the interviewer's biasing potentialities within the same unit *interview*. Such demonstrations suggest that situational determinants of a most transient sort interrupt the biasing processes.

In the course of re-interviewing a panel of respondents in the 1948 political study in Elmira,[5] the interviewer who conducted the first interview with a given respondent in June was generally not assigned to the re-interview conducted in October. Comparison of the answers obtained by the different interviewers from the same respondents shows that many respondents changed their attitudes. While most of this change must reflect processes within the respondent, some portion of it presumably derives from the particular interviewer who asked the questions. The variation in the amount of change among the samples of *different interviewers* is so large that this assumption seems warranted. For example, on a question on attitudes toward labor unions, the proportion of respondents changing ranged from a minimum of 20 per cent for one interviewer to a maximum of 69 per cent for another interviewer. On another question dealing with expectation of war, the proportion of respondents who changed their opinions varied among the different interviewers from 22 per cent to 78 per cent. On a third question dealing with the locus of blame for the Jewish-Arab conflict in Palestine, the change ranged among the samples of different interviewers from 21 per cent to 62 per cent. We can therefore feel some assurance in ranking each interviewer in terms of the magnitude of his effects on the results of any question, using as an index of his effect the proportion of his respondents who change their answers for the later interview.

If the source of such effects were purely within the interviewer himself, one would expect the interviewer who had many changers on one question to obtain many changers on the other questions. The rank-

TABLE 40

INTRA-INDIVIDUAL CONSISTENCY OF INTERVIEWER EFFECTS IN THE PROPORTION OF UN-RELIABLE ANSWERS OBTAINED FROM A PANEL ON SEVERAL QUESTIONS

	Rho
Proportion of respondents changing answers on labor vs. war question	.04
Proportion changing answers on labor vs. Palestine question	−.25
Proportion changing answers on war vs. Palestine question	−.11
Number of interviewers	32

order correlations presented in Table 40 demonstrate no consistency in effect over the three questions, suggesting that whatever effects the interviewer creates are a function of different situational factors operating from question to question.

Another demonstration of the partial inconsistency of interviewer biasing tendencies is available in the realm of probing behavior while asking open-ended questions. The tendency of particular interviewers all dealing with equivalent respondents to obtain many or few multiple answers to each of four open questions contained within the same questionnaire was determined. It was found that interviewers differed significantly in this tendency. These differences could not be allocated to intrinsic differences in respondents because of the design of the samples and must therefore represent interviewer effects.[6]

While the four questions covered different content areas, the formal task of probing was the same in each instance. The influence of situational determinants on the consistency of the interviewer's effect can be demonstrated by computing the rank-order correlations for the amount of multiple answers he obtained on pairs of questions. The median value for rho was .48, demonstrating that, while there is considerable consistency of effect in the realm of probing due to intra-personal factors, it is in part disrupted by situational factors.

Two other demonstrations of the intrusion of situational determinants are available. In these studies, wire recordings were made of the actual interviews, and by comparing the written interview with the wire recording, the number and type of errors made by each interviewer can easily be judged and scored. In both studies, the comparisons made are limited to interviews conducted by a number of interviewers interviewing the same respondent, who was prepared in advance with a "set of attitudes" (and in one study, a set of actual answers to be given).

Comparison of errors made in different parts of the interview enables us to estimate the effect of contrasted transient situational elements. While the temporal process carries with it elements of practice and fatigue, plus an opportunity for the reorganization of perception and sentiment as a result of the on-going interaction, it, of necessity, exposes the interviewer to new types of tasks as new subject matters are touched on and new forms of inquiry are used. In general, our hypothesis would hold that where the parts of the interview compared are situationally similar we would find greater consistency in the error scores for a given interviewer; where there is situational dissimilarity, such consistency should be less in evidence.

In the early study by Lester Guest, interviewers' total error scores were computed, and the relative accuracy of interviewers as between the first and second halves of the interview was compared. The data from the Guest study are presented in Table 41.[7]

The influence of situational factors is best summarized by ranking

TABLE 41

THE INTRA-INDIVIDUAL CONSISTENCY OF INTERVIEWER
ERRORS BETWEEN FIRST AND SECOND HALVES OF AN
INTERVIEW

INTERVIEWERS	TOTAL NUMBER OF ERRORS OF ALL TYPES MADE IN SUCCESSIVE PORTIONS OF AN INTERVIEW	
	First Half	Second Half
1..........................	5	11
2..........................	5	10
3..........................	6	18
4..........................	5	9
5..........................	4	8
6..........................	4	12
7..........................	4	12
8..........................	2	14
9..........................	8	10
10..........................	6	11
11..........................	4	12
12..........................	7	15
13..........................	12	24
14..........................	8	10
15..........................	8	15

the interviewers in terms of their relative tendency to make errors and correlating these ranks for the two halves of the interview. The value of rho in this instance is only .24, indicating that the relative error proneness of interviewers is a function of the specialized situations present in successive portions of the interview.

In the Guest study, two specific situational elements probably contributed to the high variation in interviewer performance, as between the two halves of the interview. First of all, the two halves are markedly different with respect to the structure of the questions. Most of the first half consists of simple multiple-choice questions; the second half contains a large proportion of free-answer questions plus some "agree-disagree" types. Secondly, in the Guest study, the respondent played the role of a "normal" respondent, in no way attempting to set up persistent situational difficulties for the interviewer. That these factors may have had an influence on interviewer consistency is suggested by the comparison of Guest's data with those collected by the American Jewish Committee in a similar study.[8]

In the AJC study, comparisons of errors over time were made for nine different interviewers questioning the same "planted" respondent. Here we find the correlations between the various temporal parts of the interview considerably higher than in the Guest study. Between the first and second thirds of the interview the rank order correlation was .75, between the second and third portions, .74, and between the first and third, .51. While the correlations are considerably less than unity, it is clear that in this experiment there was much greater interviewer consistency than in the earlier study. Of course, any number of factors might have played a part in the differences obtained, but it seems likely that two specific considerations are involved:

1. The uniformity of the role played by the planted respondent in the AJC study. While Guest's respondent gave rather "typical" responses and played the role of a normal respondent, the AJC respondent used in the present comparisons *persistently* adopted the role of a tough, recalcitrant lower-class individual in the interview. In the face of such uniform personal behavior on the part of the respondent, it seems quite logical that transient situational elements would play a smaller role in affecting interviewer error.

2. The greater similarity of question types. In the AJC study, twenty of the thirty-three attitude questions were of the agree-disagree type, and these were located in all three parts of the interview. Therefore, if, instead of dividing up the interview into temporal units, we select other criteria for division, the importance of given situational factors, as well as the relation between interviewer consistency and situational similarity, can be convincingly demonstrated. Likewise, the differences between the findings of Guest and the AJC may be more clearly understood.

The questionnaire with which the AJC experiment was performed consisted mainly of questions in four areas: (1) attitudes toward Negroes and toward discrimination against Negroes, (2) attitudes toward Jews and toward discrimination against Jews, (3) so-called "authoritarian" attitudes selected from the Berkeley scale,[9] and (4) factual questions about the respondent. With the exception of the factual data, the questions on the various areas were equally distributed throughout the questionnaire. The factual data were less well scattered, a few questions being asked in the beginning and the majority at the end. The Negro and Jewish questions were the same in content and formal structure. The authoritarian questions were similar to the Negro and Jewish questions, with one important difference—they contained no "card-type" questions. The factual questions were necessarily quite different in form from any of the others.

In Table 42, we present the rank-order correlations among the nine interviewers for errors made on the various content areas.

It may be seen from the following table that, while correlations are positive, they are far from 1.00, indicating that there is considerable inconsistency in the tendency of interviewers to make errors on questions even within closely related areas. More revealing, however, is the variation in the correlation co-efficients across different areas. Where the content is similar and the form identical (the Negro and Jewish

TABLE 42

The Effect of Situational Variation on Consistency of Errors for Nine Interviewers Interviewing the Same Respondent

Total Errors on:	Rank-Order Correlation
Negro and Jewish questions	.78
Negro and authoritarian questions	.49
Jewish and authoritarian questions	.48
Jewish and factual questions	.42
Negro and factual questions	.12
Authoritarian and factual questions	.02

questions), we obtain the highest correlation. Where the contents are dissimilar and the forms likewise dissimilar, correlations obtained are very low (for example, the authoritarian and factual correlation). These data would seem to bear out our theory that the nature of the situation plays a considerable role in the introduction of interviewer error into survey data.

All this evidence, the clues from past experience and from qualitative reports of interviewers, plus the quantitative demonstrations of the disruption of interviewer consistency in the course of interviewing, stimulates us to examine situational determinants in detail. Such study will yield substantial returns of a number of types.

At the policy level, it will invite renewed attention to aspects of survey procedure. While many aspects of the total interviewing situation are accidental, many of them are manipulable. After all, the situation in considerable degree is of our own creation—it is manufactured of the procedures we devise for the interview. If the very routine we prescribe for the interview and the interviewer in itself creates a situational basis for bias, the effect is not attributable exclusively to the interviewer. Rather the responsibility would rest on the designers and administrators of survey research. Research into situational factors will, consequently, increase general concern with procedures.

Whatever factors are operative within the interviewer to cause bias are difficult to control except by an elaborate system of selection and training. But if we can discover the factors within the interview situation that mediate, activate, or heighten these biasing tendencies, it is within our power to manipulate them and thus to reduce bias. The biasing tendencies among interviewers and respondents would still exist but would operate minimally because of the nature of the interview situation we provide.

The history of industrial psychology will demonstrate by analogy such an approach to the treatment of error. In the adjustment of the worker to the machine, psychologists initially developed selection and classification tests to find those individuals who would perform most effectively within the industrial situation. The machine was taken as a "given," and the "errors" were located within the individual and controlled by a system of selection. However, the more recent development of "psycho-engineering" reversed the procedure.[10] The limitations of the human were regarded as a given, and the problem was seen as that of re-designing the machine in such fashion that human capabilities were not overly strained.

Of course, this analogy should not be strained. Designing the survey in terms of the limitations of current interviewing staffs would lead to gains in the control of error; but in the long run, such a policy would freeze current research practice at a relatively low level. What would seem to be indicated is an approach to the problem of interviewer effect, both directly through interviewer selection and training and indirectly through control of situational factors eliciting or facilitating the biasing tendencies of interviewers and respondents.

3. PAST LITERATURE ON SITUATIONAL FACTORS AS A GUIDE TO REFINEMENT IN THEORY AND RESEARCH

While the analyses just presented establish beyond doubt the influence of situational determinants upon the operation of interviewer effects, they contribute little to an understanding of the nature of such influences. The complex of situational factors must be analyzed; experimental studies of specific factors must then be conducted, and a theory must be developed which will aid us in constructing situations which are not likely to engender the biasing processes within the interviewer. Rather than embark on an endless project in which every single segment of the total situation is subjected to experimental study, or attempt to construct a theory of situational determinants out of thin air, we shall first turn to some past research into situational factors to help clarify the problem and give leads to our own research.

While we can find little evidence in past literature as to the way in which interviewer effect is mediated by the situation, there is a considerable body of literature from self-administered questionnaire studies showing the effect of situational factors on the results obtained. For example, the situational factors of question form and anonymity have been subject to massive past research.[11] While these studies, by definition, provide no evidence on the interviewer's behavior, they are most relevant to our problem. They have the virtue of suggesting that, in part, the situational factor present in a personal interview survey may have an indirect effect on the interviewer. Since the self-administered studies show that respondents' replies can be changed by altering a situational factor, they suggest that, when an interviewer operates within a particular situation, regardless of what he himself may do, he may meet one kind of reply rather than another. In turn, his effect on the data would occur during the processes of coding, judging, recording, or probing the response rather than in the initial asking of the question. Consequently, in our specific theory of situational determinants, we are led again to stress alterations in interviewing tasks at the later stages of work rather than the influence of given situations on the opportunities for "slanting" a question or communicating an opinion.

The evidence from self-administered questionnaires also guides us in the design and analysis of experiments on the relation between situational factors and interviewer effect. It is clear from these studies that a situational factor might have an effect on results independent of the interviewer. It may operate to affect respondents even when no interviewer is present. In designing field experiments on the relation of situation to interviewer effect, it is necessary that one be careful not to interpret pure respondent reactions to situations as if they were interviewer effects deriving from the situation. The solution to the problem lies in certain kinds of controlled comparisons between given interviewers operating under contrasted conditions.

If the situation produces differential behavior among interviewers, the results obviously cannot be interpreted as pure respondent reactions to the situation independent of the interviewer. In so far as one merely examines the effect of situations on results over the total aggregation of interviewers, one cannot determine whether the change is located purely within the respondents or within the interviewers. Unfortunately, there may well be systematic effects of situations on all interviewers which are lost by such experimental comparisons, but generally there is no alternative.[12]

Such past research serves one final function. Careful examination of many independent studies of apparently the same situational factor frequently yields strange and contradictory findings. Such situational factors are either complex in their nature or complex in their possible effects, and clarification of processes normally lumped under a given situational heading is needed before one can undertake meaningful research on such a factor. To illustrate the complexity of situational variables and as a guide to such clarification we shall consider the problem and the literature in two traditional research areas—the effect of situations varying in respondent anonymity and the effect of situations where sponsorship is altered.

Anonymity.—Mere consideration of the situational factors that relate to respondent anonymity in the usual personal interview survey reveals that the *literal* fact of anonymity provides no necessary *psychological* anonymity.

Although names are usually not taken, virtually all surveys require addresses of the respondents. But even where no addresses are taken, there still exists no psychological anonymity. It is obvious to the respondent that he can easily be identified, and it is safe to say that he seldom really feels anonymous in the situation. The interviewer and the respondent have developed a relationship which, although transient, has identified the respondent in some respects to the interviewer. He is present to the interviewer as a person, and, as we have discussed in the previous chapter, interactional effects may result from the mere existence of a personal relationship.

Complete anonymity is probably most closely approximated in group administered questionnaire studies, involving unsigned questionnaires.[13] The empirical evidence from self-administered questionnaires underscores the complexity of the problem of situational factors. While the weight of evidence establishes a particular type of change when respondents are identified, qualifications become evident when the results of studies are compared. In studies in the field of personality or clinical psychology, different results are generally obtained when questionnaires or rating scales require the respondent's signature. The experiments in this area by Maller, Olson, and Fischer show consistent differences of varying significance.

In Maller's study of co-operativeness in children, he found large differences in the ratings given to themselves and others by children asked to rate the group members for "co-operativeness."[14] When the questionnaires were signed, Maller found an increase in the number of other children rated as co-operative, suggesting that the reactions when questionnaires were unsigned represented more "genuine" reactions.

Olson also found differences in responses to unsigned as opposed to signed questionnaires, using the Woodworth-Mathews Personal Data Sheet.[15] Subjects were more likely to admit statements of "feelings" associated with instability and also more physical symptoms with neurotic implications, when questionnaires were unsigned.

Similarly, Fischer, using Moody's Check List of personal problems, found that when questionnaires were unsigned there was a considerable increase in the mean number of problems considered serious.[16] He concludes that the use of signatures on personal questionnaires has an inhibiting effect on the "honesty and frankness" of the subject.

Star reports on three replicated studies of the effect of anonymity on the report of psychosomatic complaints on the self-administered neuropsychiatric screening test developed during the last war.[17] A small but consistent increase was found in each study in the tendency to report critical symptoms when the men were not identified. Star remarks that the "differences are not in themselves statistically significant." However, her results are consistent with the earlier academic studies.

Elinson and Haines, and Cisin, in more recent studies tested the effect of anonymity on the responses of soldiers to a self-administered questionnaire covering attitudes toward military service.[18] They report a significantly greater tendency for the identified group to express favorable attitudes toward their officers and greater job satisfaction. A similar trend, although *nonsignificant* was observed in five other attitude areas. Cisin, in a later analysis of these data, states that combined tests of the results over all areas show that in the aggregate the difference between identified and anonymous responses was significant at the .01 level.

While the foregoing studies suggest very strongly that actual anonymity provides a setting in which more valid data can be secured, in the sense of personal revelations, the conclusions are not as unequivocal as might at first appear. Corey, in another investigation, found no significant differences between signed and unsigned questionnaires.[19] The investigation dealt with attitudes toward cheating among students, an area which appears to be, if anything, even more sensitive to social pressures than some of the subject matters dealt with by the other investigators. The difference between the findings of Corey and the other studies is therefore surprising and emphasizes again the complexity of these problems.

The effect of anonymity is clearly a function of the subject matter of the questions. Cisin's data support this view, in that the effects were maximal in two attitude areas, but not significant in the other five areas. Furthermore, Cisin in the internal analysis of his data within the two susceptible areas (attitudes toward officers and job satisfaction) remarks: "There were instances in which a significant difference occurred between the anonymous and the identified groups in terms of distribution of *scale* scores on a given subject but a far less striking difference occurred between the two groups in terms of distribution of responses to one or more other *items* in the scale."[20]

Maller refers in his previously cited study to a similar variation in the effect of anonymity on different subject matters. The particular variation, however, points to a fundamental clarification of processes that work in two opposing directions under conditions of anonymity. Although, under conditions of anonymity, children were more inclined to rate others more critically, they also rated themselves more favorably (as more co-operative). Thus, while anonymity seems to free the respondent from fear of reprisal for *criticizing* others, it also seems to free him of inhibitions about inflating his prestige. This latter effect of anonymity seems normally neglected in past discussions. For example, Kinsey went to such great lengths to preserve confidence out of concern that respondents, unless assured of anonymity, would not report *unsanctioned* sexual activities which would subject them to reprisal or court action or deflation of prestige. But he slighted the possibility that they might feel freer to boast about or to exaggerate *sanctioned* forms of sexual activity under conditions of anonymity. Hyman and Sheatsley, in commenting on this study cite such frequent illustrative quotations from Kinsey as "Cover-up is more easily accomplished than exaggeration in giving a history." They demonstrate, however, by internal examination of Kinsey's data, that the errors actually were in both directions.[21]

There is some evidence that anonymity is more of a problem under particular cultural conditions or in a given climate of opinion. Where there is any fear on the part of respondents of possible punishment for expressing certain opinions, anonymity would seem to be crucial. It is difficult to see how anonymity can be assured to such respondents interviewed in their own residence, since they are obviously identifiable to the interviewer, and could be located with ease. That such fears are operative within the population has been documented in the previous chapter. Anecdotal material from Japan further supports the notion that the situational factor of anonymity must be seen in the context of the culture. There was some indication in that society that surveys where names were not taken might be answered in a more frivolous fashion because of the Japanese experience that any serious inquiry in the past involved the recording of names.[22] In addition to the larger climate, local environmental differences and subcultural factors may be presumed to affect the importance of anonymity. Thus, among line troops in a disciplined unit, it was usually necessary to stress the factor of anonymity, in order to get frank expressions of opinion. It is probably safe to say that very little research could have been done among soldiers were there not some assurance of anonymity.

That anonymity has different effects in given subgroups can be documented in an experiment by Festinger.[23] The voting behavior of Jewish and Catholic college girls in electing officers in an artificially created club was studied under conditions of anonymity vs. nonanonymity. The Jewish girls expressed preferences for Jewish officers only when they themselves were not identified by name and religion, whereas the Catholic girls expressed their preferences for Catholic officers even under conditions of nonanonymity.

The foregoing discussion should serve to make clear the complexity in estimating the nature and direction of effects due to identification or anonymity of the respondent. We have seen that actual anonymity may exist in varying degrees, and, also, it seems clear that whether or not this situational factor is important is in part a function of the subject matter of the study as well as the larger political and social or subcultural climate. Lastly, it is possible that anonymity may have contradictory effects and that in some situations it produces less valid data.

By extension, it should be clear that insight into the relation of a situational factor to interviewer effect requires careful clarification of the meaning or consequences of the situation for interviewer and respondent, and refined analysis of the data.

Sponsorship.—Of equal complexity as a variable in the total interview situation is the question of survey sponsorship. It should be apparent to the reader that bias may well function differentially in relation to the respondent's understanding of the purpose of the research. If the respondent understands that action in which he is concerned may follow from the research, we can expect that his opinions, and likewise the extent to which he may be affected by the interviewer, will be quite different from what it will be if he feels he is just being asked his opinion for journalistic reporting, for scientific inquiry, or to satisfy the needs of some commercial group.

Thus we would expect to find differences in certain kinds of data when the respondent has one kind of understanding as opposed to the other. It is not possible, in most cases, to know precisely what a respondent's understanding of the purposes of a survey may be. But it can be inferred that the stated sponsorship of the survey sets up certain understandings on the part of respondents, although not necessarily *the same ones* for all respondents. Thus, it is likely that the respondent will see the purpose in terms of some kind of contemplated action, if the sponsorship of the survey is governmental.[24] But beyond this, we cannot be sure of what kind of action he anticipates. If he has a belief that the government really wishes to carry out the people's desires, then his answer might be affected in one way by this knowledge. But if he believes that the government is unresponsive to the will of the people and is only trying to find out what they think for purposes of propaganda or political manipulation, then his answer might be affected in different fashion. Herein lies one difficulty in the interpretation of studies which have compared results under alternative sponsorships. In order for major differences to occur consistently in such studies, some uniform perception of the objectives of the sponsoring agency must be created. For example, it is entirely conceivable that one respondent interviewed on a government survey will try to please the interviewer (as a representative of the government) and color his answers in terms of this motivation. Another respondent, however, may want to utilize the opportunity to "gripe" to the government, and thus his responses may be more negative than those he would give to a Gallup interviewer. Still another might see the interview as an opportunity to agitate for certain ideas or programs in which he personally is interested.

Since the main way in which the respondent is able to judge the purpose of the research is by knowing the sponsorship, it is necessary that this be clearly stated so as to limit the area in which differential perceptions of purpose may operate. Public opinion interviewers have frequently found it useful to explain that their survey is "like a Gallup Poll" in order to get the purpose across to the respondent. When an organization's operations are well publicized, it seems likely that the understanding of purpose will be both more widespread and more uniform, insuring minimum differential effects due to this variable.

When the purpose is not clearly understood, respondents will unquestionably make inferences concerning the purpose. After all, the interviewer is merely the agent of some larger audience or boss for whom he is working. Hundreds of respondents in public opinion surveys ask interviewers, "What are *they* going to do with all these answers?" and are perfectly cognizant of some larger audience to whom they are declaiming. This has been revealed to NORC dramatically when interviewers have occasionally been suspected, on the one hand, of working for the FBI or, by contrast, for the Communist party. Similarly the respondent completing a self-administered questionnaire is aware that the questionnaire was brought to life by some invisible hand; he surmises or knows who it was, and may well alter his behavior in this light. Thus in the work of the Research Branch of the United States Army, "there was an abundance of evidence in the comments written in the questionnaires in studies of Negro soldiers to suggest they thought of their questionnaires as being read by a white audience."[25] Some of them even addressed the questionnaire to the President or to the White House.

Although we cannot always explain the nature of the differences that occur, it has been demonstrated quantitatively that the stated sponsorship of the survey affects responses given to certain questions. Examination of these studies shows, however, that expected effects fail to materialize in some instances and that, in other instances, effects are evident, where none had been expected. Even where no effects are demonstrable, it is possible that effects have occurred; because of differential beliefs or motivations, they may have tended to cancel out in the aggregate.

In a wartime study conducted by NORC and the OWI Surveys Division, the effect of sponsorship was examined by having half the interviewers say they were from the government while the other half stated that they were from the University of Denver.

Of the twenty-nine attitudinal questions asked, only two showed differences which could be considered significant. Significantly more respondents replied that the government is "trying to present war news accurately" when the interviewer stated that the government was sponsoring the survey. Also significantly more respondents of "government" interviewers stated that Negroes ought to have an equal chance at war jobs.[26]

The fact that results on only two questions out of twenty-nine were significantly different suggests that in general the fact of government sponsorship (as opposed to university sponsorship) was relatively unimportant for such questions at that particular time.

One would expect, in time of war, that images of the government become clearly defined and that the government impinges more on the life of the citizen. Thus, such sponsorship ought to produce effects. However, these data should not be construed to indicate that government sponsorship (or the sponsorship of any agency) makes no difference in general. It is possible that in 1942, in the United States, the policies and activities of the government were not so expansive as to precipitate any marked reactions from the respondents. That the perceived role of a government may be quite different in other circumstances, and operate strongly on responses is evident from a study done by Crespi in occupied Germany.[27] Here American military government sponsorship was contrasted with sponsorship by a fictitious "German Opinion Institute."

In this case, the government is an affect-laden object—it is imposed by a former enemy, so that we would expect that the effects of sponsorship demonstrated are probably *maximal* estimates of the effect of this variable. Admittedly the very nature of the government in this study is quite different from that of the usual case, and the results should hardly be taken as typical findings.

The differences secured by Crespi under the two contrasting sponsorships supply abundant evidence that sponsorship can have effects in such extreme situations. One-third of the thirty-six questions yielded differences which were significant at the .05 level, and five questions yielded differences significant at the .01 level. Even on questions which showed no statistically significant differences, differences were consistently in the direction that would be expected if sponsorship effects were operative. However, even in this extreme test of sponsorship effects, in which the questions were especially chosen because they might be responsive to the variable of sponsorship, the *magnitude* of the effect was not great. The mean of the maximum differences on all questions taken together was only in the neighborhood of 6 per cent.

By and large, the differences found were almost universally of the sort which indicated that respondents tended to tell the government interviewers what they thought was wanted—that is, answers were generally more favorable to the military government or toward policies advocated by the occupying authority. However, one notable exception occurred, which would seem to indicate that, in the presence of more powerful motivations, the desire to please the sponsor becomes secondary. In answer to the question, "Do you believe that the Germans have an inclination toward militarism?" the differences found (significant at the .01 level) are in the opposite direction to what would be expected if the usual motivation were the sole one operating. Crespi explains this phenomenon as follows:

The apparent MG sponsorship effects . . . are all instances of occasional respondents telling the American authorities what they like to hear. Question six (above) now suggests that this only happens, where it happens at all, when such a course does not obviously reflect unfavorably on the Germans; in other words where it does not cost anything to be more polite than truthful. What the Americans like to hear on this question—and surely the Germans know it well—is German agreement with the general American view that the Germans have an inclination toward militarism. But instead of more often giving MG interviewers such an answer—as compared to German-sponsored interviewers—the respondents are apparently inclined to do so *less* often since this latter answer is less unfavorable to the German people.

Whatever the bias that may enter into responses under government sponsorship in occupied Germany, Crespi feels that this may be more than compensated for by the reduction of other errors, which take place in German-sponsored surveys. There seemed to be less "no opinion" response and more interest among respondents when surveys were sponsored by the military government. Under German sponsorship, respondents felt some insecurity from an uncertain definition of the situation. The greater motivation and interest when the sponsorship was governmental is viewed by Crespi as common-sense realization on the part of the German respondents that only the military government was really in a position to remedy some of the difficulties they faced.

The ability of the sponsoring agency to take action with reference to his concerns may have an important influence on the respondent's answers in other fields involving the interview. This is pointed up by Hofstein's description of the structure of the army-counseling interview.[28] He states:

> The relationship to command defines the role of the personnel consultant in any interviewing or counseling situation. He cannot do anything without the implicit approval of the command. He cannot assume any role in his professional relationships except that of a representative of the command. At first thought, this relationship so characteristic of and necessary to the Army may appear to be limiting. Yet it is precisely because of this relationship that the personnel consultant can be helpful to individual soldiers.

The studies cited in the foregoing reveal that responses may be affected by the stated sponsorship of the survey under conditions where the perception of the role of the sponsoring agency is well-structured and relevant to the issues posed in the questions. Admittedly, *some* frame of reference is set in any survey situation, and the answers of respondents are always interpretable only in terms of this frame of reference. What seems to be crucial is the degree to which this frame is highly structured and what meaning it has for the respondent.

The difference in results between the NORC and Crespi studies is a demonstration of the complexity of situational factors. What is *nominally* the same kind of situational factor, government sponsorship, operates differently in the two experiments because of the different meanings of such sponsorship under the respective conditions. Further complexity is evidenced by detailed findings within the German study. The type of effect is a function of the questions used. It is dependent on whether stronger opposing motives are set in operation. While inflation of progovernmental responses is the effect observed most frequently, on occasion other effects are noted. When the questions asked involve the possibility of a remedy for existing difficulties, we find the personal needs of the respondents accentuated and criticism implicit in the answers. The lack of such effects in the NORC study may reflect the less severe need in the United States for government action to remedy existing difficulties; it may also reflect the fact that the questionnaire did not touch closely on areas where governmental action may have been deemed necessary to remedy deeply felt frustrations.

It is hoped that the foregoing discussion of these two situational factors—anonymity and sponsorship—serves to point up the complexity of situational factors and the consequent difficulty of studying appropriately their interplay with interviewer effects. Nevertheless, in studying *interviewer* effect as a function of situational factors, it is possible to demonstrate through properly designed experiments that differently structured situations may act as mediating agents for the introduction of bias. Although a multitude of factors may be operating in any given situation to induce interviewer effects, particular characteristics of given situations are frequently discernible as the probable basis for the occurrence of these effects. And in controlled situations, the existence of these effects, *originated* by the interviewer but *induced* by situations, become capable of isolation and measurement.

4. EFFECTS ARISING FROM SPECIFIC SITUATIONAL FACTORS

It seems fruitful to attempt some kind of classification of situations according to the characteristic problems which they present to interviewers. Although there are many elements in the situation itself, there are only a few ways in which these factors mediate the operation of bias.

We consider first the relation of situational structure per se to interviewer effect. All situations may be schematized along a continuum of the "degree of freedom" they permit the interviewer. Although distortion of data may arise from the imposition of a too rigidly structured interview situation, most of the evidence accumulated suggests that interviewer effect, in so far as it is related to the degree of structuring, arises from the lack of a well-defined and structured interview situation. Thus, we turn first to consider the nature of effects arising from situations characterized by this quality.

Effects Arising from Lack of Structure in Procedure

The development of large-scale opinion and attitude research brought with it an increase in the degree to which forms of inquiry were structured. The unstandardized type of interview, characteristic of clinical psychology, was of necessity unsuitable for large-scale research, for in clinical studies the interview has as its primary purpose the diagnosis or therapy of an individual, while in survey research the analysis and reporting of mass opinions or behavior and of group differences in these opinions is the principal objective.

Just as it is essential that the clinician be enabled by his technique to pursue whatever lines of inquiry seem to him to be important in the individual case, so is it necessary in survey inquiries that the interviewer be prevented from following just whatever paths *he* may think important. The entire validity of survey procedure rests upon the foundation of standardization. If we wish to report and analyze and compare group data, we must make certain that the responses of the many individuals to the different interviewers are responses to essentially the same stimuli.

Occasionally, there are research operations of a quasi-clinical type in which a few highly trained interviewers, homogeneous in background, work on a study and are guided by their uniform and thorough familiarity with the research objectives. Under such conditions, the assumption might be warranted that each interviewer would employ techniques that were ideally suited to the given respondent and yet all would work in fairly parallel and unbiased fashion. But such an assumption seems hardly warranted for the usual large-scale survey in which the massiveness of the inquiry necessitates the use of large numbers of interviewers of unequal backgrounds so widely distributed geographically that controls are difficult to enforce. Moreover, in the former instance the interviewer is at the same time often the analyst, and he can juxtapose the findings against his first-hand knowledge of the operations which elicited the data. It is essential in any analysis that the results must always be interpreted in terms of the measurement situation. Given the separation between interviewer and analyst in the usual survey, the only way in which the analyst can know the nature of the field-setting is by specifying it for the interviewers.

If the stimulus situation is really vastly different for each respondent in a survey (or even for a portion of them), then we cannot with good conscience combine these responses into group opinions or make comparisons between groups of respondents. We cannot always be sure that the same questions do have the same meaning to different respondents. There is empirical evidence that this is sometimes not the case.[29] Moreover, there are special instances where, on a priori grounds, diversity among respondents is so marked that verbal standardization would provide no insurance of uniform meaning. Such might be the case, for example, in a survey conducted in several different national populations. But where diversity is not so striking, we can at least control the conditions under which the questions are asked, so that in so far as possible we mitigate any likelihood of obtaining uncombinable responses. Whether or not we can ultimately devise techniques to assure that a question will have the same psychological meaning to different respondents is beyond the scope of this discussion. Kinsey, by allowing his interviewers to use the terminology which they felt to be applicable, attempted to standardize the *psychological meaning* of a question by unstandardizing the wording. Certainly the possibility of adapting this technique to public opinion research deserves consideration.

However, until such time as techniques are devised which make certain that stimuli will be functionally standard for all respondents, research must rest upon the assumption that verbal standardization is the nearest reliable approximation we can achieve. Though frames of reference may vary among respondents, it seems reasonable to suppose that the limits of the variation are closer if the verbal stimulus is standardized.[30]

While structuring of stimulus situations was originally developed as an aid to standardization in general, more important for our discussion is the control over interviewer effect which it provides. All other things being equal, the more controlled the interviewer's activities, the less the likelihood that variations in results can be attributed to the idiosyncrasies of the different interviewers. Although it is, of course, possible to standardize an interview situation in such a way that we facilitate the introduction of some systematic bias among all interviewers, there can be little doubt that by giving the interviewer greater freedom in the interview situation we lay ourselves open to the infinite variability in human capacities that has been so well documented in psychological literature.[31]

Differences between interviewers come into play in all phases of the interview situation. Differences in intellectual capacities may mean variation in understanding the objectives of the survey, the aims of the questions, and the meaning of responses. Sensory differences may lead to varying perceptions of significant respondent characteristics and to differential attentiveness to answers. Differential motor skills may result in recording differences.

That mere interviewer ineptitude is itself a source of error is evident from experiments done under laboratory conditions with no respondent present. Here, clearly, errors cannot result from reactional processes. In such studies, we find that error which is merely clerical and not in any way motivated by bias can be quite large in magnitude. For example, in the study by Guest and Nuckols we find that for three experimental phonographic transcriptions of interviews to which interviewers listened and recorded responses the degree of such non-biasing error is 45 per cent, 62 per cent and 66 per cent, respectively, of all errors committed.[32] Further, the interviewers—although a homogeneous group of students from the same institution—varied considerably in the degree to which they made such errors; a fact which underlines the importance of differences in interviewer skills. In the Guest and Nuckols study, the range of non-biasing error among twenty-four interviewers was from three to sixteen errors, fully as great a range as was found for biasing errors.

Beyond these differences in *ability*, however, there are others which may be even more important for the interview situation. Chief among these is the variation in "social stimulus value" among interviewers. Were interviewers selected from the population at large, such differences would of course assume tremendous proportions. But it is true that interviewers as an occupational group tend to vary far less than the population as a whole. The relative homogeneity of interviewers as a group, with respect to background characteristics, has been documented by Sheatsley.[33] While this itself may be a source of systematic bias, as discussed in the foregoing, it does limit the range within which individual differences among interviewers may operate to distort answers. However, if we examine some of the data collected by NORC on the psychological characteristics of their interviewing staff, we find, even among this relatively homogeneous group, differences in the extent and type of social relationship established with respondents. While demographically they have much in common, psychologically they are fairly diverse. Consider the following data culled from 150 of NORC's current field staff:

TABLE 43

COMPARISON OF SOME FACTUAL AND ATTITUDINAL CHARACTERISTICS
OF 150 NORC INTERVIEWERS*

	Percentage
Women	88
Men	12
Not main earner	77
Main earner	23
Have children	70
No children	30
Attended college	81
Never attended college	19

194 *Interviewing in Social Research*

TABLE 43 (Continued)

Prefer to keep problems to themselves.................... 62

Prefer to talk over with others........................... 38

Never get annoyed with respondents' opinions.............. 63

Sometimes get annoyed................................. 37

Often feel like staying and chatting with respondent.......... 48

Seldom or never feel like staying........................ 52

Have occasionally or frequently made friends with respondents. 58

Never made friends with respondents..................... 42

* Factual data from Sheatsley (*ibid.*), attitudinal data from NORC's study of interviewers using the mail questionnaire described in Chapter II.

Differences between interviewers in psychological characteristics and temperament may have crucial effects on the kind of interview situation in which they secure data. We might expect that rapport in the interview situation will vary and that the kind of spontaneous interaction that will exist between interviewer and respondent will likewise be subject to wide variation. In the absence of a structure imposed by the agency, then, such personality differences as exist among interviewers will affect the way they themselves act out their role.

The major consequence of structuring the interview is to impose restraint upon variable tendencies among interviewers. There is the accompanying danger of introducing some *constant* error through a standardized, but misguided, procedure or an excessively artificial procedure. The unstructured procedure clearly allows full sway for variations in interviewer behavior, but it may have the virtue of keeping any constant error due to bad or overly rigid procedures at a minimum. However, it should be noted that in addition to effects which result from lack of control over human variability in unstructured interview situations, such situations may also permit, under special conditions, the maximum operation of a constant error among all interviewers. This would be the case when some basic psychological process, common to the interviewers, is a source of error unless controlled. Intelligent, standardized procedures, designed in relation to such processes, can control or reduce constant errors. That such processes occur very frequently is clear from earlier chapters.

Each of the many aspects of the public opinion interview is subject to structuring by the agency. That is, we can design the situation in such a way that the task of the interviewer is clearly defined and delimited, or we can, at any point in the process, order the situation so that the interviewer's judgments come into play. Within the realm of question construction, questions themselves may be narrow in focus or very broad. We may provide answer boxes in which two or three or more categories are provided for the interviewer to check the appropriate response, or we may ask the interviewer to record verbatim everything said by the respondent. Clearly the more we specify the task, the more we have structured the situation for the interviewer.

In certain respects, the free-answer question would seem to provide maximal opportunity for the operation of interviewer effects deriving from lack of controls over variability in behavior. The tasks of asking the question and recording the answer are not nearly so rigidly defined as in pre-coded questions, since the interviewer must decide when and how often to probe, what probes to use, and what phrases in the total answer are redundant and can therefore be omitted from the recording. Consequently, studies of error in the use of such questions provide opportunity for evaluating effects occurring in unstructured situations.

In several recent studies, evidence is presented to demonstrate that error in free-answer questions, when handled by the average interviewer, is, in fact, of high frequency.[34] Two specific ways in which such effects can be manifested form the focus of these studies—(1) selective recording of responses and (2) differential probing behavior among interviewers.

In the aforementioned study by Guest and Nuckols, twenty-four subjects were asked to record interviews from three phonographic transcriptions concerned with labor-management relations.[35] The three respondents recorded gave pre-arranged answers, one predominantly pro-management, one predominantly pro-labor, and one about neutral. Both alternative type and free-response type questions were used. There were about sixty-three chances for alternative type errors and twenty-six chances for free-response type errors.

In comparing recording error on free-answer questions with similar error on pre-coded questions, Guest and Nuckols conclude that free-answer questions not only produce more total errors, but also more biasing errors.

On both the neutral and pro-management, the proportion of biasing errors to total errors is about the same for both types of questions. On the pro-labor interview, we find a fairly heavy pro-labor bias on the pre-coded questions and a rather heavy pro-management bias on the free-answer questions. That pro-labor bias in the pro-labor interview was evident only on the pre-coded questions suggests that assimilation of doubtful responses to attitude-structure expectations is characteristic of interviewers using pre-coded questions, while other sources of bias operate more strongly under the free-response form.

Guest and Nuckols suggest that on free-response questions interviewers tend to make errors *away* from the dominant theme of the interview. Although we have no empirical knowledge of why this phenomenon occurs, it seems logical that in free-response questions interviewers

TABLE 44

Type of Error as a Function of Type of Question and Type of Interview (in Per Cent)

| | Type of Question | | | | | | | |
| | Fixed Alternative | | | | Free Response | | | |
Error in Direction of:	Labor	Management	Neutral	Total	Labor	Management	Neutral	Total
Response in direction of:								
Labor..............	55	10	35	100 (29)	2	47	51	100 (47)
Management.......	29	12	59	100 (34)	33	3	64	100 (85)
Neutral...........	18	14	68	100 (71)	22	14	64	100 (28)

might tend to omit recording repeated statements of a given theme. Thus, if a particular sentiment is once expressed and recorded, interviewers might select contrary or separate themes to record rather than repetitions of the already recorded theme. If this occurred in Guest's and Nuckols' experiment, it would account for their finding that interviewers tend to record responses away from the dominant theme of the interview.

Although Guest and Nuckols found no evidence that the selective recording of free-answer material was in the direction of the interviewer's ideology, Fisher has been able to demonstrate such effects in a laboratory experiment of similar design conducted at the University of Chicago.[36] Measuring the degree of error in free-answer questions only, Fisher found a significant relationship between the interviewer's ideology and his selection of phrases to record. (See Table 45.)

Interviewers tended to record more statements which conformed with their own attitudes toward the two controversial issues. Those favoring Wallace recorded 12 per cent more of the possible pro than of the possible con statements: those opposing Wallace recorded 4 per cent more of the possible con statements than of the possible pro statements; those favoring the draft recorded 5 per cent more pro statements; and those opposing the draft recorded 16 per cent more con statements.

Differences in the types of responses most subject to interviewer effect are provided by Fisher's data, and confirm findings from other

TABLE 45

NUMBER OF PRO AND NUMBER OF CON STATEMENTS RECORDED BY THIRTY-TWO INTERVIEWERS ON DRAFT AND WALLACE ISSUES IN RELATION TO THEIR OWN POSITION ON THESE ISSUES*

	INTERVIEWERS WHO FAVORED DRAFT		INTERVIEWERS WHO OPPOSED DRAFT	
	Pro-Draft Statements	Con-Draft Statements	Pro-Draft Statements	Con-Draft Statements
Total number of statements possible to record............	279	279	713	713
Number actually recorded......	169	156	309	424
Percentage recorded..........	61	56	43	59
	INTERVIEWERS WHO FAVORED WALLACE		INTERVIEWERS WHO OPPOSED WALLACE	
	Pro-Wallace Statements	Con-Wallace Statements	Pro-Wallace Statements	Con-Wallace Statements
Total number of statements possible to record............	624	608	624	608
Number actually recorded......	331	261	331	349
Percentage recorded..........	55	43	53	57

* Total average number of statements recorded: 53 per cent.

experiments. Significantly more biasing error on free-answer questions was noted by Fisher when responses were equivocal, rather than unequivocal. Other data reported below suggest that this is also true with regard to bias resulting from pre-coded questions.[37]

Further evidence of the existence of effects in free-response questions, as well as an examination into the manifestations of these effects, is provided in a field experiment reported by Feldman, Hyman, and Hart.[38] A total of forty-five interviewers was divided into five teams of nine each, and members of each team received equivalent assignments. These investigators found little evidence of effects on traditional "polling type" questions yet a good deal on free-response questions included in the same questionnaire. The errors seemed traceable to differential probing behavior. The data are presented in Table 46.

Differential probing behavior is revealed in this study, first of all, in the number of separate answers elicited by interviewers. Here we find significant differences among interviewers working within the same sectors of a city, with equivalent samples, on all four questions tested.[39] Elicitation of multiple answers seemed to be related to the experience of the interviewer; by and large those interviewers with the greatest experience tended to elicit more multiple answers.

TABLE 46

LEVEL OF SIGNIFICANCE OF INTERVIEWER VARIATION IN NUMBER OF ANSWERS OBTAINED
ON OPEN QUESTIONS

Question	Sector I	Sector II	Sector III	Sector IV	Sector V
Suggestions for improvements in Denver..............	nonsig-nificant	.05	.05	.01	nonsig-nificant
Reason for moving to Denver*.	nonsig-nificant	nonsig-nificant	.05	nonsig-nificant	nonsig-nificant
Reasons for attitude toward neighborhood for satisfied group†.................	.01	nonsig-nificant	nonsig-nificant	nonsig-nificant	.05
Reasons for attitude toward neighbors†..............	nonsig-nificant	nonsig-nificant	.01	nonsig-nificant	.01

* While the F-ratios (variance between interviewers/variance within interviewers) do not reach the .05 level of significance in four of the sectors, the P-values are relatively low. When the exact P-values from the five sectors are combined to get an aggregate test by using Fisher's logarithmic transformation, the difference among interviewers in the aggregate is significant at the .05 level. For the other questions, no exact test was made for the five sectors aggregated because the over-all significance should be clear from mere inspection, and the laborious procedure was unnecessary.

† The number of respondents dissatisfied with their neighbors or neighborhood were too few in the total sample to permit any separate test of interviewer differences in number of reasons for this attitude.

Perhaps even more important from the point of view of validity of data secured through free-response questions is the finding of Feldman and his associates that the tendency to elicit multiple answers affects the degree to which interviewers obtain answers whose contents are "rare." The data are presented in Table 47.

In pointing out the importance of this phenomenon for the interpretation of survey data secured through free-response questioning, Feldman, Hyman and Hart state:

In drawing conclusions from survey data, it is common practice to use the infrequent occurrence of certain categories as a basis for interpretation. In all probability, the results of such categories, involving secondary opinions, are biased in the direction of under-representation because of the likelihood that at least some interviewers did not elicit multiple answers. More important, such an overall set of data will contain a mixture of primary opinions and secondary opinions due to the variation among the interviewers in ability to obtain multiple answers. If interviewers varying in probing habits are not distributed evenly over the entire sample, it is likely that some obtained differences between types of respondents may not be real differences, but merely differences in the degree to which secondary opinions have been elicited.

A demonstration of the operation of effects on primary categories of response in free-answer questions (i.e., very prevalent attitudes) is also provided by this study. In this instance, the mechanism of differential probing seems irrelevant to the ability to obtain responses of such pri-

TABLE 47

THE RELATIONSHIP BETWEEN THE NUMBER OF ANSWERS PER RESPONDENT
OBTAINED BY AN INTERVIEWER AND THE PERCENTAGE OF RESPONDENTS
GIVING ANSWERS IN A PARTICULAR SECONDARY CATEGORY
(IMPROVEMENTS IN INDUSTRY AND COMMERCE)

	PERCENTAGE OF RESPONDENTS GIVING ANSWERS IN THE SECONDARY CATEGORY OF RESPONDENTS OF:		
	The Three Interviewers Getting the Largest Number of Answers Per Respondent in Their Sector	The Three Interviewers Getting the Smallest Number of Answers Per Respondent in Their Sector	DIFFERENCE IN PERCENTAGES
Sector I............	24	7	17
Sector II..........	18	12	6
Sector III.........	12	13	−1
Sector IV.........	20	7	13
Sector V..........	15	4	11
All sectors........	18	8	10

macy from any given respondent. The study sought the explanation in some other mechanism. The authors present suggestive evidence that such effects are independent of extent of probing and are a function of expectations, i.e., the interviewer's belief that a particular category of response is important somehow affects his tendency to obtain answers within that category. Interviewers who regarded neighbors as very important in a choice of neighborhood tended to have more respondents who mentioned neighbors as a reason for their choice of neighborhood than those interviewers who regarded neighbors as of little importance, but the differences were not statistically significant. However, in view of the small numbers and the consistent direction of the findings, it seems wise not to reject the possibility that interviewer effects occur even on primary categories of response to free-answer questions.

The data just presented establish the fact that free-answer questions are subject to considerable interviewer error, arising both from inter-individual variability and from the systematic operation of psychological processes. Thus, the findings lend general support to the notion that unstructured procedures may provide a favorable milieu for the operation of interviewer effects.

We have described an "unstructured situation" as one in which the maximum opportunity exists for variations in interviewer activity. From this point of view, the procedure of asking interviewers to make "field ratings" of various respondent characteristics would seem to be a procedure in which minimal structuring exists, as far as the judgmental requirements of the task are concerned. True, the categories are provided (or points on the scale) as in pre-coded questions, but the interviewer is not "tied down" to the classification of a particular response. Since the respondent makes no "response" as such, but is classified according to some general observed characteristic, the subjective judgment of the interviewer is allowed free play. In such a situation, one would expect effects to be maximal.

In the aforementioned study by Feldman and associates, the most striking occurrence of interviewer effects was noted in the variation in field ratings. Six such ratings were tested, and five "yielded P values so microscopic that the results certainly cannot be attributed to sampling variation."

TABLE 48

TESTS OF INTERVIEWER EFFECTS ON FIELD RATINGS

	Pooled Chi-Squared Value	Pooled Degrees of Freedom	Probability
Condition of dwelling.............	193.78	120	<.0001
Condition of block................	169.89	80	<.0001
Degree of hostility of respondent......	125.56	80	.0007
Degree of respondent's interest........	151.01	64	<.0001
Respondent's intelligence............	214.73	120	<.0001
Respondent's evasiveness............	48.14	40	.18

It is worth noting that even ratings of "factual" characteristics showed immense variability. The authors point out that differences in ratings of qualities such as "intelligence" or "hostility" might reflect actual differences in interviewer-respondent interaction, but ratings of "condition of dwelling unit" and "condition of block" must represent sheer interviewer differences, under controlled sampling conditions.[40]

We must conclude that the task of making field ratings of respondents or of environmental characteristics presents the type of situation in which interviewer effects are maximized, and resultant data highly unreliable.

Of course, interviewer effect is only one of many considerations which a designer of surveys must take into account. Thus, where field ratings are indispensable for the purposes of a study, we cannot demand that they be sacrificed simply on the grounds of such imperfection. Similarly, open-ended questions may often be indispensable for revealing certain variables not amenable to study in other ways. In such instances, susceptibility to interviewer effect may become a secondary consideration in the *choice* of a procedure.

However, when such methods are applied, our findings caution us to be especially attentive to interviewer effects and to institute careful measures of control. Our findings also suggest that control may have to take the form—in part, at least—of more enlightened and effective structuring of the interview situation.

Effects Arising from Increased Opportunity for a Respondent Reaction

In Chapter IV, it will be recalled, we documented the inference that biasing reactions of respondents are likely to result from the extent and character of their social involvement in the interviewing situation. Although rapport is heightened by both *task* and *social* involvement, validity of the respondents' answers to questions seems to depend on the achievement of a nice balance between task *and* social involvement.

Bias might be expected to come into play in any situation in which we have strengthened one or more of the factors which facilitate reactional effects. Theoretically, this may occur at any point in the process.

Agencies are much concerned about the perceptions which respondents initially develop of interviewers. Thus the mere fact that an interviewer knocks at a door and gives some introductory speech might set up a tendency in the respondent to perceive him as a salesman. Agencies caution interviewers against dressing or behaving in any way that might set up some deviant kind of perception in the respondent. The interviewer is supposed to dress inconspicuously and adopt a uniformly friendly and informal manner in his approach.

Although we have a great deal of data on the existence of reactional effects per se, we have very few experiments where such effects can be traced to situational factors. One of the few such tests is available from the data collected by Mosteller and his Associates in the SSRC study of the 1948 pre-election polls.[41]

A comparison of results for several interviewers using both secret and nonsecret ballots provided us with a test in which the actual role of the interviewer is altered in two ways. We have, first of all, a comparison between situations where the question is verbalized by the interviewer, and one in which it is handed to the respondent on a written ballot. Secondly, we have a comparison of situations in which the respondent's opinion is made known to the interviewer or kept secret from him. In accordance with the theory previously stated, we would expect that when the interviewer verbalizes the question he would automatically occupy a larger part of the psychological field and therefore induce more effects. Also we would suppose that when the respondent is allowed to keep his opinion secret there will be less social involvement, due to a lesser concern for the characteristics of the interviewer, and his anticipated approval or disapproval of the responses.

The data from this study, however, do not bear out our hypothesis. Comparing the results secured by the two different Gallup interviewers working successively in two cities, we find that, for each of them in each city, the results obtained under the two methods—secret and non-secret—did not vary significantly.

However, earlier experiments of the AIPO with secret ballot techniques suggest that despite the personal presence of the interviewer, differences in results do occur on some items among urban groups when the respondent's answers are not revealed. Turnbull finds large and significant differences on questions in which the respondent's prestige might be affected and small and nonsignificant differences in other questions when the secret ballot is used.[42] Kemper and Thorndike report similar findings from a survey of 1,000 men in the city of Louisville. Student interviewers, many of them with past experience, inquired about the respondent's psychosomatic symptoms, using personal interview and secret ballot techniques. Presumably the revelation of a symptom would be prestige deflating. Significant differences were found for six of the twenty-two questions, with the secret ballot yielding a more frequent report of "maladjustment" in five of these instances. The writers note, however, that the difference in average adjustment, presumably computed from the total scale score, between the two methods was small.[43]

Another test of the same general phenomenon is reported by Huth,[44] who tested interviewer respondent agreement in opinions (as a measure of interviewer effect) in two situations. In one, an ordinary personal interview was conducted, and in the other, the questionnaire was left with the respondent "to think about," the interviewer returning at a later date to conduct the interview. Presumably, there should be less social and more task involvement in the latter situation, since the respondent has had more time to become involved in the task itself, and is in a sense "fortified" against effects deriving from the perception of the interviewer characteristics.

On two of seven questions—those dealing with a state veterans' bonus and peacetime military training—she found significant association between interviewer and respondent opinion in the nondeliberative situations, while only the bonus question showed significant association in the deliberative situations. The other five questions were concerned with prohibition, attitudes toward Negroes, war possibilities, interest in voting, and need for more industries in Denver.

Although the study tested only a small number of questions for interviewer effect, the results are most consistent. Moreover, the issues posed —e.g., drinking, race relations, voting—seem to be highly loaded with social content and therefore susceptible to reactional effects. Yet out of seven tests, in only one case was there a significant interviewer effect observable under the nondeliberative condition that was not also observable under the deliberative condition. On all other questions, interviewer effect was either absent or present under *both* conditions.

The lack of demonstrable effect in these specific tests of our hypothesis does not deny its general validity. Although we do not find bias measurably increased in situations where the interviewer is presumably occupying a larger portion of the psychological field, it is probable that, even where the interviewer had merely provided a secret ballot for the respondent, the social involvement is sufficiently large to approximate a more interpersonal situation. For, if bias could have occurred as a function of respondent reaction to perceived group membership or other characteristics of the interviewer, this would function in independence of any verbalization by the interviewer. Although the respondent's ballot is secret, there may not be psychological anonymity for him so long as there exists a face-to-face relationship with the interviewer.

The data in Chapter IV provide ample evidence of the hypothesis that the culturally defined significance of the interviewer's characteristics is a potent source of bias. We have seen that differences occur as a result of the respondent's perceiving the interviewer's color, religion, sex, class membership, and residence and his reacting in some emotional way to the characteristic.

It will be recalled, however, that the effects noted were not uniform. Significant differences were discernible on some questions and not on others for several of the studies discussed. Thus, in addition to the procedure of questioning or question form, question content may be a most important factor in the mediation of reactional effects. Where question content does not relate in some way to the group membership of respondent and/or interviewer, we would not expect reactional effects, but where the relationship between the content of the question and the group membership factor is clearly evident, reactional effects may be expected to be maximal. This difference would come under our category of *situational* differences.

This factor is illustrated by the comparison of questions from the study of Negro and white interviewers in Memphis, discussed in Chapter IV. In Table 31 the questions were classified by the level of significance of difference.

Looking back at this table, we see that questions with particular types of *content* are more likely to show differences. First of all, it is clear that, on most of the nonattitudinal questions, differences between the groups are not significant, whereas on the attitudinal questions most differences are highly significant. The only nonattitudinal questions on which differences are significant are the questions referring to automobile ownership, and the Negro newspaper read. Negro respondents were less willing to admit owning an automobile or reading a Negro newspaper when interviewed by white interviewers. While these questions are factual, it is obvious that they are clearly related to the problems raised by group membership. Negro respondents in the South are aware that white Southerners may frown on any signs of Negro affluence and might prefer that Negroes read the local "white" newspapers.

A study of the summary also reveals that questions which in any way attempt to measure attitude toward the "government" or the conduct of the war produce the most significant differences. The respondents seem to be very careful to avoid any suggestion that they might be "unpatriotic" or dissatisfied with government policies when talking with white interviewers. This is especially noticeable on the question asking who is to blame for job discrimination against Negroes. They are just as willing to blame managers and labor unions when talking with white interviewers as with Negro interviewers but are considerably less willing to blame the government when interviewed by whites. Likewise, protests over segregation are significantly more often mentioned by Negroes when talking with Negro interviewers, while complaints about "housing" are the more frequent response given to white interviewers in answer to the question, "What do Negroes feel worst about?"

These data document the importance of question content in the introduction of reactional effects. When the respondent is affected by the group membership of the interviewer, his answers will be affected on questions which are in some way related to the area of group membership. In general, the Memphis study indicates that the further removed the question is from problems of Negro-white relations in the South, the less likely it is that reactional effect will occur.

Clearly, lack of structuring in the interview and respondent conformity to the perceived social requirements of the interview situation are not the only channels through which situational factors bring about bias. Constant bias over the staff may well result from the construction and standardization of a particular kind of biasing situation by the agency. This may come about by more or less direct means (such as the construction of badly worded questions), or by indirect means such as the setting of a type of situation that presents the interviewer with a task which either mechanically or psychologically involves certain difficulties. In such cases, bias seems to arise from the attempt of interviewers to solve the problems with which they are faced. That such tasks need not necessarily be taxing to the interviewer, nor that he need even be aware that he faces a difficult task, is clear from the data which will be presented below. We consider first situations illustrative of mechanical difficulties for interviewers and the way in which effects may come into play as a task aid.

Effects Arising from Mechanical Difficulties of the Task

When demands made upon the interviewer are beyond what is realistically attainable, it may be presumed that the data are affected. For, as revealed by the case material in Chapter II, interviewers normally accept and fulfil their prescribed role, but when pressures become too great, they may be unable to maintain it. Occasionally the mere mechanical difficulties are so great that demoralization sets in, and interviewers consciously or unconsciously distort data so as to enable them to comply with the mechanical requirements of the task. Crespi in his discussion of interviewer cheating states that demoralizing demands on the interviewer are the primary causes of cheating behavior.[45] He lists as common demoralizers such features as unreasonable length of questionnaires, overly frequent probes, apparent repetition of questions, complex and difficult or antagonizing questions, part-time work, and overly difficult sample assignments. In addition, he mentions external factors, such as weather and transportation difficulties, as causing interviewer demoralization. Analysis of interviewer report forms has led Sheatsley to conclude that similar factors are prime causes of low interviewer morale.[46]

The most innocuous features of a questionnaire may conceivably cause difficulty and affect responses. For example, according to Payne, it can be demonstrated that the amount of white space allowed for the

written responses is sufficient to affect the length of the response received on free-answer questions.[47] This theory is supported by qualitative evidence gleaned from interviewers, one of whom, in recording an
interview from a phonograph record, stated: "I feel irritated; I have no
room—have to write all over the place. How can you write verbatim
when there is no place to write verbatim? . . . I get doubtful—am I
writing down the things which are really important? I may not be objective in that I'm picking out certain things and leaving out others."

However, in one empirical test of this phenomenon, Fisher reports
that the amount of space made no difference in the number of statements recorded in response to free-answer questions.[48] He found that
interviewers would simply write smaller or write in the margins, where
space was limited.

The experienced difficulty of specific situational factors must, of
course, be qualified in the light of our earlier remarks about the recruit-
ment and training of interviewers who would be capable of greater
frustration tolerance, and the fact that the larger survey requirements
may necessitate using unpleasant procedures.

When such difficult situations occur, we would not normally expect
any systematic bias over the whole staff to be evident. Rather we anticipate diffuse errors in the data, since the only psychological process at
work is the interviewer's desire to extricate himself from a difficult
situation, and often he can do this in a variety of ways. However, if
there is only one path which any interviewer may take to reduce the
difficulty of the task then one would expect systematic errors to result.
For example, difficult interviewing situations might frequently lead to
inadequate probing by interviewers, so we might expect a greater frequency of "don't know" or "no answer" responses in such situations;
or, in free-answer questions, a smaller frequency of secondary types of
responses. When frank cheating does not occur in difficult siuations, we
might expect a high degree of random error. Guest and Nuckols have
shown the degree of non-biasing error which occurs even in a simulated
easy interview situation; we might expect this to be greatly magnified
when the requirements of the task are made more difficult.

It is probably true, however, that if we constructed the interviewing
situation in such a way that the fulfilment of the task was too simple and
mechanical, we might also find an increase in cheating or random error.
There is considerable evidence in psychological literature to demonstrate that, up to a point, an increase in task difficulty makes for increased efficiency and accuracy.[49] As well, some experienced interviewers have a certain "instinct for workmanship"—a certain sense of

professional artistry—and might feel relegated to a minor clerical role by extremely simple tasks; consequently, error might result from a decrease in the interviewer's motivation for the assignment. Also, there is some evidence from NORC's survey of interviewers that research directors may underestimate the ability of the experienced interviewer to carry out difficult assignments.[50]

For example, in answer to the question: "How do you feel when someone refuses to let you interview them, or meets your approach with hostility?" 20 per cent of the inexperienced interviewers in NORC's study reported intense feelings of rejection and 8 per cent saw it as a personal failure, whereas only 12 per cent of the experienced reported intense feelings of rejection, and none saw it as a personal failure. Likewise, while only 6 per cent of the inexperienced responded to such situations as a "challenge to get the interview," 18 per cent of the experienced group perceived the situation in this way.

The contrast between experienced and inexperienced interviewers in their willingness to carry out all kinds of assignments is further revealed in answer to a subsequent question on the NORC study: "How much difference does the content of the survey make to you? That is, are you just as happy asking about one subject as another, or does your interest in the work vary a great deal depending on what we are asking about?" Here, sharp differences between the experienced and inexperienced groups are revealed. While 54 per cent of the inexperienced group say their interest depends on the subject of the survey and 38 per cent say it makes no difference, the proportions are almost exactly the opposite for the experienced group—36 per cent saying it depends on the subject and fully 60 per cent saying it makes no difference.

One field experiment conducted by NORC and reported by Sheatsley illustrates the resistance of professional interviewers to temptations to simplify their task.[51] In a test deliberately designed to "trap" the interviewer into recording the response which would save him from asking a series of annoying subquestions, no evidence was found in the aggregate of any distortion of data through such attempts to simplify the task.

The design was as follows: A survey in February contained a question which suggested that the federal government might not have enough money to do all the things it would like to do and the respondent was given a choice of two groups of services on which less money might be spent—"A" or "B." The same question was repeated on a survey the following month, but this time four subquestions were added, and a split ballot was used. On half the ballots, four tedious subquestions were asked of those who favored a cut in "A," and nothing was asked of the "don't know" or those who favored a cut in "B." On the other half, four subquestions were asked of those who wanted to cut down on "B." The samples were equivalent with each interviewer using each form on half of his respondents at random. The hypothesis would be confirmed if there were a higher "don't know" response in March, which would be one way to avoid asking the subquestions, and if there were a higher response on "A" when the subquestions applied to the "B" answer, and a higher response on "B" when the subquestions applied to the "A" answer. The results presented in Table 49 below provide no evidence whatsoever of such biasing behavior.

TABLE 49

THE INFLUENCE OF DEPENDENT SUB-QUESTIONS ON DISTORTION OF RESPONSES TO AN ORIGINAL QUESTION

RESPONSE	FEBRUARY SURVEY (IN PER CENT)	TOTAL RESULTS MARCH SURVEY (IN PER CENT)	PERCENTAGE OF RESULTS WHEN SUBQUESTIONS WOULD HAVE TO BE ASKED ONLY IF:	
			Cut Down on "A" Answer	Cut Down on "B" Answer
"Cut down on A"....	62	64	66	62
"Cut down on B".....	25	27	25	28
"Don't know"........	13	9	9	10
	100	100	100	100
	N = 1261	N = 1302	N = 654	N = 648

Effects Arising from Psychological Difficulties of the Task Assigned

Just as some interviewing situations present the interviewer with difficult problems arising from the *mechanical* procedures prescribed, so certain types of situations present *psychological* difficulties to the interviewer that are most easily solved by distortion of data in one way or another.

Demoralization, while it may result from mechanical difficulty, may also come about through the prescription of an intrinsically simple task which the interviewer finds it difficult to perform psychologically. The description by James Stern, cited in Chapter II, of the tension he experienced in questioning Germans about their reactions to the strategic bombing is an example of a kind of general demoralization which may occur because of inability psychologically to accept the task assigned. Other interviewers have reported similar experiences. One of them, assigned to obtain a detailed interview on the leisure-time activities of respondents, reported that it was extremely difficult for him to carry out this task when interviewing a working-class housewife with five small children. Clearly this respondent had little leisure time and many pressing problems, and the interviewer stated that he felt ridiculous in asking how she spent her "leisure hours." It is likely that some interviewers will fabricate data rather than continue in this kind of trying situation.

A similar demoralization occurs when the requirements of the survey are such as to cause resentment, embarrassment, or even apathy among respondents. This type of situation is one which Crespi lists as a source of cheating behavior, and it is evident from hidden recordings of interviews, obtained during a study by the American Jewish Committee, described in Chapter II, that where respondents exhibit hostility to the survey, varying kinds of distortions are introduced by the interviewer. In these experiments with "planted" hostile respondents, interviewers failed to repeat questions and occasionally skipped whole batteries of questions which might have reinforced the respondent's already expressed hostility. Other interviewers biased data by readily agreeing with the respondents' criticisms of the survey, in an apparent attempt to ease the tension in the social situation.

In the examples described above we have a conflict between the demands of the job and the demands inherent in the personal relationship of the interview situation. When an interviewer's task motivation is low and his social orientation especially intense, we may expect the social requirements to take priority in resolving the conflict. However, because the maintenance of at least a tolerable social relationship is a prerequisite for conducting any interview, the establishment of rapport is always a task requirement as well as a social requirement. Consequently, we frequently find that interviewers will sacrifice an established procedure if they feel rapport is jeopardized. Thus interviewer PB, some of whose reactions while listening to a phonograph recording of an interview were reported earlier, remarked in the same experiment:

I started to get that helpless feeling, he did not answer the question and I was forcing the answer out of him. You have to force him but as you force him he reacts by feeling more strongly.

You may not be sure what the answer is . . . so you have to repeat the question and then the respondent is up in arms and says "Didn't you listen to what I said?"

I know that he takes some interest in the Berlin question but he's getting sore now. If they were on good terms the interviewer should probe that remark of the respondent, but as it is, no probe is better.

Since the social relationship can obviously be taxed by inquiries into certain realms, the content of the questions asked can become an important situational determinant of this type of bias. Agencies have always been aware that respondents objected to certain types of questions and that they may fabricate answers when such occasions arise. But the focus of concern has been on the respondent as the source of the error. However, there is much evidence to demonstrate that, because of anticipated objections, questions on certain subjects are asked reluctantly by interviewers, and that some interviewers might skip such questions entirely. In NORC's study of interviewers an attempt was made to explore interviewers' concerns about asking questions on particular areas. About half the current staff, in answer to a direct question, indicated that they remembered questions on past surveys which they would have preferred not to ask. The table below summarizes the types of questions interviewers reported they preferred not to ask.

The data in Table 50 reveal that so-called "factual" questions are among the ones most frequently objected to by the interviewers, particularly when they disclose the respondent's economic status. In stating the reasons why they preferred not to ask particular types of questions, interviewers indicated that they thought questions were "too personal" or embarrassing to the interviewer or respondent. About a fifth of the interviewers said that respondents became hostile or suspicious at certain questions and, hence, that rapport was endangered. Others mentioned that they felt respondents didn't answer personal questions honestly.

That questions about the respondent's financial status are among those

TABLE 50

FREQUENCY WITH WHICH INTERVIEWERS SPONTANEOUSLY MENTION DISLIKE OF PARTICULAR QUESTION TYPES

Type of question	Percentage of Interviewers Who Express Dislike*
Questions relating to financial status; rent, income	38
Questions related to sex	25
Questions related to political preference	16
Questions related to religious preference	9
Questions related to age	9
Miscellaneous personal questions: mental health, physical welfare, marriage	16
Factual data, personal questions generally	8
Questions related to inter-racial subjects	4
Questions too difficult for respondent to understand	5
Miscellaneous: information, trend, card questions, questions that meet with disinterest	8
	N = 76

* The per cents add to more than 100 because some interviewers mentioned more than one type of question.

most objected to by interviewers is further documented by another set of questions asked of NORC interviewers.[52] In an attempt to find out what factors lay behind the objections of interviewers to particular types of questions, NORC formulated a list of specific questions, some previously asked in surveys and others synthetic, and asked interviewers to imagine that they were to use these on a survey and to indicate which ones they would object to asking. Various question types were included, the purpose being to cover a wide range of possible objections. While it is not possible to tell exactly why interviewers objected to some of these questions, since we did not ask for their reasons, the grounds for objection can generally be inferred from the questions. Table 51 lists the questions inquired about and the percentage of interviewers who stated that they would not object to asking them. Included in the table is our inference as to why the questions might prove objectionable to interviewers.

Although the absolute percentages in Table 51 are not necessarily reliable, since interviewers are likely to understate their objections to their employer in such a hypothetical test, the *relative* positions of the questions in terms of the frequency with which they meet objections is probably dependable.[53] It will be noted that the questions about finances again draw the most frequent objection, in spite of the fact that other questions included in the list tap extremely personal areas of investigation.

To the extent that interviewer effects result from reactions of demoralization to the content of questions, we should expect as much error in so-called factual data as in attitudinal data, and in many types of questions which are routinely used on surveys and regarded as innocuous. Apparently it is not only those surveys in which we ask about highly personal attitudes which present the interviewer with problems of establishing and maintaining rapport. Factual items on ordinary surveys (particularly, it would seem, where financial questions are asked early in the interview) may threaten rapport, and may cause the interviewer to introduce error in order to avoid the social difficulties which he might have to face by following his directions exactly.

The effects of psychologically difficult situations, created by content factors, are probably similar to the effects deriving from mechanical difficulties—diffuse and random error with a likely increase in "don't know" and "no answer" responses.

Quite apart from the *general* psychological problems of the interpersonal situation for the interviewer, there are also many specific psychological problems that present themselves during the course of an

TABLE 51

Hypothetical Question	Presumed Reason for Objection	Percentage of Staff Who State They Would Not Object*
Who do you think is mainly responsible for high prices in this country—the big businessman or the small businessman?	Loaded	97
Suppose Russia declared war on Yugoslavia—about how long do you think the war would last—just your best guess?	Requires respondent to make guess with little basis for judgment	94
Who do you think is mainly responsible for strikes in this country—the workers or their leaders?	Loaded	93
Can you whistle?	Innocuous but awkward to the interviewer because of absurdity of subject	90
What religion do you consider yourself?	Embarrassing to respondent because of personal nature of subject	89
Do you happen to know the capital of Syria?	Embarrassing to the respondent because ignorance may be revealed	88
As you may know the Reciprocal Trade Act of 1946 provides that countries in the Western Hemisphere do not have to pay a tariff over 12 per cent on certain types of industrial commodities provided they allow American goods the same privileges at their ports. Do you approve or disapprove of this policy?	Awkward to the interviewer because of length, complexity, general ignorance of respondents on technical subjects	84
What is your approximate age?	Embarrassing to respondent because of personal nature of subject	82
In the last election for President, did you vote for Dewey, Truman, Wallace, or Thurmond?	Embarrassing to respondent because of personal nature of subject	80
Are there any policies of the Communist party which you yourself admire?	Possibly incriminatory	70
How would you feel about marrying a Jew?	Embarrassing to respondent because answer may violate social credo	59
Has anyone in your family ever been in a mental hospital?	Embarrassing to respondent because subject matter is generally taboo	54
Have you provided for the Salvation Army in your will?	Embarrassing to interviewer because of absurdity for most respondents, or embarrassing to respondent because of personal nature of subject	52
Do you think masturbation can cause mental illness?	Embarrassing to both interviewer and respondent because subject matter is generally taboo	51
What was the total income of your family last year?	Embarrassing to respondent because of personal nature of subject	27

* The percentages in this table are based on 150 interviewers.

interview. Chief among these, perhaps, are the individual judgments which he must make in the classification of the responses to pre-coded questions. Of course, in many, or perhaps most cases, there exists no problem, since the majority of answers to poll questions are usually classifiable in the terms required by the question. However, in the course of completing his assignment the interviewer meets with many respondents whose answers are ambiguous, and who therefore present to the interviewer a psychological problem in making the necessary judgment in order to classify the answer.[54] It is well known from experimental studies that judgments of material which is not thoroughly objective and structured can be influenced by extraneous factors, and by the context in which the material is placed. Some of the opinions reported to the interviewer may be affected by the same processes. In addition, it is known from other experimental studies involving the use of "absolute scales" that the meaning of categories on a scale is not rigid, and that the scale may be "anchored" differently for individual judges depending on a variety of experimental factors.[55] It would seem likely, therefore, that there would be opportunity for the interviewer's beliefs, attitudes, and idiosyncrasies to influence the way he defines the categories and the task, and the way he makes the judgments entailed in classifying respondents' answers. Indeed, it might even seem essential to the interviewer to simplify the difficult task he occasionally faces by availing himself of various psychological aids to judgment.

Beyond the judgmental problems in classifying answers, there may be a motivational factor present, which would presumably make bias more likely to occur when interviewers are required to classify responses. In addition to the unconscious factors that operate to influence judgment, whatever conscious motivations there are to bias the results can operate with greater freedom under such conditions. Should an interviewer deliberately or carelessly distort the results in the process of classification, no one in the home office can tell from the mere check mark in a given answer box that such distortion has occurred.[56] However, under the requirements of verbatim recording, any bias or dishonesty on the part of the interviewer might more easily be detected by reference to the context of answers, or by the existence of patterned phrases in his completed interviews. That interviewers may well realize this was revealed in the course of the experiment in which interviewers were asked to record a dummy interview and explain aloud the process by which they did their recording. As one interviewer remarked when faced with coding a difficult answer: "You have to come to a decision —there's more of a tendency to decide there and less anxiety about how to code it because the office does not know what the respondent said. There's no danger; the office can't decide whether I did right unless they make correlations and see that the particular answer doesn't fit in."

Moreover, where responses must be classified into answer boxes, freedom for the interviewer is even sanctioned to some extent merely by the way the situation is defined in his preliminary instructions. For this method of recording, he is usually told to check "the answer that comes closest to the respondent's opinion." But under conditions of verbatim recording, he is told to record "exactly what the respondent said." Since he is given much less leeway under the latter method, we would expect bias to be less in evidence.

For all these reasons, it seemed fruitful to study this particular aspect of the interview situation. Under conditions of field classification, one might expect to find greater interviewer effects than under conditions of verbatim recording.

In an experiment conducted by NORC, the results secured for equivalent samples under contrasted methods of recording—classification versus verbatim report were compared.[57] Since this was an attempt to test the effect of the classification procedure per se, not the question type, questions with stated alternatives were used in both situations, the only difference between them consisting of the requirement that the answers be classified into pre-coded answer boxes in one case and recorded verbatim in the other.

It was found that over-all survey results on the three attitudinal questions tested were not affected by the process of field classification, but that the distribution of results on the fourth question measuring level of information was affected by field classification. Requiring interviewers to classify respondents' level of information showed a lower over-all level of awareness than when the verbatim responses were later coded in the NORC offices. (See Table 52.)

For the total field staff, specific tests of effects deriving from interviewer expectations or interviewer ideology revealed no differences under the two procedures. The data from some of these tests are presented in Tables 53 and 54. Although in *general* the over-all effects due to classification were minimal, there was suggestive evidence that the results obtained by inexperienced members of the staff were more affected by the classification procedure than those of the experienced. On two of the four questions, the differences for inexperienced interviewers were significant at the .01 level, and the aggregated Chi-square for all four questions gives a probability of only .01 that the differences

TABLE 52

THE VARIATION IN OVER-ALL RESULTS UNDER TWO METHODS OF RECORDING

	Percentage Classified by Interviewer	Percentage Recorded Verbatim
U.S. spending too much on European Recovery Program.....	43	39
Spending about right amount........................	38	38
Spending not enough...............................	4	5
Don't know.......................................	15	18
	100	100
Heard about North Atlantic Pact.....................	55	62
Had not heard about it.............................	45	38
	100	100
In favor of North Atlantic Pact......................	75	77
Opposed...	12	12
Don't know.......................................	13	11
	100	100
North Atlantic Pact makes war more likely..............	14	14
Makes peace more likely............................	65	64
It makes no difference..............................	7	4
Don't know.......................................	14	18
	100	100
	N = 646	N = 635

TABLE 53

THE EFFECT OF INTERVIEWER'S IDEOLOGY ON RESPONDENT OPINIONS UNDER TWO METHODS OF RECORDING*

PERCENTAGE OF RESPONDENTS WHO	CLASSIFIED BY INTERVIEWERS			RECORDED VERBATIM		
	Pro-Interviewers	Anti-Interviewers	Difference	Pro-Interviewers	Anti-Interviewers	Difference
Approve amount being spent on overseas aid....	52	54	2	57	44	13
Approve of the North Atlantic Pact..........	87	77	10	89	81	8
Believe North Atlantic Pact will make peace more likely..........	74	70	4	70	67	3

* The number of cases on which the percentages were based are as follows: for pro-interviewers using answer boxes, 345–354; anti-interviewers using answer boxes, 66–68; pro-interviewers using verbatim recording, 330–379; anti-interviewers using verbatim recording, 62–64.

would have occurred by chance, compared with a probability of .30 for the experienced.[58] These data are presented in Table 55. The latter findings are at variance with an earlier study reported in Cantril in which level of experience showed no relation to amount of over-all bias. However, one should note that his experiment differed in certain essential respects from the one here reported. The earlier study dealt with over-all amount of bias rather than bias introduced specifi-

TABLE 54

THE EFFECT OF ATTITUDE-STRUCTURE EXPECTATIONS UNDER TWO METHODS OF RECORDING

	CONTINGENCY CO-EFFICIENTS BETWEEN PAIRS OF ANSWERS IN WHICH THE EXPERIMENTAL QUESTION WAS*	
	Classified by Interviewer	Recorded Verbatim
Respondent's opinion on U.S. participation in world affairs and opinion about the North Atlantic Pact...............	.24	.23
Respondent's opinion on the Marshall Plan and opinion on the amount to be spent on overseas aid.....................	.59	.56
Respondent's opinion on the North Atlantic Pact and his belief that it makes war or peace likely.....................	.79	.75

* The number of cases on which the co-efficients were based under pre-coded conditions ranged from 482 to 522, whereas the number of cases for the verbatim conditions ranged from 473 to 537. Certain cells were not used in this part of the analysis because of difficulty in interpreting what pairs of answers were indicative of expectation effects. Because these calculations were made on 2 x 2 tables, the co-efficients have been corrected for the influence of broad categories. While the differences in the co-efficients under the two conditions are small, some suggestive evidence in support of our hypothesis is afforded by the fact that the difference between the co-efficients under the two conditions increases in the hypothesized direction as the pair of attitudes becomes more closely associated, despite the fact that the reverse would be expected on grounds of sampling variance.

TABLE 55

THE DIFFERENTIAL EFFECTS OF FIELD CLASSIFICATION AMONG EXPERIENCED AND INEXPERIENCED INTERVIEWERS

	THE PROBABILITY THAT THE OBTAINED DIFFERENCES IN THE OVER-ALL RESULTS UNDER TWO METHODS OF RECORDING WOULD OCCUR AS A RESULT OF SAMPLING FOR INTERVIEWERS WHO ARE	
	Experienced	Inexperienced
Attitude toward amount being spent on European recovery....	.60	.52
Awareness of North Atlantic Pact.......................	.05	.01
Attitude toward North Atlantic Pact....................	.46	.01
Belief that North Atlantic Pact makes war likely or peace likely...	.75	.28

cally in the classification process, and the interviewers defined as "inexperienced" had considerably more experience than those in the present study.[59]

If we postulate that interviewer effects in pre-coded questions arise as a function of the demand on the interviewer that he make "on-the-spot" judgments, it would seem to follow that such effects would be more frequent where the answers given by respondents are ambiguous. It has been previously pointed out that this is true for free-answer material; it would seem all the more likely to occur in pre-coded questions, since the alternative of merely writing down the verbatim responses is not available to the interviewer and he must in all such cases make a judgment of some sort. It would follow then, that if by some accident of procedure we increased the frequency of responses which might prove difficult for the interviewer to classify, we would thereby increase the likelihood that he introduces error through beliefs, desires and expectations which are activated as an aid in making the necessary judgments.

Several studies provide data bearing on this hypothesis. In the study by Cahalan and associates referred to in the foregoing, questions in which alternatives are only partially stated or in which an alternative not stated in the question may be recorded seem to be channels for the introduction of bias.[60] It seems likely that such questions actually elicit more ambiguous answers than questions of other types.

A more elaborate test of this hypothesis was provided by an experiment conducted by NORC.[61] The degree of ideological bias was measured first under a condition which strongly increased the frequency of uncodable or ambiguous answers and then under conditions which reduced such answers. This was accomplished by changing one question on half the questionnaires, so that a frequently selected middle category was omitted from the stated alternatives. Since this category was a normal repository for unstructured opinions on the question, its omission would presumably leave the interviewer with a sizeable number of ambiguous responses which required classification.

Results secured through this experiment were most revealing. It was found that on the form of the question where there was no ambiguity in the stated alternatives, differences between ideologically contrasted interviewers were not significant, whereas under the second form— where a large proportion of answers presented problems of classification —interviewers tended to classify the ambiguous responses in accordance with their own ideology. The data are presented in Table 56.

If the question form had no relation to bias arising from the inter-

TABLE 56

DISTRIBUTION OF RESPONSES UNDER TWO FORMS OF THE SAME QUESTION FOR INTER-
VIEWERS OF CONTRASTED IDEOLOGY

	FORM A (ALTERNATIVE OMITTED) AMONG INTERVIEWERS HOLDING		FORM B (ALTERNATIVE INCLUDED) AMONG INTERVIEWERS HOLDING	
	Majority Opinion	Minority Opinion	Majority Opinion	Minority Opinion
	Percentage of Respondents Answering		Percentage of Respondents Answering	
Less likely (majority)......	55	40	42	41
More likely (minority).....	19	30	18	22
No difference...........	18	9	32	27
Don't know.............	8	21	8	10
	100	100	100	100
	N = 250	N = 88	N = 249	N = 86

viewer's own ideology, we would expect differences between the distributions secured by interviewers of contrasted ideology to be about the same under both forms. However, if such bias were more operative under one form than the other, we would find greater differences between contrasted interviewers under that form. In the foregoing comparison of the two question forms, the reader can see that differences between the distributions of the two interviewer groups are in the same direction in both forms but are considerably greater under Form A than under Form B. Testing these differences by the Chi-squared method, we find that under Form B the differences are not significant,[62] while under Form A they are significant at the .01 level. Here, then, is evidence that the form of the question affects the degree of bias introduced by virtue of the interviewer's ideology. Under the question form which omitted the "no difference" alternative, ideologically contrasted interviewers got significantly different results, whereas under the other form they did not.

Detailed data presented in the original report also reveal that interviewer effects deriving from ideological factors may operate in different ways for different ideological groups. It was found that interviewers holding the "majority" political view exerted their bias by an inflation of the category in which they themselves would have responded, while those in a "minority" position biased answers by an inflation of the "don't know" category.

If the results secured here have any generality, they throw a somewhat new light on past suggestions for controlling interviewer effect.

For example, Cantril implicitly assumed that ideological bias works *in the same way* for interviewers of contrasted ideologies when he recommended:

> Although interviewer bias exists, by and large the biases in one direction cancel those in the opposite direction, so that the overall percentage of opinion is not likely to be significantly wrong. . . . If an investigator wants to minimize interviewer bias, he should choose an equal number of interviewers who are biased in different directions.[63]

Were we to follow Cantril's prescription in the use of question Form A in the foregoing, it is obvious that the biases would hardly "cancel themselves out." While the majority category is unduly inflated by the majority interviewers, the minority interviewers express their effects mainly through inflating the "don't know" and therefore do not inflate the specific minority category in a balancing fashion. In other words, a net shift of the distribution toward the explicit majority position would unquestionably take place.

Although we have no empirical evidence as to why bias works in such different fashions for the two groups of ideologically opposed interviewers, certain conjectures can be advanced as possible explanations of the phenomenon. First of all, the experimental literature gives ample evidence that the perception of scale values differs for different individuals, and that such perceptions vary with cultural, personal-historical and situational factors.[64] Therefore, it would seem likely that individuals with such different viewpoints as the majority and minority interviewer would be likely to perceive the significance of the scale categories in strikingly different ways.

Thus, even if the opposed groups of interviewers were equally *motivated* to bias responses in conformity with their own ideology, it is quite conceivable that the majority interviewers might perceive *only* the majority category as agreement with their position. By contrast, the minority interviewers might perceive *all* the categories, other than the majority one, as agreement. Merely in terms of the relativity of judgment, the interviewer who knows that the majority of people are against him, might regard it as a considerable victory to find any respondent who even goes so far as to question the validity of the prevailing viewpoint, even if the respondent does not completely espouse the minority viewpoint. They are not completely against him and might even be "won over." The interviewer who is characteristically in a minority position lives in a hostile world, with the odds stacked against him, and anyone is welcomed who even indicates mild doubts about the prevailing position. Thus, in a sense, our minority interviewer might see the "don't know" category quite differently from our majority interviewer. Interpreting it as a vote against the majority, it might serve him as a satisfactory category for the disposition of doubtful answers.

Moreover, if we conjecture about one further element of the situation, the finding that the minority interviewer does bias the responses by inflating the "don't know" category becomes even more understandable. In earlier chapters, it was noted that in addition to expectations arising from the respondent's attitude structure as revealed by cues in the interview, or from his group membership, interviewers have expectations about the attitude *any* respondent would probably have, on the basis of estimates of the prevailing sentiment on well-known issues.

We assume therefore, that both the majority and minority interviewers initially approach any given respondent with the expectation that he will probably take the majority view on an issue. What happens when the respondent gives an uncertain or "biasable" answer? The majority interviewer tends to "press" the uncertain answer into the majority category because, in him, expectation and desire coincide. The minority interviewer, however, is subject to cross-pressures. On the one hand, he expects a majority answer and, on the other hand, his ideology motivates him to desire a minority answer. To "press" this doubtful answer into the minority category is to depart a considerable distance down the scale from his prior expectation. The "don't know" category, however, is a lesser distance down the scale from his prior expectation in the direction of his ideology. Since, as we have already suggested, the minority interviewer perceives this category as partial agreement with his ideology, he can resolve these cross-pressures by assimilating answers into the "don't know" category and still satisfy whatever drive exists to inflate the percentage "on his side."

If the findings of this one experiment, *plus* the conjectural explanation, are substantiated by further research, they will have important implications for the interpretation of survey results. If this kind of differential manifestation of bias for majority versus minority interviewers occurs regularly in such situations, poll results for such question types will be systematically biased toward the majority end of the scale, especially on issues in which the prevailing sentiment is clear-cut and well-known to interviewers. Since many questions now in common use are prone to such ambiguous responses, a false picture of public sentiments may often be presented.

Further research is needed to substantiate the theory discussed in the foregoing. For example, experiments parallel to the one here reported, on issues where interviewers have no preconceptions about the prevailing viewpoint, would be instructive. If no such differential manifestations of bias occurred under these conditions, it would lend support to our speculations regarding the influence of expectations in producing such effects and would indicate within what domain such errors in interpretation are present.

Effects Arising from Increased Opportunity for Expectational Processes

In an earlier chapter, we have described expectational processes which lead to bias. While these sources of interviewer effect are latent in every interviewing situation, it is clear that the degree to which they are operative may be in part a function of the situation itself. A brief consideration of the situational facilitators of these biasing processes is given below, with some experimental demonstrations of specific situational effects.

Role effects.—In some kinds of interviewing situations, it is difficult for role expectations to operate. If the respondents are a homogeneous group, whose characteristics as individuals cannot be estimated by the interviewer on the basis of their appearance or manner, role effects would be minimal. Conversely, where there is wide disparity between individuals in the sample, we would expect an increased possibility of role effects. Likewise, where the individual is interviewed "in context" —such as his own home—it is possible that the characteristics of the home might be used by the interviewer as an aid in forming judgments about the responses of the individual.

Questions whose content is "role-linked" will certainly be more conducive to the operation of role effects. Thus the situational factor of question content may act to inhibit or heighten role expectations. The study by Feldman, reported in Chapter III, bears this out. As previously noted, these tests were made on a series of questions dealing with the purchase of various items by the respondent, almost always a woman, and by the spouse, generally the husband.

In the earlier discussion of these findings, support was adduced for the view that the significant differences obtained on the questions about gasoline, automobile repairs, housefurnishings and clothing by the matched interviewers was due to the relative "proneness" of given interviewers to expectations about the normal buying roles of husbands and wives.

However, what was not emphasized in the earlier treatment was the fact that on those items whose purchase is not thought of as the role of a particular sex, there were no significant differences between pairs of interviewers for reports about purchases either by the respondent herself or her spouse. It will be recalled from discussion earlier in this chapter that interviewer effects may be represented in fairly uniform distortions of data among all interviewers, or they may be manifest as variations among interviewers resulting from individual differences. Apparently there is no significant variation among interviewers on these items, because there is no particular problem of "role linkage" for aspects of purchasing-behavior for such items as drugs or hardware, or such services as banking, dentistry, and entertainment.

Apart from question *content* as a situational determinant of role effects, the Feldman findings also provided some evidence that other *formal* features of questionnaire design facilitated role effects. Data were presented in Chapter III to show that the presence of a question early in the questionnaire "tipped off" the interviewer to certain characteristics of the respondent and affected his handling of the subsequent questions on purchasing-behavior. While such processes are normally subsumed in our theory under "attitude-structure expectations," in this instance the prior question altered the belief of the interviewer about the *roles* of the husband and wife. Thus, the evidence has relevance to the discussion of role effects, and the influence of questionnaire design on such effects.

Attitude-structure effects.—Like role effects, attitude-structure effects may be increased by situational factors. An "interlocking" questionnaire, or one in which the questions are related to the same general area of opinion, facilitates effects by providing the interviewer many cues about the respondent's attitude structures. Thus this kind of questionnaire would be expected to induce greater effects of this nature than one in which questions asked have no presumptive attitudinal relation to each other.

One specific situational factor affecting attitude-structure expectations was studied in the experiment of Smith and Hyman. In this test, the *order* in which interviews were collected was the situational variable tested.[65] It is possible to separate those subjects who heard the interview which simulated the "ignorant" respondent *initially* from those subjects who heard that respondent only *after* they had been exposed to the markedly contrasting "intelligent" respondent. That the application of subjects to orders was fairly random is illustrated by the fact that the mean age and sex distribution of the two subgroups were identical.

This situational factor of order of interviewing carries with it the likelihood that the contrast experienced between successive respondents enhances the perception of their respective attitude structures. The incidence of expectational sources of error may therefore not be purely a function of the proneness of the interviewer, but of the accident of the sequence of interviewing. That such factors actually operate is shown in Table 57. In the five instances presented, and in three other tests, the results uniformly demonstrate that the effect of attitude-structure expectations is enhanced by the contrast experienced as a result of the specific situational factor of sequence of interviewing.

TABLE 57

THE ASSIMILATION OF EQUIVOCAL ANSWERS INTO AN "IGNORANT ISOLATIONIST" ATTI-
TUDE-EXPECTATION STRUCTURE OR "INTELLIGENT INTERNATIONALIST" STRUCTURE AS
RELATED TO THE SITUATIONAL FACTOR OF CONTRAST

	SUBJECTS WHO HEARD THE ISOLATIONIST TRANSCRIPTION	
	Initially	After Internationalist
Proportion of subjects coding the Isolationist respondent as taking no interest in U.S. policy toward Spain..........	None of the 9 subjects	4 of the 8 subjects
Mean rating on respondent's attitude toward international affairs (rating of "5" indicates maximum isolationism) ...	3.8	4.8
Mean rating on respondent's interest in international affairs (rating of "3" means no interest).....................	2.56	3.0
	SUBJECTS WHO HEARD THE INTERNATIONALIST TRANSCRIPTION	
	Initially	After Isolationist
Proportion of subjects coding the Internationalist respondent as "Approving amount U.S. is spending on European recovery"..	4 of the 8 subjects	8 of the 9 subjects
Mean rating on respondent's attitude toward international affairs (rating of "1" means maximum interventionism) ..	1.63	1.56

Probability effects.—Particular situations may give rise to some belief as to the probable distribution of opinion among the population. For example, probability effects could occur after some interviews had been conducted by any one interviewer. In such a case he might, in the course of his initial experience, develop some idea about the probable distribution of sentiments. Thus the number or sequence of interviews conducted by a given interviewer on the particular survey might affect the operation of this source of bias.

Such a theory is difficult to test empirically and we have no sub-

224 Interviewing in Social Research

stantial evidence on the problem. However, a suggestive demonstration of this phenomenon is available as a by-product of a study conducted by Curtis Publishing Company.[66] In one study of magazine readership, the material used for "confusion control" purposes was repeated in successive surveys. (In the use of this technique, interviewers are not informed that the control material has never appeared in magazine form.) Since the samples used in the successive surveys were equivalent, one would expect that each sample would contain approximately the same per cent of respondents who claim to have read the nonexistent magazine material each time. The actual results obtained on the repeated studies is presented in Table 58.

TABLE 58

Change in the Proportion of Readers of Nonexistent Magazine Content in Successive Surveys

Exhibits Used:	Percentage of "Readers"			
	1st Time	2d Time	3d Time	4th Time
4 times				
A......................	12.4	10.6	11.3	9.3
3 times				
B......................	13.1	16.4	10.4	
C......................	9.0	9.9	5.1	
D......................	17.6	16.4	14.7	
E......................	9.3	6.4	7.7	
F......................	13.3	8.6	11.0	
2 times				
G......................	12.6	11.9		
H......................	9.4	9.0		
I......................	5.5	8.3		
J......................	24.2	20.0		
K......................	18.7	7.5		

It may be seen from inspection that in general the average number claiming readership declines as the control material is used again. In the eighteen comparisons, we find that in twelve cases there is a decline in the proportion identifying the material, and in only six cases is there an increase in this proportion. Moreover, the total net decline is about three times as great as the total net increase.

Since one would expect only slight random variations due to sampling, the most logical explanation for the results secured in this study is that probability expectations were operating among interviewers. As they used the material, they came increasingly to expect that respondents would not indicate readership.

CHAPTER VI

Interviewer Effects Under Normal Operating Conditions

In the previous chapters, we have demonstrated how and why interviewers may distort survey results under *certain specific or relatively simple conditions*, but we have thus far presented little data bearing on the magnitude of such distortion in the course of *normal survey operations*.

Some of the evidence presented in Chapter III, for example, was based on laboratory-like studies. The findings of these studies contribute greatly to our understanding of a given process or component of interviewer effect in isolation from the many other factors that operate simultaneously with them in actual field situations. But they do not enable us to infer the extent of distortion under the complicated conditions of a field survey, since we cannot analyze fully enough the actual situation into its components and their interactions.

Other evidence presented in Chapters III and IV was derived within a field situation of a complex nature. However, our generalizations about the extent of distortion in normal operations are again hindered, since we concentrated our discussion on a specific determinant of interviewer effect and abstracted that factor from the total array of factors. Expectations, group membership, ideology, and the like, all operate simultaneously. While understanding is increased by the analysis of these factors separately, it is also important to study their combined effects and to find out how frequently and to what extent these effects are a problem in practical field operations. When one considers, further, the evidence presented in Chapter V that the effects of these distorting factors vary with a host of minor situational factors and realizes that previous studies have been based on a limited range of situations, it is clear that there is a need for observing these effects over many studies.

For these reasons, we must observe interviewer effect under a wide variety of complex operating conditions in order to evaluate its normal extent. In this chapter, we shall present the relatively small body of data which was specially gathered under conditions appropriate to such generalizations. We will supplement these limited data by review of the past literature in an attempt to improve our estimate of the extent of interviewer effects.

Before examining the empirical findings, it is well to distinguish several different classes of measurements of interviewer effects. These classes cannot be rigorously defined here, but even a cursory consideration of them enables us roughly to place our empirical work in the perspective of the total problem. Three such classes of measurements will be treated here.

1. GROSS EFFECTS

Strictly speaking, interviewer distortion exists whenever there is any deviation from the "true" response (defined in terms of the purposes of the study) in the response elicited and recorded by the interviewer for a given respondent to a given question. Gross interviewer effect over an entire survey may then be defined as a function of the total number of such individual deviations (each deviation weighted ideally by the degree to which it distorts the conclusions reached by the research).[1] It is obvious that in order to measure interviewer effect on this level it is necessary to have a validity criterion—some conception of what the "true" response for a given respondent to a given question is. Since any such validity criterion for attitude or opinion questions is rarely, if ever, available and the criterion data for questions of fact or behavior are seldom obtainable even when such data do exist, the measurement of gross interviewer effect in this strict sense is seriously limited even though it would be extremely desirable.

Certain approximations to the measurement of gross interviewer effect may, however, be more feasible. For instance, one can prescribe a given set of interviewing techniques as minimizing distortion (e.g., the interviewer should not use loaded probes, the interviewer should record exactly what the respondent says). Then, by direct observation or by some sort of mechanical recording of the total interview, one could measure the degree to which the interviewing prescriptions were broken. Ideally, neither the interviewer nor the respondent should be aware that his behavior is being either directly observed or recorded, but this condition has to our knowledge only rarely been met. Still, some sort of compromise where one or both parties are aware of being observed might still throw some light on the extent of gross interviewer effect, assuming that our prescriptions of "proper" interviewing technique are in line with our goals.[2]

Another conceivable way of gaining some insight into the possible extent of gross interviewer distortion is through having each respondent answer the same questions or discuss the same subject matter through several different media—for instance, through a self-administered questionnaire and a personal interview. The discrepancies in the responses gathered for each respondent for each question or subject matter through the different approaches are examined. The central difficulty with this approach is that it is almost impossible to determine in any specific instance which of the two responses, the oral or the written, is the more nearly valid. There is also the possibility that in many instances, when the two responses differ or even when they are the same, both responses are invalid.

The suggested technique could also be used by having each respondent interviewed by two or more interviewers using the same interview schedule. If one makes some assumption as to the relative skills of the interviewers, the superior one can be regarded as a criterion interviewer against which gross effects can be evaluated. Such an assumption may be warranted, under conditions where specially trained or highly professional personnel are used as check interviewers as in the Census quality check procedure. This technique has essentially the same shortcomings as the foregoing, but with even more danger that constant distortions, those common to all interviewers, will be obscured. Consequently, estimates derived from such an approach, at best, set a *lower limit* on the true extent of gross effects.

Another approximation to the measurement of gross effect involves the use of "sleeper questions"—that is, questions for which certain answers, by definition, are invalid. This would be the case, for example, in an answer by a respondent that he had read a nonexistent magazine. Such items are readily constructed and easily applicable to most surveys. Their use as measures of gross effects has not been sufficiently explored, although it must be realized that there is some limitation in generalizing about the magnitude of effects on other characteristics from the findings on bizarre, nonexistent items.

It should be noted that all these techniques are extremely difficult to use in the natural field-setting. Even if the co-operation of the respondent could be obtained, the very attempt to record an interview with a tape recorder or have the same respondent interviewed with the same schedule several times may in itself make the situation so unlike the "natural" field-setting that the findings would tell us relatively little about the magnitude of gross interviewer effect under normal operating conditions. The entire problem of the measurement of gross effect thus falls under the Principle of Indeterminacy, and thus far, no one has thought of an approach that makes the act of measurement itself intrude less into the field situation we are trying to measure. Only occasional studies attempting to measure the extent of gross interviewer effects are reported in this chapter. Only a limited number have been conducted, and most of those that have been made were done under conditions hardly comparable to normal field conditions. At this point, we can merely hope that some day the necessary resources to make further advances in the study of gross effects will become available.

It should be noted that the concept of gross interviewer effect defined in this section, by implication, attributes to the interviewer or the interviewing process all invalidity in interview material. For some purposes it might be desirable to distinguish between irremediable invalidity; i.e., invalidity which could not be remedied by any change in interviewing technique or interviewer characteristics—for example, that due solely to the respondent—and invalidity which could conceivably be removed by the alteration of some controllable element of the interview situation. A design appropriate to this problem would combine the use of criterion data of validity with the assignment of interpenetrating samples to classes of interviewers. Then the differential level of validity could be examined to determine the influence of the interviewer factor on gross effects. For other purposes, it would be well to distinguish between invalidity that would remain if the most feasible alternative method to the personal interview were used to gather the requisite data and the excess invalidity due to the use of the personal interview. A design appropriate to this problem would involve comparison of results for different enumeration procedures by reference to criterion data. Such hypothetical alternative formulations point to the fact that the degree to which gross effect need concern us depends on whether it can be remedied, whether there are other means of gathering data which would enable us to reduce or eliminate it, and whether it affects the over-all findings of the study.

2. NET EFFECTS

Net effects may be defined as the difference between the distribution of responses obtained by one or more interviewers to one or more questions from a given *population* of respondents and the "true" distribution of responses to that question or questions for that population. Here distortions in opposite directions may conceivably cancel each other so that, even though the responses of particular respondents have been distorted, there is no net distortion in the marginal distribution or even in cross-tabulations. This level of measurement is, of course, very different from gross effect, where all distortions of the individual responses of individual respondents are always considered as cumulative and never as canceling out.[3]

Net effects can be calculated relative to any body of data in the survey. They can be determined for the total group of interviewers and the total sample of respondents or for a subgroup of interviewers and/or a subgroup of respondents, or even for one interviewer and his respondents. The errors are simply determined for whatever is the group under investigation. Obviously, net effects can occur relative to any or all possible groupings of the data. From a practical point of view, the particular net effects that should be our central concern are those occurring at the specific level of cross-tabulation most crucial to the survey.

The problems of measurement discussed in connection with gross effects also arise here. However, while we would again be plagued by the problem of what the "true" responses for our given purpose are, in cases where we have defined such "true" responses, it should be simpler to obtain the *distribution* of these responses (e.g., from records or other sources) than it would be to obtain the individual true responses. That this is so is clearly indicated by the past literature. As will be seen below, the number of direct studies of gross effects is very few, whereas there have been innumerable studies of net effects. In a certain sense, the many election prediction studies approximate to measurement of net effects. Other usual examples involve the comparison of survey results with aggregate records (the distribution of true responses) of bond purchases, sales of commodities, etc., for a given population, which are readily available in the files of government or industry.

While there are many such studies, they are confined mainly to the determination of net effects on the marginals for the entire sample of respondents interviewed by all interviewers. This is no doubt due to the availability of criterion records only in this limited form. In the light of our remarks that net effects at some higher level of cross-tabulation may be most important, the general unavailability of the refined statistical distribution of the criterion data puts serious limitations on the practical value of such past literature. It not only limits us in qualifying the accuracy of specific findings; it also prevents us from drawing inferences as to the origin of net effects.

An approximation to the measurement of net effect can be made by having either the same group of respondents or different random samples of respondents from a single universe investigated by personal interview and by some other means, and then comparing the distributions of responses obtained by the different means. In practice, it is of course difficult to say definitely which of the distributions—the one obtained by interview or the one obtained by other means—approximates more closely the "true" distribution, although the investigator may often be reasonably certain that one of them is superior.[4]

Another approach to net effects involves having either the same respondents or different random samples of respondents from a single universe interviewed by different interviewers using the same schedule, and then comparing the distributions obtained by the different interviewers. This approach is again severely limited by the impossibility of determining which of the interviewers is getting the more nearly valid responses, and by the possibility that even when several interviewers get similar distributions they have all merely distorted responses in the same direction. But whenever significant variation among the distributions of responses obtained by different interviewers is found, we can be sure that at least some of the interviewers are introducing distortion. Also, in instances when most of the interviewers get quite similar distributions of responses and one or two interviewers get radically different results, it is often assumed that the interviewers getting the more common results are getting the more nearly valid results while the deviant interviewers are distorting their findings more.[5] There are, also, occasional situations where we have certain more or less a priori beliefs concerning the way people behave in the interview situation, on the basis of which we judge which of the response distributions is more nearly valid. For instance, we can assume that certain interviewers, perhaps the regular staff supervisers, are highly skilled in eliciting what for our purposes are valid responses, particularly if they use a certain type of interview schedule and procedure; the responses elicited by them can then be used as the criterion distribution against which to compare the work of other interviewers using equivalent samples of respondents.[6] Or our knowledge—or a priori belief—as to the nature of respondent opinions can be used to decide which of several distributions of responses is most nearly accurate. Or it can be assumed that an interviewer with characteristics similar to those of his respondents will obtain reasonably valid responses from these respondents.

In the following discussion, studies in which different interviewers interview samples of respondents from the same universe so that the distributions of responses can be compared without any particular criterion distribution in mind will be referred to as studies of *differential net effects*. Studies of this sort are extremely common. Although they are designed to determine the degree to which interviewers distort responses, they generally ignore biases that are constant over the entire staff of interviewers.[7] They are justified by two main arguments.

First, much of public opinion research is devoted to the determination of certain functional relations among the data rather than to precise description of the data by marginal distributions. A complete determination of interviewer effect upon a marginal distribution requires a knowledge of the net interviewer effect and, hence, of the true or criterion value. But if the effect of each interviewer on the response of every respondent is exactly the same (in magnitude and direction), the "distance" between the responses of any two individuals would be the same as if the responses were completely accurate, and correlations (which depend upon the distances between individuals) would be unaffected. It is, then, the differences among interviewers in their effect on responses that distort measures of relationship. Thus, to determine the interviewer effect on a correlation, we need to know only the differential net effect (the difference of an interviewer's results from the average for all interviewers) and not the absolute net effect (the difference of an interviewer's results from the true values). It is just the biases that are not constant which must be discovered and taken into account.

This argument, though abstract, does at least justify the study of differential net effects even in cases in which criterion distributions are not available and in which, therefore, the amount of bias in the marginals cannot be ascertained.

A second reason for special concern over differential net effects is the likelihood that the differential effects are those that are most subject to remedy. If some interviewers are known to do a better job than others, i.e., make either no errors or fewer errors of certain types than do other interviewers, then it should be possible to bring the worse interviewers up toward the level of the better interviewers, or we could at least improve the general level of interviewing through selective hiring practices. But errors common to all interviewers somehow appear to be less subject to correction because it is not yet clear that it is humanly possible to do better. While this generalization about the relation between differentiation and mutability might not hold universally, it seems well warranted in the light of our body of findings. Systematic effects of the expectational sort described in Chapter III seem firmly grounded in fundamental cognitive processes. Systematic effects deriving from group membership factors described in Chapter IV seem firmly grounded due to the current economics of the interviewer labor market. Thus to focus on differential net effects is most relevant and immediately practical.

Studies of differential net effects and/or of inter-interviewer variation are by far the easiest kind to make under operating field conditions. They can often be made at relatively little added expense as a by-product of a survey carried out for substantive purposes. In fact, if one ignores the important restriction that the samples of respondents interviewed by different interviewers be random samples from one universe (or that at least the variation between samples due to non-interviewer factors be known), studies of this general type can be done practically at will any time a survey is made. It is somewhat questionable, however, whether this type of study omitting controls over respondent factors is a desirable way of examining differential net interviewer effect.

3. INTER-INTERVIEWER VARIATION

Fundamental to the definition of inter-interviewer variation is a concept of a universe of interviewers. Then, in order to evaluate interviewer effects, we compare the distribution of responses actually obtained with the hypothetical distribution of responses that would be obtained from a given population if all the interviewers in the universe of interviewers were to interview all the respondents. Thus, there is no concern here, as there is in the case of gross and net effects, with the validity or truth of either individual responses or of a distribution of responses.

Inter-interviewer variation is the variation of the distributions of responses obtained by the different interviewers around the hypothetical distribution described in the foregoing. This variation is readily estimated by a design such as the one described under net effects, where different interviewers interview random samples from the same population of respondents and the distributions of responses thus obtained are compared with each other.

While the goal of studies of gross and net effect is to reduce the degree of invalidity in surveys or at least to determine means of taking that invalidity into account in interpreting survey results, the purpose of studies of inter-interviewer variation is to enable us to take into account an additional component of sampling variance when we set confidence intervals around estimates from survey data. This additional component of sampling variance is due to the fact that on any particular survey we are using only a sample from the universe of interviewers. Of course, the simple estimate of inter-interviewer variation is generally not the final goal of these studies. Almost all of them aim to determine ways of efficiently diminishing the contribution of interviewer variance to over-all sampling variance either through study design (e.g., determining the optimum number of interviewers to be used for a given sample design) or through interviewer hiring or training policy.

One serious difficulty underlying this approach is that the variance might sometimes be minimized around a distorted distribution (i.e., a hypothetical distribution different from the criterion distribution) if the vast majority of the universe of interviewers tended to get invalid responses. This qualification may be somewhat academic in the instance where there is no clear formulation or measure of what is a valid response. It might also overstate the danger, since it is unlikely that competent research workers would knowingly concentrate on the problem of reducing variance to the exclusion of the problem of bias. For instance, if it were found that only about half of an interviewing staff could benefit from training so that training tended to increase the differentiation in the quality of work between interviewers, it seems inconceivable that as a consequence of this anyone would forego training entirely in order to keep sampling error at a minimum. Thus, at the present, the devotion of resources to the reduction of interviewer variance is a reasonable course of action.

It should be noted here that the published papers on inter-interviewer variability that have come to our attention give at least token reference to the problem of validity. But the empirical sections of these papers usually ignore the problem of validity and devote themselves completely to variability.

4. STUDIES OF GROSS EFFECT

As was indicated earlier, there has been a paucity of studies of gross interviewer effects. On the basis of careful review of these studies the only clear conclusion is that gross effects assume no typical value but range widely depending on the specific study cited and the characteristic evaluated.[8] None of the past studies is directly informative on our current need for evidence on the influence of the interviewer on the level of validity of the data. Moreover, the character of the field staff which obtained the given findings is rarely indicated. Consequently, there is not even any inferential basis for relating variations in gross effects to given classes of interviewers over the total range of past studies.

The one major study designed to measure gross effect directly and to relate these effects to interviewer performance was the Opinion Research Center study in Denver in the Spring of 1949.[9] In this study, the individual responses to a number of factual questions were validated against official records. To questions concerning the possession of a library card, driver's license, and automobile (as well as the year and make of the automobile for owners), between 10 and 15 per cent of the respondents gave invalid responses. To questions concerning home ownership and the possession of a telephone, fewer than 5 per cent gave invalid answers. To a question concerning the age of the respondent, somewhere around 10 per cent of the answers were probably invalid. Far higher estimates were reported for the proportion of respondents giving invalid replies to a number of questions concerning whether or not the respondent voted in a series of elections or contributed to a community chest, but since the validity of the criterion records obtained in these cases is subject to some doubt, full reliance cannot be placed on these particular findings.

These data alone do not permit us to say exactly what portion of total invalidity can be ascribed to interviewer effect. But, if it could be shown that interviewers varied significantly in the proportion of invalid answers they elicited, then we could be certain that at least part of the over-all invalidity is due in a sense to some characteristics or behavior of the interviewer, or at least we could be sure of this for those interviewers who got the larger proportions of invalid responses. The statistical significance of the variation between interviewers in the proportion of respondents giving invalid responses was testable in this study since, in each of five sectors of Denver, each of nine interviewers was assigned a random sample of the respondents in his sector. Chi-squared tests of the significance of the inter-interviewer variation within sectors were made and cumulated over the five sectors. These tests failed to indicate any significant variation in validity among the forty-five interviewers. But, three other apparently more powerful tests did tend to show that there were actually real differences between interviewers in the degree to which they reported invalid responses for their respondents.[10] First of all, there were positive intercorrelations (the median value of the intercorrelations was +.39) between the proportions of invalid responses for a given interviewer for different questions.[11]

Further support from the same study for the existence of differences between interviewers may be found from the fact that members of certain classes of interviewers tended to get higher proportions of invalid responses than did the members of other classes. Inexperienced interviewers and interviewers whose performance on a response recording test indicated a tendency to allow attitude-structure expectations to distort their recording of responses tended to obtain relatively high proportions of invalid responses. These findings make it appear very likely that some of the interviewers were responsible for at least some of the invalidity found in the survey.[12]

We have thus far demonstrated that in the Denver study, a survey conducted under more or less normal field conditions, gross interviewer effects did occur. But, this particular type of study yields little direct information about the process through which this distortion occurred. Information of this latter type is best gathered through direct observation of interviews. But, as was pointed out earlier in this chapter, it would be extremely difficult to record a normal field interview without the knowledge of either the interviewer or the respondent. The closest approximations we have to this direct observation are two studies where wire or tape recordings were made of interviews between "planted" respondents and interviewers who were unaware of the "plant." In each of these studies, interviewers were given normal assignments including a number of randomly selected respondents as well as one or more respondents with whom it had previously been arranged that they answer questions in specified fashion in the interview. The interviewers were not aware that they were working on anything but a normal assignment, that any of the respondents were in any respect "planted," or that any of the interviews were being mechanically recorded. Thus, we here have controlled observations of interviewer behavior, since each respondent's behavior was essentially the same for each interviewer that interviewed him. This very stability of behavior on the part of the respondents, their failure to react spontaneously to the interviewer and be "affected" by him, does make the experiments rather unnatural, but they nevertheless yield some notion of the extent to which interviewers commit acts that are likely to produce bias in interviews.

The first of these studies was made by Lester Guest.[13] In his study, fifteen college student interviewers with varying degrees of interviewing experience all interviewed the same "planted" respondent. The respondent attempted to give, in so far as possible, the same responses to all the interviewers. The responses to different questions were prearranged to vary considerably in the degree of ingenuity in probing required on the part of the interviewer in order to elicit a full, codable answer from the respondent.

Criteria for a "good" interview were established, and the wire recording and completed schedule for the "planted" interview of each interviewer were scored for errors in terms of the criteria. The most frequent errors were all basically in the area of inadequate probing and recording of free responses. There were fifty-three instances where interviewers failed to record "side comments" or left out parts of a free response which were needed for the proper interpretation of what the respondent said. In sixty-six instances, interviewers failed to probe responses that were either vague, evasive, irrelevant, or general. In fact, in nineteen instances where the response was evasive, the interviewer circled a pre-code as if the question had actually been answered. In nineteen instances, also, the interviewers failed to probe for additional answers to a question where multiple answers were supposed to be elicited, and in twelve instances, "don't know" responses were not probed at all. Another frequent error was of a more or less clerical nature; the interviewers had been instructed to distinguish probed from unprobed answers, but they failed to do so in forty-one instances. A variety of other errors like utter fabrication of responses, changing of respondent's terminology in recording the response, changes in question wordings, and the introduction of the interviewer's own comments, ideas, and suggested answers all occurred with generally relatively smaller frequencies than did the probing and recording failures. Of course, it is difficult to evaluate these comparative findings without some idea of the number of opportunities available to the interviewer for making each type of error and some weighting of the errors in terms of the degree of resultant distortion. Nevertheless, the results show clearly that interviewers do commit certain errors which unquestionably lead to a distorted representation of the opinions or knowledge held by particular respondents.

Additional evidence from a laboratory-like study supports the Guest findings that the locus of gross effects is frequently in the area of inadequate probing behavior. In this experiment sixty-one interviewers on NORC's permanent field staff were sent questionnaires on which the verbatim answers to open-ended questions had already been recorded. They were told that these interviews had been obtained by other interviewers in the course of a regular survey, and they were instructed to code the verbatim answers into a prepared set of categories. To accomplish the task, they were sent general coding instructions and specific instructions for each question, similar to the standard coding instructions used. They were further instructed that if any particular answer did not fit any of the code categories, or if they were completely unable to decide on the appropriate code, they should indicate it as "uncodable" in its present form. In the instance of such "uncodable" answers, the interviewer was asked to indicate what additional probe he would have used to elicit a reply for the purpose of coding.

In actuality, the completed questionnaires were entirely fabricated and the answers were at different levels of codability, as indicated by the variation in the agreement among the interviewers in handling different answers.

The specific aspect of the findings relevant at this point was the extent of the tendency to probe when the answer was so vague or confusing or irrelevant as to require probing. As a criterion for scoring this aspect of interviewer performance, four judges, experienced members of the NORC professional staff, were independently given the answers and asked to perform the same task as that assigned the interviewers. Only in the instances where three out of four judges agreed on a particular answer was that answer used in scoring the interviewers. By reference to this criterion, there was a total of 701 uncodable answers among all the answers assigned to the sixty-one interviewers. The actual number of instances where the field staff suggested a probe, i.e., indicated that the answer was uncodable in its present form and listed an additional probe, was 418. Thus, in 40 per cent of the instances where expert judges claimed that the interviewers should have probed, they did not. This statistic, however, understates the frequency of total probing errors, in so far as some of the probes suggested for the remaining 60 per cent of the answers were inadequate in content. In order to determine the magnitude of error due to *poor quality of probing*, rather than to mere occurrence of probing, the specific probes suggested by the interviewers were again rated by judges according to fairly well-established and objective criteria.[14] Of the 418 probes suggested, 84 were judged to be of poor quality. In other words, error in the total realm of probing occurred for the staff as an aggregate in 52 per cent of the instances.

Of course, any generalization of this statistic is dependent in part on the similarity between the level of difficulty of the answers used in this experiment and the answers obtained in the usual survey. While no rigorous statement can be made on this problem, it can be said that most of the answers were at a middle level of difficulty, with only some at extreme levels of great ease or great difficulty, as indicated by the fact that the field staff rarely showed complete unanimity or complete disagreement in their replies. In addition, the question of the artificiality of the circumstances of the experiment limit the generalization. In some ways, the experiment was easier than the normal field situation, since the interviewers had leisure to consider their behavior, and no conflicting cues to hinder their judgment. However, they were operating in a situation where any of the normal aids to decision of a contextual or a spoken nature were eliminated. Despite these limitations, the general order of findings certainly supports the Guest finding that error may very frequently occur through the process of inadequate probing behavior.

It should be noted that many of the errors made in the Guest study need not necessarily have been biasing in any systematic direction or particularly motivated by anything but carelessness, lack of perseverance due to inadequate job involvement, or simply the inability to distinguish a full and unequivocal response from a vague, evasive, irrelevant response, and/or the inability to think of probes that would elicit the "proper" type of response. Thus, it would appear highly likely that the amount of gross effect would considerably exceed the amount of net effect because many of these errors would probably cancel each other.[15]

The Guest study also gives us some information on differential tendencies toward error among the interviewers. There was considerable variation between interviewers in the total number of errors, the range being from twelve to thirty-six with a mean of nineteen errors. But it is impossible, owing to the design of the study, to determine the degree to which this variation may be random. It is interesting, however, to note that every interviewer made at least three probing errors and at least three recording errors.[16] All but one of the interviewers made an error in asking the questions on the schedule. As for the type of error perhaps most likely to introduce bias into the interview, the introduction of the interviewer's own comments, ideas, or suggested answers, one interviewer was guilty of eight of the fifteen occurrences, while nine of the interviewers did not commit any such errors. This implies that while almost all interviewers do tend to commit errors which affect some of the responses recorded for individual respondents, relatively blatant biasing behavior is limited to a few aberrant interviewers. This conception of the operation of interviewer effect fits the theory and findings presented in Chapters II and III and the findings of the field studies of inter-interviewer variation discussed in detail later in this chapter.

The other study using recordings of interviews with planted respondents was made in New York City by the American Jewish Committee in co-operation with NORC.[17] In this study, fifteen interviewers were hired ostensibly for a special crew job. They were extremely heterogeneous with respect to previous interviewing experience and various personal characteristics. On the whole, though, they tended to be inexperienced at interviewing, two-thirds of them having had no previous interviewing experience at all. These were essentially people with little or no intrinsic interest in interviewing or in the subject matter of the study. They were merely trying to earn a little extra money on a part-time basis without necessarily intending to do any interviewing in the future. These recruits were thus more similar to the interviewers working on the usual crew job than to the permanent interviewing staff of survey agencies.

Each interviewer interviewed one to four "planted" respondents, and twelve of the interviewers interviewed eight or more uncoached respondents whom they selected in assigned households in assigned blocks.[18] The general procedure was to have the interviewer first interview a "planted" respondent playing the role of a "punctilious liberal," a person incapable of giving an unqualified, categorical response to any question. The respondent was instructed to be difficult to interview in terms of expressing ambivalent beliefs in all areas but to be friendly to the interviewer at the same time.

Following the interview with the "punctilious liberal," each interviewer interviewed several uncoached respondents. Then, he interviewed a "planted" respondent playing the role of a "hostile bigot." This respondent was instructed to be hostile, unco-operative, and suspicious of the entire situation. He generally required considerable persuasion to answer many of the questions at all and was on the whole quite vicious with the interviewer.

Following the "hostile bigot" interview, the interviewers interviewed several more uncoached respondents. Then they interviewed another "planted" respondent, who was coached to present different interviewing problems to the interviewer, rather than a specific uniform role. For example, in several instances, the respondent who was assigned to the interviewer was ostensibly not at home, but a roommate of the respondent was there and offered to act as a surrogate for the assigned person. In others, an aggressive wife was supposed to intrude into an interview with her husband, express her own opinions, and in general make a nuisance of herself. Several respondents were coached to appear more interested in the interviewer and in the interviewing than in the substance of the schedule, to make the situation difficult by trying to interview the interviewer, albeit in a friendly manner, rather than allowing themselves to be interviewed. The multiplicity of respondent roles to which the interviewers were exposed, in contrast with the unitary situation in the Guest study, carries us beyond the study of the general process by which gross error occurs. Comparing the behavior of the interviewers as they operate in the different circumstances presumably illuminates the influence of situational pressures.

The interviewers were totally unaware either of the fact that any of their cases were anything but ordinary, uncoached respondents or of the fact that any of the interviews were being tape recorded. Of course, the uncoached, regular respondent interviews were in all respects normal and were not tape recorded. These latter interviews were included mainly to establish verisimilitude to a normal survey.

The tape recordings were transcribed for the analysis. The typewritten transcriptions were then compared with the responses recorded by the interviewer on the schedule, and the errors found were tabulated. Also, the transcriptions were examined for interviewer behavior which could be considered as potentially distorting regardless of what was recorded on the interview schedule. Errors of this latter type were also tabulated.

Although for the A.J.C. study the classification and tabulation of various types of errors was not nearly so refined as that of the Guest study, we here, too, are able to learn a great deal about the processes through which gross effects occur, as well as their extent.

The errors made were classified in four broad categories:

1. *Asking errors:* omitting question or changing wording of question.

2. *Probing errors:* failing to probe when necessary, biased probing, irrelevant probing, inadequate probing, preventing the respondent from saying all he wishes to say.

3. *Recording errors:* recording something not said, not recording something said, incorrectly recording response.

4. *Flagrant cheating:* not asking question but recording a response, recording response when respondent does not answer question asked.

In tabulation, each error was counted equally. On the average, each interviewer committed thirteen asking errors, thirteen probing errors, eight recording errors, and four cheating errors on each schedule. There were fifty questions on the interview schedule, but it was possible to commit a number of errors on a single question. Still, the error rate was obviously extremely high. One should only take this finding, though, as indicative of the kinds of errors that do occur rather than as representing the extent of error on a normal survey, since it should be remembered that the "staged" situations were purposely set up in such a way as to induce the interviewer to make many errors. Although in the course of a normal survey an interviewer might well come upon a few respondents as difficult as those encountered here, a considerable proportion of respondents would normally be far easier to interview than the "planted" respondents. In easier interviewing situations, the interviewers would be far less prone to make errors. Also, it should be remembered that the interviewers employed for this experiment were on the whole inexperienced and not regular staff members of the agency conducting the survey. These latter factors might also partially account for the generally poor interviewing performance.

The errors appeared in general to be highly pervasive. Every interviewer made at least one error of each of the three non-cheating varieties. For this experiment, the number of errors committed by different interviewers did vary tremendously, but this variation could conceivably have been random. However, the study analysis suggests that the interviewer differences are real rather than random, and this seems the reasonable interpretation.

Cheating errors were less pervasive among the staff. Although every interviewer cheated at least once in the "hostile bigot" interview, four of the nine interviewers who turned in completed schedules for this respondent did not really cheat to an appreciable extent. These four recorded categorical responses to a few questions which the respondent had failed to answer or had answered in an irrelevant or equivocal fashion. However, the cheating of these four was of a completely different order of magnitude from the cheating of another four interviewers, who completely failed to ask a very large number of questions (from eighteen to thirty-three questions each), for which they recorded categorical responses as if the question had been properly asked and answered. These four interviewers clearly fabricated a large proportion of the interviews. A ninth interviewer also fabricated most of the "hostile bigot" interview, but he indicated on the schedule that he had done this because he felt he could not break through the respondent's hostility. This interviewer can really neither be classified as cheating or as not cheating.

While we cannot test statistically whether the differences in cheating behavior observed here represent true differences or whether they are simply due to sampling variation, the difference in extent of cheating behavior between the two groups of interviewers in this instance was very large. This fact and a number of other findings suggest strongly that there is some basic intra-individual determinant of cheating behavior. Thus, for example, it was demonstrated in these data that the stability of cheating behavior between split-halves of the interview was much higher than other forms of interviewer error. This demonstration, however, merely reveals that cheating is not affected much by minor types of variation occurring within a situation of some particular character. Those interviewers who blatantly cheated in the "hostile bigot" situation also resorted to cheating slightly more frequently in the "punctilious liberal" situation than did the other interviewers. But, owing to the over-all only slight incidence of cheating in the "punctilious liberal" interview, this difference can only be minor. We can say that there was slight evidence that there is a tendency for an interviewer who cheats in one situation to cheat in others, at least under the conditions of this survey. The evidence of apparent bimodality (and almost discontinuity) of the distribution of cheating among the interviewers is supported by Guest's finding that flagrant bias or cheating is aberrant behavior—an interviewer either cheats a great deal or very little in a *given* situation.

Yet, even with respect to cheating behavior, the impact of *major* situational pressures is clear. Thus, in the "punctilious liberal" situation, there was *on the whole* very little cheating. The greater extent of cheating in the more stressful "bigot" situation was clearly a function of the need to cheat in order to escape a painful situation as easily as possible. Even here, only half the interviewers interpreted the situation as requiring cheating. Consequently, interviewer cheating is a function of both individual differences and the nature of the situation.

In the Guest study, cheating was somewhat of a rarity; in the A.J.C. study, half the interviewers cheated. This was probably due to the enormous difference in the difficulty of the situations. The Guest "planted" respondent really didn't encourage the interviewer to cheat in order to finish the interview, while the "hostile bigot" situation obviously did place a premium on cheating. Since few respondents are as difficult as the "hostile bigot," the incidence of cheating on the Guest study probably approximates normal conditions more closely than the A.J.C. study.

We have thus seen that gross effects occur extensively and are mediated by certain processes. However, it does not follow that there will be serious consequences on the results. If the effect of a particular interviewer on a specific question were not consistent from respondent to respondent, these gross effects would tend to cancel out over respondents and there would be relatively little net effect on marginals. Gross effects might also cancel out over questions on a single subject matter for a given respondent. The interviewer might influence one response relating to a given subject matter in one direction and another response relating to the same subject matter in the opposite direction.

The magnitude of net effects will be dealt with directly in the next section. However, certain conclusions can be foreshadowed. There was some specific evidence from the A.J.C. study that some, although by no means all, of the effects did cancel within subject-matter areas. Further, the general evidence already presented, plus additional evidence below, indicating that much error arises from situational factors and varies over the range of different situations, suggests that there would be cancellation across respondents, and perhaps even within the interview of a single respondent. It is, then, clear that at least some gross effects would be in a sense random with respect to their influence on the substantive content of the recorded responses. However, there was also evidence in the A.J.C. experiment, reported in Chapter III, that much of the effect appeared to be due to "attitude-structure expectations." If attitude-structure expectations were prevalent, one would expect reinforcement of effects in a given subject-matter area for the same respondent. We are also led to believe that such expectations would have little net effect on marginals but relatively great effect on cross-tabulations. This is only a speculation, however. At present, we cannot determine the relative incidence of net as compared with gross effects.

While the examination of these tape-recorded interview studies leaves many questions unanswered, they provide valuable, definitive descriptions of what occurred in *particular* interview situations. Their limitations derive from their small-scale character—their use of a small number of interviewers of specific types, and of only a few "planted" respondents covering a limited number of types of situations.

In the preceding chapter, we gave some attention to the extent to which interviewer effect was persistent through time, considered in terms of the distributions of responses obtained by interviewers. Here we shall again present evidence on the persistence of effects, but use the individual respondent as the unit of analysis. We shall do this by comparing the reliability of responses of a given respondent when the responses are elicited by the *same* interviewer each time to the reliability of responses of a respondent when the responses are elicited by different interviewers. Examination of the repeat reliability data naturally bears on the problem of whether interviewer effects will be systematic. Since most of the data to be presented here refer to unchanging factual characteristics of the respondent, which do not change over time, any unreliability, by definition, represents error. Consequently, the aggregate findings of this analysis provide additional estimates of gross effects, while the refined treatment of the data provides evidence on the systematic occurrence of such effects.

If a given interviewer has an influence systematic over time on the responses of a given respondent, then one would expect less variation in response to a given question when the same interviewer interviews that respondent each time than when different interviewers interview that respondent. In order for the difference in reliability under the two different conditions to be large, the influence of any given interviewer on the responses of any given respondent (through interaction or any other means) must be highly persistent through time; i.e., if Interviewer A affects the responses of Respondent I in a particular fashion on one wave of a panel, he must affect those responses in the same way on the other waves of the panel. We are not directly measuring here whether a given interviewer affects the responses of *different* respondents similarly (our problem in the analysis of net effects). If the variable in the interview situation crucial to the determination of response is the interaction between a particular interviewer and a particular respondent and the nature of this interaction is not particularly subject to variation over time, there will be considerable systematic effects. But, if among the crucial variables are highly ephemeral aspects of the interviewing situation, like the time of day, the weather, how the interviewer and respondent happen to be feeling on the particular day of the interview, distractions, and other similar factors which might readily be expected to differ between two occasions when a given interviewer is interviewing a given respondent, then in general there will be little systematic effect over time, even though responses are unreliable.

Our data here comes from available panel studies, surveys where the same sample of individuals is interviewed two or more times. In many panel studies, through accident some respondents are interviewed on different waves by the same interviewer, while other respondents are interviewed by a different interviewer. These two sets of respondents constitute the basis of our comparisons.

Comparisons from a number of different panel studies are presented below. The results are essentially consistent in that, with rather few exceptions, the responses obtained from respondents interviewed by the same interviewers on both waves are *somewhat* more reliable than the responses elicited by different interviewers on the two waves. But, these differences in reliability are generally only of *moderate* magnitude. It is also true that there is generally a considerable degree of unreliability to the responses. Since in most instances the *actual* shift in the respondent's characteristics could only have been negligible, gross interviewer effect must have been rather widespread. This is especially true in light of the fact that whenever two interviewers produced the same error in the responses of a given respondent, or whenever a given interviewer produced the same erroneous response both times he interviewed a respondent, the interviewer effect is completely obscured in the analysis. Thus, we must conclude that some of the more ephemeral situational factors discussed earlier must be highly influential even as compared to the more persistent factors in the situation such as the personalities, relative socio-economic status, or age, etc., of the two participants in the interview situation, within the limits of the variability of the characteristics of the interviewing staffs involved.

The earliest study of this type was a study of interviewer ratings made by Mosteller.[19] In one study, a small national sample of respondents was interviewed twice with the same interviewers interviewing the same respondents on both waves. A three-week period intervened between the two waves of interviewing. In a second national study, respondents living in cities with more than 100,000 population were interviewed by different interviewers on two waves of a panel. In this study, the interviews were spaced about two months apart. Another panel study using different interviewers was also made in Chicago with interviews spaced about ten days apart. Even though for the three studies the universes differed somewhat, none of the samples was random (they were all regular quota samples), and the time lapse between interviews differed, the three studies would still appear to be essentially comparable.

The interviewers on the two national studies rated the respondents on both waves on a five-point economic status scale. When the same interviewer rated the same respondents on both waves, 77 per cent of the ratings were identical. When different interviewers rated given respondents on the two waves, only 54 per cent of the ratings were identical. The Chicago study sample contained almost completely respondents of average or higher economic status and thus the interviewers used a truncated rating scale (three categories on one wave, four categories on the other). Even in this situation, only 55 per cent of the respondents received identical classifications.

The interviewers estimated the age of the respondent and asked whether he owned a car on both waves of all three surveys. Here again there was greater reliability when the same interviewer made the rating or asked the question both times than when different interviewers were used.

The implications of the greater reliability that existed when the same interviewer interviewed the same respondent twice are not clear-cut. With only a three-week period between the first and second interview of the panel using the same interviewer, it seems very likely that at least in some instances the interviewer remembered how he had previously classified the respondent and merely classified him in an identical fashion the second time. Thus, the greater reliability attained by the same interviewer classifying the same respondent both times may in part be an artifact of memory rather than the result of persistent inter-

TABLE 59

RELIABILITY OF RESPONSES TO REPEAT QUESTIONS IN THREE PANEL STUDIES

CHARACTERISTIC	PERCENTAGE IDENTICAL CLASSIFICATIONS UNDER DIFFERENT CONDITIONS *		
	National Panel; Same Interviewers on Both Waves	National Panel; Cities over 100,000 Population; Different Interviewers on Two Waves	Chicago Panel; Different Interviewers on Two Waves
Estimate of age of respondent (10-year class intervals)......	90 (277)	71 (288)	74 (about 150)
Automobile ownership................	96 (256)	86 (288)	89 (150)

* Numbers in parentheses are the number of cases upon which the per cents are based.

viewer characteristics, which result in either stability over time in the interviewer's perception and frame of reference for classification of the respondent or in stability of the respondent's reaction to the interviewer. Thus, while the latter interpretation has some validity, it is likely that the difference in reliability overstates the systematic operation of an interviewer's effect.

A somewhat smaller difference in reliability between ratings of the economic level of respondents made by the same interviewer as against ratings made by different interviewers was observed in a panel study conducted in Cincinnati.[20] In this study, where a four-point rating was used, 78 per cent of the respondents received identical classifications on both waves when the same interviewer made the rating, and 68 per cent received identical classifications when different interviewers were rating. The difference between the differences (the difference between 23 per cent and 10 per cent) in Mosteller's and the Cincinnati study is not statistically significant but is in accord with our expectations because a six-month interval separated the first and second wave of the Cincinnati study. This longer interval would certainly have lessened considerably the possibility of an interviewer's remembering how he had previously classified a respondent. Mainly, the persistent factors tended to produce differences in reliability between the same interviewers and different interviewers in Cincinnati, while both persistent factors and memory operated in the Mosteller study. The greater difference in the Mosteller study was, therefore, to be expected.

A number of other comparisons in the reliability of factual data from the Cincinnati study are presented in Table 60 below. It should be noted in interpreting these comparisons that the study was not executed in accord with an experimental design. These comparisons are merely a by-product of a regular panel survey; consequently, extraneous, nonrandom, uncontrolled factors may have affected the results.

TABLE 60

RELIABILITY OF CINCINNATI FACTUAL DATA

CHARACTERISTIC	PERCENTAGE OF RESPONDENTS GIVING IDENTICAL RESPONSES ON BOTH WAVES	
	When Interviewed by Same Interviewer*	When Interviewed by Different Interviewer*
Education		
7-Class break...............................	77	67
Collapsed into 4-Class break...................	82	79
Frequency of church attendance		
4-Class break............................	79	67
Collapsed into dichotomy.....................	92	85
Age		
Dichotomized..............................	98	98
Service in World War II		
Dichotomized..........................	99	98
Which newspaper(s) read		
5-Classes.................................	82	82

* The reliability percentages for the "same-interviewer" respondents are based on approximately 90 respondents. The percentages for the "different-interviewer" respondents are based on approximately 410 cases.

Another panel study which enabled us to compare the reliability of certain demographic information elicited by the same interviewer with the reliability of the results obtained by different interviewers was executed in Baltimore jointly by NORC, the Bureau of Applied Social Research, and the American Jewish Committee. Here, as in Cincinnati, there was an interval of about six months between the two waves of interviewing. The same shortcomings in design as existed in the Cincinnati study apply to Baltimore, since the major purpose of the study was not experimental.

The results of the Baltimore study are essentially in confirmation of the results of the two previously discussed studies. The responses of respondents interviewed on both waves by the same interviewer were moderately more reliable than were the responses of respondents interviewed by different interviewers on the two waves.

We have presented in Tables 59–61 three completely independent demonstrations that some systematic effect of a particular interviewer on the demographic classification of a particular respondent does occur. But, by and large, the differences in reliability have not been particularly large considering the extraneous factors involved in the study de-

TABLE 61

RELIABILITY OF BALTIMORE FACTUAL DATA

CHARACTERISTIC	PERCENTAGE OF RESPONDENTS GIVING IDENTICAL RESPONSES ON BOTH WAVES	
	When Interviewed by Same Interviewer *	When Interviewed by Different Interviewer *
Education		
6-Class break	63	54
Collapsed into 4-Class break	75	67
Income		
7-Class break	57	50
Collapsed into 3-Class break	75	62
Collapsed symmetrically so that adjacent intervals are considered as identical	86	79

* The reliability percentages for the "same-interviewer" respondents are based on approximately 80 respondents. The percentages for the "different-interviewer" respondents are based on approximately 470 respondents.

sign. These comparisons clearly support the conclusion in Chapter V to the effect that there is a considerable fluctuating component to interviewer effect, in addition to a systematic component of only moderate magnitude. However, the considerable magnitude of unreliability for unchangeable factual characteristics supports the evidence presented earlier in this chapter that gross effects are large.

Some evidence on the relative reliability of opinion data collected by the same and by different interviewers is also available.[21] For opinion data also, the respondents interviewed by the same interviewers on both waves were in general more likely to give reliable responses than were those respondents interviewed by different interviewers. The size of the difference in reliability varied extremely, but it was not possible to determine whether this variation was random or connected somehow with specific question content or form.

In the 1948 Elmira panel voting study, several interviewers interviewed the same respondents on the second and third waves. These two waves of interviewing were separated by an interval of about two months. There were two questions which were asked on both waves of the study. For both of those questions, the respondent was handed a card with twelve attributes listed on it and was asked which of the attributes came closest to describing Truman and which came closest to describing Dewey. Almost every respondent mentioned several attributes as descriptive of each of the candidates.

One of the reliability comparisons is given in Table 62.

TABLE 62

RELIABILITY OF ELMIRA OPINION DATA

RESPONSES ATTRIBUTING COURAGE TO TRUMAN ON SUCCESSIVE INTERVIEWING WAVES

	SAME INTERVIEWER ON BOTH WAVES			DIFFERENT INTERVIEWERS ON THE TWO WAVES		
	First Wave				First Wave	
	Mentioned "coura-geous" as describing Truman	Did not mention "coura-geous" as describing Truman	Total		Mentioned "coura-geous" as describing Truman	Did not mention "coura-geous" as describing Truman	Total
Second Wave				Second Wave		
Mentioned "coura-geous" as describing Truman	9	4	13	Mentioned "coura-geous" as describing Truman	78	75	153
Did not mention "coura-geous" as describing Truman	7	32	39	Did not mention "coura-geous" as describing Truman	64	468	532
Total	16	36	52		142	543	685

The method we have used in computing reliability is to take the ratio of the number of respondents mentioning the attribute "courageous" on both waves to the total number of respondents mentioning the attribute on either wave; in other words, the denominator of this ratio is composed of those who mentioned the attribute on both waves plus those who mentioned it on the first wave and not the second, plus those who mentioned it on the second wave but not the first.[22] For the attribute "courageous," the reliability for the "same-interviewer" respondents would thus be 9/20 or 45 per cent and for the "different-interviewer" respondents it would be 78/217 or 36 per cent.

The reliability percentages for the questions about Truman and Dewey, computed in the manner described, are presented in Table 63.

TABLE 63

A COMPARISON OF THE RELIABILITY OF RESPONSES OBTAINED WHEN THE SAME INTERVIEWER INTERVIEWED GIVEN RESPONDENTS ON BOTH WAVES AND, WHEN DIFFERENT INTERVIEWERS INTERVIEWED GIVEN RESPONDENTS ON THE TWO WAVES*

ATTRIBUTE	ON CARD QUESTION ABOUT TRUMAN		ON CARD QUESTION ABOUT DEWEY	
	Percentage of Respondents Interviewed by Same Interviewer	Percentage of Respondents Interviewed by Different Interviewers	Percentage of Respondents Interviewed by Same Interviewer	Percentage of Respondents Interviewed by Different Interviewers
Courageous	45	36	61	53
	(20)†	(217)†	(28)†	(394)†
Conservative	100	28	50	28
	(6)	(130)	(14)	(237)
Weak	37	34	0	19
	(19)	(274)	(4)	(32)
Honest	73	54	50	52
	(33)	(446)	(36)	(478)
Inadequate	60	43	29	7
	(20)	(280)	(7)	(54)
Sound	0	20	48	34
	(4)	(104)	(23)	(317)
Confused	68	53	14	14
	(34)	(422)	(7)	(51)
Efficient	60	15	56	55
	(5)	(117)	(39)	(507)
Cold	100	19	7	23
	(1)	(27)	(15)	(78)
Well-meaning	69	57	57	34
	(35)	(520)	(21)	(344)
Thrifty	0	17	83	27
	(5)	(76)	(12)	(259)
Opportunist	20	14	70	32
	(5)	(69)	(10)	(150)

* The percentages given in the table are measures of reliability calculated in the manner described in the text.
† The numbers in parentheses indicate the number of respondents involved for each reliability percentage based on the respondents mentioning the attribute on either or both waves.

It is clear that there was a definite tendency for respondents interviewed by the same interviewers on both waves to give more reliable responses than those respondents interviewed by different interviewers. There were a few exceptions to this tendency, but almost all the large differences were in the direction of greater stability of the responses of "same-interviewer" respondents. But, the exceptions and the incidence of a number of small differences favoring the "same-interviewers" do indicate that the systematic effects that must exist are only of moderate importance.

A number of opinion questions from the first wave of the Cincinnati panel, discussed earlier, were repeated on the second wave of that study. The relative reliabilities for a sample of those questions are presented here. Again, in this study, there are definite indications that the "same-interviewer" respondents tended in general to be more stable in their responses than the "different-interviewers" respondents.

TABLE 64

RELIABILITY OF OPINION DATA IN THE CINCINNATI STUDY

QUESTION	PERCENTAGE GIVING IDENTICAL RESPONSES ON BOTH WAVES:	
	of Those Respondents Interviewed by the Same Interviewer on Both Waves*	of Those Respondents Interviewed by Different Interviewers on the Two Waves*
1. Do you think there will always be wars between countries, or do you think someday we'll find a way to prevent wars?	78	66
2. Do you think it will be best for the future of this country if we take an active part in world affairs, or if we stay out of world affairs?	77	70
3. In general, are you satisfied or dissatisfied with the progress that the United Nations organization has made so far?	69	62
4. Do you think we can count on *Russia* to meet us halfway in working out problems together?	76	72
5. Have you read anything about *the veto power* in the United Nations?	70	70
6. Do you expect the United States to fight in another war within the next ten years?	56	58

* The percentages for "same-interviewer" respondents are based on about 90 cases for Questions 1, 2, 4, and 6, and on about 55 cases for Questions 3 and 5. The percentages for "different-interviewer" respondents are based on about 400 cases for Questions 1, 2, 4, and 6, and on about 260 cases for Questions 3 and 5. The percentages for Questions 3 and 5 are based on fewer respondents because these questions were asked only of people having heard of the UN.

Another type of test of the extent of systematic interviewer effect over time can be made with the Cincinnati panel data. Two rough indices, one of interest in international affairs and the other of information concerning the UN, were set up for each wave of the panel. The magnitude of change between the first and second wave for each of the scores was computed. In comparing the changes of the two sets of respondents in this way, we are making a compound test, examining simultaneously whether effects were systematic over different questions and whether they were systematic over time.

The mean absolute value of the change in score is compared in Table

65 for the two sets of respondents for both indices. It is clear that neither of the differences in the mean magnitude of change in score is even near to being statistically significant. In fact, for the information index, the mean absolute change in score for those respondents interviewed by the same interviewer was actually greater than the mean absolute change for the respondents interviewed by different interviewers. This difference is the opposite of what we would expect if there had been systematic effects. The results certainly provide no basis for assuming that there are effects that are systematic over both questions and time.

TABLE 65

RELIABILITY OF OPINION INDICES IN THE CINCINNATI STUDY

	MEAN ABSOLUTE VALUE OF CHANGE IN SCORE FROM THE FIRST TO THE SECOND WAVE BY RESPONDENTS WHO WERE INTERVIEWED BY:		Difference Between Means	"t" (Ratio of Difference Between Means to Standard Error of Difference)
	Same Interviewer on Both Waves	Different Interviewers on the Two Waves		
Index of interest in international affairs....................	.90	.96	.06	.6
Index of information about the United Nations...............	1.42	1.34	−.08	−.5

We have thus seen that a multiplicity of comparisons from a number of different panel studies support in general the fact that there is some interviewer effect on the response which is systematic over time. But, the several anomalous comparisons and the generally small differences, as well as consideration of such spurious factors as the recollection on the part of the interviewer or respondent of the response on the preceding wave and the non-randomness involved in the design, make it clear that in general the systematic effects over time are at most only moderate in magnitude. This conclusion on the basis of these panel comparisons is in line with the discussion of systematic interviewer effects in the preceding chapter.

5. DIFFERENTIAL NET EFFECTS AND INTER-INTERVIEWER VARIATION

Differential net effects and inter-interviewer variation will be discussed together because of the similarity of the study designs used in the two areas.

A vast majority of the published studies of differential net effects and inter-interviewer variation in the course of normal field operations show a widespread occurrence of these phenomena with rather considerable magnitude in various situations and with the use of various question-forms on various subject matters. According to the general view of these studies, significant inter-interviewer variation is the rule rather than an exceptional event.[23]

In the course of our work, we have made two studies the designs of which were particularly appropriate for the examination of the incidence of significant inter-interviewer variation. In both studies, several interviewers were assigned random samples of predesignated respondents from the same universe, so that any variation in responses in excess of random variation would be ascribed to some sort of interviewer bias.

The first of the differential interviewer effect studies was made in Cleveland in 1948. This analysis was done in conjunction with an NORC survey of the residents of three Cleveland suburbs on the adequacy of their transportation facilities. A systematic random sample of households within the specified suburbs was drawn from the *Cleveland Householders' Directory*. The sample households falling into each census tract were divided into blocks of about fifty households, each on the basis of propinquity. Each of two interviewers was assigned systematic random halves (alternate sample households) of the sample households within each block. There were ten such blocks of paired interviewers in the study.

The existence of differential net effects among different interviewers was tested by comparing the amount of difference in the distributions of responses recorded by two interviewers in one block with the amount of difference in the distributions which might occur with a reasonable probability between two samples from a single universe. Statistically significant differences were taken to indicate the operation of differential net effect. Most questions were treated as dichotomies in the analysis. Chi-squared was used as a test of significance of the difference between the proportion of the respondents of one interviewer giving a specified response and the proportion of the respondents of the other interviewer in the same block giving that response.[24] Then, in order to test for the existence of differential effect on any single question, the Chi-squareds from the ten pairs of interviewers were cumulated.[25]

The questions on the survey were mainly of the fixed-response type and dealt with a variety of subject matters in the general area of shopping and travel habits. The question form also varied, there being a number of both fixed-response and free-answer questions.

Some forty-five questions were examined for differential net effects. Of these, only five questions showed significant intra-paired interviewer variation at the .05 significance level. The variation between interviewers on four of these five questions was very large and had accordingly very small probability of occurring by chance from a universe with no inter-interviewer variation. These four questions were all subquestions of the two questions on the last place of purchase of several items. The questions and results were:

Question: "The *last time* you shopped for (item) did you get them downtown or in neighborhood stores?"

	Chi-squared	Degrees of Freedom	P-value
Gasoline	30.75	10	.001
Auto repairs	43.21	10	.0001

"Now I'd like to know about the main earner (main shopper) of the household. The *last time* he (she) wanted any of the following things, did he (she) get them downtown or in some neighborhood area?"

Clothing	24.01	10	.01
Housefurnishings	38.04	10	.0001

A full exploration of the possible sources of bias on these particular questions appeared in Chapter III, Section 2, and in Chapter V of this monograph. But this does not concern us here. The important consideration here is the fact that on about forty out of forty-five opinion and factual questions on this survey there was no particular evidence of differential net effects.

An additional fact about the research design should be considered before evaluating the import of this study. The variation that was examined was in all cases the variation between the results of paired interviewers. Hence, in cases where both the interviewers in a given block biased their results in one direction and both the interviewers in some other block biased their results in the opposite direction, we would get no indication of differential net effect from our test even though such effect was in operation on the question. Since the interviewers were paired within blocks on an essentially random basis, there would be no particular tendency beyond chance for paired interviewers to be more alike in their biasing tendencies than non-paired interviewers. Still, some differential net effects may have been overlooked owing to chance pairings of similarly biasing interviewers.

Then there is the possibility that our significance tests were too weak to pick up differential interviewer effect. It is true that only extremely large differences in the universes would result in significant differences between two samples of only twenty-five cases each a reasonable proportion of the time. Nevertheless, since only one of the forty-five questions had inter-interviewer variation that would have occurred with a probability of between .05 and .01 with no true differential net effects, we can rather safely conclude that on a large proportion of the questions on the survey there was relatively little or no differential net effect.

These conclusions about the general absence of serious differential net effects were also confirmed by our second large field study designed to examine this problem. This study was part of the 1949 validity study in Denver discussed earlier in this chapter. The study was designed so that each of nine interviewers had geographically equivalent interviewing assignments of predesignated respondents in a single sector of the city. Within a sector, there was no clustering whatsoever of respondents by interviewer. This design was replicated in all five sectors of the city. The complete design is discussed very fully in the article treating the study.[26]

A Chi-squared test of significance of the variation between the results of the different interviewers was made for each sector. Then, for each question the Chi-squared tests were cumulated over the five sectors.

The interview schedule used was composed of a variety of different types of question. The schedule included fixed-response questions involving the use of a card, three- and five-point scales, dichotomies, and questions where one of the pre-coded responses was not included in the list of alternatives stated in the question. There were also several free-response questions and a number of interviewer ratings of characteristics of the respondent and his dwelling.

The subject matter of the schedule was also quite varied, dealing with respondent's attitudes to his neighborhood, interest and opinions on local and national issues, voting behavior, and factual characteristics.

The outstanding finding was that significant (at the .05 level) inter-interviewer variation appeared on only eight of twenty-one fixed-response questions. However, six of the questions with significant variation were sub-parts of a single omnibus question with ten subparts, and the remaining two which showed significant variation were almost identical. Also, significant inter-interviewer variation was found on only one of the seven traditional "factual" questions asked.[27] The questions with significant inter-interviewer variation and the results of the significance tests were:

Fixed-response opinion questions	Chi-squared	Degrees of Freedom	Probability
We are finding out how much interest people take in various problems. (Respondent was handed a card listing three degrees of interest: "A great deal," "some," and "practically none.") For example, which of those degrees of interest would you say you take in _____?			
U.S. Policy toward Spain....................	211.79	120	.0000001
City planning in Denver.....................	137.27	96	.003
Unemployment in the U.S...................	147.24	112	.013
Denver Negro situation.....................	148.15	120	.04
Denver Public Schools......................	113.15	88	.04
Presidential election.......................	120.31	96	.05
If something prevented you from voting in an election for Mayor of Denver, how much difference would it make to you *personally*—would it make a great deal of difference, quite a bit of difference, or not much difference?	163.33	112	.0008
Now if something prevented you from voting in a Presidential election, how much difference would it make to you personally—would it make a great deal of difference, quite a bit of difference, or not much difference?	136.92	104	.015
Factual questions			
Do you happen to own an automobile at the present time? (If "Yes") Is it registered in your name alone, or in your (wife's) (husband's) name also?	184.05	152	.04

The similarity of the form of the question where most of the differential net effects appeared on the Denver study, the *omnibus* interest question, to the form of the question where most of the differential net effects appeared on the Cleveland study, the *omnibus* shopping question, should be noted. In each case, we have a single question repeated over and over again, only with slight variation in the object in the question. As one would expect on a priori grounds, on both surveys a few interviewers complained about the dullness of these particular questions to the respondents. Not only were the questions deemed to be initially lusterless, but it was felt also that the respondents found the repetition boresome. Thus, it can be hypothesized that, being eager to go through this part of the questionnaire in a hurry, the interviewers may have become quite slipshod in both the asking of these dull and repetitious questions, and in the recording of answers to them.

It is interesting to note that while these seemingly innocuous questions concerning the respondent's interests showed significant interinterviewer variations, there were several questions concerning what would appear to be rather affect-laden opinion areas—e.g., political affiliation, satisfaction with the community—which did not have any such significant variation. It is hard to imagine many interviewers being even unconsciously motivated to distort responses to most of the interest subquestions by anything but a desire to get an unpleasant task over with as soon as possible, but one can imagine interviewers getting some gratification out of having respondents give some particular response to more important opinion questions. We may conjecture that the obviously greater inter-interviewer variation found on some of the interest subquestions than in the more strictly opinion questions may be due to factors which we may consider as situational, and this contributes additional evidence in support of the theory presented in Chapter V.

Another factor which may have contributed to the high incidence of inter-interviewer variation on the interest questions was an apparent confusion on the part of respondents, and possibly on the part of interviewers, as to the meaning of the questions. From reports filed by interviewers after the completion of their assignments, there was considerable evidence that many respondents tended to respond in terms of their attitudes in the various subject-matter areas or in terms of the degree of interest they felt they *should* take, rather than the interest they actually did take. Also, a really operational definition of "interest" was absent, and it is clear that the word had little meaning for some respondents and variant meanings among those who did understand it. Thus, a great deal was left to the discretion of the interviewer. The opinion questions were relatively straightforward in comparison with these interest questions. There would seem to have been little chance of a respondent failing to comprehend their meaning and so the interviewer's discretion impinged less upon the response. The degree to which, on a given question, the interviewer must engage in behavior not strictly prescribed—i.e., where he has alternative courses of action— would seem, as indicated in Chapter V, to be highly related to the degree of inter-interviewer variation to be found on a question.

Although the incidence of substantial inter-interviewer variation was generally absent for the fixed-response *opinion* questions and on the factual questions, there were highly substantial and statistically significant variations between interviewers in their ratings of characteristics of the respondents and the respondents' dwellings. Also, there was significant variation between interviewers in the number of responses per respondent they obtained to free-response questions.[28] These latter findings do not at all contradict the Cleveland findings, though, because the form of the questions from that interview was similar to that of the fixed-response and factual questions of the Denver study. Thus, in the area where our two studies overlap, the findings are in essential agreement: that there was little evidence of substantial inter-interviewer variation on fixed-response opinion questions and factual questions.

Parallel questions arise in connection with both the Denver and the Cleveland studies. The first arises out of the fact that only the nine interviewers within a given sector are compared with each other. If for some reason interviewers within the same sector tended to have the same biases while interviewers in different sectors had different biases, we would not have discovered differential net effects even though they did occur. It is extremely unlikely that this could have occurred on the Denver study because the interviewers within each sector were purposely contrasted in terms of a number of their characteristics such as age, sex, interviewing experience, etc. Since there is no known characteristic on which interviewers within a given sector were more homogeneous than interviewers in different sectors and since each sector had nine interviewers (one-fifth of the forty-five interviewers used), it seems inconceivable that much differential net effect could have been overlooked owing to this cluster aspect of the design.

Of course, the degree of differential net effects found in any study is a function of the heterogeneity of the total group of interviewers used. In the two studies discussed in the foregoing, the interviewing staffs used were certainly as heterogeneous as a staff working within a single city on a particular normal survey generally would be. In Cleveland, the interviewing staff was composed of a few regular NORC interviewers and a great many people of varying interviewing experience recruited through newspaper ads and similar means. In Denver the interviewing crew was even more heterogeneous. Here the interviewers used came chiefly from two groups: experienced professional interviewers on the staffs of national and local research agencies, and students of social science at the University of Denver. Thus, there is no reason to assume that there was any appreciably less opportunity for differential net effects to occur on the Denver or Cleveland surveys than there would be on most regular surveys. If anything, the heterogeneity provided greater opportunity than under usual survey operations, thus making the negative findings even more compelling.

Before going further into the nature of the inter-interviewer variation that has been found, it would be well to examine our conclusion that "for most fixed-response opinion questions there is relatively little inter-interviewer variation" in the light of other studies which seem to indicate the general existence of a considerable amount of such variation. Some differences between the design and analysis of the two studies discussed and earlier studies with conclusions at variance from ours may account for the different conclusions.

First, there are a number of studies where the over-all distributions of responses elicited by different groups of interviewers are compared. In several instances, interviewers have not been assigned randomly to respondents. When these studies have been based on a national interviewing staff, there has been a correlation between the town or at least the general area in which the interviewer and respondent live. This correlation could of course lead to spurious differences between the respondents interviewed by interviewers contrasted in terms of their own opinions if there are positive intra-class correlations between sampling place and both interviewer and respondent opinion. The differences between the responses obtained by the different groups of interviewers are generally tested for significance using a doubtful assumption. It is assumed that if there were no inter-interviewer variation, the responses of the respondents interviewed by different groups of interviewers would differ from each other to the same extent as would responses of respondents in simple random samples of the same sizes as those of the aggregates of respondents interviewed by the given groups of interviewers. This testing procedure unquestionably leads to a gross underestimate of the possibility of getting such differences by chance. Given research workers have been aware of this spurious factor in their analyses and have tried to correct for it. For instance, Cahalan, Tamulonis, and Verner excluded questions showing substantial regional variation from their analysis. Still, it is probable that even on the remaining questions there was substantial intra-class correlation between specific place and opinion remaining to inflate the differences between the responses of interviewers with different opinions. One need simply picture the differences in opinions that may exist between the residents of a wealthy suburb and the residents of a medium-sized industrial town or the residents of a small farming community even *within* a single region to see the possibility that such a spurious factor may produce differences in responses obtained by different groups of interviewers in such a design. Even within a single city, if interviewers are assigned to interview near their own homes, the same sort of spurious factor could account for the relationship between the interviewer's and the respondent's opinion. Thus, we cannot be sure whether studies employing this design which have found significant differences between the responses obtained by different interviewers really contradict our negative findings.[29]

A related problem involved in a number of studies is the absence of interpenetrating samples of respondents for different interviewers. An analytic problem arises, even though there is no reason to assume correlation of interviewer and respondent opinion, since the different interviewers or the different groups of interviewers whose results are compared for the determination of the incidence of inter-interviewer variation generally do not interview within the same spatial clusters. There is very likely to be a positive correlation between the place where a *respondent* lives and his opinions and characteristics. In such case, the geographical clustering of respondents would generally result in larger differences between the distributions of responses obtained by different interviewers than would appear if the interviewers had been assigned *simple* random samples. This statement would hold even if there were no real interviewer effect. Thus, when these studies are analyzed using assumptions of *simple* random sampling, or at least failing fully to take account of the extent of clustering, one underestimates the probability of finding variations between the results of interviewers as large or larger than those actually found, by chance, when there is no true inter-interviewer variation.

In discussing these studies, we shall assume there is no outside knowledge from other studies as to variance between the different cluster areas. If such information were available, it could be used to compute the sampling error between different interviewers' assignments.

There have been two basic designs in the analysis of such studies. First, the responses obtained by interviewers having a given characteristic are compared with the responses obtained by interviewers having a contrasted characteristic. We shall assume here that the interviewers were assigned to clusters of respondents in a random fashion, although often this is not the case, as was pointed out earlier. We shall also assume that the interviewers used in a particular study constitute a random sample from the universe of available interviewers.

Now, if there is no interpenetration of the clusters assigned to the different interviewers, it is impossible to determine the random sampling error between the responses of the several groups of respondents because of a confounding of variation between the clusters with the variation between interviewers having the same characteristic. But, as will be pointed out later, if the purpose of the study is to examine the differences in results obtained by interviewers with the different characteristics and not simply to establish the existence of variation between interviewers per se, this confounding of variances does not prevent one from testing his hypothesis. One can simply use, with only a minor adjustment, the observed variance between the results of interviewers with a given characteristic in this particular study, divided by the number of interviewers, as the estimate of the variance of the mean for the distribution of responses obtained by interviewers with this characteristic.[30] Thus, one can readily estimate the sampling variance of the difference between the means of the distributions of responses obtained by the groups of interviewers with differing characteristics and test for the significance of this difference.

As we pointed out earlier, in most analyses of such material, the assumption of simple random sampling is made, i.e., the variance of the means of distributions of responses obtained by different groups of interviewers is estimated by assuming that the entire group of respondents interviewed by the interviewers with a given characteristic constitute a simple random sample from a universe of all interviewers interviewing all respondents (in the given area of the survey). But there is good reason to believe that the true sampling variance, the variance correctly estimated by the procedure previously described, is considerably larger than the expected value of the estimate of variance made on the assumption of simple random sampling, owing both to the positive correlation between area of residence and opinion of the respondent and to the variation between interviewers within a classification. Hence, it is probable that past studies have overestimated the extent of the incidence of differences in results obtained by different groups of interviewers.[31]

The second analytic procedure used in the analysis of studies using interviewers with non-interpenetrating clusters of respondents involves the testing of significance of the inter-interviewer variation, without any grouping of the interviewers in terms of their characteristics. The distributions of responses obtained by different interviewers are simply compared with each other. Sometimes only the results of interviewers working within the same city, having received similar initial assignments, and having interviewed respondents with similar distributions on several demographic variables are compared. Still, *there is no way of telling* to what degree the respondents in the clusters interviewed by different interviewers might be expected to differ from each other on the relevant variables even if there were no inter-interviewer variation. Thus, here again we cannot take the findings of such studies at face value and must try to judge the validity of the findings in terms of outside knowledge.

A third important factor to be considered in comparing the findings from the Cleveland and Denver studies with those from a number of the earlier studies is the confounding of inter-interviewer variation in the selection or sampling of respondents with inter-interviewer variation within the interview itself. In many of the earlier studies, the interviewers were simply given identical quota assignments rather than a random sample of predesignated respondents. Thus, it is impossible in such studies to determine whether a difference in the opinions of the respondents of different interviewers is due merely to varying biases in the selection of respondents or whether there is also variation in performance during the actual interview.

Since the Cleveland and Denver studies involved predesignated respondents, there was minimal opportunity for the interviewer to obtain deviant results merely through bias in the selection of respondents. Therefore, it is not surprising that there is less evidence of general inter-interviewer variation from these studies than there is from studies where the interviewer was free to choose his own respondents. This fact, as well as evidence from two studies devoted specifically to comparing inter-interviewing variation under different conditions of sampling,[32] indicates that much of what has been previously interpreted as differential net distortion *within* the interview may well be simply varying bias in the selection of respondents.[33] While this is, of course, a significant component of interviewer performance worthy of investigation, its true character should not be misinterpreted. In addition, even when probability samples are used, inter-interviewer variation could be a function of the differential ability of interviewers to obtain interviews with all their predesignated respondents. In so far as there is a correlation between a respondent's availability for an interview and his opinions, a variation in response rates would account for some of the observed differences in the distributions of responses found for different interviewers in studies of inter-interviewer variation. That interviewers differ in their abilities to complete their assignments of predesignated respondents is clearly demonstrated in a large-scale study conducted in England by Durbin and Stuart under the direction of M. G. Kendall.[34] The detailed findings are reported below in the discussion of inter-interviewer variation.

Consequently, unless the respondent loss-rate is small in magnitude, as in the Cleveland study, or the losses are examined to determine their distribution and consequent effects among interviewers as in the Denver study, there is the danger of misinterpreting the origin of the total inter-interviewer variation found.

As was discussed earlier, studies where the distributions of responses obtained by several different groups of interviewers are compared generally fail to take account of variation between interviewers within a given group (i.e., between interviewers having a given characteristic). This factor should be considered in estimating sampling variance under the null hypothesis whether or not the different interviewers have been assigned interpenetrating random samples. We have discussed using the observed variance between interviewers within a classification as the basis for estimating the random error when non-interpenetrating clusters of respondents were assigned to interviewers. This same observed variance could also be used as the basis of estimation even when the interviewing assignments are interpenetrating.

Another factor that may partially account for the general view that inter-interviewer variation is prevalent is the probable tendency to publish only positive findings. Although this supposition cannot be substantiated, it seems likely on a priori grounds that examinations of inter-interviewer variation which showed significant variation were more likely to be published, being in line with expectations and being, in a sense, less equivocal than studies which failed to find significant variation between interviewers. When an examination of the data—particularly when only few interviewers are involved or when each interviewer interviewed a rather small sample of respondents—fails to show statistically significant variation between interviewers, there is the omnipresent danger that the weakness of the significance tests has led to the neglect of differences that are really there, and so one hesitates to publish such negative findings. Now, of course, even if there were no real inter-interviewer variation, 5 per cent of all the significance tests made would indicate that observed variation was significant at the 5 per cent level. If our supposition that many tests which failed to show significant variation were not published is correct, then it becomes more likely that a fair proportion of the published tests showing significant variation are actually in error—i.e., that they reject the null hypothesis that there are no differences between interviewers when actually the null hypothesis is true, the extreme variation observed in those instances being simply due to chance. Thus, our findings of a rather low incidence of inter-interviewer variation again may not be as much in contradiction to the findings of earlier studies as it appeared to be at first sight.

There have been several studies made with designs similar to those of our Cleveland and Denver studies. In these studies, interviewers were assigned interpenetrating samples of predesignated respondents or households. Thus, the results of these studies are comparable with our results.

Mahalanobis has reported several studies of the variation in the results obtained by different interviewers. In connection with the Bengal Labour Enquiry, the results obtained by five interviewers were compared. Significant inter-interviewer variation was found on two of the five questions examined. In connection with the Nagpur Labour Enquiry, the results obtained by four interviewers were compared. Here, significant inter-interviewer variation was absent from all four of the questions examined. In connection with two cost-of-living studies, cost-of-living indices were computed separately on the basis of each interviewer's work. In one of the studies, cost-of-living indices based on five different interviewers were compared without finding significant variation. In the other study, indices based on three different interviewers were compared with the same failure to find significant variation. Thus, significant variation was found on only two of the eleven comparisons made. Mahalanobis also reports an additional study, the Radio Programme Preference Survey. Here, each of three independent teams of investigators interviewed in one of three interpenetrating samples of respondents. The variation between the three samples was compared to the variation that would be expected if the three samples had been simple random samples from a binomial population. On fifteen of the eighteen questions examined, the observed variance was larger than the expected variance, and in seven of those instances the observed variation was significantly larger than the expected. But, it is not clear whether the three samples were actually simple random samples or whether there was clustering involved, and so we cannot tell whether the excess in observed variance should be ascribed to inter-interviewer variation or to the spatial intra-class correlation of opinions. We also have no information about whether the three sets of interviewers differed from each other in terms of training or any other characteristics.[35]

Shapiro and Eberhart examined differences in the distributions of responses obtained by four interviewers conducting essentially intensive interviews with comparable samples of respondents in a non-field survey situation. Interviews were conducted with respondents at local VA offices rather than at their homes, but since the general form of the questionnaire, the subject matter, and general interviewing procedure were not too far different from what might be found in an ordinary field survey, the findings are probably reasonably relevant to field surveys. The authors report significant or near significant variation between interviewers was found on ten of the thirty-four questions on the questionnaire.[36] But, it should be noted that the interviewer's task on this survey was somewhat more complex than his task on most of the other studies reported here, including the Cleveland and Denver studies. Even though a number of the questions used were pre-coded, the interviewers were supposed to probe intensively on the questions before coding the response. Thus, opportunity for variant behavior existed in the situation to a greater extent than on the pre-coded questions used in the other surveys presented here; in these, the interviewer was expected to accept the initial response of the respondent or at least the first codable response after a minimum of probing. When one considers the opportunities for variation in the intensive interview situation, confirmed by our very own findings from the Denver study on variation in open-ended questions, reported in Chapter V, the Shapiro and Eberhart findings are well in accord with our own.[37] It should be noted, however, that the interviewers involved in their study were all highly motivated, and three of the four were highly experienced. All four were very well acquainted with the interview schedule and had a clear understanding of the goals of the study.[38]

Stock and Hochstim have reported a number of different analyses of inter-interviewer variation in studies using probability samples, but it is not clear in which, if any, the interviewers actually had interpenetrating samples.[39] For the sake of the present discussion, we shall assume that in those cases where the samples did not interpenetrate, the overestimate of interviewer variance was relatively slight, although we cannot be sure of this. They report an experiment made in a medium-sized Eastern city, designed primarily to examine relative inter-interviewer variation when the interviewer is assigned to a predesignated respondent, and when he is assigned to a specified block but can choose respondents within the block on a quota basis. The probability sample part of the design is comparable to our own study. All the data needed to test the significance of the inter-interviewer variation on the probability sample is not available, but, from the data that are available, it is clear that, at most, only one of the six questions examined showed variation significant at the .05 level (in fact, a negative interviewer variance was estimated on two of the six questions, due no doubt to sampling error but still indicative of the fact that the actual interviewer variance could not be very large).[40] The one question with considerable variation was a free response question.

Stock and Hochstim also report a Bureau of Labor Statistics study in Chicago, where each of six interviewers had to determine the selling price of a number of different articles in three different types of store. This task was, in essence, an interviewer rating because the interviewer had to decide which of the many articles of clothing in the store met the requisite specifications and was to be priced. From the data presented in the article, it is impossible to test the statistical significance of the variation on most of the nine items priced. It is clear that there was significant variation on one of the items and that there was no significant variation on two others, but nothing can be said about the remaining six. But even if most of the remaining items did show statistically significant variation, this would only again substantiate the previous references to the high degree of inter-interviewer variation resulting when the interviewer's task involves considerable judgment on his part.

Additional evidence is available from a survey conducted by the Bureau of the Census designed to measure inter-interviewer variation in connection with their Monthly Labor Force Survey in Baltimore in December, 1947.[41] The design of this study was somewhat unusual in that only pairs of interviewers handled interpenetrating assignments, but the same interviewer was generally paired with several different interviewers in different segments. This slight modification in design does not affect the comparability of the findings of this study to the findings of the other studies already discussed. In the Census study, the results of four different interviewers were compared on five questions. The data by which significance tests could be made are not presented in the publication on the study, but it is obvious that on three of the questions, where the estimate of inter-interviewer variance is negative, the variation could not have been statistically significant. Although from the data presented they cannot be tested precisely, it is very doubtful if the inter-interviewer variation on either of the other two questions presented was significant. Thus here again there is little evidence for prevalent inter-interviewer variation.

A well-designed study of inter-interviewer variation, made in London in 1950 under the direction of M. G. Kendall, adds much to our knowledge of the prevalence of inter-interviewer variation. This study was designed to examine differences in various aspects of performance of three groups of interviewers: experienced, practically full-time interviewers for the Government Social Survey; experienced, part-time interviewers for the British Institute of Public Opinion; and a group of inexperienced, volunteer, unpaid student interviewers from the London School of Economics.

The study was executed through a factorial design so that the variations due to a number of different factors—questionnaires, interviewer groups, districts, age and sex of subject—could be examined simultaneously with full efficiency.

The only factor to concern us here is the interviewer factor. Owing to the factorial design, all factors interpenetrate. Hence, each interviewer group was assigned an equal number of interviews, to be divided equally among each of the three specific types of questionnaires, and within each interviewer group each type of questionnaire was administered to an equal number of respondents within each age-sex category within each district. Thus, except for random variation with respect to dependent variables between equivalent four-factor specific groups, the three interviewer groups were given completely identical assignments.

The findings of the Kendall study have appeared in two papers.[42] The Durbin and Stuart paper was concerned mainly with variation in performance in obtaining interviews with assigned respondents. It seems possible that the variation in this aspect of performance may account for some observed differences in the distributions of responses obtained by different interviewers (assuming a correlation between a respondent's availability for interview and his responses) in studies with rather high respondent loss-rates.

The main finding of the response rate analysis was that the students were decidedly inferior to the interviewers of the two professional organizations in obtaining interviews. "Within each group of interviewers, there is no evidence of marked heterogeneity among the individual interviewers. The results show that the main differences are between the classes of interviewers rather than between individuals."[43]

It is worth noting that a large part of the excess losses of the inexperienced interviewers was due to refusals. A far larger proportion of the assigned respondents of the inexperienced interviewers refused to be interviewed than of the experienced interviewers. This fact would seem to indicate that inexperienced interviewers lack the temerity, ability, and/or the will to overcome the resistance of respondents to being interviewed. It would also appear likely, then, that in the interviewing situation itself, the inexperienced interviewers might fail to press a reticent respondent as fully as necessary; the inexperienced interviewer might be prone to accept refusals on individual questions or "don't knows" of an evasive nature without an adequate attempt to overcome the resistance; he might also fail to probe as fully as necessary in many instances. This consideration is in accord with our explanations of the finding reported in the preceding chapter that the more experienced interviewers elicited fuller responses to open questions than did the less experienced.[44]

Booker and David found no clear evidence that differences between experienced and student interviewers in results obtained *within* the interview were significant.[45] One noteworthy finding on omission of questions was that the L.S.E. omission rate was markedly highest on the factual questions appearing at the end of the interview, again perhaps owing to the reticence or inability on the part of the inexperienced interviewer to press the respondent after having already asked a number of questions.[46]

The interviewers of all three organizations obtained practically identical proportions of noncommittal responses (responses like "don't know," "no preference," "nothing in particular," and "all parts" when the respondents were supposed to choose between alternatives that were matters of opinion rather than information). The absence of difference in this respect between experienced and inexperienced interviewers is rather remarkable. This result certainly detracts from the credibility of our hypothesis in the Denver study of greater reticence and inability to probe on the part of inexperienced interviewers.

No consistent pattern of differences was found with respect to the number of responses obtained to questions permitting multiple answers. Thus, these results question the generality of our finding in the Denver study that experienced interviewers elicited more multiple responses than inexperienced interviewers. The basis of the contradiction is not clear-cut, although conceivably the British experienced interviewers had less practice with open or other multiple-response questions than had their American counterparts.

Thus far we have discussed variations in performance between the three groups in terms of certain formal characteristics of responses instead of the content of the responses themselves. Booker and David also examined such differences in the distribution of responses themselves reported by the three different groups of interviewers. They found variation significant at the .10 level for only 20 of the 119 questions. While it is clear that not all of the observed differences can be accounted for in terms of sampling variation alone, it should be remembered that some of the significant variation may have been due to previously discussed differences in refusal rates or similar factors extraneous to the interview proper. Thus, here again there is relatively little evidence for the existence of *widespread* variation in results due to behavior during the interview itself.

By and large, there seemed to be no reason to assume that any of the differences in the distributions of recorded answers had anything to do with the fact that one group of interviewers was inexperienced and the other two were experienced. This fact confirms our general notion that much of the inter-interviewer variation that does occur is non-systematic in character.

Actually, there is little reason to expect variation in the *substantive content* of responses obtained by groups of interviewers contrasted merely in experience. Variation between groups of this sort would be expected to be along more formal lines—e.g., the number of responses elicited, number of evasive responses, etc. The variation in substantive responses would be perhaps more affected by a factor like interviewer expectations than by the experience factor. Nevertheless, the Kendall study is significant because of its unique application of a factorial design to the study of interviewer effect, and because of the contribution of its specific findings.

We have thus far seen that, in studies where the equivalence of the assignments of different interviewers has been insured through the pre-designation of *randomly selected* respondents, the prevalence of statistically significant inter-interviewer variation has been rather low. It is, of course, true that in most of these studies each interviewer interviewed rather few respondents. Thus, the significance tests were on the whole rather weak, and so real but small differences between interviewers were often overlooked. Still, when one considers the extent of the tests made and their general agreement as to the absence of significant variation on at least a majority of the fixed response pre-coded questions requiring a minimum of interviewer judgment, it does not seem possible that substantial inter-interviewer variation could be very widely prevalent on such questions.

Yet, in earlier chapters, we showed that certain processes of interviewer distortion (expectation effects, clerical errors, reaction effects, etc.) did occur, and in the earlier parts of this chapter, we indicated through the validity studies, the recorded interview studies, and the panel studies that gross effects did occur in field studies. These findings of gross interviewer effects on responses would appear to be somewhat in contradiction to our conclusion that substantial inter-interviewer variation was not particularly prevalent. Two important considerations help reconcile these divergent findings.

First, gross effects need not vary particularly from interviewer to interviewer. All interviewers can bias their results in more or less the same fashion, and thus the distributions of responses obtained by different interviewers need not differ particularly even though they are all affected.

The second consideration involves the fact that only net effects show up as inter-interviewer variation. If we consider an interviewer as having a strong need to find all of his respondents agreeing with him on every issue (or even disagreeing with him) and if there are differences in opinion among the members of the interviewing staff, then we'd expect large net effects to occur and along with them substantial inter-interviewer variation. But, if we view the interviewer as being essentially task oriented and as engaging in biasing behavior or making other interviewing errors solely to expedite getting his job done as painlessly as possible, then there is no particular reason why distortions of individual responses may not simply cancel out over a number of respondents. In general, the preceding chapters tend to support a view of an interviewing situation in which the interviewer is mainly task oriented—involved in getting his job done, not so much concerned with what his respondents say. Thus, it is not contradictory that each interviewer should distort a large number of individual responses, but that the distributions of responses obtained by different interviewers should in general look much the same.

There is no particular reason to assume from this that different interviewers will get the same responses from a single respondent or a group of respondents. As was indicated earlier in this chapter, a single interviewer interviewing the same respondent twice is more likely to get the same answers than are two different interviewers interviewing the same respondent. Although there is undoubtedly a great deal of random or situational error in interviews, it still seems very possible that different interviewers may exert differential net biases on *given* respondents or subgroups of respondents.[47] These individual biases may cancel out to a large extent when the total assignment per interviewer contains a number of respondents or a number of groups of respondents.

Some interesting findings in a study by Mahalanobis illustrate just such a situation where net differential biases over one group of respondents may be canceled out by differential net biases in the opposing direction in some other group. In the study done in connection with the Nagpur Labour Enquiry, discussed earlier in this chapter, the four interviewers obtained different results within certain given areas, but the differences they obtained were not constant from area to area. Yet, on *none* of the four questions analyzed did the aggregate distributions of responses for the different interviewers vary significantly. The biases apparently canceled out over the five areas. Thus, if the study had been made in only one or two of the five areas, we might have concluded that there was significant inter-interviewer variation.

It is doubtful that such situations are very common, but this particular finding is interesting as an indication of how differential interviewer bias can exist and still not be manifested in marginal distributions.[48]

On almost every study examined, some questions did show variation between interviewers. Two questions arise about the nature of this variation: In what manner did the distributions of responses differ from each other, and how were the variant distributions compounded out of the total interviewing staff?

With respect to the first question, the only reasonable answer seems to be that absolutely anything can happen. If the interviewer distortion stemmed mainly from the desire of the interviewer to have respondents hold certain opinions, then one might expect the responses obtained to be pushed in a *single* direction or conceivably toward a "don't know" category.[49]

In practice, we occasionally find distributions of responses differing in this manner. These differences may have arisen in a situation where the interviewers were concerned with the content of the response. But there are numerous situations where we find differences which could not readily arise through a content bias. For instance, there are situations where there are too few responses at both ends of the continuum and too many heaped into the middle category. There are situations where the middle category has too few responses, and both ends of the continuum have too many. There are even situations where the "don't know" category has too many responses, and both ends and the middle of the continuum all have too few. One gets the feeling from viewing such cases that it is not so much concern with the substantive content of the response that leads to inter-interviewer variation as it is differences in the perceptual frame of reference of interviewers when they code responses in the field, when they select parts of answers to open questions to record, or when they decide which answers need probing and which don't. Interviewers have different criteria for judging whether a response adequately answers a question or whether it requires further probing. Then, there are, of course, variations in interviewers' ability to think of proper probes for vague responses, as well as variation in their morale, or their desire to do a good interviewing job. Factors like these can explain how the distributions of responses can vary with no apparent relation to the substantive contents of the questions.

Similar conclusions as to the nonsubstantive source of much of the variation between interviewers were reached by Shapiro and Eberhart. It should be remembered that, in their study, extremely large differences were found between the distributions of responses obtained by different interviewers on a number of questions. These differences occurred in the proportion of "don't know" and "not ascertainable" responses as well as in positive response categories on attitude questions. We shall quote at length from their discussion of interviewer variation because of its relevance for our own discussion here.

The study of interviewer bias has most often been concerned with the influence of such factors as the interviewer's social or racial status and personal opinion on responses obtained to attitude questions. The emphasis on these sources of bias should not lead one to assume that controlling them will solve all or even the greater part of the problem of bias. Unfortunately the problem of interviewer bias is frequently complicated by the presence of factors which are unrelated to status and opinion but which are a direct function of interviewer performance.

The characteristics of the interviewers ruled out the possibility that differences in status were large enough to produce differential biases among them. Furthermore, it was clear . . . that they were thoroughly aware of the necessity for not influencing responses by suggestion.

In the analysis of the interviews with on-the-job trainees it was possible to separate from the general area of interviewer bias the following deviations from 'good' interviewer performance which contribute to bias: (*a*) reliance on an initial response; (*b*) incomplete reporting of the respondent's answers; and (*c*) independent decisions by an interviewer concerning the necessity for asking questions included in the schedule. The succeeding paragraphs demonstrate how each of these variations operated in a specific attitude question to produce a bias.[50]

It is apparent from the analysis that the errors were not equally distributed among the four interviewers. In about half the instances of interviewer difference, *A* was the principal variant . . . his interviews reveal the effects of some attitudes that did not characterize the other interviewers. These attitudes had to do essentially with method, and not with the subject matter covered by the interview.

. . . it is useful to comment briefly about the kinds of interviewer difference found in the present survey. . . .

Instances of apparent interviewer bias on attitude questions were discovered. These appeared to result not from variations in the interviewers' own attitudes toward the topics covered by the questions, but from differences in the interviewing methods used. . . .

There were fewer differences between interviewers in classifying respondents' answers, but instances did occur. This kind of variation can occur as frequently as interviewers are required to perform also as coders. In classifying information after the respondent has given it to him the interviewer must use his own judgment as to the meaning of the reply and the meaning of the answer categories he is supplied with. These judgments can vary widely from interviewer to interviewer if the categories lack precision or if the interviewers are inadequately trained.[51]

This explanation of inter-interviewer variation fits very well with the fact that, on the whole, variation is not highly prevalent. For, if the substantive content of the response is not the main factor underlying interviewer distortion, it can readily be seen that various distorting errors made by an interviewer could cancel each other frequently over a series of respondents. This consideration gives further credence to our view of the nonsubstantive source of a great deal of inter-interviewer variation.

We do not wish to imply here that no interviewer variation originates out of the classical substantive source. Obviously, there are some interviewers who on some questions on some surveys have a strong predisposition to get certain responses owing to their own expectations or ideology. We certainly have viewed distributions distorted unidirectionally as in the models presented earlier, and in many instances this distortion was in the direction of the interviewer's own ideology. But, we cannot tell in any particular case what the basis of the distortion was, and we wish to stress here that in many instances neither the interviewer's own ideology nor even his expectations need have been the basis for his distortion of responses.

With regard to the distribution of variant tendencies throughout the interviewing staff, we have relatively little evidence owing to the small number of cases interviewed by each interviewer on most studies and owing especially to the small number of interviewers used in most of these studies. It is our general impression, though, that for most questions, most interviewers get more or less the same distributions of responses while a few interviewers get highly aberrant distributions. For instance, the significant variation on the interest subquestions on the Denver study, discussed earlier in this chapter, was due in several instances to the fact that one or two of the nine interviewers in each of two or three sectors reported a large proportion of "don't know" responses while all the remaining interviewers reported very few such responses. In other cases, the variation was significant because one or two interviewers in one sector got far fewer responses in the middle category than did other interviewers, while on the same question in some other sector, one interviewer pushed most of the responses in the direction of an extreme category.[52]

Only in the rarest instances have we noted a bimodal distribution—two nearly equal-sized groups of interviewers where each member of one group obtained one type of distribution while each member of the other group obtained a considerably different distribution of responses.

Thus, either there is little net interviewer effect or most interviewers tend to distort their responses in the same fashion. But, on some particular questions, a few aberrant interviewers engage in highly idiosyncratic behavior and turn in results considerably different from those of the majority interviewers. This phenomenon of the aberrant interviewer emphasizes the danger of predicating generalizations about interviewer effect on experiments involving the comparisons of only a limited number of interviewers. Only when the results of the aberrant interviewer who happens to be included in the study can be incorporated into a large body of results from many interviewers, can we attenuate his influence on our generalizations.

This distribution of distortion throughout the interviewing staff on particular questions fits well with our conception of the basis of distortion. If the substantive content of the response were the main determinant of distortion, then one would expect that on questions where interviewer opinions or expectations were reasonably equally divided, the interviewers would obtain some sort of bimodal distribution of response distributions—a considerable proportion of interviewers would get response distributions biased one way while a considerable proportion would get response distributions biased in the opposite way. But, if distortion enters through the misunderstanding or the disobedience of instructions, then a J-Curve situation would exist—most of the interviewers would get about the same results, but a few would occasionally get highly deviant distributions.

It also should be noted that it is not always the same interviewers who are aberrant on different questions. Although we have shown that there is some systematic component to interviewer performance in that there is a positive intercorrelation in the number of multiple answers obtained by interviewers on different questions and a positive intercorrelation in the proportion of invalid responses obtained by interviewers on different questions, these intercorrelations are generally of only a moderate magnitude. There is plenty of room left for interviewer performance to vary from question to question as illustrated by the low intercorrelations in unreliability over different questions from the Elmira political study discussed in Chapter V. Actually, there are many instances where an interviewer obtained a highly deviant distribution of responses on one or two questions but not on others, while interviewers who were not deviant on these first questions were deviant on one or two other questions. Thus, inter-interviewer variation appears generally to be a highly idiosyncratic rather than a systematic phenomenon.

CHAPTER VII

Reduction and Control of Error

An underlying purpose of the interviewer effect study was to lay the groundwork for a systematic approach to the reduction and control of error arising from the interview process. Before we could consider methods of accomplishing this control, it was necessary to learn as much as possible about how, under what conditions, and to what extent interviewer effects operate. In the preceding chapters, therefore, we have explored the nature of the interview situation, examined some of the specific factors which bring about interviewer effect or error, and provided some evidence on the total amount of error actually occurring under normal field conditions.

On the basis of the evidence presented in Chapter VI, it might appear that the magnitude of error under normal field conditions is so negligible that there is no need for lengthy discussion of methods for control or reduction of error. This would be a most hasty conclusion for a number of reasons. Even if one were to grant that the sources of potential error seem to be under control at the present time, since error is not manifest, this might simply mean that survey agencies have managed to hit upon lucky procedures. Such luck is hardly insurance against error in general. The history of election forecasting provides a most appropriate analogy to the present problem. The successful forecasts of a dozen years did not preclude a failure in 1948, and upon analysis it seems that the success was based on a precarious system in which certain errors had temporarily been under control, or had been in abeyance, given certain situations, or operated in totality in such a way as not to jeopardize the final results. A far better insurance of future success than mere past success is systematic knowledge of the process underlying interviewer effect, and systematic discussion of methods of control.

It should also be noted that the evidence presented in Chapter VI on the magnitude of error under normal field conditions is neither massive enough in quantity nor based on a sufficient sampling of types of field conditions to permit us to conclude that the results of normal surveys are not seriously distorted by interviewer effect. The two large-scale studies reported in that chapter are both based on the staffs of one field agency, NORC, and cover, of necessity, a limited range of contents and situational factors. These studies were supplemented by evidence from other studies in an attempt to get an estimate of the problem that would be more typical. But still the question of evidence on *normal field surveys* poses a sampling problem far more difficult than the sampling of humans, and one which the statisticians have hardly touched.

For these reasons, it is desirable to deal with the reduction and control of interviewer effect, and to summarize the implications of the earlier chapters for the problem.

It will require time and research to develop the implications of this study for error control. Greater understanding of the interview situation provides no magical formula for eliminating interview bias or error, but it should help to define the appropriate directions for research to take and to correct misapprehension as to the factors which need most attention. Immediate or short-run solutions will have to be explored within the framework of the particular problem and the administrative and operating limitations involved. But the conditions of present-day research must not be regarded as fixed and unalterable, if a serious attack on some of the fundamental sources of bias is to be made. In this chapter, we shall discuss some of the methods which may be effective in reducing or controlling error as suggested by this study and by the research of others.

Approaches to the problem of reducing error may be classified into three groups:

1. Empirical methods which attempt to remove or diminish the *source* of error, so that minimum error will occur in the interview.

2. Empirical methods which may allow effects to operate in the interview, but seek to bring about a cancellation of effects over all interviewers or to produce homogeneity among interviewers so as to eliminate at least the differential effects of different interviewers.

3. Formal or mathematical methods which allow effects to operate in the interview, but attempt by analysis or measurement of the magnitude of the effects to minimize or estimate their influence on final results.

The methods employed to remove the *source* of error will depend on what the source is. Methods which aim at the cancellation of effects or at minimizing or estimating them by analysis and measurement apply generally to error from all sources.

1. CONTROL OF ERROR ARISING FROM FACTORS WITHIN THE INTERVIEWER

Empirical approaches to the control of interviewer effects through the manipulation of the interviewer may take the form of improvements in selection and training of interviewers or improvements in general personnel policy which will reduce turnover among the better interviewers or attract people of superior ability to interviewing work.

Improvement in the selection of interviewers requires some decision on the part of survey agencies as to what particular traits are desirable in an interviewer. If all kinds of interviewer error were positively and highly correlated, this problem would not arise, but in so far as skills are independent, some choice has to be made as to which skills are primary.

The essential phases of the interviewer's work are:

1. *Sampling.* The interviewer must be able to follow instructions for probability sampling or to use good judgment in selection under quota controls.

2. *Obtaining accurate information.* The interviewer must be able to get respondents to answer fully and truthfully, so that the opinions they express are not influenced by the interviewer. Social skills, accuracy in asking questions, and skill in probing are required in this phase of the work.

3. *Recording.* The interviewer must be thorough and accurate in recording the respondent's answers.

An interviewer may be skilful in one of these phases but not in another. The interviewer who is careless in the clerical work of recording answers may use excellent judgment in probing equivocal or vague answers in an unbiased manner. An interviewer skilful at getting the respondent to "open up" may find it difficult to follow complicated sampling instructions or may be prone to obtain or record too many responses in accord with his own expectations or opinions.

Before improvement in selection of interviewing personnel can come, it is essential to know to what degree these skills are compatible with each other and what types of individuals are most likely to have combined skills.

Intercorrelations of Interviewer Skills

An unpublished study of the American Jewish Committee described in some detail in Chapters III and VI provides some evidence on the intercorrelations of interviewer skills based on actual observation of the interview itself by means of concealed wire recorders and on comparison of the recordings with the completed schedules. Where interviewer performance is judged only by examination of the completed schedules, some of the more important components of interviewer skill cannot be adequately evaluated. The schedule may be completely filled out, with adequate replies on free-answer questions, but the central office can only infer the interviewer's skill in probing, his ability to obtain good rapport with the respondent, or his accuracy in asking the questions and recording the answers. There is nothing to show definitely whether the answers on the schedule really represent the respondent's views, whether the interviewer exhibited biasing behavior by projecting his own opinions into the interviewer situation or even "made up" the answers himself when he failed to ask the question or the respondent did not reply.

Table 66[1] gives the intercorrelations among four types of errors and the correlation of each type of error with the total number of errors.

TABLE 66

INTERCORRELATIONS OF TYPES OF ERRORS IN A.J.C. STUDY

	Probing Errors	Recording Errors	Cheating Errors	Total Errors
Asking errors..................	.23	.40	−.12	.53
Probing errors.................		.58	.24	.81
Recording errors..............			.04	.71
Cheating errors...............				.53

The intercorrelations among asking, probing, and recording errors are all positive, although only the probing-recording correlation is significant at the 5 per cent level.[2] The results suggest a moderate degree of association between the various abilities. The low correlations of cheating errors with the other kinds are largely an artifact of the method of scoring; when the interviewer failed to ask the question but nevertheless supplied an answer, no other error could occur on that item. This also explains the negative correlation between cheating and asking errors. However, the correlations do indicate that cheating behavior is not closely related to errors in general.

Since each interviewer had only two or three respondents and these respondents played the same roles for all fifteen interviewers, the validity of the intercorrelations is not certain. They may partly measure characteristics of the particular respondents, as well as those of interviewers. Intercorrelations based on a large sample of respondents in situations offering a more normal variety of stresses might be different.

A laboratory experiment to test probing ability of NORC interviewers, which was described in Chapter VI, gives an opportunity to compare probing skill in a laboratory situation with the regular over-all interviewer ratings based on field performance as determined from the completed schedules. From the results of the experiment, a "probing tendency" score was calculated for each of sixty-one interviewers. A score of 100 means that the interviewer probed the answers he received with the average frequency for all interviewers receiving these answers. The scores ranged from 26 to 171. In order to examine the association between probing behavior and the regular interviewer ratings, the average of the last three ratings was used to obtain greater stability. Interviewers were divided into two roughly equal groups—the thirty highest in this average rating compared with the remaining thirty-one. The distribution of "probing-tendency" scores for high- and low-rating interviewers is shown in Table 67 below.

TABLE 67

COMPARISON OF PROBING SKILLS WITH REGULAR RATINGS
(61 NORC Interviewers)

"Probing Tendency" Score	High-Rating Group	Low-Rating Group	Total
Less than 50............	1	3	4
51–70.................	1	4	5
71–90.................	5	7	12
91–110................	9	7	16
111–130...............	8	6	14
131–150...............	3	3	6
Over 150.............	3	1	4
	30	31	61

There seems to be some association here, but it is not very strong. The mean probing tendency score for the high-rating group was 106 as compared with a mean score of 94 for the low-rating group. The biserial correlation between ratings and probing scores is .25. The difference between means and the biserial correlation co-efficient are both a little short of significance at the 5 per cent level. It does seem to be true that the very low probing scores, which indicate that the interviewer was far below the average in ability to perceive uncodable answers which needed further probing, were obtained almost entirely by the low-rating group; of the fourteen probing scores below 80, eleven were obtained by interviewers in the low-rating group.

Further evidence on intercorrelations of interviewer skills is given in Sheatsley's study of the interviewer labor market.[3] Each NORC interviewer is rated regularly on (1) his performance on free-answer questions, as measured by the completeness and relevance of his verbatim and free-answer material, (2) his clerical ability, as defined by the interviewer's apparent skill in asking the questions properly and recording the answers accurately, and (3) his sampling ability, which is determined by his faithfulness in following instructions in making his selections under quota controls. These three ratings provide some measure of the interviewer's performance in the three essential aspects of his work, in so far as this can be determined from examination of the completed schedules.

Table 68 presents the correlation co-efficients among these measures of performance, based on average ratings over a period of time.

TABLE 68

INTERCORRELATIONS BETWEEN INTERVIEWER SKILLS
(Based on 1161 NORC interviewers)

	Tetrachoric Correlation Co-efficient
Free-answer ability and clerical ability	.52
Clerical ability and sampling ability	.46
Free-answer ability and sampling ability	.33

There is no question as to the statistical significance of the correlations based on 1,161 interviewers. The fact that they are all positive and moderately high indicates that the skills measured are not completely discrete.

It was not possible to determine how the intercorrelations vary with experience or by type of interviewer. The lower correlations of sampling ability with free-answer ability may be partly spurious, for an interviewer who rates low on sampling ability because he selects too many upper-class educated persons may rate higher in free-answer ability simply because such respondents are more likely to talk freely. Also free-answer ratings, based only on the completed schedules, had to be taken as a measure of the interviewer's ability in probing and rapport as well.

Sheatsley concludes that "nevertheless, the data do indicate that *most NORC interviewers tend to be generally good, generally fair, or generally poor.*"

The relatively high correlation between free-answer ability and clerical ability does not seem to support the notion that precise, meticulous persons are likely to lack social skills. Several explanations may be suggested:

1. A person *markedly* lacking in either social skills or clerical ability is not likely to be hired as an interviewer.

2. "Clerical ability," as measured by the ratings, is quite different

from traditional clerical ability, as measured, for example, by the standard Minnesota Clerical Test. Ability in asking questions and recording answers in a social situation like the interview requires some social skill, as well as the exercise of judgment and intelligence. Guest and Nuckols found practically no association between scores on the Minnesota Clerical Test with interviewer recording errors, even in a laboratory experiment.[4] But they point out that a special kind of clerical ability is required in interviewing, and that the type of clerical task performed on the Minnesota Clerical Test could not with certainty be expected to predict this type of performance. McRae found that cleri- cal ability (measured by omission of questions or failure to record answers in the interview) was associated with ability to handle the enumeration process which involves an interpersonal relationship with the respondent, but not with the other paper work involved in follow- ing directions on an area sample such as listing dwelling units, etc.[5] If we consider that "free-answer ability" requires the most skill in inter- personal relationships, "clerical ability" the next greatest skill, and sampling ability the least, it is consistent that "free-answer ability" should be most highly correlated with "clerical ability" and least with sampling ability.

3. "Free-answer ability" is not solely a matter of social skill or ability to obtain good rapport, but also requires the exercise of judgment and intelligence in probing and recording responses, qualities which would seem related to "clerical ability." The moderately high positive correla- tion (.58) between skill in probing, an element of "free-answer ability," and recording accuracy, an element of "clerical ability," cited earlier from the A.J.C. study, is further confirmation that the two abilities are related through common underlying elements, so that we would expect a fair degree of correlation between the two ratings. Even if we supposed that "free-answer ability" consisted of 75 per cent social skill and 25 per cent intelligence, while clerical ability consisted of 25 per cent social skill and 75 per cent intelligence, the correlation be- tween them would be about .60.[6] There is reason to believe moreover, that social skills are not as important a determinant of the free-answer rating as in this example, for there is evidence that some of the ele- ments that enter into "free-answer ability"—probing skills, for ex- ample—may not be closely related to social skills. In the A.J.C. study referred to previously, judges' ratings of the naturalness, friendliness, and rapport of the interviewers show no positive correlations with either recording or probing skill.

Guest also obtained results in an earlier study which suggest that the correlation between "naturalness" and interviewer competence as measured by lack of errors is low or negative.[7] In a later study, Guest and Nuckols found a negative correlation (.32) between "agreeableness" and performance, as measured by lack of errors.[8] In another study, Keyes noted some tendency to superior performance for "introvertive" personality groups and those with "low social adjustment" generally, especially in probing ability, although the differences were not clearly significant.[9] Finally, over-all NORC ratings for interviewers whose past job experience involved persuasion or approach were lower than for other interviewers, although their average scores on "free-answer ability" were fairly high.

The cumulation of this evidence leads to the tentative conclusion that, although social skill plays some part in the survey interviewer's work, it is not closely related to the other skills demanded by the job, and that excessive social orientation of the interviewer is not conducive to superior performance. This view is reinforced by the qualitative material presented in chapter II. Earlier conceptions of the interview process have emphasized its social nature and in consequence have tended to enthrone good rapport as the *sine qua non* of the successful interview, and to over-evaluate the socially oriented personality as the most desirable interviewer type. Some of the current interviewer manuals sound like the pep talks of sales managers. But the phenomenological investigation of the nature of the interview situation seems to show that the analogy with "selling" has been pressed too far. True, a moderate degree of sociableness and ability to meet people is an essential for getting respondents to consent to the interview and to answer questions willingly. Survey agencies are not likely to hire people for interviewing work who do not possess at least this minimum degree of "sociality." Beyond this point, however, there seems to be little relation between social skills and interviewing success over most of the range, and, in fact, there is reason to believe that too great rapport or too much social orientation in the interviewer may actually be detrimental. "The Creep" and "Tough Guy" cases cited in chapter II were instances where, from the usual point of view, rapport was poor, hostility of either interviewer or respondent was present, and yet there was no evidence that bias was introduced. In the "Hen Party" case, on the other hand, the respondent was completely "sold," rapport was excellent, but there was evidence that the respondent was aware of the interviewer's opinions and may have deferred to those opinions in giving her answers. The kind of situation which the salesman attempts to produce may be precisely the one which is least suitable for the accurate measurement of opinion. And the interviewer who is most adept at producing such situations may be as unsuitable for the interviewing task as the one who encounters too many refusals.

Other evidence was presented in chapter II to show that the respondent is often much more detached from the social aspects of the interview situation and from the personality of the interviewer than he is usually considered to be; and that the interviewer himself usually has a kind of professional task orientation which enables him to preserve objectivity; that interviewers themselves regard over-involvement in the interview socially as a fault to be avoided, and that interviewers as a group show less "sociality," as measured by the inclination to discuss personal problems with others, than the general norm of college-educated women with whom they may be compared.

Some general conclusions of a tentative nature emerge. Over-all skill, in the various phases of the interviewing task (getting respondents to answer easily and truthfully, recording answers accurately, and sampling efficiently) show a fair degree of association. However, each element of the job requires social skills and other abilities—carefulness, judgment, intelligence, etc.—in varying proportions, and these underlying skills, particularly the social and nonsocial, do not appear to be closely related.

The implications for the survey agency are that the current practice of rejecting applicants who are *markedly* lacking in either ability to approach people or ability to understand and follow instructions, and fill out questionnaires accurately is a sound one; but also that caution should be exercised in having interviewers who are excessively socially oriented. In order to apply these findings efficiently, these skills and traits need to be measured. Hence we need to know how they are related to other more easily determined characteristics. If we can find correlations between skills and independent variables, such as test scores or interviewer characteristics, we would have some basis for the selection of good interviewers within the limitations imposed by interviewer labor market conditions. Before taking up this question, however, we need to examine the relationship of interviewer performance in the routine tasks to his biasing tendencies.

Correlations Between Routine Skills and Biasing Behavior

The A.J.C. study described earlier also provides some data on the relationship between performance in the routine interview tasks—asking questions, probing, and recording answers—and biasing behavior in the interview.

Measures of biasing behavior were computed, based on a subjective evaluation of each error occurring on a Negro, Jewish, or Authoritarian item to determine whether the error was of a nature to influence the direction of the respondent's reply, or to distort his answer in the process of recording. Any error which seemed to increase spuriously the respondent's apparent pro-Negro, pro-Jewish or anti-Authoritarian attitude received a value of 1 to 3, depending on the estimated distortion potential. Errors tending to bias toward anti-Negro, anti-Jewish or pro-Authoritarian attitudes were scored −1 to −3 similarly. In addition, comments of the interviewer in his conversation with the respondent were examined and scored for bias in the same fashion, depending on direction and distortion potential.

However, in correlating biasing behavior with errors of the various kinds, the direction of bias was ignored and the scores on Negro, Jewish, and Authoritarian items were added together. Correlations of this total arithmetic bias with errors are shown in Table 69.

TABLE 69
CORRELATIONS OF TOTAL ARITHMETIC BIAS IN A.J.C. STUDY
WITH VARIOUS KINDS OF ERRORS

With asking errors. 26
With probing errors. 42
With recording errors. 38
With cheating errors. 35
With total errors. 55

Since each kind of error *includes* biasing as well as neutral errors, the correlations with biasing errors would not be very meaningful if they were high. Correlations of biasing errors of each kind with neutral errors of the same kind would have been more interpretable. However, the fact that the correlations are so low in spite of the procedure used indicates *virtual independence* between biasing and neutral errors.[10] This result is rather surprising, since we might have expected that those interviewers most affected by the strain of difficult interviews would have made more errors of *both* kinds than interviewers who could remain more detached from the situation. However, the intercorrelations in Tables 66 and 69 suggest that the reactional effect of the respondent on the interviewer is not uniform across all aspects of his work or that the interviewer does not have a generalized error tendency.

Somewhat different results were obtained by Guest and Nuckols in their laboratory experiment using three electrically transcribed interviews concerned with labor-management relations.[11] Answers were prearranged, one respondent giving predominantly pro-management answers, another predominantly pro-labor, and a third answers which were about neutral. The subjects were twenty-four college student interviewers who had had a small amount of experience in public opinion studies. The questionnaires filled out by those interviewers from the transcribed interviews were scored for errors in the direction of management, errors in the direction of labor, and neutral errors. A fairly high correlation, .52, between the number of biased errors and the number of neutral errors was obtained, indicating that interviewers who made more neutral errors also tended to make more biasing errors. The biasing errors, however, tended to cancel each other, as is shown by the low correlation of .13 between number of biasing errors and net resultant bias.

In this same study, the correlation between the direction of bias (pro-management or pro-labor) and interviewers' predispositions in favor of management or labor as measured by the Leaman labor-relations scale, was only .19, indicating that the biasing errors were not, for the most part, attributable to the interviewers' own predilections. These results, taken together, suggest to the authors that biased errors, at least those which arise in the process of recording, are really random clerical errors.[12] This conclusion is in accord with the theory of interviewer bias set forth in chapters II and VI, where the interviewer was described as essentially task-oriented, and error was traced not so much to the concern of the interviewer with the substantive content of the response as to the difference in judgment, and in the perceptual frame of reference of interviewers in coding responses or in selecting what parts of the answers to open questions should be recorded. In this view, the main sources of bias are misunderstanding of instructions; mistakes in judgment of equivocal responses; idiosyncratic definition of his role by the interviewer himself, proceeding from his own beliefs as to the nature of attitudes and of respondent behavior; and nonobservance of prescribed procedures when situational pressures are strong.

Since at least a substantial part of the biased errors occurring in the interview seem to arise from the same set of causes that produce errors in general, the selection of interviewers on the basis of skill in the routine tasks of the interview should also have the effect of minimizing at least one of the determinants of interviewer bias.[13]

The relation between expectational or stereotypic tendencies and routine skills has not, to our knowledge, been thoroughly explored, although some evidence will be presented later on their association with experience and with validity in general.[14]

Correlations between Skills and Independent Variables

Menefee lists as some necessary qualifications of good interviewers:[15] stability, honesty, and dependability, ability to meet people, intelligence, interest in the work, objectivity, and experience. Many more have been suggested by others.

While these qualifications may have some empirical basis in the cumulative experience with field investigations, they cannot have the weight of generalizations based on experimental study of the problem over a wide range of interviewing conditions. This can be clearly demonstrated in the wide variability in the qualifications recommended in the literature. Years ago, Cavan tabulated the suggestions of thirty-eight different investigators writing in the decade of the twenties on the common subject of the good interviewer.[16] The maximum agreement was on one trait which nineteen of the writers mentioned. In all other instances, traits mentioned by any writer were omitted by the majority of the other writers. With respect to one trait, "sympathetic attitude toward the respondent," there is actually a complete contradiction in the suggestions, with almost equal numbers recommending and opposing the presence of the trait in the good interviewer.[17] Cavan's tabulation is reproduced in Table 70, below.

It seems that different past writers may either be sampling different types of interviewing behavior in establishing the correlates of performance or may have no objective criteria by which they have determined the correlates. However, it may be that the different writers are talking about different kinds of interviews.

Attempts to establish objective criteria of interviewer competence and the correlates of such competence were made by Guest and by Guest and Nuckols in the two studies referred to in the foregoing. In the first of these,[18] fifteen college students interviewed the same "stooge" respondent. The interviews were transcribed from concealed wire recorders. Performance of the interviewers based on number of errors of recording, question wording, omission of questions, failure to probe, etc., was correlated with their scores on the Bernreuter Personality Inventory, the Moore-Hill College Aptitude Examination, and the Strong Vocational Interest Blank. Few of the positive rank-order correlations were high enough to be of predictive value. Such personality factors as emotional stability and dominance showed negative correlations with interviewing skill. Total score on the college aptitude test showed a positive correlation of only .11. A few fairly high correlations with some occupations on the Strong Vocational Interest Blank were found. Guest suggests that these might be used in combination with each other and with aptitude test scores to develop a multiple predictor or test battery of high value.

TABLE 70

THE QUALITIES AND ATTITUDES OF A SUCCESSFUL INTERVIEWER SUGGESTED BY THIRTY-EIGHT DIFFERENT INVESTIGATORS

	No. of Times Mentioned
Expert knowledge in the field of investigation	5
Broad general knowledge	2
Previous knowledge of the interviewee	1
Poise, interviewer should be organized emotionally, should understand himself	5
Good personal appearance, pleasant manner, well-dressed	5
Attitude toward interviewee:	
Respect interviewee, understand his point of view, do not ridicule or talk to him	19
Helpfulness, "here is a friend"	13
Non-moralistic or noncritical attitude, without emphasis on misdeeds of interviewee	13
Impersonal, detached, unsentimental, unsympathetic	11
Sympathetic	10
Unemotional, never feel surprise or shock	8
Responsiveness to interviewee, never bored	6
Impartial, unprejudiced	5
Be a good listener, give interviewee complete attention	4
General qualities, mentioned by only one or two persons:	
Health, drive, perseverance, humor, patience, jollying, cheerfulness, punctuality, courage, business-likeness, ease in talking	

In the more recent laboratory study by Guest and Nuckols,[19] twenty-four college student interviewers were first given a number of standard tests, including an auditory number-span test and sentence-span test, an abridgment of a labor-relations scale developed by Leaman, the Minnesota Clerical Test, the Guilford-Martin Personnel Inventory I, and the Wonderlic Personnel Test, this last being considered to measure academic aptitude or intelligence. The subjects were later tested for accuracy in recording three recorded interviews concerned with labor-management relations, with prearranged answers developed by the authors. Correlations between total number of errors and the various test scores are shown below.

The most positive results of the study are the indications that the more intelligent interviewers are less likely to make errors, as shown by the negative correlation of .55 between the Wonderlic test and total error score. Since scores on the auditory number-span test showed a correlation of only .02 with error scores, the authors reason that it is not memory-span, but some other aspect of intelligence that is responsible for the better performance of the more intelligent interviewers. Whatever the reason, there is a strong suggestion to select intelligent interviewers—even at high cost—"but mere college education is no guarantee of the intelligence needed."[20]

TABLE 71

CORRELATIONS BETWEEN TEST SCORES AND TOTAL NUMBER OF ERRORS IN GUEST-NUCKOLS EXPERIMENT

Minnesota Clerical Test....................	.08
Wonderlic Personnel Test (intelligence)......	−.55
Guilford-Martin	
Objectivity...........................	.12
Agreeableness........................	.32
Co-operativeness......................	−.06
Auditory Number-Span Test (memory).......	.02

The only other statistically significant finding is the positive correlation of .32 between agreeableness and error. The authors suggest that "agreeable" interviewers may record extreme viewpoints in a less extreme category or use less forceful words when recording free-response answers, leading to biasing errors, or that they are just less careful generally. If we consider "agreeableness" as related to social interest, this finding is in accord with the apparent negative association between social skills and other interviewer skills mentioned earlier. The personality factors of objectivity and co-operativeness show little relation to errors in recording.

In a recently published study by Herbert Fisher, test scores of recording ability (determined by reading a dull passage and having the interviewers record as much of it as they could) were found to be a good measure of ability to record responses in an interview situation.[21] The good recorders—those interviewers who made good scores on the test—recorded a consistently larger proportion of the responses in subsequent laboratory interviews, with the author acting as respondent. Furthermore, the poor recorders showed a slightly greater tendency to select responses which were in accord with their own opinions, but this difference does not approach statistical significance.

A large-scale analysis of the differential performance of various *types* of interviewers, according to their factual characteristics, was made by Sheatsley in his study of the interviewer labor market. He examined the quality of the work and stability (length of time on staff) of 1,161 present and former NORC interviewers.[22] Quality of work is based on median over-all ratings of each group on a five-point scale ranging from 1.00 (poor) to 5.00 (excellent). The three components of the over-all ratings, as mentioned before, were free-answers, clerical performance, and sampling performance.

The median rating for all 1,161 interviewers was 3.06, but the rating for those on the current staff averages much higher (3.62), reflecting the process of weeding out of the interviewers with poorer performance. Table 72 gives some results of the analysis for a number of the factual characteristics.

Summarily stated, the salient findings are:

Sex and marital status: Women had better average ratings than men (3.12 against 2.95), and the married women were superior to single women (3.15 to 2.91). Furthermore, the married women remain longer on the staff than the other groups.

Age: The 30–39 age group showed up best on both ratings and length of service. Below 25 and over 50, the quality of the interviewer's work is below standard, and the younger age groups also had higher turnover.

Education: College-educated interviewers achieved somewhat higher than average ratings, though the differences are not statistically significant and are offset by lower turnover of the less-educated group.

Field of study: The college-educated interviewers who majored in psychology, sociology, or anthropology received the highest ratings, followed by those trained in one of the physical sciences. Fine-arts majors received the lowest ratings of all, while those trained in business, humanities, or law also received inferior ratings.

Outside employment: Interviewers with full-time jobs in other work were below average on both ratings and length of service. Interviewers employed part-time on other work also were below average in ratings, though not in longevity.

Length of past job experience: Little relation between this factor and the ratings or longevity was noted, except that those with *no* past job experience did obtain somewhat lower ratings.

Type of job experience: Surprisingly, interviewers whose past job experiences involved least contact with the outside public, e.g., office and clerical work, medical technician, etc., averaged highest in the ratings, while those whose experience had been in jobs involving approach or persuasion of other people, e.g., salesmen, reporters, social workers, etc., had the lowest average ratings. In the middle, were those whose jobs involved considerable contact with the public, but little approach or persuasion—salesgirls, etc. Sheatsley points to the varied

TABLE 72

PERFORMANCE OF NORC INTERVIEWERS AS RELATED TO PERSONAL CHARACTERISTICS

	NUMBER OF MONTHS ON STAFF	MEDIAN AVERAGE OVER-ALL RATING	PERCENTAGE RATED ABOVE AVERAGE ON		
			Free-Answers	Clerical Performance	Sampling Performance
All interviewers...............	7.98	3.06	35	33	30
Current staff.................	25.20	3.62	50	48	34
Men........................	5.08	2.95	32	34	31
Women.....................	8.32	3.12	35	32	30
Single women................	6.23	2.91	35	31	22
Married women..............	9.71	3.15	35	32	33
Age:					
Under 21..................	4.79	2.68	27	24	20
21–25.....................	4.65	2.98	38	39	35
26–29.....................	7.38	3.13	39	38	35
30–39.....................	9.40	3.20	37	32	34
40–49.....................	11.42	3.04	35	33	25
50–up.....................	7.70	2.91	28	21	26
Education:					
Some graduate work........	7.28	3.20	39	35	36
Completed college..........	7.48	3.17	40	30	35
Some college...............	8.44	2.99	35	35	29
No college.................	10.06	3.00	28	29	24
Major field of study:					
Psychology, sociology, anthropology..............	6.40	3.33	48	36	39
Other social science.........	7.12	3.09	40	27	29
Business and commercial......	7.62	2.99	45	28	24
Physical science............	6.70	3.22	38	36	38
Humanities, law............	7.03	2.99	35	29	32
Fine arts..................	7.90	2.67	33	28	33
Employed full time............	5.92	2.95	34	30	27
Employed part time...........	9.12	2.99	40	31	33
No other employment.........	8.75	3.12	35	33	31
Past job experience:					
None.....................	8.70	3.00	29	34	26
Less than 2 yrs..............	6.82	3.11	42	34	37
2–5 yrs...................	8.35	3.12	38	37	32
Over 5–10 yrs..............	5.77	3.06	35	28	33
Over 10 yrs................	9.04	3.07	33	27	26
Experience with job:					
As teacher.................	8.45	3.16	38	30	35
Involving approach, persuasion	7.66	2.96	38	30	28
Involving public contact but little approach, persuasion...	8.95	3.05	31	28	24
Involving no public contact....	8.10	3.17	36	38	35
Type of past interviewing experience:					
Student, academic surveys.....	7.60	3.38	44	44	46
Other opinion research.......	10.10	3.17	36	43	26

TABLE 72—*Continued*

	NUMBER OF MONTHS ON STAFF	MEDIAN AVERAGE OVER-ALL RATING	PERCENTAGE RATED ABOVE AVERAGE ON		
			Free-Answers	Clerical Performance	Sampling Performance
Consumer, market research....	10.16	3.09	34	36	28
Informal unscientific surveys...	7.55	3.00	35	27	27
No past experience...........	7.64	3.05	36	30	35
Supervision:					
Independent interviewer......	8.64	3.05	35	31	31
Assistant to supervisor.......	7.00	3.17	32	40	26

nature of the interviewer's job as the explanation: "The group experienced in approach and persuasion, for example, averaged well on 'free-answer' performance, but fell down slightly on the clerical and sampling aspects of the work, while those with only clerical or allied experience carried out the last two aspects of their work in a superior manner."

Type of past (pre-NORC) interviewing experience: Interviewers experienced in student or academic surveys at college achieved the highest ratings of any experience group (3.38), but those experienced with other opinion survey organizations also earned better-than-average ratings and have lower turnover.

Supervision: Interviewers whose work is directly supervised (mostly those in the large cities) obtained higher ratings than those receiving their assignments from the central office. This is largely attributable to superior clerical work, an expected finding, since the clerical aspects of the work are most easily verified by the supervisor.

Some of these findings will not be unexpected to those in the field of public opinion or market research, but they are useful in providing an objective confirmation of long-held opinions and impressions. Others furnish new evidence on hitherto disputed questions, such as the evidence that experience with other agencies appears to be an advantage rather than a disadvantage, as some have held. Still others completely upset prevailing notions, notably the evidence that those with prior experience in approach and persuasion do poorer interviewing work than those without such experience. Yet the differences found are small in most cases, and none of the factual characteristics has in itself high value for selecting the superior interviewers, since no group shows an average rating of better than 3.38. In this sense, the study may be considered somewhat disappointing, but Sheatsley reminds us that interviewing is a complex of many different skills and cites the two Guest studies, already mentioned, to show that other investigators have had difficulty in finding factors related to even one isolated aspect of interviewing skill, such as recording ability. Moreover, if some of the factual characteristics are combined, the chances of successful prediction are increased. He states: "We find, for example, that housewives aged 30 to 50, with some past opinion or market research interviewing experience, achieve average ratings of 3.29 and remain an average of 14.9 months on the NORC staff. These are a great deal better than the averages for all interviewers, and a staff hired merely on such a basis would be expected to perform with above-average skill, all other factors being equal." Sheatsley concludes with the suggestion that co-operative research in the development of new and more appropriate tests offers the best prospect of success and emphasizes that these tests must measure not only skills, but also job motivations, attitudes to research, etc., if they are to predict *total* performance.

Another extensive experimental attempt to find the correlates of good interviewer performance is reported by Keyes.[23] The group of forty-five interviewers employed on a community survey of Denver by the Opinion Research Center described in chapter VI were the subjects of the experiment. The interviewers were given seven psychological tests, and their test scores together with interviewer factual data were compared with survey performance as judged from the number of "DK" responses, ratings of adequacy of respondent answers, evidence of probing, and completion of assignments.

The major findings are summarized below:

Factual characteristics:

1. *Education*—College graduates showed higher competence than the interviewers with some or no college. Those who had received training in public opinion theory showed outstanding performance.

2. *Experience*—Interviewers who had worked on twenty-five or more surveys achieved better scores than those with less or no experience.

3. *Sex*—Women obtained higher competence scores than men.

4. *Age*—The 35–44 age group were most competent.

Personality: A tendency to introversion and low social adjustment was associated with superior performance.

Interests: Aesthetic and theoretical value orientations were associated with better performances, while interviewers whose values were chiefly economic, political, or religious were inferior.[24] In terms of occupational interests, those interested in literary pursuits did best, while interest in "persuasive" occupations was associated with lower competence.

Intelligence: Somewhat superior performance was shown by those who obtained high scores on the California test of mental maturity.

Clerical ability and recording ability: Clerical ability, as measured by the Minnesota Clerical Test, and recording ability, as determined from tests constructed especially for this study, were both somewhat related to superior performance.

The study was not successful in finding psychological tests of high predictive value. Correlation co-efficients of the test scores with performance criteria were all too low to insure confidence in predictions made from the scores. Furthermore, some of the relationships previously cited may be spurious or confounded, since the *partial* association or correlation between the test variables and factual characteristics and the performance scores are not available. Nevertheless, the general profile which emerges of the better interviewer as female, 35–44 years old, possessing superior education, experience, and intelligence, with introversion tendencies is in general agreement with the findings of other investigators already cited. It will be remembered that the Guest studies showed a high positive association between intelligence and interviewing performance, with a suggestion of a negative correlation between social orientation and performance, and that the Sheatsley labor market study found that women, those in the 30–40 age group, those with superior education, and those whose background was in the non-persuasive occupations obtained better interviewer ratings.

A study by Taft gives support to this somewhat paradoxical finding of a relation between social tendencies and poor performance and provides insight into the dynamics involved.[25] Taft studied the correlates of ability to judge or rate both the traits of other individuals and the proportion of a group which would collectively show certain traits. The correlates were determined for a group of forty male graduate students on the basis of an elaborate three-day personality assessment program. Such specific findings as the following were obtained: The physical science majors were superior to social science students. There was a moderate positive correlation between accuracy of judgment and "carefulness." The good judges were significantly more alert, calm, cautious, logical, reserved, and serious. The poor judges were more often outgoing, talkative, and imaginative. The good judges were task-oriented rather than person-oriented. They possessed an "organized, socially passive, serious, unemotional and realistic personality." Taft concludes that: ". . . the good judges of others are extraceptive persons possessing a hard headed judging attitude . . . while poor judges are intraceptive persons who view other people in terms of their relationship with themselves; they are socially dependent and err in the direction of being over-generous."

While these findings bear specifically on only that component of the interviewer's task involving judgment or rating of traits, they seem germane to the larger findings reported earlier, and they suggest that objectivity in other realms of performance may also be jeopardized by excessive sociality.

Additional confirmation of this general finding is available from an exploratory study done under widely different conditions. A group of ten interviewers listened to a transcription of an interview, took notes of the contents, and later wrote a report of the interview. Their reports were rated by two independent judges on clarity of expression, organization of the material, completeness of recording of details, and freedom from distortion. The interviewers were also rated on their tendency to be "person-oriented" or "content-oriented" (analogous to our concepts of social vs. task involvement), as determined by judges' ratings of the comments and evaluations the interviewers were asked to make on the technique used in the transcribed interview. Correlations of the skills with type of orientation revealed a negative association between person-orientation and skill. What is again suggested by these data is that too great a social orientation in some manner interfered with the performance of the more routine duties of interviewing.[26]

Relation of Experience to Interviewer Effects

There is considerable disagreement in the survey field concerning the effect of experience on interviewer performance. Many research workers claim that the improvement in skills and understanding which comes with experience is offset by greater knowledge of short cuts and cheating practices and development of idiosyncrasies of interviewing. There is a general tendency to hire inexperienced interviewers who can be more easily trained in the research agency's particular techniques and procedures.

The factual evidence available does not settle all the issues in this controversy, especially since current measurements of performance rely largely on the evidence which appears on completed questionnaires and do not demonstrate what actually goes on in the interview.

Nevertheless, studies relating experience to various aspects of interviewer performance deserve some attention in any consideration of desirable interviewer characteristics.

The most comprehensive examination of the relation between experience and performance is again found in Sheatsley's study of the interviewer labor market. Table 73, reproduced below, shows how NORC interviewers' ratings changed with the length of time on the staff. A simple comparison of ratings of interviewers with various lengths of experience would not answer the question, because selective firing and resignation tends to weed out the poorer interviewers in time. Therefore the table compares the ratings over time of the *same* interviewers.

We see from the table that (1) the ratings for each group showed consistent improvement over time, with the single exception of the fifth and later years, when there is a slight drop; (2) interviewers who remained longest on the staff turned in the highest first-year ratings, and the longer-lived interviewers received consistently higher ratings at equivalent points.

TABLE 73

MEDIAN ANNUAL RATINGS OF NORC INTERVIEWERS

	N	First Year	Second Year	Third Year	Fourth Year	Succeeding Years
All interviewers:						
Rating for first year........	932	3.04				
Interviewers who lasted more than one year:						
Rating in first two years....	369	3.29	3.32			
Interviewers who lasted more than two years:						
Rating in first three years...	192	3.33	3.53	3.65		
Interviewers who lasted more than three years:						
Rating in first four years....	115	3.38	3.53	3.73	3.82	
Interviewers who lasted more than four years:						
Rating in each year........	67	3.43	3.65	3.82	4.06	3.88

As Sheatsley says, the findings "cast grave doubt on the hypothesis that interviewers do their best work early in their careers, and then tend to lose interest or to grow careless. On the contrary, there is, for the most part, a steady though not sensational improvement from year to year." This seems true enough for the interviewers who remain on the staff a long time, but it may be accounted for by loss from firing or resignation of interviewers who *do not* improve or whose performance deteriorates. In other words, those who remain on the staff are much more likely to be those interviewers who for one reason or another sustain their interest so that they are able to profit from experience. It is clear from the table that they were the better interviewers from the beginning. Sheatsley gives the median second-year rating of 3.11 for those who lasted only two years compared with a median of 3.53 for those who lasted more than two years, with the median for the entire group of 3.32. Examining the median first-year ratings, it seems certain that this must have been higher than 3.11 for those who were to last *only* two years. Apparently those interviewers who last only two years *do not* improve in their second year, but actually receive poorer ratings.

From Table 74 below, it appears that an interviewer's work during his first year on the staff is a pretty reliable predictor of how he will do

TABLE 74

RELATIVE PERFORMANCE BY GROUPS
(NORC Interviewers)

SECOND-YEAR RATING	FIRST-YEAR RATING		
	Percentage Below Average	Percentage Average	Percentage Above Average
Below average........	63	34	17
Average............	17	26	21
Above average.......	20	40	62
	100	100	100
	N = 137	N = 100	N = 132

TABLE 75

LENGTH OF TIME ON STAFF BY FIRST-YEAR RATING
(NORC Interviewers)

FIRST-YEAR GRADE	N	LENGTH OF TIME ON STAFF		
		Percentage Less Than One Year	Percentage One to Two Years	Percentage Over Two Years
Poor........................	33	82	12	6
Below average..................	104	63	18	19
Average......................	100	43	27	30
Above average.................	84	53	20	27
Excellent.....................	48	55	22	23

in his second year. This is perhaps the most important finding. As Sheatsley says, "It now appears that if an interviewer is not turning in satisfactory work at the end of the first year, the money spent on educational correspondence or personal re-training had better be spent on the hiring of someone else."

Fortunately, most of the poorer interviewers do not remain long on the staff—82 per cent of those with poor ratings in their first year remain less than one year and only 6 per cent of them stay more than two years. On the other hand, interviewers receiving the very best ratings at the start do not remain as long as those with "average" ratings, probably because of the competition of better-paying jobs.

We have been discussing the relationship of performance ratings to experience with NORC. In terms of prior experience with other agencies, the picture is somewhat different. We cited earlier the slightly superior performance of NORC interviewers with *some* previous experience in interviewing with other agencies. However, those with very long prior experience—over five years—show much poorer-than-average ratings; the differences shown in Table 76 between the distri-

TABLE 76

Average Rating of NORC Interviewers by Prior Interviewing Experience

	N	Percentage Below Average	Percentage Average	Percentage Above Average
No past interviewing experience....	430	48	17	35
Up to 6 mos. past "	139	43	18	39
6 mos.–2 yrs. past "	103	42	20	38
Over 2 yrs.–5 yrs. past "	70	41	22	37
Over 5 yrs. past experience........	45	54	27	19

bution of interviewers with over five years prior experience over the groups below average, average, and above average, and the corresponding distribution for all interviewers is significant at the 5 per cent level. This tends to support the contention that interviewers with a long record of past experience with other agencies find it difficult to adjust to the demands of a new agency.

Evidence of superiority of experienced interviewers in obtaining multiple answers on open-ended questions is available from unpublished data from the NORC Denver Community Survey described elsewhere in this report. In this study, nine interviewers were assigned to each of five sectors, with assignments in each sector randomized. On all four open-ended questions shown in Table 77 below, a higher percentage of the experienced interviewers (those who had worked previously on seven or more surveys) were among the top three in their sector in number of answers obtained.

TABLE 77

THE RELATION OF EXPERIENCE TO ABILITY TO OBTAIN MULTIPLE ANSWERS ON OPEN-ENDED QUESTIONS

QUESTION	PERCENTAGE FALLING IN TOP THREE IN SECTOR	
	Experienced	Inexperienced
	N = 19	N = 26
Suggestions for improvements in Denver...............	42	27
Reasons for attitude toward neighborhood.............	42	27
Reasons for moving to Denver......................	47	23
Reasons for attitude toward neighbors...............	42	27

It seems that these data can be interpreted in terms of greater probing skill for the more experienced interviewers. Evidence tending in the same direction, although not statistically significant, is available in the results of the experimental measurement of interview probing skills in a laboratory situation described in Chapter VI. Of the sixty-one interviewers who participated in the experiment, thirteen might be called inexperienced—arbitrarily defined as those who had worked on less than nine surveys for NORC. The "probing tendency" score, measuring tendency to probe answers which should be probed, averaged 93 for these thirteen against a score of 103 for the remaining interviewers.

In the Denver study, it was possible to determine the validity of respondent answers on a number of characteristics from outside records. Table 78 shows that, on two of the three items validated, the experienced interviewers obtained results of greater validity, while on the third item, the difference is negligible.

When the Chi-squared values for the three items are pooled, the results are significant at the .02 level.

How experience develops in interviewers an ability to get valid answers is not revealed by the study. It should be noted that inexperienced interviewers in this study, though lacking field experience, had taken courses in interviewing and other phases of survey method.

Suggestive evidence was reported in chapter V that inexperienced interviewers are more likely to introduce interviewer effect in the classification of responses into pre-coded boxes because they would have greater need of the aids furnished by unconscious biasing tendencies in simplifying the task of classifying answers.[27]

In their experiment on attitude-structure expectations described in Chapter III, Smith and Hyman tested the hypothesis that inexperienced interviewers would be more prone than the experienced to allow their expectations based on the whole attitude structure of the respondent to influence their coding of respondents' answers, owing to insufficient

TABLE 78

THE RELATION OF INTERVIEWER EXPERIENCE TO INVALIDITY OF RESULTS

	AMONG INTERVIEWERS WHO ARE	
	EXPERIENCED	INEXPERIENCED
	Percentage Who Fall into Groups Shown	
	N = 19	N = 26
Ownership of driver's license		
In the upper three in amount of invalidity.........	26	38
In the middle three..........................	21	43
In the lower three........................	53	19
	100	100
Personal contribution to Community Chest		
In the upper three..........................	10	50
In the middle three..........................	37	31
In the lower three..........................	53	19
	100	100
Voting in 1948 presidential election		
In the upper three..........................	37	31
In the middle three..........................	26	38
In the lower three..........................	37	31
	100	100

training or lack of conscientiousness.[28] In this case, a phonograph transcription of an interview with a respondent whose attitudes were predominantly isolationist was used. In Table 79 below, we see that, on both the questions tested, the inexperienced subjects had more incorrect codes and seem more likely to code in terms of expectation effects, but the differences are not statistically significant so that no definite conclusions can be drawn.

In Chapter VI we cited the findings of the Kendall study that inexperienced student interviewers were less successful in obtaining interviews than the experienced interviewers of two professional British polling organizations. Their lesser ability to overcome respondent resistance resulted in more refusals and a higher proportion of "Don't knows" on completed interviews, although it was not clearly demonstrated that the less experienced interviewers recorded opinions, preferences, or facts significantly different from those of the experienced interviewers. However, the fact that the inexperienced interviewers

TABLE 79

THE RELATION OF EXPERIENCE TO EXPECTATION EFFECTS AS SHOWN BY CODING OF THE
ISOLATIONIST RESPONDENT'S REPLIES*

	PERCENTAGE AMONG INTERVIEWERS WITH	
	No Experience	One Year or More
Attitude toward foreign spending	$N = 33$	$N = 36$
Spending too much money (incorrect)............	58	45
Spending right amount (correct), other codes......	42	55
	100	100
Interest in Spain	$N = 34$	$N = 37$
Take no interest in policy toward Spain (incorrect).	29	16
Some interest (correct), other codes............	71	84
	100	100

* Separate Chi-squared tests yield P-values of .28 and .16, and a combined test based on the aggregated Chi-square yields a value of .21.

had higher non-response rates is significant, because this difference might lead to differential biases in other cases where the characteristics being measured were more closely related to differential tendencies to respond.

All the studies just mentioned (and the Keyes study cited earlier) have shown some tendency for the experienced interviewers to be superior, either in one or another aspect of interviewer competence or in the avoidance of bias. It is true that an earlier study by Cantril, discussed in chapter V, found no relation between experience and bias,[29] but the inexperienced interviewers actually had participated on the average in ten surveys and therefore may not furnish a real test of the effects of inexperience.

In summary, the weight of the evidence supports the conclusion that we may expect superior performance from the more experienced interviewer. Two qualifications should be made, however:

1. Any apparent superiority of experienced interviewers may be due

as much to selective turnover (the better interviewer generally remains longer on the staff) as to the beneficial effects of experience itself. Whatever the reason, the length of experience still seems valid as a predictor of performance.

2. It seems that the research agency should be cautious about hiring interviewers with particularly long experience with another agency, but this should obviously depend on the degree of similarity of the work of the two agencies.

Correlation of Bias and Independent Variables

Very little information on the relationship between biasing tendencies and other interviewer characteristics is available. We have already cited some suggestive evidence that experienced interviewers may be less likely to bias results. In the Guest-Nuckols study already described, the number of biased errors of recording in an artificial interview situation were compared with psychological test scores for twenty-four college students. Errors were scored by the judges as in a pro-management direction, pro-labor direction, or neutral. The excess of errors in one direction over errors in the other direction was divided by the total number of biasing errors to obtain a *resultant bias index* (net bias). The correlations between these bias measures and test characteristics are shown in Table 80 below:

TABLE 80

RELATION OF BIAS TO VARIOUS INTERVIEWER CHARACTERISTICS

TEST CHARACTERISTIC	CORRELATION WITH	
	Total Number Biased Errors	Resultant Bias Index
Clerical ability (Minnesota Clerical Test)	.04	−.08
Guilford-Martin Personnel Inventory:		
Objectivity	−.07	.04
Agreeableness	.35	.24
Co-operativeness	−.11	.30
Intelligence (Wonderlic Test)	−.53	−.24

These results are not conclusive; the correlations of less than .35 are not significant at the 5 per cent level. In their general direction, however, they are corroborative of the persistent tendency we have noted for superior performance to be positively associated with superior intelligence, as shown by the negative correlations of intelligence with both total number of biased errors and net bias, and for characteristics which seem associated with social skills or social orientation, agreeableness, or co-operativeness to be somewhat negatively associated with performance, although this relationship is not a strong one.

Evidence on what variables might be used as predictors of tendencies to ideological or expectation biases is almost nonexistent. It might be expected that ideological bias would be most likely to be introduced by interviewers whose viewpoints are nearer the extremes. In the Guest-Nuckols study, interviewers were tested by the Leaman labor-relations scale, which had been shown to differentiate between persons who, because of their background, might be expected to be pro-management or pro-labor. However, the low correlations of .19 between scores on this scale and the direction of the net bias revealed little tendency for interviewers to record respondents' answers to accord with their own point of view.[30]

The quantitative material presented in Chapter II, particularly the phenomenological interviews, seemed to show that interviewers differ widely in their proneness to expectation effect. Some interviewers do not accept the notion of a consistency or unity of attitudes, and apparently this is particularly true of the interviewer who shows little "intrusiveness" or social orientation to the respondent, a fact which may prevent him from synthesizing his impressions. On the other hand, about a third of the interviewers said they could size up the respondent and predict his answers in advance half the time or better, an indication of role-expectation tendencies, and many interviewers reported using "contextual aids of a stereotyped sort" in classifying ambiguous answers.

When interviewers were classified as stereotypic or non-stereotypic on the basis of the F-scale derived from the Berkeley study of authoritarianism, found to be correlated with stereotypicality, a larger proportion of the "stereotypic" interviewers reported in a subsequent questionnaire that they could predict respondent answers half the time or better (44 per cent against 30 per cent for the "non-stereotypic" interviewers). From psychological studies of stereotypicality, tests might be developed which would be more efficient diagnostic indicators of tendencies to expectation biases.

The sources we have cited thus far all attempt to relate interviewer performance to classical traits or characteristics. The individual correlations found are too low to be very useful for selection purposes, although a test combining a number of characteristics might be found which would have good predictive value. The relative weakness of individual psychological tests for predicting performance is not unique to interviewing. Ghiselli found the same thing to be true of tests for predicting worker's performance in many other occupations, after examining some 120 published references on the subject.[31] Furthermore, he points out that tests which may be useful for one organization may not suit the requirements of another.

Possibly a more fruitful approach would be found in the use of tests which do not attempt to find the correlates of interviewing skill as such but rather attempt to measure performance in a situation which simulates that of the interview itself. This quasi-interview situation may be so designed that some of the more important components of interviewing ability and skill may be measured. A number of tests of this kind have been described in this report, though they were undertaken as experiments in interviewer effect rather than for the selection of interviewers. Comprehensive tests designed to measure freedom from bias, recording ability, and even probing skill and rapport in simulated interview situations would probably be very expensive and certainly would not always be practical as a regular procedure in personnel selection, but under some conditions, they might be used profitably, perhaps supplemented by batteries of psychological tests.

There is some suggestive evidence that such performance tests involving a quasi-interview situation may be superior instruments. A number of organizations now make use of a "test narrative," in which a fictitious interview is described in detail, with each question by the fictitious interviewer and each answer by the respondent written out. On the basis of these answers, the interviewers or prospective interviewers taking the test fill out the schedule or questionnaire. This procedure gives an opportunity to introduce knotty problems which will test at least the ability of the interviewer to understand and follow complicated instructions and his accuracy in recording respondents' answers. The Census Bureau makes effective use of such test narratives. In 1948, as a part of the pretest of the forthcoming census, the Bureau made a quality recheck of schedules in a few counties, using personnel from the central office to carry out the re-interviews. Comparison of test narrative scores with measures of field work accuracy of the original interviews, as determined by agreement with the quality check re-interview, suggests that the test narrative may be useful as a predictor of performance in the field, although, statistically, the sample is too small and the differences too unreliable to constitute definite proof.[32] Researchers working for the British Social Survey report that they have found the "test narrative" approach useful in the selection of interviewers.[33] For the purpose of devising an upgrading scheme for interviewers of proven competence, the Social Survey used two tests:

one, a simple clerical test, the other, a series of dummy interviews with prepared answers (i.e., interviews in which the informant supplies identical information to each candidate). By this means, the researchers report they found important differences between interviewers in clerical ability and accuracy of recording, although admittedly they could not measure by this means alone, all the factors, many of them intangible, which go to make up the good interviewer.

The Smith-Hyman study of expectation bias, described in Chapter III,[34] provided an instance in which performance in a quasi-interview situation could be compared with quality of work in an actual field survey. Proneness to expectation effects, as determined from a laboratory experiment, was found to be somewhat associated with greater invalidity of results in the Denver Community Survey, in which independent checks for some questions were available in official records.

Minimizing Bias Through Training Procedures

Research agencies depend largely on careful instruction and training of interviewers in correct interviewing procedures for the avoidance of bias. These training procedures have been developed naturally out of experience and from the experimental studies of interviewer bias which have appeared in the literature, and the emphasis in training manuals reflects the prevalent beliefs as to the sources and locus of bias. Examination of a number of the training manuals currently in use by market and opinion survey agencies discloses that the principal source of bias is conceived to be ideological and that the locus of bias is considered to be chiefly in the process of asking questions.[35] By contrast, biases arising in the process of recording respondents' answers have received less attention, and the operation of perceptual and cognitive factors such as expectations has been almost completely neglected. We may hope that one result of this study of interviewer effect will be to shift some of the emphasis in training to those sources and loci of error which this study has shown to be of hitherto unsuspected importance.

Every one of the interviewing manuals examined has included admonitions to the interviewer to ask questions using the exact wording of the questionnaire and in the exact sequence in which the questions appear on the questionnaire, and every one of them has cautioned the interviewer to avoid influencing the answer of the respondent either by actual suggestion of answers or by conscious or unconscious verbal emphasis or mannerisms, and to refrain from expressing his own opinions, even when asked to do so by the respondent. But with the exception of the NORC manual, most of them have scant material on the biases which may arise in the recording process. None of them that we have seen makes any mention of possible biases arising from interviewer expectations, including the NORC interview manual, which is the most voluminous and has twenty-five separate references to biasing factors, including even a warning concerning biases arising from differences in race, economic class, or sex between interviewer and respondent.

Curiously enough, one manual contains an admonition which would seem to encourage the introduction of bias through the employment of attitude-structure expectations. We quote: "Should the respondent change his opinion during the course of an interview, you must check over the questionnaire from the beginning and make sure all answers are consistent." And again: "Make sure *all* answers are properly coordinated and provide a complete story."

This insistence on consistency seems to require that the interviewer *reject* any answer not in accord with his expectations based on the attitudes revealed by answers to the earlier questions!

However, it should be stated that agencies have made and are making continuous efforts to eliminate or reduce bias in interviewing by intensive instruction and training, by means of manuals, specifications for particular surveys, and by continuing supervision and inspection of the interviewer's work. Every effort is made to enforce uniform practices in interviewing so that the results will at least be comparable. The degree of supervision exercised varies depending on the kind of work and the size of staff of the particular agency. Some of the larger agencies have regional supervisors who are in at least occasional contact with the interviewers. NORC training and supervision procedures are described at length in an appendix to this report. Each interviewer's work is rated regularly, and upon the completion of each assignment, the interviewer receives a personal letter from the central office in which errors of procedure, in so far as they can be detected from examination of the completed schedules, are pointed out to him. For example, marked or unusual patterns in the responses, the repetition of particular words or phrases in free-answer replies, indications that suggestive probes have been used, deviant behavior as revealed by comments on the interviewer's report form, and the like faults are noted and called to the attention of the interviewers.

Similar procedures are used by other agencies. This intensive training is designed not only to reduce error but to produce homogeneity, which is useful in itself in error control, as we shall have occasion to elaborate later on.

When the interviewer is first hired, he receives individual training in NORC techniques and procedures under the personal direction of an office or regional supervisor. This training includes study of the manual, basic instructions, and trial interviews, which are observed and criticized by the supervisor. During the course of this training, the supervisor will point out weaknesses and biasing tendencies in the interviewer's work. Applicants with obviously biasing personal characteristics are never hired, and the new interviewer is indoctrinated early in his training with such precepts as "Never suggest an answer," "Ask all questions exactly as worded," "Never show surprise at a person's answer," "Never reveal your own opinions," etc. The interviewer manual devotes particular and detailed attention to the subjects of field ratings and probing behavior—two of the areas in which studies have found greatest evidence of bias. The specifications for each survey point out the areas in which bias is most likely to occur on the survey.

Improvement in Personnel Policies and Working Conditions

To one familiar with the status of present-day interviewing and the conditions under which interviewers work, there must appear to be a certain futility in elaborate research to find methods of selecting the best interviewers, without at the same time finding ways to make interviewing work sufficiently attractive to appeal to such hypothetically superior personnel. Lists of the qualifications required for good interviewers have been made to sound like a catalog of all the virtues—a high degree of intelligence, pleasing personality, carefulness, dependability, honesty, good physical condition, good education, and many others. But what does the research agency offer for this paragon? Work which is physically and mentally demanding, low pay, sporadic assignments given with little advance notice, and no opportunity for advancement. Present average pay rates for interviewing work run as low as $1.00 per hour, compared with the average rates of 70–75 cents common ten years ago. Although we sometimes see interviewing characterized as "professional" work, such pay rates could hardly be expected to attract persons with professional qualifications, certainly not for full-time work.

But interviewing, as market and opinion research is currently organized, is not full-time work. The frequency and size of assignments varies somewhat from one agency to another, but the range is probably from about eight to twenty assignments per year, of a few hours to four or five days in length. Hence, most of the agencies rely on housewives and others who do not have to work full-time for a living, who may be able to use a little pin-money, or who accept the work because it relieves the tedium of household duties. For the compensation received, it seems that they produce a high caliber of work! Thirty-eight per cent of NORC interviewers, in reply to a mail questionnaire thought they would continue to do NORC interviewing even if paid only 75¢ an hour, and only 29 per cent thought they would be better interviewers if paid $1.50 an hour.[36] However, it may very well be true that if interviewers were employed on a full-time basis and given more of a professional status and higher rates of pay improvement in results would be obtained. Opinion survey agencies in particular, because of the presumed effect of their findings in the determination of public policy, have a responsibility to increase the reliability of these findings. And a mere statement of the undoubted difficulties in the way of employment of full-time interviewers at higher rates of pay does not discharge this responsibility. If current limitations imposed by financial and operating conditions are accepted as fixed and unalterable, it is doubtful if any thoroughgoing improvement in interviewing standards can be achieved.

Improvement in the conditions of interviewing work might not only attract a superior type of interviewer but might also bring about a reduction in turnover of the better interviewers. As matters now stand, many of the better interviewers leave after a short period to take better-paying jobs. Of all NORC interviewers hired over a period of years, only one in five remained as long as two years or completed as many as twenty assignments. The NORC experience is fairly typical of most research organizations. In contrast, of interviewers hired by the Bureau of Agricultural Economics during four war years, almost half remained two years or more. BAE interviewers were employed full-time, had professional status, and received considerably higher-than-average pay. This comparison implies that interviewer turnover would be greatly reduced if the job could be made to offer greater security, more regularity, higher pay, and higher status.

On the other hand, as long as interviewing remains an occasional or part-time job at low pay, turnover in the staff will be minimized by hiring persons who are not in the full-time labor market and who will therefore not be attracted by other jobs. Under present conditions, the frequency and size of assignments and the type of work determine almost completely the type of interviewer hired. The cities and counties in which the services of interviewers are required are specified by the sampling requirements, and hence the field department is restricted in its ability to act on independent applications, or to increase the fre-

308

quency of assignments. If interviewing were to be made a full-time job, research agencies would probably not only have to pool their interviewing staffs (a practice already followed to some extent) but might also be forced to use the same national samples of primary areas. And higher rates of pay for interviewing would mean drastic changes in the economics of the industry. It is unlikely that such changes will come about without great pressure from outside.

2. CONTROL OF ERRORS ARISING FROM RESPONDENT REACTIONS

In Chapter IV, it was pointed out that certain respondent reactions arise from the interpersonal nature of the interview *situation* itself, independently of the particular interviewer. Reduction of the error from this source can be effected therefore only through modification of the interview *situation*, as discussed in the next section.

Bias arising from the group membership disparities between interviewers and respondents has long been recognized by research agencies, which have modified certain practices to control error. As Sheatsley remarks:

It has become more and more unlikely that any research agency today, except for experimental purposes, would use white interviewers to survey the opinions of a cross-section of Negroes, would hire "Jewish-looking" interviewers to conduct a poll on the subject of anti-Semitism or would employ a crew of upper class clubwomen to carry out a survey on the attitudes of the slum dwellers.

But aside from such precautions in special cases where it is clear that the group membership disparity could seriously affect the results, such disparities continue to exist as a potential source of bias. In his study of the composition of existing field staffs, Sheatsley shows that interviewers are of a considerably higher education and socio-economic status than the general population. "The 'typical' interviewer, in fact, is an upper-middle class woman, about 40 years old, with at least one or two years of college."

The Katz study, referred to in Chapter IV, provided evidence that the use of middle-class interviewers to interview the working-class population tends to distort results in the direction of conservatism. Selection of respondents under quota sampling, as has been shown repeatedly, tends to produce an under-representation of lower-income and lower-education groups, and such an under-representation also distorts results in the conservative direction.[37] This compounded bias against lower-class opinion is probably the largest and most systematic of all biases operating in opinion survey work and is probably responsible for the Republican bias in the results of many of past election polls. More serious in its effects would be the continual pro-conservative bias in the studies of opinion on important public issues in the interim between elections.

What can survey agencies do to minimize such biases? An approach involving matching or dovetailing characteristics of interviewer and respondent is severely limited by labor market and administrative conditions. First of all, the existing composition of interviewer staffs is determined largely by the nature of the work—the fact that interviewing is a white-collar part-time job with a low hourly pay rate means necessarily that most interviewers will be people who do not have primary responsibility for a family and will be drawn predominantly from among middle-class housewives. Hence, apart from such experiments as Katz made, the economics of survey work exclude most working-class people from interviewing. So under existing conditions, the general composition of interviewing staffs cannot be greatly altered. And even for special types of surveys in which group disparities might be considered as particularly great potential sources of bias, operating conditions impose severe limitations on any approach to minimizing biases through matching characteristics of interviewer and respondent.

Sheatsley states the problem clearly:[38]

Although most research agencies handle a wide variety of studies, the composition of their field staffs can be modified in only very minor ways. . . . By and large, the same interviewers must be used for all types of studies because they have been trained for our work, at considerable expense, and because it would not be possible to recruit and train a different nationwide field staff for each particular type of study we conduct.

Furthermore, most market and opinion surveys are national cross-sectional studies, so that each interviewer must interview a representative sample of *all* types of people in his own town. Even if it were feasible to employ many different interviewers in the same town, there is no sure means of "matching" interviewer and respondent in advance.

However, some of the survey agencies have made some attempt to achieve a partial "matching" by trying to make the field staff a miniature sample of the population being studied—usually a national cross section with respect to certain characteristics, e.g., by hiring approximately equal numbers of men and women or proportionate numbers of Republicans and Democrats, on the theory that biases will cancel out, a sort of application of Mosteller's expedient of equal numbers of pro- and con-interviewers to be discussed later on. Agencies which maintain large field staffs, such as AIPO, tend to emphasize this solution, since greater flexibility of the large staff enables the agency to select its interviewers to fit the study. Such attempts have not been completely successful, and in any case, do not greatly affect potential reactional biases, since they are directed mainly toward minimizing ideological bias of the *interviewer* rather than differential *respondent* reaction to the interviewer.

Smaller agencies cannot use this approach and hence rely largely on training methods to avoid bias. It is possible for these agencies to exercise closer supervision over their smaller staffs and to train each interviewer in talking to all kinds of people. No matter how intensive the training in correct interviewing procedures may be, however, it cannot eliminate biases from respondent reactions to the *appearance* of the interviewer himself.

3. CONTROL OF ERROR THROUGH MODIFICATION OF THE SITUATION

Perhaps the most practical approach to the reduction of interviewer effect lies in greater control over or modification of the situational factors which mediate effects. The discussion in Chapter V points out that the psychological processes and tendencies in interviewer and respondent which lead to bias remain latent until the conditions of the interview situation permit their manifestation. Where the effects manifested by an interviewer are consistent, they are caused mainly by personal factors, and the approach of better interviewer selection and training would be most fruitful. But where effects are *inconsistent*, situational factors are chiefly responsible, and our aim should be to modify these conditions in so far as possible to render them less favorable to the realization of the latent biasing tendencies.

Implicit in the standardization of instructions and interview procedure, which is common practice in survey work, is the continuing effort to minimize interviewer effect by control over the situational conditions and over the interviewer's behavior in response to these conditions. But as our study has shown, this control has not always been effective against situational stresses.

Some aspects of the interview situation which may lead to bias are not manipulable as we pointed out in Chapter V. Aside from the difficulty of controlling the personal factors or psychological propensities within the interviewer which lead to bias in certain situations, the respondent himself cannot be controlled, and the broader objectives of the survey may conflict with the effort to modify biases inherent in the situation, e.g., we may have to ask a series of questions on interrelated attitudes even though such a series may dispose toward maximum operation of attitude-structure expectation effects. Other limitations were mentioned in Chapter V. Controls must not be applied to the extent that they reduce the interviewer's ability to use his skills or the respondent's feeling of ease in the interview. Nevertheless, the theory of effects of situational factors elaborated in chapter V contains many implications for modifying the situation so as to eliminate or reduce interviewer effects. The reader must weigh these potential gains against other considerations and make decisions most appropriate to his own research problems. Thus, for example, the evidence that lack of structure in procedures is a major source of error would normally lead to the conclusion that the use of field ratings and open-ended questions should be avoided. However, there may well be overriding considerations dictating the use of such procedures. Under such conditions of a need to use potentially dangerous procedures, one must seek the control of error through the other means suggested. One would then seek by training and selection and appropriate administrative policies to produce a staff which would undertake such procedures with impunity.

Although the mere presence of the interviewer is often sufficient to induce *some* bias, effects will increase in the degree that the personality of the interviewer enters the situation as a focus for the respondent. The available techniques for collecting information may be scaled according to the degree to which they "socially involve" the respondent in this manner from minimum to maximum involvement.

1. Self-administered questionnaires, which may be mail questionnaires or self-enumeration schedules picked up by the interviewer.

2. Secret ballots, handed to the respondent by the interviewer, but filled out in the interviewer's presence.

3. The "deliberative" technique, by which the interviewer leaves the questionnaire for the respondent to "think about" and returns later to conduct the interview.

4. The personal interview of the usual type.

The tests cited in Chapter V do not *conclusively* demonstrate that effects uniformly increase with the presumed increase in opportunity for respondent reaction from the first to the fourth of these techniques, and it was pointed out that respondent reaction to perceived group membership could function partly independently of verbalization by the interviewer. However, where the respondent's prestige is involved in the answer to the question, or where the questions are of a highly personal nature or otherwise embarrassing to either interviewer or respondent, there is some evidence that effects will tend to be greater as the technique employed increases the ratio of "social involvement" to "total involvement." For questions of this type, research agencies might consider more frequent employment of the less socially involving techniques, or at least a combination of techniques, with the usual type of personal interview reserved for those questions which experience has shown are less productive of bias, unless other gains to be derived through the agency of the interviewer are paramount. Where these other gains dictate the use of the personal interview, variations within the interview should be attempted of such a nature as to alter the respondent's perception of the saliency of the interactional process. One such modification involving interview techniques by which the interviewer asks the questions but does not record the answers in the respondent's presence has been used in the past, on the theory that the respondent may feel more at ease and talk more freely than when paper and pencil are used in his presence. Under one method, the "reconstructed" interview, the interviewer fills out his schedule after he leaves the respondent. This procedure, of course, places a severe strain on the interviewer's memory. It seems that possible reductions in bias through better rapport would be offset by increased opportunity for the interviewer's biasing tendencies to come into play as a substitute for his imperfect recollection of the respondent's answers. Particularly attitude-structure expectations might influence recording, because the interviewer would probably recall at least the general attitude of the respondent and might use it as a clue to the answers imperfectly recalled. Payne reports errors in one-fourth of the cases when the "reconstructed" schedule was compared with tape recordings of the same interview, though many of the errors were trivial.[39] Probably this is a conservative measure of the reconstruction error that would normally occur, since the interviewers in this case knew they were being checked. Another example of error in the "reconstructed interview" is given in an experimental investigation of the counseling interview cited in Chapter I.[40] The completeness and accuracy of the reports were determined by comparing them with phonographic recordings of the corresponding interviews. The reports were written immediately after the interviews and the counselors were aware that the interviews were recorded. Most of the material actually reported was accurate (75–95 per cent), but over 70 per cent of the interview material was omitted. Some of the omissions were important, so that, according to the author, the reports "gave a somewhat distorted picture of the contents of the original interview" and were a poor substitute for the typewritten transcription of the phonographic recording.

Bevis describes a survey of gasoline station attendants in which tape recordings were used to take down the respondent's exact words through the device of concealing a microphone and recording apparatus in the interviewer's car.[41] Employment of tape recorders would, if unknown to the respondent, not only increase his feeling of ease but would eliminate all recording bias, as well as provide a check on bias in asking questions and in probing. However, besides the technical difficulties of using and concealing bulky apparatus in a home interview, the method seems highly objectionable on grounds of ethics and public relations: The secret would "out" sooner or later, and public reaction against the polls might be disastrous, since such records could conceivably be used to the respondent's disadvantage by a third party.

Mechanical demands upon the interviewer may result in pressure so great as to demoralize him, causing him to cheat or distort the data, consciously or unconsciously, to comply with the mechanical requirements of the task. Psychological difficulties for the interviewer may arise from requirements of the survey, which lead to respondent resentment, embarrassment or apathy, or simply from general respondent hostility. Again distortion and cheating behavior may result because in the conflict between the demands of the job and those of personal relationship with the respondent, the latter may take precedence, especially since maintenance of good rapport may be necessary to get the job done at all.

Frequently, these difficulties are beyond the control of the survey organization. However, in so far as they stem from survey procedures, these should be modified so far as possible to avoid such difficulties. Specific aspects of procedure which should be carefully considered are the content and form of questions. Types of questions which are likely to produce psychological difficulties for the interviewer or unfavorable reactions in the respondent should be avoided as much as possible or special techniques employed to mitigate the psychological difficulties involved.

Now of course, it is evident that all such questions cannot be eliminated. Frequently they may be essential objectives of the survey or essential to the analysis of survey results. However, it may be possible to lessen their biasing possibilities in other ways: (1) By use of the less "socially involving" data collecting technique. Income questions might, for example, be obtained via the secret ballot, even where the rest of the questions are asked personally by the interviewer. (2) By careful attention to *question sequence* on the schedule. Personal questions or other types likely to arouse resentment, embarrassment, or apathy should not be placed at the beginning of the interview, where they may destroy rapport at the outset, unless the survey purpose makes this order mandatory, as, for example, when necessary to determine whom to interview. (3) By greater attention to simplification of wording.[42]

In some cases, attitude-structure expectation effects might be minimized by embedding the significant attitude questions in a context of questions which have no presumptive attitudinal relation to each other, or by placing related questions as far apart as possible to prevent the carry-over in the interviewer's mind.

The situational pressures which bring into play certain biasing tendencies as an aid in coping with the difficulties of the interviewing task are attenuated by experience. The experienced interviewer has had practice in learning how to overcome many of the difficulties that arise in interviewing, and hence he is less hostile to such difficulties, is able to maintain a more detached or professional attitude in cases where the inexperienced interviewer might try to find a way out of his troubles by the conscious or unconscious employment of his own preconceptions or expectations. Thus the implications of Chapter V for the modification or control of the situation to minimize bias are most relevant when inexperienced interviewers have to be employed.

4. CONTROL THROUGH CANCELLATION OF EFFECTS

The empirical approaches to the control of interviewer effect which we have discussed so far are concerned with control of error at the source, through better selection and training of interviewers, matching interviewer and respondent characteristics, and elimination of situational pressures. Another approach simply attempts to produce greater homogeneity or zero *net* effects in the behavior of interviewers by selection or training methods, or by designing assignments so that effects are cancelled in total, even though they may continue to operate in the field.

Cantril and Mosteller suggest that interviewer bias may be minimized by selecting an equal number of interviewers on each side of an issue.[43] This conclusion is based on formulas worked out by Mosteller for the relation between total bias and the distribution of interviewers' opinions, and hence applies only to the minimizing of *ideological* bias—that arising from tendencies of the interviewer to obtain too many responses favorable to his own point of view. Unless the different interviewer assignments are interpenetrating, the effect will be confined chiefly to the minimizing of ideological sources of bias affecting the accuracy of *marginal totals*. The device has no bearing on biases arising from other sources, such as expectation, class differences, or question wording. Furthermore, there are a number of practical difficulties in applying this expedient. The labor market and operating conditions involved in hiring and maintaining an interviewing staff do not permit the continual juggling that would be necessary to insure an equal number of pro- and con-interviewers on every issue. Even in a single survey, usually a number of different issues are involved, so that it would be impossible to obtain an equal division of opinion on all of them. However, the principle might profitably be applied in situations which experience has shown to be most productive of ideological bias, or where recurring surveys of the same or similar type are undertaken. For example, opinion research agencies engaged in pre-election polls and in studying other issues highly correlated with political party affiliation might, on this principle, maintain approximately equal numbers of Republican and Democratic interviewers on the staff, as some of them try to do. But since labor market conditions and the nature of interviewing work bring about a high degree of homogeneity of interviewers' characteristics, equal distribution of opinions on most issues would seem to be difficult to obtain.

We refer the reader to the original source for Mosteller's detailed formulation of the problem. To summarize the argument here, note that the net bias may be stated as:

Net bias equals
pro-bias per pro-interviewer times per cent pro-interviewers
minus
con-bias per con-interviewer times per cent con-interviewers.

Now, if the tendencies of pro-interviewers to get too many pro-responses are, on the average, equal in strength to the tendencies of con-interviewers to get too many con-responses, it is clear from the equation above that the opposing biases will cancel if—and only if—the numbers of pro- and con-interviewers are equal. For every Republican interviewer who obtains, say, 5 per cent too many pro-Republican answers, there will be a Democratic interviewer who gets 5 per cent too many pro-Democratic answers. In most practical situations, there will be no basis for assuming a differential biasing tendency, so that on practical grounds equalization of the number of pro- and con-interviewers is indicated.

If we are unwilling to make the assumption that the opposing biases are equal in strength, Mosteller argues that an equal distribution of pro-

and con-interviewers is preferable on the grounds of symmetry—that is, the possible biases, under all possible assumptions, would distribute themselves *symmetrically* about zero if—and only if—we have an equal distribution of interviewers. For example, suppose that there is a 10 per cent difference in results between pro- and con-interviewers. If we make in turn the extreme assumptions that all of this bias were attributable to the pro-interviewers or to the con-interviewers, the maximum possible biases are plus and minus 5 per cent if the interviewers are equally divided. If the interviewers are not equally divided, one of the limits will be above 5 per cent in one direction, the other below 5 per cent in the other direction. Suppose there are 70 per cent pro-interviewers and 30 per cent con-interviewers. Then, under all possible assumptions, the biases range from plus 7 per cent to minus 3 per cent, so that the maximum possible net bias is greater in absolute magnitude than for the case with an equal distribution of interviewers.

It can also be shown that the *average* absolute distortion over all *possible* (not *probable*) divisions of the total bias is smaller for the equal-distribution case. Since the possible biases in this case range from −5 per cent to +5 per cent, the average absolute bias (without regard to sign) is 2½ per cent. Consider again the case where 70 per cent of the interviewers are pro, 30 per cent con, with possible biases ranging from −3 to +7 per cent. The possible biases from −3 to −5 per cent are replaced (as compared with the equal distribution case) by possible biases ranging from +5 to +7 per cent, a difference of 2 per cent absolute on the average over one-fifth of the range. Hence the *average possible* bias in this case is 0.4 per cent greater than in the equal distribution case.[44]

In case the interviewers are not equally divided on an issue but an estimate of the total bias is available, the assumption of equal biasing tendencies could be used to correct the results, providing we can be sure that pro- and con-interviewers were assigned equivalent samples. Suppose that the interviewing staff consists of 60 per cent Republicans and 40 per cent Democrats, and that the Republican interviewers obtain 57 per cent pro-Republican responses as against 47 per cent for the Democratic interviewers. The unadjusted estimate of the pro-Republicans in the population is 53 per cent (60 per cent × 57 per cent + 40 per cent × 47 per cent). The biases are not self-canceling, since we do not have an equal distribution of interviewers. To correct for this, we might assume that the 10 per cent difference is composed of a 5 per cent pro-Republican bias for the Republican interviewers, and a 5 per cent pro-Democratic bias for the Democratic interviewers. In other words, we assume that both groups should have obtained 52 per cent pro-Republican responses, so that this would be the corrected estimate. Clearly, however, adjustments of this kind would be risky unless extensive experience had shown them to be reliable.

Chapter V, however, provided a demonstration that biases in opposing directions do not necessarily cancel each other. There it was shown that in a particular case of bias connected with omission of an alternative, majority interviewers exercised their bias by inflating the category which they themselves would have selected, while the bias of minority interviewers usually took the form of inflation of the "Don't know" category. In this case, at least, the result is a systematic net bias in the majority direction. In view of this finding and the general lack of information about how biases operate, the uncritical application of the Mosteller-Cantril formula seems unwise.

In the unlikely case that we have actual information about the relative strength of the opposing biases, the number of pro- and con-interviewers assigned should be in inverse relation to the biases. If, for example, we have a total of thirty interviewers, and we know that pro-interviewers exert a 10 per cent bias, con-interviewers a 5 per cent con-bias, then ten of the interviewers should be favorable on the issue, while twenty should be opposed. The total bias in each direction will then be equal, since the greater strength of the pro-bias is offset by a proportionately smaller number of interviewers exercising this bias.

Since the Mosteller procedure deals only with marginals, some other device would be desirable to minimize interviewer effect for subgroup characteristics and for comparisons between subgroups. In fact, as we pointed out in Chapter VI, in public opinion research particularly, the main interest of the analysis is not so much in marginal totals as in certain functional relations, as, for example, comparisons between classes of the population. We can often tolerate considerable error in the marginals, provided these functional relations are relatively free from distortion.

One device that may be effective in minimizing such distortion is the use of interpenetrating samples. In the first place, the use of interpenetrating samples gives assurance that no single subgroup estimate will be unduly influenced by the idiosyncrasies of one or a few interviewers. For example, if we are studying the attitudes of various classes on some public issue, the ideal distribution of assignments would be to give each interviewer an equal random sample of the cases within each class. If a single interviewer tended to bias results for some particular class of respondents, the distortion introduced into the results for the class by this interviewer would be attenuated by the data obtained by the other interviewers. More important, the bias in comparisons between subgroups will be minimized. Even though the biases for the different subgroups tend to be fairly constant where a large number of interviewers are employed, a high degree of clustering of assignments is likely to result in distortion of subgroup comparisons because of interviewer variability and also because of interaction between interviewers and classes (certain interviewers may bias results particularly for certain classes). Use of interpenetrating samples will tend to insure the constancy of biases over the different subgroups so that no distortion or very small distortion in the comparisons between classes will occur.

Interpenetrating samples have also often been used for experimental purposes in the control of error, particularly for measurement of interviewer or sampling variability. Their most extensive use for this purpose has been in the experimental work of Mahalanobis in India, discussed later on.[45]

Financial and operating considerations usually dictate a considerable degree of clustering of assignments. However, the repeated evidence from experimental studies of interviewer effect that bias tends to concentrate among a few aberrant interviewers suggests the desirability of employing this principle of spreading risk as much as possible.

Methods of error control may be directed toward ironing out the variability between interviewers, as, for example, training methods which may at least produce homogeneous standards within the interviewing staff, although they may also leave some constant error. Like interpenetrating samples, reduction of interviewer variability brought about by the uniformizing effect of training will have the useful effect of reducing the error in subgroup comparisons. Such a reduction would occur when whatever bias produced by, or remaining after, the homogenizing effect of training was in the same direction for both subgroups being compared, which seems fairly probable. As an example, suppose Interviewer A's respondents are largely middle- and upper-class, while Interviewer B's respondents are lower in the social scale. On some opinion questions, more intensive probing might tend to push the majority of the responses which were initially "DK's" into the "yes" column. If Interviewer A probes more frequently and intensively than Interviewer B, his higher-class respondents will show a higher proportion "yes" merely because of the difference in probing behavior. If training methods succeeded in producing greater uniformity in the probing behavior of A and B, differences arising from the different "DK" rate would be reduced.

It is conceivable, though, that homogeneity might increase the error in cross-tabulation. This would be true if the result of training was to produce greater bias for one subgroup than another, or biases in different directions for two subgroups. This might even occur as a result of a procedure designed to *reduce* bias in the marginals, if, for example, the procedure could be applied more easily to some classes of respondents than others, but such an effect of homogeneity would seem unlikely.

A classic example in the use of training methods to produce uniformity in personnel interviewing was presented by L. J. O'Rourke of the Civil Service Commission in 1929.[46] The qualifications of 4,000 applicants for positions as prohibition officers had to be evaluated by thirty oral examiners. A set of hypothetical, but realistic problems, concerned with the investigation of reported prohibition law violations, was constructed to test the judgment, resourcefulness, and skill of the applicants. The problem was presented to applicants by the examiner or interviewer in a uniform manner; the possible questions the applicant might ask the interviewer were anticipated and worked out in advance; and a prepared list of answers or statements was available for the interviewer's use in replying to each of the possible questions. Next, the applicant was asked to tell how he would go about investigating the case. Again, every procedure which the applicant might reasonably suggest was listed for the interviewer, and for each suggestion, a series of probes or follow-up questions was listed, so that the interviewer was prepared with a logical and uniform method of probing that suggestion. A scale of numerical values was preassigned to the anticipated answers, questions, and suggestions of the applicant, and the interviewer was supplied with a table of these values applicable to all problems involving the applicants. On this basis, objective ratings of the applicant could be made.

Examiners were given an intensive training course, during which the entire group of thirty trainees witnessed the same oral examinations, with Commission employees playing the role of "applicants," and each trainee had to assign each "applicant" one of four possible ratings, say A, B, C, or D. The first three "applicants" were rated before the training course began. Comparison of the distribution of interviewers' ratings for these three with their ratings for the eighth, fifteenth and twenty-second "applicants," given in Table 81, below, shows how the training course tended to increase uniformity in the ratings:

TABLE 81

INCREASE IN UNIFORMITY IN RATING OF APPLICANTS AS A RESULT OF TRAINING*

RATING	BEFORE TRAINING Applicant Number			AFTER TRAINING Applicant Number		
	1	2	3	8	15	22
A	1	9	13	1	—	—
B	5	14	11	9	27	—
C	14	6	6	20	3	3
D	10	1	—	—	—	27
Percentage in largest rating group	47	47	43	67	90	90

* The numbers given in the table are approximate, having been inferred from the original graphic distribution.

Although the training of civil service examiners provides an extreme case of standardization, it is possible that this approach might be more extensively used in certain types of recurring opinion surveys, where most of the possible answers of respondents, both direct and equivocal, might be anticipated and probes worked out in advance for the guidance of the interviewer. To a limited extent, such a procedure is followed now by opinion research agencies in their instruction manuals, but the recommendations given in these manuals usually apply to general situations encountered in many surveys, rather than to a specific survey, though the procedure is used to some extent in the specifications or instructions for individual surveys.

However, training and other methods of handling interviewers (selection, dismissal, contacts, etc.) may not only produce homogeneity but also diminish error.[47] Occasional checks for bias may be instituted in nonexperimental surveys through the use of supplementary questions, minor modifications in survey design, or in assignment of sample cases to interviewers, which will enable the survey agency to single out the most defective interviewers most prone to bias, and either intensive retraining or dismissal of the aberrant interviewers may be effective in reducing bias. These, together possibly with infrequent specially designed studies, could be used to supplement the usual ratings of interviewer performance as a guide in handling dismissals. The evidence already given for generally superior performance of experienced interviewers seems to show that present training and dismissal practices do tend to weed out the poor interviewers and thus reduce interviewer bias.

Most studies of interviewer effect, however, have not been so designed as to yield evidence on *which* interviewers were biasing results. Conceivably erroneous judgments as to which interviewers are superior could eliminate interviewer variability by eliminating the deviant interviewers while giving results of complete invalidity, because a homogeneously bad staff had been selected. Sometimes internal evidence will furnish a clue to the relative validity of the results. Occasionally, independent checks may be available, as in the NORC Denver Community Survey, in which official records of the characteristics of each respondent gave an opportunity to measure the relative validity of the results obtained by the different interviewers.

5. CONTROL THROUGH FORMAL OR MATHEMATICAL METHODS

The approaches to reduction of interviewer error discussed thus far have all been concerned with manipulation of the factors responsible for error. Another approach involves estimation of the magnitude of error. Such estimates are of considerable value in the analysis and interpretation of the data, and they are useful in determining how the error arising from the interview process may be minimized in future surveys. The detailed discussion of the advantages of the approach will be presented shortly.

In Chapter VI, several different classes of measurement of interviewer effect were distinguished. *Gross interviewer effect* referred to all deviations of responses recorded by the interviewer from the "true" response, as defined for the study.[48] *Net effects* were defined as the difference between the distribution of responses obtained by one or more interviewers and the "true" distribution of responses for the population interviewed. Since errors in opposite directions may cancel each other, net effects may be negligible or absent even when a considerable amount of gross effect occurs. Also net effect may occur for particular interviewers while canceling out over all interviewers, leaving no resultant net effect or bias in the distribution of the responses for the total population of respondents interviewed by all interviewers. The definition of *inter-interviewer variation* is based on the concept of a potentially infinite universe of interviewers. Each of these interviewers, under given conditions, would obtain a particular distribution of responses if he interviewed all persons in the universe. Inter-interviewer variation is thought of as the variation of these separate distributions of individual interviewers about the combined distribution of responses for all interviewers. If the criterion distribution of responses differs from the distribution of "true" values for the population, there is net effect or bias so that the measurement of inter-interviewer variability does not provide a measure of the constant bias or net sum of biases over all interviewers. In fact inter-interviewer variation may be zero even when a large net effect exists, if the bias is constant over all interviewers, a condition which may sometimes be approximated in practice because of homogeneity produced by training methods or by the composition of the interviewing staff. In sum, interviewer variance represents the error about the "expected value" for all the interviewers, while net interviewer bias represents the deviation of this expected value from the true population mean. Total interviewer error is the sum of the two kinds of errors.

The condition for the absence of bias is that the response errors of different interviewers (deviations from the true values) be compensating, while the condition for the absence of inter-interviewer variability is zero correlation between the response errors obtained by a single interviewer. If the response errors of any interviewer tend to deviate in the same direction from the average error for all interviewers, his errors will be correlated. Hence, both the presence and absence of inter-interviewer variability may occur in conjunction with the presence or absence of net bias, depending on the co-existence of the two conditions. But if inter-interviewer variability is present, it means that at least *some* of the interviewers are introducing distortion, and it is not safe to assume that the individual biases will cancel in the aggregate.

There are a number of ways in which the measurement of interviewer error, in the form of measurement of gross or net effects or measurement of inter-interviewer variability, may contribute to the reduction and control of error:

1. By showing whether there is a problem, that is whether interviewer effect is large enough to be of special concern.

2. In interpreting survey results, measurements of gross and net effects make it possible to take account of the degree of *invalidity* of the data, while measures of inter-interviewer variation as a component of sampling variability enable us to state the degree of *reliability* of survey results.

3. A series of such measurements may localize the interviewer error. If it is found that particular questions or particular content areas are most productive of effects, attention can be directed toward improving survey procedures in such areas, and the survey organization will know where to place the emphasis in the training of interviewers. Studies of inter-interviewer variability as well as studies of gross and net effects may serve this purpose, since, as we mentioned before, significant inter-

viewer variation indicates that at least some of the interviewers are distorting the results. However, only studies of gross and net effects can reveal the presence of biases which are fairly constant over all interviewers or show clearly which interviewers are biasing the data. It may be that the interviewers whose results show the greatest departure from the average are obtaining the more valid data, but if we assume that the opposite is true, we may sometimes be able to track down the error by spot checks of the schedules for the aberrant interviewers or by reference to a priori considerations or experience. Where the error is successfully localized in particular interviewers, intensive retraining or dismissal may be effective in reducing error.

4. Isolation of the component of sampling error due to interviewer variation may enable us, under certain assumptions, to determine how great an increase in the number of interviewers is necessary to bring about a desired reduction in interviewer contribution to the sampling error, or to determine the optimum number of interviewers to give minimum variance for a fixed cost, or minimum costs for a fixed degree of reliability.

5. Alternative survey methods may be employed experimentally on subsamples within a single survey. If one method (such as the use of supervisors or supposedly superior interviewers) can be assumed for some reason to be relatively unbiased, the bias under the less accurate method can be estimated as the difference between the results for the two methods. Then comparison of interviewer variability and relative costs for the two methods will enable us to select the procedure for use in later surveys which gives the minimum total error (bias plus variance) for a given cost, or to combine the two methods most efficiently in a double sampling design.

6. Measurement of differential net effects of groups of interviewers of contrasting ideology, expectation, or group membership, if correctly made, would show the sources of bias to be attacked.

Problems in the measurement of gross and net effects were explored rather thoroughly in Chapter VI and need not be re-examined here. In general, such measurement is extremely difficult and usually not feasible under practical operating conditions, especially in the field of public opinion studies, where independent validity criteria are rarely available. For this reason, most studies of methods of estimating interviewer or response errors in surveys have been confined almost exclusively to estimation of interviewer variation. Since such estimates, as indicated in the foregoing, can be useful in the control of error in a number of ways, we will discuss here the conditions under which it is possible to estimate interviewer variability and methods by which the estimate may be accomplished.

The fundamental conditions for the estimation of interviewer variance for any characteristic are that the assignments of different interviewers must be interpenetrating, that is, they must be equivalent samples of the same population, and each assignment must consist of two or more sample units. The interviewer subsamples themselves may be simple random, stratified random, or systematic samples, and the units of sampling may be individual persons, households, or clusters of persons or households. Under these conditions, the variation among the distributions obtained by the different interviewers in the survey would be equal, on the average, to the variation among samples of the same kind and size taken by any one interviewer, provided there is no inter-interviewer variability, that is, provided the effect of different interviewers on recorded responses is not significantly different. Hence, by testing the significance of the ratio of observed variation between interviewers to the variation between respondents of the same interviewer, we can determine whether interviewer variability exists.

It is, of course, not necessary that *all* the interviewer subsamples interpenetrate. If assignments are equivalent for pairs of interviewers or within groups of interviewers in geographic areas or other subclasses of the population, interviewer variation can be estimated. Such an interpenetrating design was the type used in the Denver and Cleveland studies described in Chapter VI.

When the condition of equivalence of assignments is not met, interviewer variation is confounded with locational variability or variability between subclasses of the population. In normal survey practice, a considerable degree of clustering of interviewer assignments is usually necessary because of the expense and time required for travel between scattered units. In many opinion and market surveys, the population under study is the entire country, and in many of the sample places, only one interviewer is employed. In many others, the number of sample cases and the number of interviewers is very small, necessitating clustering to save travel costs. Therefore, it is not ordinarily feasible to assign equivalent samples to interviewers, even in sets. Thus under ordinary survey conditions, interviewer variability cannot be measured in any strict sense. This fact is often glossed over lightly and equivalence of interviewer assignments assumed without adequate justification. A number of instances of this kind in published studies of interviewer error were cited in Chapter VI, where the reasonable suggestion was made that interviewer variability has been greatly exaggerated on this account.

Under quota sampling, in particular, interviewer variation in the responses obtained cannot be measured in the strict sense, since the probability that a given individual will fall into the sample or be interviewed by a given interviewer is indeterminate. Interviewer variation in responses is confounded with variation between the different interviewer subsamples arising from the latitude allowed the interviewer in the selection of respondents. Where block-quota samples are used, as in the traditional NORC procedure in the larger cities (see Appendix B), this freedom is restricted by the predesignation of the blocks from which the quotas are to be filled. In this case, the assumption of equivalence of interviewer assignments may not be so greatly in error, provided the samples of blocks are equivalent. Maximum limits of interviewer variation in responses elicited, calculated from the observed variation in the obtained distributions of the different interviewers, may sometimes be low enough to justify a conclusion that interviewer variation is absent or negligible.

Moreover, from a practical standpoint, there may be some value in measurement of the variation even though it cannot be separated into the response and selection components, when the *blocks* in different interviewer subsamples represent equivalent samples of blocks in the survey area or within subdivisions of the survey area. The observed variation between interviewers, divided by the number of interviewers, could be used to calculate a rough approximation to the total sampling error (including the error arising from *sampling* interviewers as well as error arising from *sampling* respondents) or at least a rough approximation to upper limits of the sampling error of sample statistics about the corresponding parameters of the criterion distribution—the distribution which would be obtained if all interviewers in the universe of interviewers interviewed all respondents under the specified survey conditions. Also some idea of *differential* interviewer variability between types of questions may be obtained, although variations in selection of respondents may also have differential effects for different types of questions, so that even for this purpose, the comparisons would not be *conclusive*. A number of studies of this kind which provide clues or suggestions about interviewer variability rather than definite conclusions are reported by Stock and Hochstim and will be discussed further on.[49]

Sometimes the non-interviewer component of the observed variation between the results of different interviewers may be known from other sources, so that interviewer variation can be separated. This might rarely happen in the case of certain factual characteristics which might be known for different small geographic areas from a recent census. Of course, response errors are present in complete censuses and response bias is probably larger usually, but the contribution of *variance* between interviewers might be small because of the larger number of interviewers. In practically all cases, however, no such information is available.

In sum, the precise determination of interviewer variance requires that the study be specially designed for this purpose. Under ordinary survey procedures in the assignment of cases to interviewers, the variance between interviewers in small groups or pairs within the same geographic small area or in areas presumed to have closely similar characteristics might be used to approximate interviewer variance. Where each interviewer is assigned a single segment or area at random, a closer approximation could be obtained by spotting the sample cases for each interviewer on a map, subdividing the area covered by the interviewer into two or more smaller areas, and taking the variation between paired adjacent small subareas of different interviewers as an approximation of the true interviewer variance. Such methods would usually give overestimates of the variance, but at least they would set reasonable upper limits. Perhaps one practical procedure which may be used when recurring surveys of the same type are made would be to design an occasional survey to measure interviewer variance, and assume that this variance will be the same for other surveys of the same type. However, the repeated evidence given in earlier chapters, reinforced by some of the data cited later in this chapter, that much of the interviewer error and bias which occur are situational in character or occur randomly, or in the form of aberrancies of one or two deviant interviewers, counsels caution in imputation of the same variance to later surveys.

The concept of interviewer variability as formulated here as a form of statistical variability implies that its effect on sample estimates will diminish as the number of interviewers increases in the same way that sampling error in the usual sense diminishes with the increase in the number of units drawn into the sample, that is, in inverse ratio to the square root of the number of interviewers. A little reflection will show that the model does not conform to the limitations and demands of reality. If we doubled the number of interviewers and the variation between interviewers remained the same, then the effect of interviewer variability on the variance of sample estimates would be halved. Actually, in this case, the variation between interviewers would probably change because training procedures might have to be altered, possibly less time given to intensive training of each interviewer, and because a change in the size of assignment given each interviewer would probably affect the magnitude of response errors and the correlation of response errors within interviewer assignments. For example, with a large assignment, fatigue or time pressure might increase the tendency of the interviewer to cheat or to employ his own expectations or opinions in the interpretation of equivocal responses. In effect, then, any change in the number of interviewers results in a different set of survey conditions, and the strict definition of interviewer variability becomes the variation in the distribution of responses obtained by different interviewers *when a specified number of interviewers is employed* about the distribution of responses over all possible samples of this specified number of interviewers.

In practice, moreover, when the number of interviewers is increased markedly, the universe from which the additional interviewers are drawn differs from the universe from which the smaller or more usual number of interviewers is drawn. The additional interviewers may be less experienced, less able, or college students instead of housewives, and so on. Hence the variability between interviewers would probably be greater. The effect of interviewer variability on the variance of sample estimates is probably in approximately inverse ratio to the number of interviewers up to some number which does not greatly exceed the usual number employed, but thereafter the decrease probably becomes smaller, or there may even be an increase. Moreover, interviewer *bias* may increase if the additional interviewers are less able or cannot be given the usual training. Over a fairly small range, however, the assumption of constancy of interviewer variability may hold fairly well. Suggestions for reducing interviewer effect or response error by manipulation of the number of interviewers should be considered in the light of this discussion.

Methods of Measuring Interviewer Variability

The analysis of variance technique may be used to determine the presence of interviewer variability. This is the approach used by Stock and Hochstim and we shall cite some of their reported studies as illustrations.[50]

In one case, three interviewers were sent out in the same car and given an over-all quota by sex, age, and occupation. The total number of respondents for the three interviewers was 1,015. The results obtained are shown in Table 82.

TABLE 82

VARIATION OF RESULTS OF THREE DIFFERENT INTERVIEWERS ON THREE DIFFERENT QUESTIONS

QUESTION	PROPORTION OF RESPONDENTS GIVING THE SPECIFIED ANSWER			
	All 1,015 Respondents	Interviewer A (326 Cases)	Interviewer B (346 Cases)	Interviewer C (343 Cases)
Factual question: Do you know how to drive an automobile? (Answer—"Yes")	66.1	66.9	63.3	68.2
Information question: So far as you know does State X have any laws that limit the size of trucks, etc.? (Answer—"Yes")	67.4	64.4	65.0	72.6
Opinion question: Do you think bigger trucks should be allowed or are they big enough now? (Answer—"Big enough now")	74.0	73.3	71.1	77.6

The numbers of sample cases for the different interviewers are approximately equal. Taking this average as 340, and assuming for the moment that the interviewer subsamples were equivalent random samples from the same universe, the standard errors of the individual interviewer percentages on the three questions would be approximately 2.6, 2.5 and 2.3 per cent respectively. The difference obtained by Interviewer C on the information question does not seem to be accounted for by sampling error. However, on all three questions, the analysis of variance was made, breaking up the total mean square into interviewer mean square and mean square between respondents within interviewer subsamples. On the information question, the interviewer mean square, as expected, turned out to be significantly larger than the respondent or sampling mean square, but not on the factual and opinion questions. Thus interviewer variability was indicated for the information question. The analysis of variance for this question is shown below:

The total sampling error including the interviewer contribution was calculated, again on the assumption of equivalence of assignments. For this purpose, we can consider the analogy of cluster sampling. The responses that would be obtained by a single interviewer from all individuals in the population would be a single "cluster" of responses. A sample of k of these clusters or k interviewers is selected, and within each cluster a subsample of responses is taken. Thus the variance, σ^2_p, of the sample estimate of P, the proportion answering "yes" would be taken as the usual variance for cluster sampling. Assuming that the universe of respondents and the universe of interviewers are very large,

TABLE 83

ANALYSIS OF VARIANCE FOR INFORMATION QUESTION

SOURCE OF VARIATION	SUM OF SQUARES*	DEGREES OF FREEDOM	MEAN SQUARE
Total....................	223.0581	1014	
Among interviewers..........	1.4101	2	$.7051 = B$
Among respondents (within interviewer)...............	221.6480	1012	$.2190 = A$

F-ratio $= \dfrac{\text{Mean square among interviewers}}{\text{Mean square among respondents}} = 3.22$, which is significant at the 5 per cent level.

* The total sum of squares $= npq = 1015\ (67.4)(32.6) = 223.02$ (difference from above figure due to rounding p). The interviewer sum of squares can be obtained approximately by squaring the differences between the interviewer percentages and the over-all percentages and weighting each square by the number of cases.

and that interviewers had equal numbers of cases, this variance would be approximately

$$\sigma^2_p = \frac{\sigma^2_I}{k} + \frac{\sigma^2_R}{n}$$

where:

k is the number of interviewers in the sample $= 3$

n is the total number of respondents $= 1,015$

σ^2_I represents the variation between the proportions that would be obtained by different interviewers if all interviewers in the universe of interviewers interviewed all respondents in the population.

σ^2_R represents the average variation between all possible respondents of the same interviewer.

From the sample mean squares B and A, estimates of σ^2_I and σ^2_R can be calculated:

Estimate of $\sigma^2_I = \dfrac{k(B - A)}{n} = \dfrac{3(.7051 - .2190)}{1015} = .001437$

Estimate of $\sigma^2_R = A = .2190$

Variance of $p = \sigma^2_p = \dfrac{.001437}{3} + \dfrac{.2190}{1015} = .000479 + .000216 = .000695$

The variance of p can also be calculated directly from $\sigma^2_p = \dfrac{B}{n} = \dfrac{.7051}{1015}$

$= .000695.$[51]

The first term in the variance (.000479) represents the interviewer contribution to the sampling variance. The standard error of p is $\sqrt{.000695}$ $= .026$ or 2.6 per cent. If interviewer variability were not taken into account, the standard error of p would be calculated from $\sigma_p = \sqrt{\dfrac{pq}{n}} =$ 1.5 per cent. The net effect of taking into account interviewer variance was to triple the variance and almost double the standard error.

The conditions necessary for strict measurement of interviewer variability and for calculation of the sampling error were not present in this example. Since this was a quota sample, the comparability of interviewer subsamples cannot be assumed, even if the three interviewers were working in the same geographic area. However, the fact that the factual and opinion questions did not show significant interviewer variation suggests to the authors that it was not differences in sample selection which caused the variability on the information question and that there was some peculiarity in the way C interviewed as contrasted with A and B.

The explanation is reasonable enough but we could also hypothesize that C might have tended to select respondents of slightly higher education or class on the average, and that it is precisely on information questions such as the one in this case, concerned with fairly obscure state laws, that respondents of higher education or class might be expected to show differences from the average, while the differences between classes of respondents would be likely to be negligible on questions like "Do you know how to drive an automobile?" or "Do you think bigger trucks should be allowed?" In any case, the attempt to measure interviewer variability has at least the merit of suggesting the type of question on which variation is most probable.

Suggestive evidence that such selection variability may often be confounded with variability within the interview is provided by another study reported by Stock and Hochstim. In this case, the survey was especially designed to test the effect of sample design on interviewer variability. Two interpenetrating systematic block samples were used. In one sample, sex-by-age quotas were assigned within the selected blocks, in the other, specified respondents in specified blocks were assigned to the interviewers. Results on questions of six different types were first analyzed for the two samples combined.

The contributions of interviewer variability varied considerably with the type of question. To measure the effect of sample design, the interviewer variances were determined separately for the block-quota and

TABLE 84

CONTRIBUTIONS OF VARIANCES TO STATISTICAL ERROR

Type of Question	Percentage Contribution of Interviewer Variance to Total Variance of Estimate
Interviewer judgment (economic status of respondent)	55.2
Factual (car ownership)	16.7
Information (whether Store A owned by local people)	—
Multiple choice (which of 5 businesses most important to city)	43.7
Pro-con opinion (whether locally owned stores benefit shoppers more)	70.0
Free response opinion (variety main reason for shopping at certain stores)	64.1

the probability sample. The separate variances are shown in Table 85. On four of the six questions, the estimated interviewer variability is practically negligible for the probability sample, suggesting that inter-

TABLE 85

SAMPLE DESIGN AND INTERVIEWER VARIANCE

	INTERVIEWER VARIANCE		INTERVIEWER VARIANCE AS A PERCENTAGE OF TOTAL VARIANCE*	
	Probability Sample	Block-Quota Sample	Probability Sample	Block-Quota Sample
Lower socio-economic status	.0034	.04889	.14	16.60
Own car	−.00861†	.01003	.00	3.30
Store A owned by local people	.00430	.00442	2.38	1.10
Electric Company most important	−.00891†	.01133	.00	2.56
Store locally owned benefits shoppers more	.00145	.02445	.66	7.38
Variety main reason for shopping at Store A	.03228	−.00231†	15.84	.00

* The percentages in Table 85 represent merely the fraction of the total variance (sum of squares) due to interviewer variation. In arriving at the per cent *contribution to variance of sample estimates* given in Table 84, the interviewer variances of Table 85 would be divided by a small number (number of interviewers), whereas the remaining variance would be divided by a large number (number of sample cases), hence the *contribution of* interviewer variance to *sample estimate* would be much larger relatively than its proportion of the total variance.

† Although variances are positive, estimates of them are themselves variable, and hence may be negative. To estimate interviewing variance, the mean square between blocks within interviewer assignments is subtracted from the mean square between interviewers, and the result is divided by the average number of cases per interviewer (corrected by a function of variation in block size). If there is no real variability between interviewers, we would expect the two mean squares to be equal. But in such a case, the block mean square might be greater than the interviewer mean square because of random sampling fluctuations, and hence the formal estimate of interviewer variance may be negative.

interviewer variability measured from a quota sample is likely to reflect chiefly variation in the selection of respondents. However, the results are not conclusive, since the interviewer variability was higher on two questions for the probability sample.

The authors state that reassignment of sample blocks among interviewers resulted in a condition approaching randomness of interviewer subsamples, so that the analysis of variance seemed justifiable. The fact that most of the interviewer variances for the probability sample were very small lends some support to this conclusion.

The most extensive measurements of interviewer variability under rigidly controlled conditions of equivalence of interviewer assignments are found in the continuing series of studies using interpenetrating samples carried out by the Indian Statistical Institute and reported by Mahalanobis.[52] Surveys of housing and economic conditions of factory workers in the Jagaddal area conducted in 1941, 1942, and 1945 provide an example. The survey area was divided into five geographic subareas or strata. Within each subarea the sample units were divided into five equal subsamples, each of which was an independent random sample of the whole subarea. Thus the five subsamples constituted five independent interpenetrating networks of sample units within each subarea. Each of the five subsamples in a subarea was assigned to a different interviewer, and the same five interviewers were used in all five areas.

With such a design, an analysis of variance of the results could be made to show the contribution to total variance of areas, interviewers, and area-interviewer interaction. The results of this analysis for 1942 are shown in Table 86 below. Only three of the five areas were used in the analysis, as the numbers of cases in the other two areas were too small. The numbers of cases in each of the resulting fifteen area-cells were equalized by rejecting an appropriate number of schedules at random.

The various components of the variance were compared with variance within "area-investigator cells," that is with the variance between respondents in the same area interviewed by the same interviewer, and F-ratios computed. In the case of age and monthly expenditures for cereals, the interviewer variance was significant.

From the analysis of variance, estimates of the total sampling error could be calculated. We will illustrate by the calculation of sampling error for per capita expenditures on cereals. If B is the mean square between investigators, the variance of the sample estimate will be approximately

$$\sigma^2_{\bar{x}} = \frac{B}{n} = \frac{1.25}{525} = .00238$$

$$\sigma_{\bar{x}} = .049$$

The estimate of mean per capita expenditure for cereals was 3.09. The standard error of this estimate is approximately .05. The variance of the sample estimate calculated in the usual manner (without taking

TABLE 86

BENGAL LABOR INQUIRY, JAGADDAL AREA, 1942—ANALYSIS OF VARIANCE
(Analysis Using Equalized Cell Frequencies)

SOURCE OF VARIATION	DEGREES OF FREEDOM	AGE	VALUES OF VARIANCE FOR FOLLOWING CHARACTERISTICS			Consumption of Cereals in Pounds Per Head Per Month
			Expenditures in Rupees Per Month Per Capita			
			Total	Food	Cereals	
Between areas	2	62.13	805.52	36.5	0.07	79.6
Between investigators .	4	304.84	275.78	22.3	1.25	114.7
Areas x investigators . .	8	78.47	129.38	9.6	1.47	152.8
Between subsamples . .	14	140.81	267.80	16.8	1.21	132.0
Within subsamples . . .	510	127.74	168.12	9.9	0.49	100.3
Total	524	128.00	170.78	10.1	0.51	100.8

F-ratios of Variances (Ratios to Variance Within Subsamples)

Between areas	0.40	4.79†	3.69	0.14	0.80
Between investigators .	2.39*	1.64	2.26	2.55*	1.15
Areas x investigators . .	0.61	0.77	0.98	3.00†	1.53
Between subsamples . .	1.10	1.59	1.70	2.47†	1.52

* Significant at 5 per cent level.
† Significant at 1 per cent level.

account of interviewer variation) would be the mean square between respondents within strata (areas) divided by the total number of respondents calculated as follows:

	Mean Square	D. F.	Sum of Squares
Between all respondents	0.51 ×	524	267.24
Between areas	0.07 ×	2	0.14
Between respondents within areas	0.51	522	267.10

The usual calculated variance would be $\frac{0.51}{525} = .00097$ which gives a standard error of .031. Thus the effect of interviewer variability was to increase the sampling error by something over 50 per cent.

It will be noticed that the interaction variance for cereal expenditures was the only significant interaction variance, indicating in this case a *differential* interviewer effect for different areas. Accordingly, the significant values were analyzed by area-investigator cells, and it was found that the abnormally high values were due to a single interviewer in one particular area.[53] Where *replicated* interpenetrating samples of this kind are used, it sometimes becomes possible to localize the error not only to a particular interviewer, but also to a particular area, so that the control of error is greatly facilitated.

A similar survey using interpenetrating samples was conducted in Nagpur in 1943. The design was arranged in the form of a randomized block, with five zones and four investigators each having approximately the same number of family schedules, about fifty, in each zone-investigator cell. F-ratios are shown in Table 87. Again the variances were divided by the error variance—the mean square within subsamples.

TABLE 87

F-Ratios of Variances in Nagpur Family Budget Inquiry, 1943

SOURCE OF VARIATION	TOTAL INCOME	MONTHLY TOTAL	EXPENDITURES	
			Food	Cereals
Between zones............	11.06†	9.64†	8.36†	8.28†
Between interviewers........	0.21	1.55	0.91	0.15
Zones x interviewers........	0.95	1.03	2.10*	2.00*
Between subsamples.........	2.96†	2.93†	2.80†	3.00†

* Significant at 5 per cent level.
† Significant at 1 per cent level.

In this case, the zones were set up purposely to differ as much as possible, but *interviewer variation* was negligible. As Mahalanobis expresses it, "Personal equations had been completely eliminated."[54]

It is interesting to notice that the interaction variances found in these two studies are confirmatory of the theory and findings of chapters IV and V. In Table 87, significant interaction is shown in two cases—monthly expenditures for food and cereals. Since the zones were purposely made as different as possible and all the between-zone variances are significant, this may be interpreted to mean that the significant interaction between interviewers and zones is really evidence also of the existence of a "reactional" effect in the sense that the term reaction was used in Chapter IV, that is, an effect deriving from the reaction of a particular group of respondents to a particular interviewer and vice versa. Here the respondents of each of the widely different zones may be considered as a particular group or class of respondents, interacting differently with different interviewers.

In the earlier Jagaddal study, expenditures for cereals showed a significant interaction variance. In this case, the significant interaction variance also indicates an interaction between a particular set of respondents (those in certain zones) and particular interviewers. But since there was no significant variation between areas, the interaction evidently does not mean a reaction between a particular interviewer and particular respondents as such, but rather the operation of *situational* factors. One possibility is that some temporal factor, such as fatigue, could be the explanation. If, for example, a particular interviewer was tired out while interviewing in the last zone, significant zone-interviewer interaction could occur.

Several other studies with similar designs are cited by Mahalanobis with varying results. Cost-of-living studies showed no significant interviewer variability. On the other hand, studies of radio program preferences showed significant departures from the binomial probabilities for the frequency of listening for most types of programs. One cannot be sure, however, that these departures mean significant interviewer variation, since it is not clear from the report whether there was any clustering of units which might have accounted for the significant departures from the binomial.

The studies cited by Stock and Hochstim and those of Mahalanobis, with their occasional findings of interviewer bias on some studies and on some questions but not on others, show that, while the bias seems to vary somewhat with content and question type, the occurrence of bias is rather capricious and unpredictable. The occasional character of the findings of bias confirms the theory of Chapters V and VI as to the situational and random nature of the occurrence of bias and furnishes a warning against the use of formal methods of bias measurement on a sporadic basis. Historical data of this kind must be applied to limited classes or the experimental measurement must be repeated.

Hitherto, we have assumed that interviewer variance and sampling error of estimates taking into account interviewer variation were the same as in cluster sampling, with the responses of all individuals in the population to a single interviewer as the cluster. But the response of a given individual to a given interviewer is not fixed—that is, there are a number of possible responses, and associated with each of the possible responses is a certain probability. So we may conceive of the responses of a given respondent to a given interviewer as a random variate. This concept of response error as a random variate has been used by Hansen, Hurwitz, Marks, and Mauldin to formulate a mathematical model for response errors and to derive formulas for estimating interviewer variance and total variance under this model.[55] The formulas are derived first for the case in which assignments are randomized within groups of interviewers. Since this is a condition which may be approximated in practice much more often than randomization of assignment of the *whole* sample over *all* the survey interviewers, the practical utility of the formulas is increased.

Under this approach, there is a "true value" for each individual in the population, defined in terms of the purposes of the survey. An "individual response" is the value obtained in a particular interview by a specified interviewer with a specified respondent at a given time, so that the individual response will vary with any alteration in the survey conditions. The "individual response error" is the difference between an individual response and the true value for the individual. The variability of individual responses is conceived to be random, so that the response error of a particular individual in a given survey has an expected value (the individual response bias) and a random component of variation around that expected value. If the value to be estimated from the survey is an average or aggregate of the "true values" for the individuals in the population, this estimate will have a response bias, the difference between the expected value of the average or aggregate of observed responses and the average or aggregate of the true values, and a response variance of the average of observed responses about the expected value of this average.

The analysis assumes that the random components of the response error for different individuals interviewed by different interviewers are uncorrelated. It is true that there may be correlation between responses even in this case. This might occur because of the influence of a common supervisor or common training for two different interviewers, but such correlations will probably have a negligible effect on sampling variances. It is assumed that response errors for different individuals interviewed by the same interviewer may be correlated. The alternative assumption of zero correlation between the random component of response errors of a particular interviewer would imply that there is no differential effect of different interviewers on responses and hence no inter-interviewer variability.

The model assumes that interviewers are divided into groups, each group being available to interview only certain classes of the population or in certain geographic areas. A number of interviewers are selected at random from each group and assigned an equal number of cases selected at random from among the sample individuals in the class or area assigned to the group. Sample individuals are selected independently of the groups, that is, the sample is not selected separately for each area or class corresponding to a group so that the total number of sample individuals interviewed by each group is a random variate.

With the assumptions outlined above the mathematical model includes

1. a population of N individuals and a population of K interviewers
2. n of the N individuals are selected at random, without restriction
3. k_A interviewers are selected at random, without restriction, from A-th group to interview the n_A sample cases available for interview by this group. If the total number of groups is L, the total number of interviewers will be $k = \sum^{L} k_A$

4. The same number $\bar{n}$ of individuals is assigned to each of the interviewers, and the $\bar{n}$ individuals assigned to any interviewer are a random subsample of all the sample individuals available for interview by this group.

From this model, the formula for the variance, $\sigma^2_{\bar{y}}$ of the sample mean $\bar{y}$, is derived:

$$\sigma^2_{\bar{y}} = \frac{1}{n}\left\{\sigma^2_y + \sigma_{yI}(\mathrm{T}\bar{n} - 1)\right\} \tag{1}$$

where

σ^2_y represents the variance of all individual responses around the mean of all individual responses in the population that would be obtained if every interviewer interviewed all individuals in the population. Each of the possible responses of each individual to each interviewer is weighted by the probability of that response.

σ_{yI} represents the covariance between responses obtained from different individuals by the same interviewer, the covariance being taken within interviewer groups.

Unbiased estimates of σ_{yI} and σ^2_y can be obtained from the sample. It is necessary to obtain the following mean squares:

Mean square between all respondents. This is simply the sum of squares of all deviations between sample responses and the sample mean of those responses divided by the degrees of freedom $(n - 1)$. Designate this by M_R where the M stands for "mean square."

Mean square between respondents within interviewer subsamples. This is the sum of squares of deviations between responses of an interviewer and the mean of all responses for that interviewer, summed over all interviewers and divided by the degrees of freedom $(n - k)$. Designate this by M_{RI}.

Weighted average of mean squares between interviewers within groups. First the sum of squares of deviations between interviewer means and group mean for each group is divided by the degrees of freedom for that group $(k_a - 1)$, to get the mean square for each group. Then the *average* of these mean squares is obtained by multiplying each one by k_A, the number of interviewers in the group, summing the products and dividing by k, the total number of interviewers. Designate this by M_{IG}.

Then we have

$$S_{yI} = \text{estimate of } \sigma_{yI} = \frac{M_{IG} - M_{RI}}{n} \tag{2}$$

$$S^2_y = \text{estimate of } \sigma^2_y = M_R + \frac{n - k}{n - 1} \frac{S_{yI}}{k} \tag{3}$$

$$S^2_{\bar{y}} = \text{estimate of } \sigma^2_{\bar{y}} = \frac{1}{n} \left\{ S^2_y + S_{yI} (n - 1) \right\} \tag{4}$$

$$= \frac{M_R}{n} + \frac{n - k}{n - 1} \left(\frac{M_{IG} - M_{RI}}{n} \right)$$

The first term of this last formula is the usual formula for estimating the variance of a sample mean from a random sample of n units from an infinite universe. The second term represents approximately the increase from taking into account intra-interviewer correlation. Testing the ratio (M_{IG}/M_{RI}) of the average interviewer mean square to the mean square between respondents for significance by the F-test will show whether significant inter-interviewer variability is present.

Looking back at the formula for the variance of the sample mean, we see that it can be put in the form

$$\sigma^2_{\bar{y}} = \frac{\sigma^2_y}{n} \left\{ 1 + \frac{\sigma_{yI}}{\sigma^2_y} (n - 1) \right\} \tag{5}$$

Now, if we had only one interviewer group—that is, if the assignments of all the different interviewers were equivalent samples of the entire population, σ_{YI}/σ^2_y would represent the *correlation*, ρ, between responses obtained for different individuals by the same interviewer.

$$\sigma^2_{\bar{y}} = \frac{\sigma^2_y}{n} \left\{ 1 + \rho (n - 1) \right\} \tag{6}$$

This expression shows the analogy to cluster sampling, since it is the formula for the variance of a sample mean with a sample of k clusters of $\bar{n}\left(=\frac{n}{k}\right)$ units each.

In this case (a single interviewer group) the estimate of the variance of the mean given in (4) reduces to:

$$S^2_{\bar{y}} = \frac{\text{Mean square between interviewers}}{n} \qquad (7)$$

This is the same estimate of the sample variance used by Stock and Hochstim in the analysis of variance approach.

Reducing Effect of Interviewer Variance

We discussed earlier some reasons why interviewer variability (or intra-interviewer correlation) may change with a change in the number of interviewers. If we assume, though, that interviewer variability is independent of the number of interviewers employed, its effect on sample estimates will decrease as the number of interviewers employed is increased. Under this assumption, we could minimize the effects of interviewer variability by assigning one sample unit to each interviewer. But increasing the number of interviewers would increase costs of training, supervision, and travel and require reduction of costs at some other point—for example, by reducing sample size. The solution offered by Hansen *et al.* is to determine the optimum combination of sample size (n) and number of interviewers (k) to give minimum variance for a fixed cost. If the cost is:

$$C = nC_R + kC_I$$

where

C = total budget available for field work in the survey
C_R = cost per respondent
C_I = cost per interviewer
(Here it is assumed that per unit and per interviewer costs do not change with changes in sample size and number.)

Then the optimum values of n and k are:

$$n = A\sqrt{\frac{\sigma_y^2 - \sigma_{yI}}{C_R}} \qquad k = A\sqrt{\frac{\sigma_{yI}}{C_I}}$$

where

$$A = \frac{C}{\sqrt{C_R(\sigma_y^2 - \sigma_{yI})} + \sqrt{C_I + \sigma_{yI}}}$$

We need to emphasize that the general inverse relationship between interviewer variability and number of interviewers, as well as the equations for determining the optimum number of interviewers based on this relationship, apply to estimates of marginals only. If interpenetrating samples were used, an increase in the number of interviewers would have the effect of decreasing interviewer variability in subgroup estimates and subgroup comparisons, inasmuch as the number of interviewers for the respondents of each subgroup would also be increased.

But we have to consider the effect of an increase in the number of interviewers under normal survey conditions, where economy of time and money require that assignments be made in clusters of units. Under these conditions, if the number of interviewers is small, units assigned to each interviewer may cover a fairly large geographic area and hence may be fairly heterogeneous in character. Any systematic biasing tendency of a particular interviewer, that is, a tendency of the interviewer to obtain too many answers in one direction from *all* groups of respondents, will tend to affect all subgroups leaving the subgroup comparisons unbiased. If the number of interviewers is increased, normally each interviewer will interview in a smaller area and his respondents will usually be more homogeneous in character. Thus subgroup comparisons will tend to a greater extent to be comparisons between respondents of *different* interviewers and will be affected to a correspondingly greater degree by interviewer variability. Of course, if the degree of interpenetration is increased in proportion to the increase in the number of interviewers so that the respondents of each of the larger number of interviewers are scattered over as wide an area as when fewer interviewers were employed, some reduction in the effect of interviewer variability on subgroup comparisons would result. But this would increase cost of travel between units and render the optimum equations inapplicable.

In public opinion research where, for many analytical purposes, the greatest interest is in the functional relationships between classes of respondents, the application of this approach to minimizing variability in the marginals may therefore be unwise in some cases, since it may actually decrease the reliance to be placed on the comparisons between classes.

The mathematical model given here can serve as the basis for an approach to minimizing *both* bias and variance. A particular survey may be regarded as subject to considerable response bias, but there may be alternative techniques that will reduce the bias, possibly with substantial increases in cost. First each of the alternative methods can be tested in the field, and from these tests, the optimum values of n and k can be determined, as before, to minimize the *variance* for a specified total cost. The chief difficulty is in estimating the net response *bias*. Experience or reasoning may lead to the conclusion that one of the alternative methods is probably subject to negligible response bias. Assuming this to be true, the bias for any other method may be estimated from experience or pilot studies from the difference obtained between this method and the method presumed to be most accurate.

As an example of alternative methods, farm expenditures might be determined by direct questioning of farmers or by detailed examination of purchase records, the latter method being presumably more accurate but also more expensive. Actually, in opinion and market survey work, there would ordinarily be great difficulty in finding a practical alternative to the usual survey techniques which would result in lower bias. Factual characteristics can sometimes be validated at great cost from independent records, as in the Denver Community Survey described elsewhere in this report. Some alternative methods to the usual personal interview for ascertaining opinion were described earlier, particularly in Chapters V and VI, such as the use of mail questionnaires, secret ballots, self-enumeration schedules, "depth interviewing," employment of interviewers with superior training and experience or presumed superior qualifications, post-interview recording of responses, and others. The results of experimental studies to compare alternative methods for validity have been inconclusive for the most part, although there have been indications that certain methods produce more valid results under certain conditions, as, for example, the use of the more anonymous techniques, like the secret ballot, on questions involving respondent prestige or questions of a highly personal nature. Criteria for the evaluation of relative validity may sometimes be developed from internal evidence of the data or from a priori reasoning and psychological theory. The problem of finding such criteria has been discussed earlier in this report.

Assuming that we can make a reasonable evaluation of relative validity, we could choose the method which minimizes mean square errors for a given cost, or we could combine two methods in the same survey by using the device of double sampling, which might be more efficient in some cases. First, a relatively large number of cases would be interviewed by one of the cheaper and presumably less accurate methods. Then a subsample of cases would be selected from the original sample and re-interviewed by one of the more expensive and presumably more accurate methods. Thus we would have a subsample of respondents interviewed by both methods. To obtain the final estimate, the ratio of estimates for the more accurate method to estimates for the less accurate method for the subsample would be multiplied by the estimate from *all* cases obtained from the interviews recorded under the less accurate method. We refer the reader to the paper by Hansen and his associates for formulas for the variances of such estimates.

The approach of Hansen and his associates to reducing error provides a logical mathematical framework for identifying and measuring interviewer error, and this clarifies the problem of error control. The applicability of this approach in actual practice depends on the particular survey conditions. To summarize some of the limitations which usual public opinion and market survey conditions impose:

1. Most surveys are multi-purpose in character. Estimates are usually desired for a number of major characteristics in marginal totals as well as cross tabulations to show the relationships for subclasses in the population. The possible conflict between the optima for marginals and for subgroup comparisons has already been discussed. But even where the chief interest centers in the marginals, the optima for the major characteristics will often differ widely. In the illustrative example given in the Hansen paper, the optima ranged from two to nine interviewers for five labor force characteristics. If some average optimum is used, the combined efficacy in minimizing variance for a given cost will often be slight.

2. The number of interviewers employed on a survey must ordinarily be determined by administrative and operating considerations, particularly limitations of time allotted to complete the survey. For three of the five characteristics in the illustrative example, the optimum number of interviewers for minimizing the variance for a given cost turned out to be only two. In actual practice, it would be extremely unlikely to find a survey for which the time limitations were sufficiently flexible to permit the use of only two interviewers, each of whom had to cover thirty-two sample segments. Hence the optimum equations will be applicable only over the usually relatively narrow range permitted by the survey conditions. Also the economics of public opinion and market surveys require the employment of a regular staff of part-time interviewers whose assignments must be spaced so that they get neither too much nor too little work, and the number of interviewers to be employed in surveys cannot be manipulated to a great extent without upsetting the existing arrangements.

The national cross sections used in most public opinion and market surveys permit little manipulation of the number of interviewers in many localities where it is feasible to employ only one or a few interviewers.

3. Determination of the optimum number of interviewers depends on the assumption that interviewer variability does not change with the number of interviewers, an assumption which is probably valid only over a limited range for the reasons discussed earlier. Also, in practice, whatever the effect on interviewer *variability*, the effect of increasing the number of interviewers is quite likely to be an increase in the net *bias*, since the additional interviewers usually have to be drawn from a different universe of persons with inferior training and experience.

4. Many surveys are limited in scope and nonrecurring in character so that variances and costs cannot be estimated from a previous survey. Pilot studies used for this purpose would be very expensive if satisfactory estimates of variances and costs, that is, estimates based on a sufficiently large sample, are to be obtained, and the conditions of such studies do not usually simulate those of the final survey.

5. Assuming that cost-accounting methods are capable of determining separately costs per interviewer and cost per respondent, these unit costs are probably not constant but vary in some manner with the number of interviewers. For example, cost per interviewer for training and supervision would probably decrease as the number of interviewers increases, but costs per respondent would go up because of the increased travel between the units assigned to each interviewer, assuming that the assignments were *interpenetrating in equal degree.*

6. Interviewer assignments have to be clustered under ordinary cost and time conditions. Equivalence of assignments, even within groups of interviewers, is unusual, though sometimes the overlapping of assignments is sufficiently great so that the necessary conditions for the measurement of error may be approximated.

7. In using the approach to minimize both variance and bias, criteria for determining the "most accurate method" or least biased among alternative methods are very difficult to find.

8. Under a double-sampling scheme, the fact that a respondent is interviewed twice may result in a different set of responses under the presumed more accurate method than would have been obtained if this method had been used alone, either because of respondent's resentment or his desire for consistency. Hence estimates of variances and differential biases may be affected.

In spite of these limitations, the mathematical model for response error and the approach given for reducing error under the model can be used on occasion by survey agencies when the necessary conditions are approximately fulfilled or special survey designs are used, and the results of such studies will have some applicability to later surveys, even when the necessary conditions are less closely approximated.

Correction for Interviewer Bias Associated with Differential Net Effects

Methods of measuring differential net effects of interviewers of contrasting ideology, expectations, or group membership through the use of Chi-squared analysis and other techniques have been illustrated frequently in this report and in the literature of interviewer bias. Earlier we mentioned the suggestion of Mosteller and Cantril that final results might be corrected for ideological bias if we can make certain assumptions, usually the assumption of equivalence, about the relative strengths of opposing biases.

But other methods of correcting the final results may also be used in cases where differential net effects have been demonstrated. One such method is the elimination of the data collected by some of the interviewers on the basis of certain assumptions about which interviewers are biasing the data. Ferber and Wales describe a procedure of this kind used in a 1950 study of attitudes to pre-fabricated housing in the Champaign-Urbana, Illinois, area.[56] The fourteen interviewers were required to fill out the questionnaire themselves before the survey. Respondents' replies were classified according to the answer of the interviewer and Chi-squared values were computed to determine whether interviewers obtained significantly more replies in line with their own opinions, using a 5 per cent level of significance. On four of the eight questions, over-all biases were indicated by the tests. To determine bias for individual interviewers the distribution of the replies turned in by each interviewer was compared with the corresponding distribution for the total sample, excluding the replies of that interviewer.[57] If the distributions differed significantly, the interviewer's returns were taken to be biased. Final results for these questions were then corrected by eliminating the data obtained by the "biased" interviewers.

This procedure, of course, involves the dubious assumption that the distribution of replies obtained by the other interviewers is unbiased. Furthermore, as we have pointed out before, significance tests often indicate bias where none really exists, so that unrestricted application of this procedure is not recommended.

Estimates of Error Based on Experience or Independent Information

Sometimes the effects of interviewer error and bias on final estimates may be removed or reduced by adjustment or qualification of the estimates on the basis of experience or of independent information. The only instances of such procedures that we can cite from the past literature involve adjustments for the *total* system of errors, i.e., sampling and response error in addition to interviewer error. However, in theory, such adjustments could be derived purely for that component of error due to interviewer effects. As an example of an adjustment for the *total* system of errors, we may mention the age-sex adjustments of labor force estimates by the Census Bureau. Results of the monthly labor force surveys of the Census Bureau are adjusted by inflating the estimates of labor force characteristics for each age-sex group to independent current estimates of the total number of persons in that age-sex group derived by actuarial methods.[58]

Opinion and market survey agencies are aware of the tendency in quota sampling to obtain too few respondents in the lower educational status and lower socio-economic categories, and have sometimes corrected the results by re-weighting the data for the various economic or educational groupings, in accordance with independent information on the educational or economic distribution of the population. This procedure was used by Gallup in the 1948 election polls. The sample showed 17.9, 46.8 and 35.4 per cent of the respondents in the college, high-school and grammar-school educational groups respectively, but the census educational distribution of the population aged twenty-one and over showed 13, 42 and 45 per cent in the three groups. Of the college-educated respondents 61.6 per cent indicated an intention to vote for Dewey, compared with 43.1 per cent for the high-school group, with 42.1 as the per cent for the entire sample.

Multiplying the percentage intending to vote for Dewey in each group by the corresponding Census percentages for the population in each group gave a revised estimate of *40 per cent* Dewey supporters for the entire sample.[59] Another example of the adjustment of final estimates for 1948 by Gallup was the correction of estimates of voting intentions to allow for the inflation known to occur in the number of respondents who say they voted in 1944 and in the number who say they voted for Roosevelt. The estimated inflation is determined by studying a large number of past surveys, and the inflation factors were then applied to the actual distribution of the major-party vote in 1944 to give revised weights to be applied to the groups set up on the basis of 1948 voting intentions.

Still another example of such an approach is available in the "quality check" of the 1950 Census. We alluded to the quality check procedure earlier, but there its relevance was to *measuring* gross or net effects, rather than as procedure for *reduction* of error by empirical adjustments. An estimate of error is obtained by comparing the results of the original enumeration with the results obtained by intensive re-interviewing of a sample of the original households on selected items, using specially trained, superior enumerators. Naturally, the superiority of the check interview is assumed to yield the more accurate results. On the basis of these check figures, qualifications of the findings can be published, and the original results can even be corrected.[60]

Use of Scale Scores To Minimize Bias

The recent development of question scales for the measurement of attitudes,[61] for example, the Guttman scales, may prove to be useful in minimizing the effects of interviewer bias under certain conditions. If the bias is not systematic in character, that is, is not manifested uniformly by the interviewer, but tends to occur randomly or is situational in character, then we might expect that the employment of indices or scale scores from batteries of questions would tend to attenuate the effects of bias, since the random bias occurring on one question might be lessened by "burying" this question in with a battery of others. In this case, the use of the scale scores tends to average out the biases, insuring against the risk from reliance on a single question.

There are, of course, instances where the bias is of such a systematic character that a scaling procedure would simply compound or aggravate the effect. Such would seem to be the case in instances involving attitude-structure expectations as exemplified in Chapter III. However, there was also considerable evidence presented in Section 1 of Chapter V that bias varies with situational factors, and in Chapter VI that bias may simply be random in character. For such instances, scaling would be recommended.

An actual example of the value of using scales or batteries as attenuators of bias can be constructed from some data of the Denver Community Survey not previously presented in Chapter VI. One omnibus question contained ten subparts asking about the respondent's degree of interest in various public problems. Three of the items represented logical components of a battery or scale of interest in local affairs. These dealt with city planning, the public school system, and the activities of the city administration. On the first two of these, interviewer differences in the results obtained from equivalent samples were highly significant, indicating that the results per item were not reliable. This unreliability would have been reduced, however, if the three items had been pooled into a common scale of interest in local affairs, since the deviant results for given interviewers were not consistent over the three items. This can be indicated by ranking the nine interviewers in each sector on the degree of interest their samples manifested in each item and intercorrelating the ranks over questions, sector by sector. The fifteen co-efficients ranged from $-.13$ to $.80$ with a median value of $.33$. Since the expected value of these co-efficients, even if there were no interviewer effect, would be of some positive magnitude because of the sheer generality of interest among human beings, the median value of $.33$ is all the more compelling in arguing that the ranking of respondents by the use of a scale would be less affected by the interviewers' own bias, then ranking by individual questions.

Additional evidence of the attenuation of effects through the use of scores based on the pooled answers to a battery of questions was available in Chapter VI, in the finding that there was no difference in the relative reliability of scores on two indices when respondents were re-interviewed by the same vs. different interviewers. This was in contrast with the finding that answers to *single* questions were affected systematically by the particular interviewer used.

Besides the possible use of the scale scores for attenuation of bias, they might also provide a better measurement, or test, of whether bias is present. Chapter VI offered a good argument for the belief that many of the findings of interviewer bias may represent simply chance fluctuations. Thus the erratic character of results when testing for bias on individual questions could be decreased by the employment of the more stable scores for a whole scale of questions.

Procedural and Methodological Data Bearing on the Qualitative Materials for Chapter II, the Definition of the Interview Situation

The purpose of this appendix is to describe the procedures by which the phenomenological reports drawn upon in Chapter II were collected. In so far as readers are impressed with the value of a phenomenological description of the interview for future research into interviewer effect, this appendix might serve as a guide to others who would collect new data to add to the fragmentary picture we now have. In addition, the reader can assess the quality of the original findings in the light of the procedure and specific evidence to be presented on the problem of validity.

Admittedly, the procedures necessary to obtain the type of data we were seeking will never satisfy the positivistically minded reader in the way that experimental and statistical data would. But experimental and statistical data would never have been adequate to our purpose. We sought the subjective view of the interview situation, and this called for subjective data which for some readers, unfortunately, has the connotation of unreliability. For such readers, nothing would buttress their faith in the data. But in relation to such categorical criticism, it should be pointed out with clarity and emphasis that the use we made of such data was tentative. Generalizations, in so far as they were advanced, were qualified. The data were the basis essentially for speculation and theorizing; the verification of such theories involved other more orthodox procedures of a statistical and experimental sort. The support for these suggestive findings in Chapter II, therefore, rests ultimately on the entire body of evidence in this project and not merely on the evidence of the quality of the procedures here reported.

Three procedures were relied upon for reconstructing the definition of the situation: First, intensive interviews with interviewers to obtain a picture of the *totality* of their experiences. Secondly, a reconstruction of a series of particular *single* interviews through reports from both parties. Third, accounts of the interviewer's experiences while listening to a transcription representing a recorded interview. Each of these will be discussed in turn.

1. THE INTENSIVE INTERVIEWS WITH INTERVIEWERS

Sampling Considerations

Seven such interviews were conducted. All seven of the interviewers were long experienced, professional survey interviewers. Five of them were women. Five of them had had their main experience in the New York Metropolitan District, one had worked in the Middle West, and the other had worked in every conceivable area. All but one were on the staff of NORC (the non-NORC interviewer had had longest experience with intensive interview surveys for government agencies), but five of them had worked for a variety of agencies doing field work of all types. It is obvious that they constituted no representative sample of survey interviewers. But this is no serious criticism. The interviews were deliberately restricted to interviewers who would have the greatest fund of experience as a basis for communicating a richness of material to us. Further, the interviewers were deliberately selected in terms of ability to reminisce, to introspect, to analyze their experience, and to report it to us in detailed terms. If one seeks a phenomenology of the interview, he must obtain it where it can be found. That what was obtained consisted of private and unique experiences is perfectly possible. But out of such revelations might come the stimulation for a theory, which would be regarded as *provisional* until verified in precise ways and found to have generality.

The Procedure Followed and the Validity of Reports

Six of the seven were interviewed by one interviewer, Hyman. The seventh was interviewed by a highly experienced professional survey interviewer. The interview was conducted privately. The procedure followed was simply to tell the interviewer that we wished the benefit of his broad experience in order to improve our future work, and to ask him to start by telling us what he felt was important. Often, this led to an immediate outpouring of something the interviewer felt strongly about. After this, or in occasional instances where there were no spontaneous remarks, the suggestion was given that we try to recollect some of his experiences by thinking back to some concrete day's work as an interviewer, to start with his approach to the respondent, and to report his recollection of his feelings. Such spontaneous reports were interrupted periodically by probes to clarify some point, but generally the interview proceeded with exceedingly little structuring, and the order and content of remarks were determined naturally. The answers were recorded verbatim by manual procedures.

No standardized questionnaire was used. While the attempt was made to cover particular areas of experience, wherever possible no questions on the particular area were mentioned until late in the interview so that much of the material was liberated spontaneously. It is unlikely, therefore, that the phenomena reported are in any considerable degree artifacts of direct questioning. The particular areas which we attempted to cover included: the gratifications they derived from interviewing, the interviewers' reactions to the respondents' attitudes and to the treatment respondents accord them, their beliefs about the existence of certain attitude patterns within the respondent and in different groups of respondents, the role interviewers feel it is desirable for them to assume, their attitude toward probing and experiences in probing; the reaction of the respondent to the approach, the questions, the interviewer's personal characteristics, and to certain interviewing circumstances; and finally in the sequence some direct questioning about bias. Naturally, in such a lengthy interview, with a minimum of structuring, and with the respondents themselves being interviewers, there was a very discursive quality to the reports, and many other areas of experience were brought into discussion.

A number of questions immediately arise with respect to the quality of the reports given:

Bias due to the interviewer-subject wanting to present an account to his employer that would insure or enhance his security.—Since the interviewer who conducted these interviews was known as a permanent member of the NORC staff, it might well be that an interviewer-subject would deliberately conceal certain kinds of experiences and behavior out of fear that such revelations might be a basis for discharge. With respect to this possible error, it might be pointed out that there is no proper norm for interviewer conduct in most of the areas discussed to which the interviewer-subjects could orient themselves. Explicit admissions of interviewer bias constitute the only violation of known norms, and this was incidental to the main contents of the interview. In addition, the general atmosphere of the interview was exceedingly permissive, and the subjects with one exception were on exceedingly good and friendly terms with the interviewer. Finally, it may be noted that in the very place where concealment would be most likely to occur, in reports of flagrant bias or violations of established procedures, there were explicit reports by two of the subjects of such behavior. We are quoting these in order to convey the lack of inhibition of the interviewer-subject in the situation. G remarks spontaneously: "I'm afraid I often reword the questions. First I read it as it's printed. But then when they look blank—suppose the question says: 'how do you feel about another war'—maybe they don't say anything. So then you say 'well, when you think of bombs falling and your sons or your husband going to war,' well, then, as one woman replied, she said: 'I wake up every morning being scared stiff of a war.'"

M admits these "crimes": In describing how he conducted an interview with a foreign respondent, he reports: "I went ahead and interviewed her. When she didn't understand a word, I would have her son explain it to her and with simple words and pantomime I would make clear to him and her what was meant by the words in the question. . . . I realize I was guilty in arrogating to myself the authority to make such an interview."

Later in reporting that he may reword the questions, he remarks: "I must confess to a shortcoming. I do not believe that I sufficiently do as the good book suggests. . . . I confess that originality is probably indefensible, but it is a freedom I take upon myself because I am quite sure, in my own mind, that I have sufficient understanding of words and the niceties of their distinctions to phrase the question differently without altering its sense."

Omissions due to lack of coverage, to forgetting, and to selectivity.— The intensive interviews with interviewers were used to obtain a picture of the cumulative pattern, the totality, of their experience, and not the details of a *given* interview situation. Consequently, the problem of memory factors is not of great consequence. In addition, we were interested in the interview situation as seen through the eyes of the interviewer, and not in a report of the objective facts. The intrusion of subjective elements was exactly what was called for in relation to most of the objectives of these interviews. But even with respect to the quality of these protocols as detailed reports of *reality*, they seem to have considerable validity. They are exceedingly rich in detail, and not gross, blurred pictures as would be the case in the recall of distant and forgotten events. In addition to detail, the experiences were elaborated at great length. Four of these accounts ran approximately 2500 words in length, two of them ran 7000 words, and, as mentioned in the text, the interview with M was of such detail that it exceeded 17,000 words in length. The material is full of such detailed recollections as "I had a bad experience in Williamsburg once"; "On Survey 152, the women were not well informed on the Marshall plan"; "On one survey I was in a C-D neighborhood—I was speaking to a woman—another woman overheard it and burst forth and said 'stop talking, she's a Communist.' " The descriptions seem to be fluent accounts of experience, reported with great ease.

Faulty inferences and analyses made on the basis of examining the protocols.—The treatment of the data in these interviews was not statistical. Data were not coded or tabulated in any uniform way. The material was simply examined and inferences drawn about certain phenomena. Since no claim is made for the frequency of these phenomena among the seven interviewers or among interviewers in general, it was felt that statistical treatment was not essential. These reports are presented as case material from discrete interviewers. The inferences may at times be faulty, but the original data are presented in detail in the text, so that the reader can easily judge for himself. The original interviews are, of course, on file at the National Opinion Research Center and can be examined for a check on the present analysis.

2. THE CASE STUDIES OF PARTICULAR INTERVIEW SITUATIONS

Sampling Considerations

The three case studies presented in the text are part of a larger series of descriptions of particular interview situations. The series was based on phenomenological data covering the mutual experiences of both respondent and interviewer in fifty actual survey interviews. These particular interviews were conducted in the course of only *one* national survey on political issues at a particular moment in time. The fifty subjects were selected from those who had been interviewed in the three sample points, New York City, Chicago, and Denver, by a total of ten interviewers and further restricted by the fact that only certain respondents were co-operative enough to submit to the procedure to be reported below. The reader might well raise certain questions about the sampling. The interviews are not many in number and are based on the work of only a few interviewers, interviewing only respondents in big cities. These interviews may also be biased with respect to the sampling of *conditions* of the interview in that they refer only to situations where political contents were collected at a certain historical moment. Moreover, they are obviously biased in that some respondents who would qualify for inclusion in the group we initially planned to study refused to co-operate or were not available, and in that we selected particular cases from the larger series for presentation in the text. Criticisms on such grounds of sampling do not seem crucial. This material, like the intensive interview data, is not presented as a basis for final generalization. However, with respect to the influence of the content of the survey, we might remark that the processes illuminated are of a fundamental sort and do not appear bound to the specific opinions originally solicited. With respect to those who refused to co-operate, it might be ventured that, if anything, they would be even more detached from the impact of the interview—one of the major points made in the text. With respect to the three cases presented, they are deliberately a biased selection intended to illuminate unusual processes in the interview. It is the unusual that makes us revise our theory in a more comprehensive direction, and not what we have known before. The data for all these cases are available in the National Opinion Research Center office for examination by anyone interested in evaluating them for himself.

The Procedure Followed and the Validity of Reports

Ostensibly with the purpose of improving our general field procedures, the interviewers were given a detailed questionnaire which they were supposed to complete immediately following the original interview. The questions were intended to reveal first a picture of the situation as they saw it—the way they pictured the respondent, his motivation in being interviewed, his reaction to the questions, etc., their reaction to the respondent as a person and to his attitude. Data were also collected on the objective circumstances of the interview, and reports of the respondents' own behavior—particularly with respect to bias—were also elicited. The interviewers had no idea that they were singled out for special study, or that the respondents would also be queried. As a vivid proof of this, it might be remarked that one of the interviewers involved turned in completed forms on a series of respondents, who when called upon were found not to exist or never to have been interviewed. The discovery of this "cheater interviewer" was incidental to the project, but it certainly suggests that at least this interviewer had no suspicion that the special form was to be followed by a re-interview.

The respondent's view of the situation was obtained by a detailed re-interview with him within a short period of time after the original interview. This re-interview was conducted, naturally, by a different interviewer, and the attempt was made to pick only highly skilled interviewers for this assignment. Since it is customary procedure on NORC surveys to obtain the address of the respondent plus detailed factual data, the original respondent could in most instances be identified for the re-interview. His name was not recorded on the original interview, partly because of established practices about anonymity and partly so as not to warn the original interviewer of the likelihood of the respondent's being revisited. In the re-interview, the respondent was informed that we believed he had been interviewed on one of our recent surveys, and that we would like to know his reactions so as to improve our general field procedures. The re-interview was initiated by asking him if he remembered the original interview. This provided an opportunity to study the impact of the total experience and his orientation to specific features of it. Later questions dealt with his feelings about being interviewed, his motivation for accepting the interview, his reaction to the experience, the way he conceived of the situation (e.g., like a quiz, an argument, a friendly conversation, etc.), his reaction to the interviewer as a person, and his report of the interviewer's behavior, particularly with respect to the communication of bias. In general, there was a deliberate parallelism in the coverage in the original interviewer's report and in the respondent's re-interview so as to obtain the mutual views and appraisals of the same aspects of the interview situation. These procedures presumably yielded data on the undercurrent of the interview situation. Of course, we also had the actual record of the respondent's answers to the questions in the original interview, and we had also obtained the original interviewer's own attitudes by having him complete the regular questionnaire for the survey. Data were thus provided for evaluating the disparities that existed between the two parties in their ideology and group membership, and the measured attitudes revealed in the original interview could be examined in the light of the interview setting in which they had been elicited. Many questions about the validity of these reports arise:

Biased reports of the original interviewer's experiences in order to protect his own employment.—While the original interviewer was instructed that our purpose in having him complete the questionnaire about the situation was purely for improvement of *general* procedures, and although he seemed not to sense that a re-interview would occur, he may well have felt that this was a method of surveillance over his performance. Consequently, he may have presented distorted reports to put himself in a better light. This factor would have operated mainly to reduce reports associated with flagrant biases on his part, which reports were only incidental to our purposes. This source of error might also have operated to reduce reports of unfavorable reactions from respondents, and reports that the interviewer himself reacted in hostile fashion. That it certainly did not eradicate the latter reports is clear from the case presented in the text of "The Creep." That it may have reduced reports of interviewers about the hostility they sensed in the respondent is possible.

Inadequate reports of the respondent's experience due to the lapse of time between original interview and re-interview.—Every attempt was made to conduct the re-interview as soon after the original experience as possible. However, because of the difficulty of finding the original respondents and arranging for a re-interview, several days generally intervened. The time between original and re-interview ranged from two to eight days, with a median figure of five days. For purposes of studying the detailed experiences of respondents, this was not ideal, but in terms of studying the *impact* of the experience, it yielded the finding that the experience was soon dissipated. With respect to losses due to forgetting, it is our impression that any lack of detail was not due to the time lag. It seemed to be more a function of the particular respondent's orientation toward the experience. Those who were detached, for whom the interview was trivial, who were lost in their private worlds, were the ones who did not remember. Table 88 presents some quantitative evidence on the influence of this possible error factor by showing the relation of lapse of time to clarity of respondent report. The lack of linear relationship supports our argument. While this comparison between groups re-interviewed after different time periods does not control the type of respondent, there is no reason to suspect that such characteristics are not distributed randomly among the groups interviewed after different time lags.

TABLE 88

THE RELATION BETWEEN TIME LAPSE PRIOR TO RE-INTERVIEW AND MEMORY OF ORIGINAL SITUATION

	Percentage Reporting "Almost Forgotten Original Interview"
Two-three day interval	8
Four-five day interval	29
Six-eight day interval	17

Biased reporting by respondent due to the desire not to complain about the original interviewer to his employer.—There were strong attempts made to impress the respondent with the fact that this was not a "checkup" on the work of the original interviewer, that the respondent's answers were to be used merely as a basis for improvement of *general* procedures rather than for a screening of the staff. Despite such attempts, the impression was that many respondents were suspicious of our motives and did not want to jeopardize the employment of the original interviewer. There seems therefore to be a diminution of reports of feelings of hostility to the original interviewer, or of reports that the interviewers engaged in practices which respondents might sense were against the rules. That such reports by respondents about unsatisfactory behavior on the part of interviewers, or about unsatisfactory reactions to the interviewer, were not *completely* suppressed is clear from the two case histories presented in the text—the "Hen Party" and "The Tough Guy." Nevertheless, there seems to be no general control over this source of error, and certain findings must be qualified in the light of its operation on the respondent.

Inability of the respondent to separate his reaction to the re-interview itself from his report of feelings in the original interview.—Just as the original interviewer created a certain atmosphere and effect, so too must the re-interviewer. Perhaps the reactions to the new situation in some way have contaminated the memory of the original event. There seems to be some suggestion from reading the re-interviews that this did happen.

In general, the re-interviewer was a somewhat more skilled individual, so we may assume that the atmosphere he created was one of better rapport, perhaps greater social interaction, less hostility and disparity between respondent and interviewer, and less tension. In occasional instances, the respondent did react with greater hostility to the re-interviewer. In all these instances, however, the effect of such a biasing factor would be to distort the respondent's statement of the original situation in a *predictable* direction.

In reconstructing the case histories of these situations, the analyst reported wherever he sensed the operation of such a factor and the material reported in the text was evaluated in that light. Nevertheless, such a source of error may still be operative.

Method of integrating materials independently derived from interviewers and respondents.—The foregoing discussion covers the major types of response errors that might have affected our reconstruction of the interview situation. However, another major possibility of error arises during the analytic phase of the work. The mutual reports of interviewer and respondent were only the *raw* data for the phenomenological description of the concrete interview situation. The actual descriptions were derived by an analyst who immersed himself in the four lengthy sets of materials—interviewer's description, respondent's description, interviewer's expressed attitudes, and respondent's expressed attitudes—and then wrote a reconstruction of the original situation. For certain purposes the data were tabulated and cross-tabulated. But this statistical processing was found inadequate to the richness and complexity of the material. Consequently, most of the findings are predicated on the analyst's sensitivity in integrating these materials into a coherent picture. At first, no guiding scheme was given the analyst, and he simply read each case separately for suggestions of the special process involved. After much reading of the materials, a scheme was developed for the description of the situation, and the final cases, such as those reported in the text, were analyzed under these headings and the descriptive report of the situation written.

It is obvious in such a procedure that there is much opportunity for the analyst to exercise his bias in the interpretation or simply to misinterpret the data. The check upon this was to have a second analyst read the identical materials and examine the interpretations given by the first analyst and confer with him. All the materials presented are based on at least the combined judgments of two analysts, and thus there is considerable protection against idiosyncratic interpretations. The original data are of course available for others to examine in checking upon this source of error.

In summary, it is quite clear that many types of errors may be operating to affect the quality of these case studies, and they must be regarded as tentative. However, their fruitfulness for new lines of theory compensates for their tentativeness. It would perhaps have been possible to describe concrete interview situations with greater objectivity and preciseness, e.g., by hidden mechanical recordings of the event or by hidden observers' ratings of the event. But such procedures, while reliable, would have given a picture of only the *externals* of the interview. The inner world of the interview would have been inevitably lost as any attempts to infer these subtleties from the objective content of the interview would have been subject to great, but unknown errors.

3. INTERVIEWER EXPERIENCES AS REVEALED WHILE LISTENING TO A TRANSCRIPTION OF AN INTERVIEW

Sampling Considerations

Only two interviewer-subjects were used in this procedure. They were both fairly experienced, and both were men. The two inquiries were conducted by different investigators, both of whom followed a relatively standard procedure and both of whom had had long experience in surveys. The subjects were chosen deliberately because of the belief that they were sensitive individuals who could co-operate and would be capable of analyzing the flow of their experience and making it articulate to us. It is obvious that the two are not in any sense a sample of interviewers, but again it should be stressed that their reported experiences are not the basis for firm generalizations.

The Procedure Followed and the Validity of the Reports

The background of the procedure used in this study is reported in detail in chapter III. Each interviewer-subject listened to two transcriptions which presumably were obtained during actual interviews. Each was instructed to record the answer of the respondent on a copy of the questionnaire which corresponded to the questions used on the transcription. These interviews had been produced artificially by a professional radio actor of long experience acting as respondent and reading a set of prepared answers to an interviewer who questioned him. They were specifically designed for an experiment on attitude-structure expectations and consequently with the exception of occasional ambiguous or contradictory answers, they conveyed pictures of two contrasted types of respondents, each with a unified pattern of attitudes. The subject was instructed to report whatever came to his mind in the process of listening to the interview and recording the respondent's answers. Whenever necessary, the transcription was interrupted for as long as the subject cared to talk, and if he wished, a portion of the interview was replayed for him. Such playbacks tended to destroy some of the unity of the original interview and to give it a fragmentary character.

No prepared list of questions was asked. Periodically, remarks made by the subject were followed up by informal probing. In relation to points in the transcription that were regarded as crucial moments in the development or reorganization of an impression, it was sometimes necessary to inquire whether the interviewer-subject had anything to say. But for the most part a great deal of vivid imagery, affect, and judgment were spontaneously reported. While the purpose of the procedure was to obtain a report on the development of attitude-structure expectations in the course of interviewing, no suggestion whatsoever was given that the subject describe the respondent or report his expectations about him. He was free to report about anything, and the protocols included details as inconsequential for our purposes as the reaction to the "hmm" sound made by the original interviewer at one point. Consequently, we can assume that the phenomenon of expectations revealed in this way is in no way an artifact of any explicit suggestions in the procedure.

Other possibilities of error present themselves. The phenomenological data previously obtained derived from the realities of an actual interview or many interviews. This new procedure had a somewhat artificial laboratory-like character, and on this basis may not be analogous to the interviewer's experiences in the real interview. There were a number of ways in which the artificiality of the situation might jeopardize the results, and these will be discussed in turn.

Realization that the transcriptions were simulated interviews and consequent artificiality in the report.—Neither of the interviewer-subjects reported any suspicion of the transcriptions. In their accounts, there is detailed reference to the supposed interviewer and respondent and much attributing to them of various characteristics. Neither subject recognized that the respondent was in actuality the same person on both transcriptions, and one subject contrasted one of the "interviewers" with the other, despite the fact that they were in actuality the same person.

Various remarks are illustrations of the genuineness of the transcriptions in the subject's mind. Thus:

"That interviewer is so unlike myself," "Rapport is breaking down. I'd strongly reassure the respondent right here that his opinions are important," "I like this interviewer better than the other one—he's a softer individual," "I think the interviewer should have pinned him down," "The interviewer doesn't put enough emphasis on his questions."

Factors in the situation minimizing the formation of impressions of the respondent.—In certain ways, the situation artificially reduced the cues which would be likely to create beliefs in the interviewer about his respondent. The subject heard only the auditory record of the interview, and had none of the cues of gesture, clothing, possessions, and the like, which would have been present in interviewing a real respondent. While there is of course the possibility that in the real-life situation, such a complexity of cues would operate in contradictory rather than summative fashion, we can probably make the assumption that the addition of cues would have increased the formation of unified impressions. In so far as the protocols convey a definite attitude-structure expectation process, we can regard it as a compelling proof that one would occur in more normal circumstances. In addition, the episodic character of the transcription, due to frequent playbacks and periodic probes, probably disrupted the formation of impressions and reduced them in comparison with the real-life situation.

Factors in the situation accentuating the formation of an impression of the respondent.—Two factors might have worked in this direction. Since we wished to highlight the dynamics of such cognitive processes, it was felt necessary to magnify the pictures presented. Consequently, the two simulated interviews were deliberately with contrasted types of respondents and the characterizations were somewhat extreme. Since some respondents met in real life would have less integrated ideologies, these transcriptions might convey an exaggerated picture of the operation of attitude-structure expectations.

Granted that this is true, it does not jeopardize the inferences drawn in Chapter II. Conclusions are not drawn that such expectations *always* occur, or *frequently* occur. The phenomenological data were intended to demonstrate that they *did* occur, and something of their dynamics, and there is assuredly in real life a certain number of respondents of the type pictured on the transcriptions.

In addition, such criticism is predicated on the assumption of the rarity of these types of respondents in the normal opinion survey, but the reality and frequent occurrence of such extreme types is well known to all in public opinion research. The fact that many of the opinions in the transcriptions were taken from answers actually obtained in past surveys supports this point. Moreover, data presented in the original published account of the study show that the characterizations were not always regarded as extreme, so that this error may not be as serious as would at first appear. Whether this bias is completely compensated for in magnitude by the factors previously mentioned which minimize the formation of impressions is not known, but of necessity the total error must be reduced to some extent.

NORC Training and Field Procedures*

Since so many of the experimental findings reported in this monograph are based upon NORC interviewers, it is important to describe briefly the characteristics, training, and supervision of this field staff, and the nature of their work, so that the reader may judge for himself the extent to which our findings may be generalized to other interviewing groups. To the degree that the NORC interviewers are representative of other field staffs, the findings which are based on this group would appear to have general applicability. To the degree that the NORC interviewers differ from other field staffs, such findings would require qualification.

The demographic characteristics of the NORC national field staff have been reported in some detail by Sheatsley, and comparisons with certain other national field staffs are available.† The staff is predominantly composed of women (88 per cent), in the 30–50 age group (70 per cent), with at least some college education (81 per cent). The great majority are part-time workers, only 29 per cent having employment on a full-time job elsewhere. The staff differs from that of the Gallup Poll, which employs more men and more people with full-time jobs, but in background factual characteristics, the NORC interviewers seem quite representative of the total pool of part-time interviewers employed by most national opinion and market research organizations.

Although comparative figures from other agencies are not available, it is not unlikely that the NORC staff differs in several other respects from this "total pool" of interviewers which it resembles demographically. Almost two-thirds of the NORC staff, for example, interview only for NORC, and most of these have had no experience with any other agency's questionnaires.‡ They are perhaps less dependent financially upon their interviewer's pay, since their NORC assignments are small and relatively infrequent, and the NORC pay rates have generally lagged slightly behind those of the larger market research

---

* This appendix was written by Paul B. Sheatsley and is descriptive of NORC procedures during the period 1947–50, when most of the studies reported on were conducted. Minor changes and refinements have naturally occurred since that time.

† See Chap. II.

‡ Statements made in this paragraph are based on findings from the mail questionnaire to the NORC staff described in Chap. II.

companies. And they are perhaps more highly motivated in other respects because they tend to dislike consumer and market studies and to take particular interest in the types of surveys conducted by NORC. NORC performs no market or consumer research, and all its surveys are financed by means of foundation grants or by such clients as government agencies, universities, or private institutions of an educational, charitable or scientific nature. The questions that NORC interviewers ask, therefore, generally concern social, economic, or political issues. Methodologically, however, the type of question and format of the questionnaire do not differ materially from those employed by any other market or opinion research agency, and essentially the same interviewing rules are followed. All interviews are conducted face-to-face, with the interviewer reading the questions and then recording on the questionnaire the respondent's answer—either by reporting his language verbatim or by checking or circling the appropriate pre-code. Sometimes all of the questions concern a single broad issue or subject; sometimes they take up a variety of topics which may not be closely related. At the conclusion of each interview, a series of factual questions such as age, education, occupation, etc., are asked of the respondent. Though the majority of the questions are pre-coded in form and offer the respondent his choice of two or more suggested responses, there are frequent subquestions of the "Why do you feel that way?" type, and occasionally there will be other open-ended questions inviting a free-answer response. Some of the questions are factual in nature (i.e., "What newspaper do you read?"), but most solicit the person's opinion. Interviewers are encouraged to avoid "No opinion" or "Don't know" responses, and to urge the respondent to consider the question, to answer it "Just in general" or "Taking everything into consideration," and to select the one alternative that comes closest to his own opinion or impression. Many of the pre-coded questions are of the dichotomous type, but others are in the form of a scale, and some occasionally require the use of a card on which three or more somewhat lengthy statements or alternatives are presented for the respondent's choice.

All of the NORC interviewers have been hired in person; none was employed by mail. The hiring agent was in most cases one of the salaried field supervisors in either the Chicago or New York office, although about one-fourth of the interviewers were hired by a "regional supervisor"—another NORC part-time interviewer, but one with several years of NORC experience, who has been entrusted with supervisory duties in the general geographical area in which she resides.

About one-third of the staff were hired as a result of their independent inquiry and application; they wrote in or appeared at the office seeking employment as interviewers, and when openings occurred on the staff, they were hired. The remaining two-thirds were sought out by the NORC representative, most usually through inquiries from local officials or the heads of community organizations. Except in the few cities where NORC maintains offices or regional supervisors, all hiring was accomplished on "field trips" in which the NORC representative would visit the town or city where new interviewers were required. In such cases, approximately fifteen or twenty applicants are usually screened for every three or four that are hired.

All of the NORC interviewers have received training in NORC techniques and procedures under the personal direction of an office or regional supervisor, and except when large numbers of interviewers are being trained for a special study in a particular locality, the training is always given individually. The amount of time spent on this training has varied from a single afternoon to several days, depending upon the applicant's aptitude and experience and the amount of time available. In general, the procedure is as follows: After studying certain basic instructions and preliminary materials and after a short talk by the supervisor, the applicant obtains, by himself, two or three trial interviews on the NORC training questionnaire, the first with a friend or relative, the last with a stranger. These interviews are subsequently criticized by the supervisor, with appropriate comments upon any obvious errors or weaknesses. The applicant then interviews the supervisor, who gives prepared answers of a difficult or problem type and who acts, in general, the part of a difficult respondent in order to test the applicant's ability to handle a variety of situations. Following this interview and discussion, the applicant is taken into the field and directed to obtain two or three interviews with strangers of varying socio-economic levels in the presence of the supervisor, who notes any particular errors or weaknesses and later comments upon them. The supervisor himself may often give one or more demonstration interviews as an example. A final discussion between the two, in which any remaining problems or difficulties are taken up, ends the training.

Once hired and trained by the supervisor, the new interviewer, unless he lives near by or resides in a city frequently visited by NORC personnel, usually is completely without personal contact with the office. He may at long intervals be visited by a traveling supervisor, but most members of the national staff have had only mail contact with the office since they were first hired. This appears to be a common situation among nationwide interviewing staffs, although some agencies have been able to meet the problem better than others through periodic regional conferences or through the employment of a full-time traveling supervisor who can in the course of time visit almost all of them.

In general, there is no personal supervision of the NORC interviewer's actual work. Unless he should be a new interviewer in a large city, working under the direct supervision of an office or regional supervisor, he receives his assignments by mail, directly from the office, and after completing his interviews, returns the material by mail, directly to the office. He works alone, from written instructions, and the results of his work are entirely dependent upon his own skills, initiative, and understanding of the NORC directions. The names of his respondents are not recorded, and unless his interviews reveal some suspicious pattern or otherwise lead the office to suspect fabrication, there is no direct check on the validity of his calls.

To offset the lack of personal contact and supervision once the interviewer is enrolled on the staff, NORC has instituted a variety of quality controls and morale-building devices. Each interviewer, for example, receives at the time of his enrollment on the staff a hard-cover copy of the field manual, "Interviewing for NORC." This manual, published in 1945 and revised slightly in 1947, is the interviewer's "blue book." Its 150 pages cover every aspect of his work, and he is held responsible for a thorough mastery of its contents. A 100-item "True-or-False" test has been prepared to test interviewers' familiarity with the manual, and while the interviewer is free to look up any doubtful answers, mere reference to the manual for the correct response achieves one of the purposes of the test. In addition to the basic manual, detailed specifications, or specific instructions for that particular survey, accompany each interviewing assignment. These specifications, which usually include six or eight single-spaced mimeographed pages to cover a twenty-question questionnaire, tell something of the background of the survey and its purposes, contain general advice and suggestions on how to handle particular problems which may arise, and discuss each of the separate questions in detail. The specifications are written on the basis of the office's pretesting experience, and they carefully instruct interviewers on the proper handling of particular types of vague, qualified, or irrelevant responses which may occur. The precise meaning and objective of each question are elaborated for the interviewer's benefit, and occasionally specific alternative phrases are authorized, in the event that certain respondents do not understand the question as it is worded.

Every interviewer knows that his interviews receive a rigorous examination and analysis in the office, and that his work is "rated" from the standpoint of quality. In actual practice, not every interviewer is rated on every survey; but all new interviewers and all "borderline" interviewers have each of their assignments rated, and even veteran members of the staff are rated on every alternate assignment. These office ratings cover the interviewer's handling of free-answer questions, the degree and manner in which he probed replies which were not clear, relevant, or specific; the number and type of comments he elicited on pre-coded questions, the degree to which he seems to be reporting completely and verbatim; the care with which he studied the instructions and filled out the questionnaire, the number of checking errors or omissions he made, the clarity and completeness with which he described such characteristics as "Occupation"; and his sampling performance, which on probability surveys would include his following of instructions and the care and accuracy with which he filled out his forms, and in quota sampling, would include his accurate filling of the assigned quotas and the representativeness of his cross section in terms of such unassigned characteristics as geographical location, education, occupation, etc. These ratings are recorded in detail on "rating sheets" and are the subject of a considerable amount of correspondence from the office to the field staff. Every interviewer receives a personal letter following every assignment or two, announcing his rating and discussing whatever errors or weaknesses have been revealed. Thus the training process is carried on, as long as the interviewer is on the staff. Interviewers are encouraged to interest themselves in survey methodology and, at the conclusion of every assignment, must fill out a report form detailing their reactions to the various questions and offering whatever criticism or suggestions occur to them. These criticisms are acknowledged in the office's letters to each interviewer, and often serve as the basis for a paragraph or two which will add to the interviewer's understanding of research problems. Interviewers are also encouraged to tell the office, either on the report form which they fill out at the conclusion of each survey or in separate letters, about any problems or questions they have about the work; and these communications are answered by office supervisors in personal letters.

Although the regular national staff was aware that NORC had received a grant for the study of "interviewer bias," it is extremely doubtful that this knowledge affected their performance in any way. The purpose of any of the interviewer-effect studies reported here was always either disguised or left unstated. But in the NORC training and education program, special attention always has been given to the problem of bias. Applicants with obviously biasing characteristics are never hired, and the new interviewer is indoctrinated early in his training with such precepts as "Never suggest an answer," "Ask all questions exactly as worded," "Never show surprise at a person's answer," "Never reveal your own opinions," etc. The index to the NORC interviewing manual lists no fewer than twenty-five separate references to "biasing factors," and entire sections of that volume are devoted to two areas of interviewer performance in which our studies have found the greatest evidence of bias—field ratings and probing behavior. The specifications for each survey further alert the interviewer against bias by noting the areas in which it is most likely to occur, and they endeavor to standardize just such matters as probing behavior on each question and the criteria to be used in field ratings. Evidences of bias are also considered in determining the NORC interviewers' performance ratings on each survey. Marked or unusual patterns in the responses, the repetition of particular words or phrases in free-answer replies, indications that suggestive probes have been used, deviant behavior as revealed by comments on the interviewer's report form— such weaknesses are always noted and pointed out to the interviewers in the letters they receive from the office.

The frequent letters from the office, in addition to their purposes of training and also education, are designed to maintain and improve the interviewer's morale by demonstrating that his problems are understood, that his work is appreciated and used, and that his complaints or difficulties receive sympathetic attention. Letters containing a great deal of criticism are so phrased as not to discourage the interviewer, and the more skilful members of the staff often receive personal communications which contain only praise and thanks for their good work. Even these superior workers, however, are constantly encouraged to think about interviewing problems and to work toward still greater skill and efficiency. Various other devices are employed in these letters to make the distant interviewer feel that he is an integral part of the organization: events in his personal life which come to the office's attention (for example, a child's illness or a daughter's graduation) are acknowledged and commented on; he may be given some unpublished information about a forthcoming survey or about the uses to which a past survey was actually put; he may be asked to supply us with descriptive or statistical data about the community he lives in, etc.

Further to keep the isolated interviewer in touch with the office, a monthly newsletter (usually four mimeographed pages in newspaper layout) is mailed to each member of the staff, including those who are temporarily inactive. This newsletter, designed to be both informative and entertaining, contains humorous anecdotes submitted by the interviewers, results of past surveys, suggestions on interviewing techniques, stories about particular interviewers who have distinguished themselves in one way or another, news about plans for prospective surveys and the schedule for the immediate future, occasional stories about the activities of the office staff, etc. Inexpensive gifts are sent to each member of the staff at Christmas time, and occasionally interviewers with very superior records or long service receive special awards.

A further incentive to conscientious work lies in a sliding scale of pay, based in part on the interviewer's ratings and in part on his length of service. He starts at the minimum figure, which, after his completion of four assignments with satisfactory ratings, is advanced to a somewhat higher rate. On the completion of ten assignments (usually about a year later), and provided his ratings are above average (in the upper 40 per cent), he is raised to the highest rate. Thus, at least until he attains the maximum rate, there is a financial incentive for the interviewer to accept as many assignments as are offered to him and to strive to correct any deficiencies reported to him in letters from the office. By the time he attains the highest rate, interest in the work and pride in his performance generally assure his continued diligence.

NORC interviewers are paid by the hour, on a "portal-to-portal" basis, and are reimbursed for all necessary expenses such as transportation, phone calls, postage, parking fees, etc. The hourly rate produces considerable variation in charges from one interviewer to another, as a result of differential interviewing efficiency and of differences in the type of quota assigned, the weather, etc. But this method of payment is believed to encourage more skilful and more conscientious interviewing, since it removes the temptation to do careless or dishonest work for the sake of speed. The interviewer is paid for all the time he spends on the job, and if he is handicapped by bad weather or is forced to make an unusual number of callbacks or is detained by a particularly garrulous respondent, he is not penalized for these mischances. Any attempts to take advantage of the hourly method of payment, by "padding" the number of hours listed as spent on the job, are readily apparent from a routine cost analysis. Interviewers whose charges appear unusually high, when compared to other members of the staff having comparable assignments, are apprised of the fact, urged to increase their efficiency on future surveys, and invited to write the office of any trouble they have in this respect. Those whose costs remain consistently much higher than average are soon dropped from the staff unless special circumstances are involved.

The volume of interviewing handled by the average NORC interviewer is not great. As we have noted, the great majority do not interview for any other agency, and NORC does not demand a great deal of their time. The typical NORC interviewer will complete about eight assignments per year, although the number may range from four to fourteen, depending upon his location, availability, competence, and the number of national surveys NORC has scheduled. Not only is he called on less than once a month, but when an assignment does come, it is usually a small one which can easily be completed in two or three days. Assignments generally range from twelve to twenty interviews, and the interviews themselves usually average about a half hour with each respondent. Most interviewers who can put in full days complete about ten interviews per day, although many of the staff prefer to interview only part-time and to distribute the work over the three or four days usually granted to them for completion. Assignments are generally sent on very short notice. An advance postal card is mailed to interviewers selected for the survey as soon as the mailing date is known, but this card usually arrives only three or four days in advance of the actual survey materials. The interviewer is free to telegraph his inability to accept the assignment, without prejudicing his position on the staff, although frequent or consistent refusals will generally draw a letter from the office suggesting that the interviewer be placed on the "temporarily inactive" list until such time as he can accept a larger share of the assignments offered him. Though interviewers always work in or near their home area, their specific assignments are usually rotated to avoid monotony. Thus, one assignment may call for near-by farms, the next one may specify residents of the interviewer's own town, and the following quota may send him to some adjacent city or county.

NORC's *national* surveys of the period covered in this report were based on a form of quota sampling, restricted by the designation of preselected blocks in most urban areas. Where such restrictions do not occur, the interviewer has quotas in terms of sex, two age groups, and four rental brackets, and each cell must be correctly filled. The interviewer generally knows in what parts of the city he can find people with homes of the assigned rental values, and within those neighborhoods he strives to fill his sex and age quotas. At the beginning of his assignment he can accept virtually anybody for his sample, but he soon begins to fill the small cells, and a considerable number of calls is usually necessary before he can fill the last few holes in his cross section. The interviewer is not supposed to interview his friends or relatives, he is supposed to keep in mind the importance of such uncontrolled factors as nationality, religion, education, etc.; and he is asked to scatter his interviews geographically by obtaining no more than three in any block nor six in any neighborhood. The recording of background data about each respondent, including his address, provides a check on the degree to which the interviewer complies with these requirements. Under the block-sampling procedure, a city's blocks are stratified by rent in the NORC office, and pairs of blocks are drawn at random from each stratum. Two sides of each of the designated blocks are then randomly specified for the interview, so that the total assignment consists of clusters of four interviews on two blocks. The interviewer is free to select any dwelling unit on the assigned side of the assigned block, so long as he stays within his sex and age quotas. Callbacks are sometimes required when the block-side contains only a few dwelling units, and a substituting procedure is specified when no units at all are available.

All of the above considerations apply, of course, only to the regular NORC national field staff. Some of the findings cited in this report are based on special surveys conducted in particular areas and using a staff of interviewers specially hired and trained for that job. Usually these surveys employed some kind of probability sample. On such surveys, the type of interviewer hired and the nature of the employment and training are probably not much different from those involved in any other one-time survey in a particular community. Two or more office supervisors travel to the selected community, invite applications for employment on the interviewing staff, screen the applicants who materialize, and then train them in a group, in a series of training sessions arranged over a period of two or three days. Each interviewer is then given his assignment, he checks in at the office periodically, and his work is closely supervised by the office people who are there on the spot. Although full-time work is encouraged, some members of the staff may interview only evenings and weekends. Hourly, and somewhat higher rates of pay are generally the rule, with bonuses occasionally awarded for successful completion of the more difficult assignments or for willingness to do nighttime interviewing. Usually about half of such a crew has had previous experience, as part-time resident interviewers for nationwide or local research companies or as students in connection with their course work, while the other half will be totally inexperienced. Once the particular survey is completed, the interviewers are dismissed, although one or two of those who showed superior aptitude may be retained for the national staff provided their community can be used as a regular sampling point.

Since hiring and training procedures, administrative and supervisory practices, rates of pay, and volume of work will inevitably differ from one research agency to another, the findings we have cited in this report which are based on the NORC staff must be weighed in conjunction with the descriptive information provided in the foregoing. It is most probable, however, that the similarities in the interviewer's task, from one agency to another, are immeasurably greater than the differences among his employers, and that, except in very unusual circumstances, what has been found true of the NORC interviewers will equally hold true for other people performing the same job.

Bibliography for Chapter VI

This bibliography is a partial list of published studies dealing with interviewer effect which were examined in an effort to appraise the extent of such effects in the course of normal field operations. From the hundreds of studies examined, we cite here only those which bear on those aspects of interviewer effect treated in our study. A separate monograph, obtainable from the University of Chicago Press, gives a summary of the relevant features of each of these studies—character of interviewing staff, sample and character of population, content and form of questions, method of analysis and type of significance test, findings of interviewer effect, etc.

ACKERLEY, LOIS. "A Comparision of Attitude Scales and the Interview Method," *Journal of Experimental Education*, V (1936), 137–46.

BLANKENSHIP, ALBERT. "The Effect of the Interviewer upon the Response in a Public Opinion Poll," *Journal of Consulting Psychology*, IV (1940), 134–36.

CAHALAN, DON; TAMULONIS, VALERIE; and VERNER, HELEN. "Interviewer Bias Involved in Certain Types of Opinion Survey Questions," *International Journal of Opinion and Attitude Research*, I, No. 1 (1947), 63–77.

CAMPBELL, ANGUS. "Two Problems in the Use of the Open Question," *Journal of Abnormal and Social Psychology*, XL (1945), 340–43.

CANTRIL, HADLEY. "Interviewer Bias and Rapport," in *Gauging Public Opinion*. Princeton: Princeton University Press, 1947, pp. 107–18.

CLARKE, E. "Values of Student Interviewers," *Journal of Personnel Research*, V (1926), 204–7.

DINERMAN, HELEN. "1948 Votes in the Making—a Preview," *Public Opinion Quarterly*, XII (1948), 585–98.

DURBIN, J., and STUART, A. "Differences in Response Rates of Experienced and Inexperienced Interviewers," *Journal of the Royal Statistical Society*, Series A, CXIV (1951), 163–206.

FEARING, FRANKLIN. "The Appraisal Interview," in MACNEMAR, Q., and MERRILL, M. (ed.). *Studies in Personality*. New York: McGraw-Hill, 1942, pp. 47–87.

FELDMAN, J.; HYMAN, H.; and HART, C. "A Field Study of Interviewer Effects on the Quality of Survey Data," *Public Opinion Quarterly*, XV (1951), 734–61.

FERBER, ROBERT, and WALES, HUGH. "Detection and Correction of Interviewer Bias," *Public Opinion Quarterly*, XVI (1952), 107–27.

GUEST, LESTER. "A Study of Interviewer Competence," *International Journal of Opinion and Attitude Research*, I, No. 4 (1947), 17–30.

HANSEN, M.; HURWITZ, W.; MARKS, E.; and MAULDIN, W. "Response Errors in Surveys," *Journal of the American Statistical Association*, XLVI (1951), 147–90.

HEPNER, HARRY. *Psychology Applied to Life and Work*. New York: Prentice-Hall, 1950.

HOFFER, CHARLES. "Medical Needs of the Rural Population in Michigan," *Rural Sociology*, XII (1947), 162–68.

HORVITZ, DANIEL. "Sampling and Field Procedures of the Pittsburgh Morbidity Survey," *Public Health Reports*, LXVII (1952), 1003–12.

HOVLAND, CARL, and WONDERLIC, E. "Prediction of Industrial Success from a Standardized Interview," *Journal of Applied Psychology*, XXIII (1939), 537–46.

HYMAN, HERBERT. "Do They Tell the Truth?" *Public Opinion Quarterly*, VIII (1944), 557–59.

JENKINS, JOHN, and CORBIN, HOARCE. "Dependability of Psychological Brand Barometers, II, The Problem of Validity," *Journal of Applied Psychology*, XXII (1938), 252–60.

KATZ, DANIEL. "Do Interviewers Bias Polls?" *Public Opinion Quarterly*, VI (1942), 248–69.

KEATING, ELIZABETH; PATERSON, DONALD; and STONE, C. HAROLD. "Validity of Work Histories Obtained by Interview," *Journal of Applied Psychology*, XXXIV (1950), 6–11.

KINSEY, ALFRED; POMEROY, W.; and MARTIN, C. *Sexual Behavior in the Human Male*. Philadelphia: W. B. Saunders, 1948. Chapters on methodology.

LIENAU, C. "Selection, Training and Performance of the National Health Survey Field Staff," *American Journal of Hygiene*, XXXIV (1941), 110–32.

MAHALANOBIS, P. "On Large-Scale Sample Surveys," *Philosophical Transactions of the Royal Society of London*, Ser. B, CCXXXI (1944), 329–451.

_____. "Recent Experiments in Statistical Sampling in the Indian Statistical Institute," *Journal of the Royal Statistical Society*, CIX (1946), 325–70.

MOSTELLER, FREDERICK. "The Reliability of Interviewers' Ratings," in CANTRIL, HADLEY (ed.). *Gauging Public Opinion*. Princeton: Princeton University Press, 1947, pp. 98–106.

NEELY, TWILA. *Study of Error in the Interview*. Unpublished Dissertation, Columbia University, 1937.

PARRY, HUGH, and CROSSLEY, HELEN. "Validity of Responses to Survey Questions," *Public Opinion Quarterly*, XIV (1950), 61–80.

RICE, STUART. "Contagious Bias in the Interview," *American Journal of Sociology*, XXXV (1929), 420–23.

SHAPIRO, S., and EBERHART, J. "Interviewer Differences in an Intensive Interview Survey," *International Journal of Opinion and Attitude Research*, I, No. 2 (1947), 1–17.

SMITH, HARRY, and HYMAN, HERBERT. "The Biasing Effect of Interviewer Expectations on Survey Results," *Public Opinion Quarterly*, XIV (1950), 491–506.

STEMBER, HERBERT, and HYMAN, HERBERT. "Interviewer Effects in Classification of Responses," *Public Opinion Quarterly*, XIII (1949–50), 669–82.

STOCK, J. STEVENS, and HOCHSTIM, JOSEPH. "A Method of Measuring Interviewer Variability," *Public Opinion Quarterly*, XV (1951), 322–34.

UDOW, ALFRED. "The Interviewer Effect in Public Opinion and Market Research Surveys," *Archives of Psychology*, 1942, No. 277.

WILLIAMS, F., and CANTRIL, H. "The Use of Interviewer Rapport as a Method of Detecting Differences Between 'Public' and Private Opinion," *Journal of Social Psychology*, XXII (1945), 171–75.

WYATT, DALE. *Interviewers' Opinions Compared to Interviewers' Expectations as Sources of Bias in a Public Opinion Poll*. Master's thesis, Ohio State University, 1949.

Previous NORC Publications, Interviewer Effect Series

FELDMAN, J. J.; HYMAN, HERBERT; and HART, CLYDE W. "A Field Study of Interviewer Effects on the Quality of Survey Data," *Public Opinion Quarterly*, XV (1951–52), 734–761.

FISHER, HERBERT. "Interviewer Bias in the Recording Operation," *International Journal of Opinion and Attitude Research*, IV (1950), 391–411.

GUEST, LESTER, and NUCKOLS, ROBERT. "A Laboratory Experiment in Recording in Public Opinion Interviewing," *International Journal of Opinion and Attitude Research*, IV (1950), 336–52.

HART, CLYDE W. "Bias in Interviewing in Studies of Opinions, Attitudes, and Consumer Wants," *Proceedings of the American Philosophical Society*, XCII (1948), 399–404.

HART, CLYDE W. "Interviewer Bias," American Society for Testing Materials, *Special Technical Publication* No. 117, 1951, pp. 38–45.

HYMAN, HERBERT. "Inconsistencies as a Problem in Attitude Measurement," *Journal of Social Issues*, V (1949), 38–42.

————. "Interviewing as a Scientific Procedure," in LERNER, DANIEL, and LASSWELL, HAROLD D., *The Policy Sciences: Recent Developments in Scope and Method*. Stanford University Press, 1951.

————. "Problems in the Collection of Opinion-Research Data," *American Journal of Sociology*, LV (1950), 362–70.

HYMAN, HERBERT, and STEMBER, HERBERT. "Interviewer Effects in the Classification of Responses," *Public Opinion Quarterly*, XIII (1949–50), 669–82.

MANHEIMER, DEAN, and HYMAN, HERBERT. "Interviewer Performance in Area Sampling," *Public Opinion Quarterly*, XIII (1949), 63–77.

PARRY, HUGH J., and CROSSLEY, HELEN M. "Validity of Responses to Survey Questions," *Public Opinion Quarterly*, XIV (1950), 61–80.

SHEATSLEY, PAUL B. "An Analysis of Interviewer Characteristics and Their Relationship to Performance," *International Journal of Opinion and Attitude Research*, IV (1950–51), 473–98; V (1951), 80–94, 192–220.

SHEATSLEY, PAUL B. "Some Uses of Interviewer-Report Forms," *Public Opinion Quarterly*, XI (1947–48), 601–11.

SHEATSLEY, PAUL B. "The Influence of Sub-questions on Interviewer Performance," *Public Opinion Quarterly*, XIII (1949), 310–13.

SHEATSLEY, PAUL B. "The Art of Interviewing and a Guide to Interviewer Selection and Training," in JAHODA, MARIE; DEUTSCH, MORTON; and COOK, STUART W. *Research Methods in Social Relations*, Dryden Press, 1951.

SMITH, HARRY L., and HYMAN, HERBERT. "The Biasing Effect of Interviewer Expectations on Survey Results," *Public Opinion Quarterly*, XIV (1950), 491–506.

STEMBER, HERBERT. "Which Respondents Are Reliable?" *International Journal of Opinion and Attitude Research*, V (1951), 475.

STEMBER, HERBERT, and HYMAN, HERBERT. "How Interviewer Effects Operate Through Question Form," *International Journal of Opinion and Attitude Research*, III (1949–50), 493–512.

NOTES TO CHAPTER I

1. D. K. Lieu, "Collecting Statistics in China," *American Statistician,* 1948, pp. 12–13. (Reprinted from the *Statistical Reporter,* Division of Statistical Standards, Bureau of the Budget, No. 130 [Washington, D.C., 1948].)

2. F. J. Roethlisberger and W. J. Dickson, *Management and the Worker* (Cambridge: Harvard University Press, 9th printing, 1949), p. 286.

3. G. P. Murdock, *Social Structure* (New York: Macmillan, 1949), p. 111.

4. J. W. Bennett reviews this entire literature and shows the striking contrasts in the accounts of a large number of different observers. It should be noted, however, that Bennett emphasizes not errors in the original field work but errors in the manipulation and handling of data during the analytic stages. See *Southwestern Journal of Anthropology,* II (1946), 361–74.

5. Oscar Lewis, *Life in a Mexican Village: Tepoztlan Restudied* (Urbana: University of Illinois, 1951), pp. 428–29. We are indebted to Professor Milton Singer for bringing this comparison to our attention.

6. Reo Fortune, "Arapesh Warfare," *American Anthropologist,* XLI (1939), 36.

7. B. Stavrianos, "Research Methods in Cultural Anthropology in Relation to Scientific Criteria," *Psychological Review,* LVII (1950), 334–44.

8. Lewis, *op. cit.*

9. Ralph Linton, *The Cultural Background of Personality* (New York: Appleton-Century, 1945). Paul Radin, *The Method and Theory of Ethnology* (New York: McGraw-Hill, 1933).

10. Margaret Mead, "The Training of the Cultural Anthropologist," *Amer. Anthro.,* LIV (1952), 343–46.

11. Clyde Kluckhohn, "The Personal Document in Anthropological Science," in *Social Science Research Council Bulletin No. 53* (New York: SSRC, 1945).

12. F. C. Bartlett *et al., The Study of Society* (4th ed.; London: Routledge and Kegan Paul, 1949).

13. E. J. Kempf, *Psychopathology* (St. Louis: Mosby, 1920).

14. R. K. Merton, *Social Theory and Social Structure* (Glencoe: The Free Press, 1949), p. 214.

15. S. Tomkins, *Contemporary Psychopathology* (Cambridge: Harvard University Press, 1943), p. 448.

16. R. Christie, "Experimental Naivete and Experential Naivete," *Psychological Bulletin,* XLVIII (1951), 327–39.

17. For another instance of a method subject to indeterminacy due to the interpersonal nature of the data collection procedure, but one in which the indeterminacy is again not patent and often neglected, the reader is referred to the discussion of the self-administered questionnaire in Chapter IV. Of course, the best example of indeterminacy is the classic Hawthorne study, in which the experimenters' behavior turned out to be the crucial factor in producing changes in the workers. However, in this instance, what would

normally have been a hidden liability in the research was converted into an asset and made the central finding of the study. The writers describe the study as follows: "In the endeavor to keep the major variables in the situation constant and the girls' attitudes cooperative, the investigators *inadvertently* altered the social situation of the group. . . . They were trying to maintain a controlled experiment in which they could test for the effects of single variables while holding all other factors constant. . . . By Period XIII it had become evident that in human situations not only was it practically impossible to keep all other factors constant, but trying to do so in itself introduced the biggest change of all; in other words, the investigators had not been studying an ordinary shop situation but a socially contrived situation of their own making. The experiment they had planned to conduct was quite different from the experiment they had actually performed. They had not studied the relation between output and fatigue, monotony, etc., so much as they had performed a most interesting psychological and sociological experiment. In the process of setting the conditions for the test, they had altered completely the social situation of the operators and their customary attitudes and interpersonal relations." See Roethlisberger and Dickson, *op. cit.*, 182–83.

18. For a unique and striking instance to the contrary, the reader is referred to Newman, Bobbitt, and Cameron who obtained exceedingly high reliability in ratings by different interviewers screening U.S. Coast Guard Officer candidates. See "The Reliability of the Interview Method in an Officer Candidate Evaluation Program," *American Psychologist*, I (1946), 103–9.

19. S. Stouffer *et al.*, *Measurement and Prediction*, Vol. IV, *The American Soldier* (Princeton: Princeton University Press, 1950), chap. 14.

20. Elsewhere Star presents other evidence against the interpretation that these differences represent real differences between the soldier populations of the different centers. She reports that the variability in results among different stations on a standardized test of disability (Neuropsychiatric Screening Adjunct) was small, suggesting that the populations truly did not differ so markedly. For example, while the Detroit examiners rejected three times as many candidates as the Chicago examiners, the proportions screened in the two centers by the test were 26.9 per cent and 24.1 per cent respectively.

21. W. A. Hunt and C. L. Wittson, "Some Sources of Error in the Neuropsychiatric Statistics of World War II," *Journal of Clinical Psychology*, V (1949), 350–58.

22. P. E. Vernon and J. B. Parry, *Personnel Selection in the British Forces* (London: University of London Press, 1949), p. 126. It should be noted that this demonstration of unreliability does not adequately represent the high level of *validity* obtained by the British generally through the application of such selection processes. Elsewhere in their report, Vernon and Parry present clear and striking evidence of the reduction in failure rates during training for various army personnel, following the institution of such psychological selection methods.

23. Great Britain Air Ministry, *Psychological Disorders in Flying Personnel of the Royal Air Force, Investigated during the War 1939–45*, Air Publication 3139 (London: H. M. Stationery, 1947).

24. P. Ash, "The Reliability of Psychiatric Diagnoses," *Journal of Abnormal and Social Psychology*, XLIV (1949), 272–76.

25. B. Mehlman, "The Reliability of Psychiatric Diagnoses," *Jour. Abn. Soc. Psychol.*, XLVII (1952), 577–78.

26. Harry M. Grayson and R. S. Tolman, "A Semantic Study of Concepts of Clinical Psychologists and Psychiatrists," *Jour. Abn. Soc. Psychol.*, XLV (1950), 216–31.

27. J. H. Masserman and H. T. Carmichael, "Diagnosis and Prognosis in Psychiatry," *Jour. Mental Sciences*, LXXXIV (1938), 893–946.

28. E. B. Brody, R. Newman, and F. C. Redlich, "Sound Recording and the Problem of Evidence in Psychiatry," *Science*, CXIII (1951), 379–80.

29. E. Chapple and C. Arensberg, "Measuring Human Relations: An Introduction to the Study of the Interaction of Individuals," *Genetic Psychology Monographs*, XXII (1940).

30. E. D. Chapple, "The Interaction Chronograph: its evolution and present application," *Personnel* (1949).

31. Julius Seeman, "A Study of Preliminary Interview Methods in Vocational Counseling," *Journal of Consulting Psychology*, XII (1948), 321–30.

W. V. Snyder, "An Investigation of the Nature of Non-Directive Psychotherapy," *Journal of General Psychology*, XXXIII (1945), 193–223.

32. B. J. Covner, "Studies in Phonographic Recordings of Verbal Material, IV. Written Reports of Interviews," *Journal of Applied Psychology*, XXVIII (1944), 89–98.

33. W. A. McClelland and H. W. Sinaiko, "An Investigation of a Counselor Attitude Questionnaire," *Educational and Psychological Measurement*, X (1950), 128–34.

34. U.S. Army Air Forces, Aviation Psychology Program, Research Report No. 5, Printed Classification Tests.

35. E. Baughman, "Rorschach Scores as a Function of Examiner Difference," *Journal of Projective Techniques*, XV (1951), 243–49.

36. Else Frenkel-Brunswik, "Motivation and Behavior," *Genetic Psychol. Mono.*, XXVI (1942), 121–265.

We shall return in Chapter III, in the discussion of "attitude structure expectations," to this interesting phenomenon demonstrated both in the Brunswik study and in the RAF study of psychiatric interviewing—namely, the variations among interviewers in the structure or constellation or patterning observed for separate traits.

37. In certain fields, there is no process of collection of primary data; by definition, therefore no "interviewer" error. The scientist selects and interprets previously existing information. In such instances, the analogy to errors of interviewing or collection would be errors in selection or interpretation or inadequacies in the original body of material. For the prevalence of such errors in economics, the reader is referred to O. Morgenstern, *On the Accuracy of Economic Observations* (Princeton: Princeton University Press, 1950). For a detailed case study of such errors among historians, the reader is referred to Howard K. Beale, "What Historians Have Said About the Causes of the Civil War," in *Theory and Practice in Historical Study: A Report of the Committee on Historiography*, Bulletin No. 54 (New York: Soc. Sci. Res. Council, 1946).

38. J. Yerushalmy, "Statistical Problems in Assessing Methods of Medical Diagnosis, with special reference to X-Ray Techniques," *Public Health Reports*, LXII (1947), 1432–49.

J. Neymann, remarks from a paper read before the American Statistical Association, Cleveland, December, 1948, with reference to League of Nations Publication C6 M5 1924 III and personal communication.

R. H. Jones, "Physical Indices and Clinical Assessments of the Nutrition of School Children," Jour. Roy. Stat. Soc., CI (1938), 1–34.

A. L. Cochrane, P. J. Chapman, and P. D. Oldham, "Observer's Errors in Taking Medical Histories," Lancet, CCLX (1951), 1007–9.

W. E. Deming, "On the Sampling of Physical Materials," (Paper read at the meeting of the International Statistical Institute, Bern, Switzerland, September, 1949) (ditto).

R. Lippitt, "Social Psychology as Science and as Profession," (Presidential Address, Society for the Psychological Study of Social Issues, Denver, Colorado, September 5, 1949) (mimeo).

R. S. Woodworth, *Experimental Psychology* (New York: Henry Holt, 1938), pp. 300–301.

39. Bertrand Russell, *Philosophy* (New York: Norton, 1927), p. 30.

40. H. A. Murray *et al.*, *Explorations in Personality* (New York: Oxford University Press, 1938), pp. 21–22.

41. For discussion of personal documents see Kluckhohn, *op. cit.*

42. One study in the literature based on samples of captured uncensored German mail demonstrated empirically that the estimates thus obtained agreed with independent data for the entire population, writers and non-writers combined. Consequently, this limitation may not always hold, although in the absence of an empirical demonstration, one has no way of knowing whether bias is present. See United States Strategic Bombing Survey of Germany (Washington, D.C.: Government Printing Office, 1946), Vol. II, chap. 2. It should be noted that this limitation does not apply to idiographic science. See G. Allport, *The Use of Personal Documents in Psychological Science*, Bulletin No. 49 (New York: Soc. Sci. Res. Council, 1942).

43. G. Allport, J. S. Bruner, and E. M. Jandorf, "Personality Under Social Catastrophe: Ninety Life Histories of the Nazi Revolution," *Character and Personality*, X (1941–42), 1–22.

44. S. Stouffer *et al.*, *The American Soldier* (4 vols.; Princeton: Princeton University Press, 1949).

45. For a discussion of the use of saliency questions, see D. Krech and R. Crutchfield, *Theory and Problems of Social Psychology* (New York: McGraw-Hill, 1948), p. 279.

46. H. Cantril, *Gauging Public Opinion* (Princeton: Princeton University Press, 1944).

47. P. E. Vernon, *The Assessment of Psychological Qualities by Verbal Methods*, Medical Research Council, Industrial Health Research Board, Report No. 83 (London: H. M. Stationery, 1938). Quoted by permission of the Controller of Her Brittanic Majesty's Stationery's Office.

48. G. Eckstrand and A. R. Gilliland, "The Psychogalvanometric Method for Measuring the Effectiveness of Advertising," *Jour. App. Psychol.*, XXXII (1948), 415–25.

R. R. Willoughby, "Liberalism, Prosperity and Urbanization," *Journal of Genetic Psychology*, XXXV (1928), 134–36.

G. Seward, "Sex Roles in Post War Planning," *Journal of Social Psychology*, XVIV (1944), 163–85.

49. U.S. Strategic Bombing Survey, *op. cit.*

50. Vernon, *op. cit.*

51. E. Herzog, "Pending Perfection: A Qualitative Complement to Quantitative Methods," *International Journal of Opinion and Attitude Research*, I, No. 3 (1947), 32–48.

52. The lack of realization that observation under natural conditions may be bound by situational factors is vividly demonstrated in one study involving the covert observation of "natural" conversations. The themes of the conversation were cross-classified by the sex and estimated age and class of the speaker, but *not by the characteristics of the listener*, which would have been perfectly easy for the observer to record. Surely what a woman may say in everyday conversation would be expected to vary when she talks to a man rather than to a woman, just as the respondent's remarks in a formal interview might vary with the group membership of the interviewer. While the factor is not taken into consideration in the former case, it is often used as a basis of criticism in evaluating the formal interview. See J. Watson, W. Breed, and H. Posman, "A Study in Urban Conversation," *Jour. Soc. Psychol.*, XXVIII (1948), 121–33.

53. By extension, the same consideration should be kept in mind in evaluating specific alternative forms of interviewing. Even though a given interviewing procedure may be demonstrated to be more precise and reliable than another method of interviewing, one might nevertheless reject the precise method in the interest of obtaining information. Accuracy is desirable but not at the price of triviality.

54. In the rare instance, where our purposes are experimental, differences between interviewers might be deliberately enhanced if the effect of such factors were a central subject of study. Such deliberate introduction of interviewer effects could be regarded as an experimental equivalent of larger social forces and an easy method for studying certain social psychological problems. See H. Hyman, "Inconsistencies as a Problem in Attitude Measurement," *Journal of Social Issues*, V (1949), 38–42.

55. The full technical treatment of these types of error is presented in Chapters VI and VII. The distinction is old and described variously as bias vs. variance, validity vs. reliability, variable vs. constant error, etc. Here we will not dwell on the formal problem, since we wish to discuss rather its larger implications.

56. We are indebted to Robert O. Carlson for suggesting this procedure, which he has been using experimentally. This same procedure of "tandem interviews" was found to be the most effective means of getting information bearing on the selection of medical college students in investigations sponsored by the Markle Foundation. See their *Annual Report* (1952), p. 36.

57. For a discussion of such situational factors within the interview, see Hyman, *op. cit.*

58. One can resolve this problem of validity by operational definition and regard attitude or opinion as the answer revealed to the question. In such instances, it is not necessary to specify any other setting within which one

tries to predict the expressed attitude or to be concerned about the under-lying state.

59. Murray, *op. cit.*

60. M. Woodside, "The Psychiatric Approach to Research Interviewing," in *Studies in Population, Proceedings of the annual meeting of the Population Association of America*, ed. G. F. Mair (Princeton: Princeton University Press, 1949), 166–69. Italics ours. The two quotations that follow are from the same pages.

61. H. Hyman and P. B. Sheatsley, "The Kinsey Report and Survey Methodology," *International Journal of Opinion and Attitude Research*, II (1948), 183–95.

62. This quotation is from L. R. England, "Little Kinsey, An Outline of Sex Attitudes in Britain," *Public Opinion Quarterly*, XIII (1949–50), 587–600. For a study of the national urban population in United States see J. W. Riley and Matilda White, "The Use of Various Methods of Contraception," *American Sociological Review*, V (1940), 890–903.

63. F. W. Finger, "Sex Beliefs and Practices among Male College Students," *Jour. Abn. Soc. Psychol.*, XLII (1947), 64.

64. Ruth Shonle Cavan, "Interviewing for Life History Material," *American Journal of Sociology*, XXXV (1929–30), 100–15.

65. Roethlisberger and Dickson, *op. cit.*, chap. 13.

66. A. C. Kinsey, W. B. Pomeroy, and C. E. Martin, *Sexual Behavior in the Human Male* (Philadelphia: Saunders, 1948).

67. G. V. Hamilton, *A Research in Marriage* (New York: Boni, 1929).

68. P. B. Sheatsley, "Some Uses of Interviewer Report Forms," *Pub. Opin. Quart.*, XI (1947), 601–11.

NOTES TO CHAPTER II

1. E. S. Bogardus, "Interviewing as a Social Process," *Sociology and Social Research*, XIX (1934), 70–75. See also Nicholas Spykman, *The Social Theory of Georg Simmel* (Chicago: University of Chicago Press, 1925), and Robert E. Park and Ernest W. Burgess, *Introduction to the Science of Sociology* (Chicago: University of Chicago Press, 1921).

2. S. A. Rice, "Contagious Bias in the Interview," *Amer. Jour. Sociol.*, XXXV (1929), 420–23.

3. Italics ours.

4. Hadley Cantril, *Gauging Public Opinion* (Princeton: Princeton University Press, 1944), chap. viii and Appendix II.

5. Frederick Mosteller *et al.*, *The Pre-Election Polls of 1948* (New York: Soc. Sci. Res. Council, 1949), chap. vii.

6. G. A. Lundberg, *Social Research* (New York: Longmans Green, 1946), p. 368.

7. R. B. MacLeod, "The Phenomenological Approach to Social Psychology," *Psychol. Rev.*, LIV (1947), 193–210.

8. Ruth Cooperstock analyzed the data on which these case histories were based and wrote the initial descriptions of the situations.

9. For a detailed report of the procedure the reader is referred to Appendix A.

10. This interviewer was Jewish.

11. For more evidence of such a discipline over conduct, particularly within the experienced interviewer, the reader is referred to H. Smith and H. Hyman, "The Biasing Effect of Interviewer Expectations on Survey Results," *Pub. Opin. Quart.*, XIV (1950), 491–506, and to J. Feldman, H. Hyman, and C. W. Hart, "A Field Study of Interviewer Effects on the Quality of Survey Data," *Pub. Opin. Quart.*, XV (1951), 734–61.

12. James Stern, *The Hidden Damage* (New York: Harcourt Brace, 1947), p. 230.

13. *Ibid.*, p. 236.

14. Italics ours.

15. D. Riesman and N. Glazer, in a most provocative discussion of public opinion research, based on characterological and structural concepts, subject the concept of rapport to a somewhat similar critical treatment. They suggest that the emphasis upon rapport may distort the true picture of *lower-class* political attitudes. In so far as the lower-class person's real-life situation does not contain the elements of consideration and warmth characteristic of the interview, and these very elements are likely to enhance the report of political involvement, an artificial picture may be obtained. See "The Meaning of Opinion," *Pub. Opin. Quart.*, XII (1948), 633–48.

16. In the instance of issues of an intimate and deep-lying nature, it may be that rapport in the extreme is an essential, but such issues seem outside the usual domain of social research.

17. Italics ours.

18. Italics ours.

19. It is of some significance that a social scientist, not associated with this study, with long clinical experience, discussed interviewing with both K and M and ventures this very interpretation. "K reported . . . that many people are ashamed not to know what they feel they ought to know about political questions. M also encountered this but I would guess to a much lesser extent. For K lives in a world where it matters very much what we 'know.' . . . Is it not likely that such a person will give respondents even more of a feeling that they ought to know than they would have anyway?" (Private communication from David Riesman.)

20. Riesman independently remarks about this interviewer: "She wants to establish an animated ultra-interview transference state with the respondent."

21. Italics ours.

22. Italics ours.

23. For a detailed discussion of the procedure, the reader is referred to Chapter III and Appendix A.

24. Italics ours.

25. The form on which the interviewer recorded the answers contained the questions and allowed only a limited amount of space for the free answers.

26. Italics ours to indicate emphasis in interviewer's speech.

27. Similar evidence on variations in the role assumed by interviewers is available from studies in other fields. For example, in the study cited in Chapter I on the reliability of psychiatric assessments in the RAF, the two

psychiatrists reported the way in which they had conducted their interviews and defined the procedures prescribed for them. While considerable latitude was allowed them, they had been instructed as to what factors should enter into their assessment, the nature of the interview procedure had been schematized, and they were required to score a series of ten presumably predisposing traits. Nevertheless, from their reports, it was clearly seen that each adopted an individual method of interview. For example, "one established rapport by talking about service life and then proceeded to obtain a detailed account of performance in the service before enquiring into the personality before service, while the other did just the opposite, obtaining a chronological life story which ended with the service experiences." See Great Britain Air Ministry, *Psychological Disorders in Flying Personnel of the Royal Air Force, Investigated during the War 1939–45*, Air Publication 3139 (London: H. M. Stationery, 1947), p. 225. Quoted by permission of Her Brittanic Majesty's Stationery's Office. In another study of interviewing procedures used in classification of American naval personnel, from inspection of the mechanical transcriptions of the total interview process, it was clear that the eight interviewers observed gave their own individual definitions to a common assignment. With respect to structuring of the interview, there was no consistency among the interviewers. For example, some explained the purpose—others did not. There were large differences in the acceptance of the interviewee as an individual. Some interviewers misused their authority. Some saw the situation as tedious and tiring; others did not. The analysts concluded that the original interviewers had worked out no clear conception of their role and function. See E. Ingraham and A. Sheriff, "The Use of Proficiency Tests in Classification of Personnel," Office of Scientific Research and Development Memorandum (Microfilm).

28. Much of the theorizing about such cognitive factors has already been reported in previous publications of this project. See for example: H. L. Smith and H. Hyman, *op. cit.* and H. Hyman, "Isolation, Measurement, and Control of Interviewer Effect," *SSRC Items*, III (1949).

29. G. Ichheiser, "Misunderstandings in Human Relations: A Study in False Social Perception," *Amer. Jour. Sociol.*, LV (1949).

30. D. Krech and R. Crutchfield, *Theory and Problems of Social Psychology* (New York: McGraw-Hill, 1948), p. 84.

31. Frederic C. Bartlett, *Remembering* (Cambridge: Harvard University Press, 1932).

32. S. Asch, "Forming Impressions of Personality," *Jour. Abn. Soc. Psychol.*, XLI (1946), 261.

33. Italics ours.

34. Krech and Crutchfield, *op. cit.*, especially chap. 4.

35. Asch's finding that the *initial* term sets the direction for the organization of the perception, and the intrinsic feature of an attitude-structure expectation, that subsequent answers are expected to be consistent with the *first* answers rather than with some basic prior characteristic of the respondent are worthy of special note. They suggest the general significance of situational determinants in liberating interview effects, for the effect is clearly seen to be dependent on the accident of what question is put first, or what type of answer might be casually mentioned at the beginning of an inter-

view. This foreshadows and supports the general theory of Situational Factors to be presented in Chapter V.

36. J. J. Feldman first noted this phenomenon in the data and coined the term "role expectations."

37. For a discussion of findings on stereotypes, the reader is referred to O. Klineberg, *Tensions Affecting International Understanding*, Bulletin No. 62 (New York: Soc. Sci. Res. Council, 1950), chap. 3.

38. Krech and Crutchfield, *op. cit.*, p. 96.

39. N. S. Shaler, *The Neighbor* (Boston: Houghton, Mifflin, 1904), quoted in R. E. Park and E. W. Burgess, *Introduction to the Science of Sociology* (Chicago: University of Chicago Press, 1921), pp. 294–98. See also William Graham Sumner, *Folkways* (New York: Ginn & Co., 1906).

40. E. L. Horowitz and R. E. Horowitz, "Development of Social Attitudes in Children," *Sociometry*, I (1937), 301–38.

41. The term was coined by Herbert Stember and the concept originally developed by him in the course of this project. See Herbert Stember and Herbert Hyman. "How Interviewer Effects Operate Through Question Form," *Internat. J. Opin. Attit. Res. 3* (1949), 493–511.

42. K. E. Clark, "A Note on the Meaning of Poll Results," *Internat. Jour. Opin. Attit. Res.*, III (1949), 109–12.

43. The summary findings of this study are reported in D. Wyatt and D. Campbell, "A Study of Interviewer Bias as related to Interviewers' Expectations and Own Opinions," *Internat. Jour. Opin. Attit. Res.*, IV (1950), 77–83. For the particular statistic cited above the reader is referred to Wyatt, Unpublished Master's Thesis, Ohio State University Library.

44. See, for example, the discussion of first principles of interviewing in W. Bingham and B. Moore, *How to Interview* (3d. ed.; New York: Harper, 1941). It is interesting to note that the only reference to such cognitive factors by these authors is in their discussion of interviewing to appraise candidates. In their chapter on public opinion interviewing, no reference to such sources of bias is made. Again this suggests the fact that we thought of the *survey* interview as involving essentially the communication of questions and answers and neglected the subtle judgmental processes involved.

45. R. C. Oldfield, *The Psychology of the Interview* (2d. ed.; London: Methuen, 1943).

46. L. L. Thurstone, *A Factorial Study of Perception* (Chicago: University of Chicago Press, 1944).

47. For a summary of such theorizing, see Else Frenkel-Brunswik, "Intolerance of Ambiguity as an Emotional and Perceptual Personality Variable," *Journal of Personality*, XVIII (1949), 108–43.

48. *Ibid.*

49. For one demonstration of such tests, the reader is referred to M. Rokeach, "Generalized Mental Rigidity as a Factor in Ethnocentrism," *Jour. Abn. Soc. Psychol.*, XLIII (1948), 259–78.

50. P. B. Sheatsley, "The Public Relations of the Polls," *Internat. Jour. Opin. Attit. Res.*, II (1948), 453–68.

51. Sheatsley also presents data on refusals and the attitudes of the *noncooperative* to complete the picture of public sentiments, but since our purpose

is simply to describe the attitudes of those who are interviewed, this group is here omitted from discussion.

52. This study was designed by Marshall Brown in co-operation with members of the NORC staff. The complete report was submitted in the form of a doctoral dissertation under the direction of Professor Lester Guest at the Pennsylvania State College.

53. This survey was done in January, 1949, when these events had just occurred.

54. This questionnaire and the general project were planned by Paul B. Sheatsley and analyzed with the assistance of Ruth Cooperstock. A more complete report of the findings will be published as a separate journal article.

55. Eighty-eight per cent of the current field staff are women and 81 per cent of the total staff have had some college education. See P. B. Sheatsley, "An Analysis of Interviewer Characteristics and their Relationship to Performance," *Internat. Jour. Opin. Attit. Res.*, IV (1950), 473–98.

56. When the national sample was queried, this question came at the end of a long interview on political matters. It may be that those who consented to be interviewed are that segment of the national population who are somewhat more sociable. Nevertheless, the difference is so striking that it supports our general conclusion.

57. Details of this experiment are reported in Chapter V.

58. Tetrachoric correlation co-efficients were inferred from Thurstone's computing diagrams.

59. The reader is referred to Theodor Adorno *et al.*, *The Authoritarian Personality* (New York: Harper, 1950), for a full discussion of these scales.

60. See H. Stember and H. Hyman, "How Interviewer Effects Operate Through Question Form," *Internat. Jour. Opin. Attit. Res.*, III (1949–50), 493–512.

NOTES TO CHAPTER III

1. C. Kluckhohn, "The Personal Document in Anthropological Science," in *Social Science Research Council Bulletin, Number 53* (New York: SSRC, 1945), p. 140.

2. R. C. Oldfield, *The Psychology of the Interview* (2d ed.; London: Methuen, 1943), p. 112.

3. A quantitative demonstration of this phenomenon is available in the published report of the intensive surveys conducted in conjunction with the Bikini test of the atom bomb. In occasional questions, the proportion of respondents whose opinions were not ascertained ran as high as 40 per cent, and Cottrell and Eberhart in explaining this finding state: "There may be other unascertained answers resulting mainly from the fact that interviewers have refrained from subjecting to the entire questionnaire those respondents who have repeatedly said they 'don't know,' 'don't think about those things.' " L. Cottrell and S. Eberhart, *American Opinion on World Affairs in the Atomic Age* (Princeton: Princeton University Press, 1948), p. 94.

4. This study was conducted by the Department of Scientific Research of the American Jewish Committee in conjunction with NORC.

5. Italics ours.

6. R. C. Oldfield, *op. cit.*, p. 104.

7. R. C. Oldfield, *op. cit.*, p. 111.

8. H. H. Kelley, "The Warm-Cold Variable in First Impressions of Persons," *Journal of Personality*, XVIII (1949), 431–39.

9. M. Haire and W. F. Grunes, "Perceptual Defenses, Processes Protecting the Organized Perception of another Personality," *Human Relations*, III (1950), 403–12.

10. For the effects of initial context as in classic "ideo-motor" suggestion experiments, the reader is referred to the summary discussion in O. Klineberg, *Social Psychology* (New York: Holt, 1940), pp. 322–28; for a critical review of experiments on "prestige" suggestion, the reader is referred to S. Asch, "The Doctrine of Suggestion, Prestige and Imitation in Social Psychology," *Psychol. Rev.*, LV (1948), 250–76.

11. Karl Marbe, "Bemerkungen zum vorhergehenden Aufsatz Luetgebrunes," *Archiv für die Gesamte Psychologie*, LVIX (1927), 173–78.

12. None of these experiments should be confused with the large literature on autistic perception, in which *motivational* factors cause *individual* distortions of reality. The experiments cited show the well-nigh *universal* effect of initial experience in creating an organized perception which affects subsequent discrete experiences.

13. Haire and Grunes, *op. cit.*

14. Here we have as pure an example of a role expectation as one could imagine.

15. G. Ichheiser, "Misunderstandings in Human Relations: A Study in False Social Perception," *Amer. Jour. Sociol.*, Vol. LV (1949).

16. Traditional research on "halo effect" emphasizes how a general evaluation of another person affects the judgment of specific traits, and suggests a globalness of expectational effects, but such a concept does not seem in accord with modern evidence that some intellectual process intervenes to reduce mechanical and global generalization.

17. A replication of Asch's basic experiment by Wishner and Mensch also reveals a specificity to these effects rather than a global halo effect. See I. Mensch and J. Wishner, "Asch on 'forming impressions of personality,'" *Journal of Personality*, XVI (1947), 188–191.

18. Else Frenkel-Brunswik, "Motivation and Behavior," *Genetic Psychol. Mono.*, XXVI (1942), 121–265.

19. Frenkel-Brunswik, *op. cit.*

20. Haire and Grunes, in reporting the different defenses by which their subjects protected the description of the workingman from the contradictory evidence that he was "intelligent," note that one small group actually changed the basic description so as to give full place for the characteristic of intelligence. This group seems either free of the usual role expectation or holds it in only a labile form. The magnitude of this group was at maximum seventeen out of the forty-three subjects, *op. cit.*

Similarly, Asch, in his analysis of experiments on prestige suggestion, on the effect of an imputed authorship on judgment of a text, notes that there were some subjects "who did not wish to be affected by external factors and took the fairly intelligent step of hiding the authors' names from themselves," *op. cit.*

21. While a matrix of intercorrelations among all pairs of nine drives involves only thirty-six co-efficients, the relationships were computed separately for boys and girls, thus accounting for a total of seventy-two co-efficients for each judge.

22. F. Elkin, "Specialists Interpret the Case of Harold Holzer," *Jour. Abn. Soc. Psychol.*, XLII (1947), 99–111. Italics ours.

23. Great Britain Air Ministry, *Psychological Disorders in Flying Personnel of the Royal Air Force, Investigated during the War, 1939–45*, Air Publication 3139 (London: H.M. Stationery, 1947). Quoted by permission of the Controller of Her Britannic Majesty's stationery office.

24. *Ibid.*, p. 227.

25. Frenkel-Brunswik, *op. cit.*

26. See Chapter II.

27. *Labor Force Definition and Measurement* (New York: SSRC, 1947), pp. 25–27.

28. These data and the detailed experiment are reported in H. L. Smith and H. Hyman, "The Biasing Effect of Interviewer Expectations on Survey Results," *Pub. Opin. Quart.*, XIV (1950), 491–506.

29. The description of the attitude-structure expectation experiment is taken almost entirely from the original published report of the study. See Smith and Hyman, *ibid.*

30. The writers wish to express their appreciation to Robert E. Dryden, who contributed his unusual dramatic talents in the service of survey research.

31. The writers are grateful for the co-operation of Don Cahalan, formerly of the University of Denver, Eugene Hartley, of the City College of New York, Patricia Kendall, of Columbia University, Elmo Roper, and Robert Seashore, of Northwestern University, for making subjects available.

32. For a detailed description of the survey, method of assignments, and the validity procedures, see Hugh J. Parry and Helen Crossley, "Validity of Responses to Survey Questions," *Pub. Opin. Quart.*, XIV (1950), 61–80. For the discussion of findings on interviewer effect, Feldman, Hyman, and Hart, "A Field Study of Interviewer Effects on the Quality of Survey Data," *Pub. Opin. Quart.*, XV (1951), 734–61. See also chapters v and vi.

33. Asch postulates a similar process in explaining the results of prestige suggestion experiments. The experimental subject when confronted with the difficult task of evaluating some text "feels himself under the necessity of arriving at a judgment for which he has no reasonable basis. . . . He then proceeds to clutch at whatever clues he can find" (*op. cit.*, p. 273).

34. That these experiments could not have been completely artificial, however, is suggested by the fact already reported that performance in the laboratory-setting correlated with the validity of reports obtained in the course of a regular field survey.

35. The clothing item was dichotomized differently from the other three. Because of the nature of the distribution, the dichotomy was downtown purchase vs. neighborhood, no purchase, or don't remember.

36. The universe was not all of Cleveland, but merely three suburban areas making the assumption of cultural homogeneity more tenable.

37. Further support for a situational determinant of interviewer effects on these questions is presented in Chapter VI, where it is shown that parallel findings are available for another field study.

38. Air Ministry, *op. cit.,* pp. 308–19.

39. In the study of reliability of psychiatric diagnosis reported by Asch and referred to in Chapter I, the same phenomenon seems to be at work, although the data are not presented in such a way as to establish the pattern precisely. While Doctors "X" and "Y" agreed in their classification of thirty-eight patients into major diagnostic categories in only 66 per cent of the cases, the marginal distributions by major categories for the two psychiatrists seem much more similar. *Ibid.*

40. R. K. Merton, "The Self-Fulfilling Prophecy," *Antioch Review*, VIII (1948), 193–210.

41. F. Stanton and K. Baker, "Interviewer Bias and the Recall of Incompletely Learned Materials," *Sociometry*, V (1942), 123–34.

42. Replications of this experiment have been performed by two independent investigators. Friedman obtained negative findings for nonprofessional interviewers who were students. Lindsey obtained negative findings using graduate students with some past experience in interviewing. These two experiments certainly cast doubt on the *generality* of Stanton and Baker's original finding. While it is impossible to explain the discrepant findings because of the many different factors operating, later investigators suggest a number of hypotheses. See G. Lindsey, "A Note on Interviewer Bias," *Jour. Appl. Psychol.*, XXXV (1951), and P. Friedman, "A Second Experiment on Interviewer Bias," *Sociom.*, V (1942), 378–81.

43. See Chapter V.

44. D. Wyatt and D. Campbell, "A Study of Interviewer Bias as Related to Interviewers' Expectations and Own Opinions," *Internat. Jour. Opin. Attit. Res.*, IV (1950), 77–83.

45. These tests of significance underestimate the probability of obtaining the observed differences by chance when there are no true differences. The tests are posited on an assumption of simple random sampling. This assumption leads to an overstatement of the statistical significance of a difference because it fails to take into account the clustering of the cases obtained by each interviewer and the variations between interviewers with common expectations.

46. The original data are presented in Feldman, Hyman, and Hart, *op. cit.*

47. The distribution of such estimates was presented in chapter ii.

48. L. J. Cronbach and B. M. Davis, "Belief and Desire in Wartime," *Jour. Abn. Soc. Psychol.*, XXXIX (1944), 446–58.

R. Wallen, "Individuals' Estimates of Group Opinion," *Jour. Soc. Psychol.*, XVII (1943), 269–74.

R. M. W. Travers, "A Study in Judging the Opinions of Groups," *Archives of Psychology*, No. 266 (1941).

49. Some of the expectational data have already been presented in Chapter II on page 70. These were abstracted from the original article. See K. E. Clark, "A Note on the Meaning of Poll Results," *Internat. Jour. Opin. Attit.*

Res., III (1949), 109–12. The relation between expectation and ideology comes from a personal communication from Dr. Clark whose co-operation is gratefully acknowledged.

50. Wyatt and Campbell, *op. cit.*

51. For a discussion of the error-choice method, see K. Hammond, "Measuring Attitudes by Error-Choice: An Indirect Method," *Jour. Abn. Soc. Psychol.,* XLIII (1948), 38–48.

52. L. Guest and R. Nuckols, "A Laboratory Experiment in Recording in Public Opinion Interviewing," *Internat. Jour. Opin. Attit. Res.,* IV (1950), 336–52. This experiment was conducted under a grant-in-aid from the NORC project.

53. H. Fisher, "Interviewer Bias in the Recording Operation," *Internat. Jour. Opin. Attit. Res.,* IV (1950), 391–411. This experiment was conducted under a grant-in-aid from the NORC project.

54. The experiment was originally described in H. Stember and H. Hyman, "How Interviewer Effects Operate through Question Form," *Internat. Jour. Opin. Attit. Res.,* III (1949), 493–512.

55. These findings are discussed in detail in Chapter VI, and in Feldman, Hyman, and Hart, *op. cit.*

56. These data were made available to us through the courtesy of the Elmira 1948 political study.

57. This model was developed by J. J. Feldman.

58. The theory, of course, is not limited to any one respondent characteristic such as "sex." More generally stated, projection would occur where the respondent was similar to the interviewer in some significant observable respect. Sex merely provided one appropriate example.

59. Wyatt and Campbell, *op. cit.*

60. Moreover, this latter difference only borders on significance when tested by Chi-squared yielding a *P*-value of .09.

NOTES TO CHAPTER IV

1. See chap. v.

2. Albert Ellis, "Questionnaire vs. Interview Method in the Study of Human Love Relationships," *Amer. Soc. Rev.,* XII (1947), 541–53; also XIII (1948), 61–65.

3. Finger, in comparing data secured through questionnaire and personal interview methods in the study of sex beliefs and practices, concludes that on most items results secured are quite similar. Frank W. Finger, "Sex Beliefs and Practices Among Male College Students," *Jour. Abn. Soc. Psychol.,* XLII (1947), 57.

4. Helen Metzner and Floyd Mann, "A Limited Comparison of Two Methods of Data Collection: The Fixed Alternative Questionnaire and the Open-Ended Interview," *Amer. Soc. Rev.,* XVII (1952), 486–91.

5. Paul F. Lazarsfeld and Raymond Franzen, "The Validity of Mail Questionnaires in Upper Income Groups," October 1, 1945, and May 15, 1946 (Privately distributed).

6. We are indebted to John F. Maloney for the data cited.

7. Maloney, however, goes on to point out that past experience with mail questionnaires indicates that significantly higher ratings for prestige articles

and for book sections usually result from this method. This conclusion would support our view that the interviewer's presence can act as a check on any respondent tendencies toward prestige-motivated exaggeration.

8. Eli S. Marks and W. Parker Mauldin, "Response Errors in Census Research," *Journal of the American Statistical Association,* XLV (1950), 424–38.

9. C. Wedell and K. Smith, "Consistency of Interview Methods in Appraisal of Attitudes," *Jour. Appl. Psychol.,* XXXV (1951), 392–96.

10. H. Metzner and F. Mann, *op. cit.*

11. O. Larsen, "The Comparative Validity of the Telephone and Face-to-Face Interviews in the Measurement of Message Diffusion from Leaflets," *Amer. Soc. Rev.,* XVII (1952), 471–76.

12. Leo Crespi, "The Influence of Military Government Sponsorship in German Opinion Polling," *Internat. Jour. Opin. Att. Res.,* IV (1950), 151–78.

13. While this demonstration supports the view that a respondent's expressed opinions may often not conform to his private opinions, it may be that the measured data are still valid. In so far as public opinion aims to predict the *action* consequences of opinions, it may well be that opinions which are suppressed in a permissive interview situation because of fear would be even less likely to influence behavior which occurs in the more threatening real-life situation.

14. Paul B. Sheatsley, "An Analysis of Interviewer Characteristics and their Relationship to Performance," *Internat. Jour. Opin. Attit. Res.,* IV (1950), 473–98.

15. Sheatsley, *ibid,* p. 487.

16. P. Fay and W. Middleton, "Judgment of Specific Personality Types from Voice as Transmitted over a Public Address System," *Character and Personality,* VIII (1931), 144–55.

E. L. Kelly, "Personality as Revealed by Voice and Conversation without Face to Face Contact," *Psychological Bulletin,* XXXV (1938), 710–38.

G. Allport and H. Cantril, "Judging Personality from Voice," *Jour. Soc. Psychol.,* V (1934), 37–55.

17. Stuart Rice, *Quantitative Methods in Politics* (New York: Knopf, 1928), pp. 51–70.

Irvin Child, "Judging Occupation from Printed Photographs," *Jour. Psychol.,* VII (1936), 117–18.

Lawrence Gahagan, "Judgments of Occupations from Printed Photographs," *Jour. Soc. Psychol.,* IV (1933), 128–34.

18. Gertrude Abramson, *The Effect of a Stereotype on Judgment of Group Membership* (Master's thesis, New York University, 1949). This study was conducted under the auspices of the Department of Scientific Research of the American Jewish Committee.

19. Herbert Hyman in F. Mosteller *et al., The Pre-Election Polls in 1948* (New York: SSRC, 1949), chap. 7.

20. H. F. Gosnell and S. DeGrazia, "Critique of Polling Methods," *Pub. Opin. Quart.,* VI (1942), 378–90.

21. For example, see Hadley Cantril, *Gauging Public Opinion* (Princeton University Press, 1944), pp. 115–18.

22. The middle-class character of the interviewer labor market is such that

it is difficult to find interviewers who really represent the poorest stratum. Consequently our C and D interviewer group are not sufficiently like D respondents to permit a crucial test of the hypothesis.

23. The general hypothesis that unfavorable situational factors would be less obstructive for experienced interviewers is supported by other phases of this research. See Feldman, Hyman, and Hart, "Interviewer Effects on the Quality of Survey Data," *Pub. Opin. Quart.,* XV (1951), 749–50, and Stember and Hyman, "Interviewer Effects in the Classification of Responses," *Pub. Opin. Quart.,* XIII (1949), 680–82.

See also the finding of Katz on how experience reduced the effect of class disparity, reported later in this section.

24. See Paul B. Sheatsley, "An Analysis of Interviewer Characteristics and their Relation to Performance; Part III," *Internat. Jour. Opin. Attit. Res.,* V (1951), 206.

25. While the positive relationship between rapport and validity seems supported, this relationship should not be regarded as a continuous and linear one. There may exist a condition of over-rapport which may act as a biasing condition in an interview situation, as pointed out in Chapter II. It is interesting to note that Miller also observed the possible negative effects of high rapport in using participant observation techniques in a study of labor union members. See S. M. Miller, "The Participant-Observer and 'Over-Rapport,'" *Amer. Sociol. Rev.,* XVII (1952), 97–99.

26. For a comparison of reliable and unreliable respondents, see Herbert Stember, "Which Respondents are Reliable?" *Internat. Jour. Opin. Attit. Res.,* V (1951), 475.

27. H. Cantril, *op. cit.,* p. 115, for a previous report of some of the findings.

28. S. Stouffer *et al., The American Soldier* (4 vols.). (Princeton: Princeton University Press, 1949), p. 720. That reactional effects arising from disparities in the color of the interviewer and respondent may be a general problem in research situations other than the survey interview is evidenced by a study of the influence of Negro vs. white examiners on the productivity of Negro and white subjects responding to the thematic apperception test. The tentative findings support the fact that the color of the examiner has an effect in particular instances. See E. Schwartz, B. Riess, and A. Cottingham, "Further Critcal Evaluation of the Negro Version of the TAT," *Jour. Proj. Tech.,* XV (1951), 394–400.

29. D. Robinson and S. Rohde, "Two Experiments with an Anti-Semitism Poll," *Jour. Abn. Soc. Psychol.,* XLI (1946), 136–44.

30. Apparently when interviewers do not "look Jewish" the effect of adding a non-Jewish name makes little difference. However, differences when the names are used in both cases could result from the possibly greater social involvement present when an interviewer uses *any* kind of name to introduce himself. This could operate so as to reduce the frequency of anti-Semitic responses.

31. We are indebted to Don Cahalan for these data.

32. This survey was sponsored by the Department of Scientific Research of the American Jewish Committee.

33. Pixie S. Wilson and Virginia Barker, "The Campaign Against Vene-

real Diseases," Wartime Social Survey, Ministry of Information, January 1944. (Mimeo.)

A related finding is reported by Curtis and Wolf in studying the effect of the sex of the interviewer on Rorschach responses. These investigators obtained significant differences in the proportion of sex replies to the Rorschach for male subjects tested by males as compared with those tested by females. Henry S. Curtis and Elizabeth B. Wolf, paper read at the 59th Annual Meeting of the APA, reported in the *American Psychologist*, VI (1951), 345.

However, it should be noted that an equivalent experiment reports negative results. See P. Alden and A. Benton, "Relationship of Sex of Examiner to Incidence of Rorschach Responses with Sexual Content," *Jour. Project. Tech.*, XV (1951), 231–34.

34. Daniel Katz, "Do Interviewers Bias Polls?" *Pub. Opin. Quart.*, VI (1942), 248–68.

35. H. Hyman and P. B. Sheatsley, "The Kinsey Report and Survey Methodology," *Internat. Jour. Opin. Attit. Res.*, II (1948), 183–95.

36. A. Rose, "Public Opinion Research Techniques Suggested by Sociological Theory," *Pub. Opin. Quart.*, XIV (1950), 205–14; also see R. K. Merton, "Selected Problems of Field Work in the Planned Community," *Amer. Sociol. Rev.*, XII (1947), 304–12.

37. This survey was conducted by the Division of Surveys of the Office of War Information under the direction of Elmo C. Wilson.

38. The cultural milieu, of course, also defines the meaning of any interview situation, irrespective of the characteristics of the individual interviewer as suggested previously.

NOTES TO CHAPTER V

1. We are indebted to Professor Hadley Cantril, Mrs. Elizabeth Deyo, and Mrs. Mildred Strunk of the Princeton Office of Public Opinion Research for allowing us to use these data.

2. In appraising degree of stability of bias by reference to this co-efficient, one should not use the maximum theoretical value for rho of 1.00 as the criterion of complete interviewer stability. Sampling variation from survey to survey would reduce the value below unity even if bias were completely consistent.

3. On the basis of the analysis of these rank-order correlations, it seems clear that the cause of the change is not some orderly growth or training process within the interviewers. If it were, one would expect the consistency to decrease regularly, as the surveys that are paired for the computations are further apart in time. This is not found to occur. For example, the median rho for pairs of *adjacent* surveys is .52. For pairs of surveys, six surveys apart, the value is .53, for pairs which are seven surveys apart, the value is .50. Consequently, the situational factors that reduce consistency do not seem to involve orderly growth or learning. They are just as likely to change in short as in long periods of time.

4. S. Asch and H. A. Witkin, "Studies in Space Orientation," *Journal of*

Experimental Psychology, XXXVIII (1948), 325–37, 455–77, 603–14, 762–82. See also, H. A. Witkin *et al.*, Personality through Perception (New York: Harper and Brothers, 1954).

5. These data were made available to us through the courtesy of the 1948 Political Study.

6. The detailed discussion of these data and the experimental procedure used for studying interviewer effects is reported in Feldman, Hyman, and Hart, "A Field Study of Interviewer Effects on the Quality of Survey Data," *Pub. Opin. Quart.*, XV (1951), 734–61. See also Chapter VI.

7. The details of this study are reported in "A Study of Interviewer Competence," *Internat. Jour. Opin. Attit. Res.*, I, No. 1 (1947), 17–30. We are indebted to Professor Guest for the special analysis of changes in the course of the temporal process.

8. This study was conducted by the Department of Scientific Research of the American Jewish Committee with the assistance of a grant-in-aid from the National Opinion Research Center. We are grateful to the committee for their courtesy in making the data available.

9. See Adorno *et al.*, *The Authoritarian Personality* (New York: Harper, 1950).

10. For detailed treatment of this development, see S. S. Stevens, *Handbook of Experimental Psychology* (New York: Wiley, 1951).

11. See, for example, on question form: S. C. Menefee, "The Effect of Stereotyped Words on Political Judgments," *Amer. Soc. Rev.*, I (1936), 614–21; E. Raskin and S. Cook, "A Further Investigation of the Measurement of an Attitude toward Fascism," *Jour. Soc. Psychol.*, IX (1938), 201–6; E. R. Wembridge and E. R. Means, "Obscurities in Voting upon Measures Due to Double-Negative," *Jour. App. Psychol.*, II (1918), 156–63.

12. One could isolate the influence of situation on *all* interviewers rather than on respondents per se by wire recording of real interviews, or by laboratory studies of interviewer behavior in handling simulated replies under different situations, or in occasional special areas of interviewing where the task cannot involve the respondent—e.g., field ratings. All these procedures are used and referred to in the text, but are not general or practical solutions.

13. The point is underscored by Kinsey who in order to maintain the confidence of the record (and of the respondent) went far beyond the procedure of not recording names. All interviews were recorded in a "cryptic code." "The code is never translated into words. . . . Each interviewer has memorized the code, and there is no key to the code in existence." With respect to the code identification of the respondent for purposes of follow-up, "it is the judgment of the cryptographer who tried to break the final form that decoding would be impossible unless one had access to all of the histories and all of the files for a considerable period of time. . . . It should be added that the histories are kept behind locked doors and in fireproof files with locks that are unique for this project." A. C. Kinsey, W. B. Pomeroy, and C. E. Martin, *Sexual Behavior in the Human Male* (Philadelphia, Saunders, 1948), p. 44.

14. J. B. Maller, "The Effect of Signing One's Name," *School and Society*, XXXI (1930), 88.

15. W. C. Olson, "The Waiver of Signature in Personal Reports," *Jour. App. Psychol.*, XX (1936), 442.

16. R. F. Fischer, "Signed vs. Unsigned Questionnaires," *Jour. App. Psychol.*, XXX (1946), 220.

17. S. A. Star, "The Screening of Psychoneurotics in the Army," in Stouffer *et al.*, *Measurement and Prediction* (Princeton: Princeton University Press, 1950).

18. J. Elinson and V. T. Haines, "Role of Anonymity in Attitude Surveys," (paper read before American Psychological Association, 1950); I. Cisin, *Anonymity vs. Identification in Studies of Public Opinion* (Unpublished Master's thesis, the American University, Washington, 1951).

19. S. M. Corey, "Signed vs. Unsigned Questionnaires," *Journal of Educational Psychology*, XXVIII (1937), 144.

20. Cisin, *op cit.*, p. 50. Italics ours.

21. H. Hyman and P. B. Sheatsley, "The Kinsey Report and Survey Methodology," *Internat. Jour. Opin. Attit. Res.*, II (1948), 183–95.

22. Personal communication from Herbert Passin.

23. Leon Festinger, "The Role of Group Belongingness," in J. G. Miller, *Experiments in Social Process* (New York: McGraw-Hill, 1950).

24. That the problem of sponsorship is not peculiar to the survey method is evidenced by the report of one ethnologist: "A considerable number of misstatements may be understood in the context of the relation of the ethnologist to the community under observation. If the ethnologist is connected with a government, especially one which is viewed hostilely by the Indians, certain information may be concealed for fear of taxation and punishment. If the Indians punish children by the whip in violation of a governmental decree, then one may expect that the physical punishment of children will probably be hidden from the observer. Or if taxation is based on harvest-returns there will be an attempt to conceal these. Similarly, if the ethnologist works out from a mission house as his center of operations, certain religious ceremonies which are disapproved by the missionaries may be concealed for a long period of time. . . . This is so considerable and delicate a problem that the ethnologist must devote careful attention to the choice of his affiliation with the outside 'they' group as well as the form of his own relations with the Indian community." See H. Passin, "Tarahumara Prevarication: A Problem in Field Method," *American Anthropologist*, XLIV (1942), 240–41.

25. S. A. Star, personal communication.

26. Significant at the .01 and .02 level respectively. A wartime study conducted by the Program Surveys Division, USDA, also found substantially negative results in comparing government and university sponsorships. (R. Crutchfield, private communication.)

27. Leo Crespi, "The Influence of Military Government Sponsorship in German Opinion Polling," *Internat. Jour. Opin. Attit. Res.*, IV (1950), 151.

28. Saul Hofstein, "Military Counseling as Practiced by the Personnel Consultant," *Family*, XXV (1945), 337–44.

29. See Richard S. Crutchfield and Donald A. Gordon, "Variations in Respondents' Interpretation of an Opinion-Poll Question," *Internat. Jour. Opin. Attit. Res.*, I, No. 3 (1947), 1.

30. Stanley Payne, "Variable or Standardized Questions?" Address to the American Association for Public Opinion Research, Princeton, June, 1951, reported in *Pub. Opin. Quart.*, XV (1951), 788.

31. For a summary of data on variability see A. Anastasi and J. Foley, *Differential Psychology* (New York: Macmillan, 1949).

32. Lester Guest and Robert Nuckols, "A Laboratory Experiment in Recording in Public Opinion Interviewing," *Internat. Jour. Opin. Attit. Res.*, IV (1950), 336. Experiment conducted with grant from NORC.

33. Paul B. Sheatsley, "An Analysis of Interviewer Characteristics and their Relationship to Performance," *Internat. Jour. Opin. Attit. Res.*, IV (1950).

34. In one pioneering study of question types, it was suggested that free-answer questions seem to show little evidence of interviewer effects. Don Cahalan, Valerie Tamulonis, and Helen Verner, "Interviewer Bias Involved in Certain Types of Opinion Survey Questions," *Internat. Jour. Opin. Attit. Res.*, I, No. 1 (1947), 63. However, the data used in this study were collected incidentally during a succession of NORC studies, and it was impossible to control such factors as time, context, subject matter, sample, and personnel in the analysis of varying question types.

35. For a full description of this experiment see Guest and Nuckols, *op. cit.*

36. For a full description of this study see the original report: Herbert Fisher, "Interviewer Bias in the Recording Operation," *Internat. Jour. Opin. Attit. Res.*, IV (1950), 391.

37. See Stember and Hyman, "How Interviewer Effects Operate through Question Form," *Internat. Jour. Opin. Attit. Res.*, III (1949), 4.

38. Feldman, Hyman, and Hart, *op. cit.* See also chap. vi for a detailed discussion of the study.

39. Shapiro and Eberhart report similar evidence for an open question involving field coding of the answers. The question called for multiple answers as to the respondent's fixed monthly expenses. Range in Mean Number of Expenses obtained from respondents by the four interviewers was 1.2–1.7. See "Interviewer Differences in an Intensive Interview Survey," *Internat. Jour. Opin. Attit. Res.*, I, No. 2 (1947), 1–17. For a detailed discussion of this study also see Chapter VI.

40. Stock and Hochstim also present evidence on the susceptibility of different types of questions to interviewer effect. They demonstrate that there is greater interviewer variance for ratings, including the rating of factual characteristics, than for questions of a factual, information, or opinion nature which are put to the respondent. See "A Method of Measuring Interviewer Variability," *Pub. Opin. Quart.*, XV (1951), 322–34.

41. F. Mosteller *et al.*, *The Pre-Election Polls of 1948* (New York: SSRC, 1949), pp. 128–33.

42. W. Turnbull, "Secret vs. Nonsecret Ballots," in H. Cantril, *Gauging Public Opinion* (Princeton: Princeton University Press, 1944), 77–82.

43. R. A. Kemper and R. L. Thorndike, "Interview vs. Secret Ballot in the Survey Administration of a Personality Inventory," *American Psychologist*, VI (1951), 362 (abstract). The attenuation of the effect when total scale scores are used bears on the point elaborated in Chapter VII.

For another study of the problem, see R. A. Kemper, "Secret Ballots, Open Ballots, and Personal Interviews in Opinion Polling" (Unpublished Doctoral Dissertation, Columbia University, 1950).

44. Helen V. Huth, *The Effect of a Deliberative Interviewing Technique on a Public Opinion Survey* (Master's thesis, University of Denver, 1949). (Done under grant from NORC.)

45. Leo Crespi, "The Cheater Problem in Polling," *Pub. Opin. Quart.*, IX (1945), 431.

46. Paul B. Sheatsley, "Some Uses of Interviewer-Report Forms," *Pub. Opin. Quart.*, XI (1947), 601.

47. Stanley Payne, *The Art of Asking Questions* (Princeton: Princeton University Press, 1951), p. 51.

48. Herbert Fisher, *op. cit.*, p. 410.

49. A. T. Poffenberger, *Applied Psychology* (New York: Appleton, 1927).

50. Based on the study of 150 members of the current staff described in Chapter II. The two groups compared are 50 interviewers who have completed less than six surveys for NORC and 49 interviewers who have completed thirty or more such surveys.

51. Paul B. Sheatsley, "The Influence of Sub-Questions on Interviewer Performance," *Pub. Opin. Quart.*, XIII (1949), 310–13.

52. Maccoby, in reporting on the long experiences of the Survey Research Center with surveys of consumer finances, notes these same problems. She remarks: "Consumers in the United States will not discuss their finances as readily as they will give their opinions on social and political questions." She also describes the variety of situational and interviewing factors which aid in the conduct of such inquiries. See "Interviewing Problems in Financial Surveys," *Internat. Jour. Opin. Attit. Res.*, I, No. 1 (1947), 31–39.

53. In an effort to determine to what extent the frequency of interviewers' anticipated objections to particular questions represented the frequency with which they would object if they actually had to ask such questions, NORC included two of the questions in Table 51 in a national survey in January, 1952, and obtained interviewer reactions to the actual experience. Although the interviewers used are not identical with the group reported, and only 75 in number rather than 150, the comparisons between hypothetical attitudes and actual attitudes reveal that at least for one of the questions actual objection runs somewhat higher than hypothetical objection. Only 72 per cent of the interviewers actually offered no objections to asking the question "Can you whistle?", while 95 per cent actually had no objections to the question in the table concerning Russia and Yugoslavia.

54. As one interviewer put it when explaining why he preferred free-answer questions: "I guess I'm lazy about trying to get at the exact idea that will enable me to code."

55. See, for example, H. R. McGarvey, "Anchoring Effects in the Absolute Judgment of Verbal Materials," *Archives of Psychology*, No. 281 (1943).

56. It is common practice in NORC surveys to instruct the interviewer to write in any comments the respondent makes, whenever he is doubtful of the proper classification. These comments provide some check on the inter-

viewer's judgment. However, some polling organizations discourage the practice of taking down comments.

57. Herbert Stember and Herbert Hyman, "Interviewer Effects in the Classification of Responses," *Pub. Opin. Quart.*, XIII (1949), 669.

58. Since the same respondents are answering all questions and the same interviewers are using both forms, the Chi-squareds may be intercorrelated, and the validity of the aggregate test might be questioned. However, there seems clearly a significant difference, in view of the two questions which yielded P-values of .01 for the inexperienced interviewers.

59. Those who had completed twenty or more NORC surveys were regarded as having had long experience, and those who had completed three or less surveys were regarded as inexperienced. This great discrepancy in level of experience, we felt, would compensate for any crudities in regarding each NORC survey (no matter how much work had been entailed) as one unit of experience. The number of interviews available for the comparisons within the experienced group ranged from 573 to 580 and for the inexperienced, from 307 to 316. The exact P-values were determined by interpolation from R. A. Fisher's tables.

60. Cahalan, Tamulonis, and Verner, *op. cit.*

61. Herbert Stember and Herbert Hyman, "How Interviewer Effects Operate through Question Form," *Internat. Jour. Opin. Attit. Res.*, III (1949), 493–512.

62. P-value is .58.

63. Hadley Cantril, *Gauging Public Opinion* (Princeton: Princeton University Press, 1944), p. 118.

This quotation from Cantril, though it does imply that the biases cancel, does not adequately convey the basis for Mosteller's conclusion that bias will generally be minimized by having an equal distribution of interviewers biased in opposite directions. Mosteller (in the Appendix of Cantril's book) considers the case where the opposite biases may not cancel. Given then a knowledge of the *total* bias which cannot be broken into pro and con components, the limits of the possible bias, positive and negative, are equidistant from the "true value." It is on these grounds of symmetry of limits for the noncanceling case, as well as zero bias for the canceling case with equal distribution of interviewers, that Mosteller bases his conclusion.

Nevertheless, it may be that consideration of best possible distributions of interviewers should be based not on possible limits of bias with no assumptions about relative magnitudes of the contrasted biases, but rather on the hypothesis of a systematic resultant majority bias. See Chapter VII.

64. For a summary of this literature see M. Sherif and H. Cantril, *The Psychology of Ego-Involvement* (New York: Wiley, 1947), chap. 3.

65. For a full description of the method used in this study see chap. III.

66. We are indebted to Herbert C. Ludeke of Curtis Publishing Company for making these data available to us.

NOTES TO CHAPTER VI

1. It should be noted that gross interviewer effect may not be the same as the *total number of errors* occurring in a survey. Many errors, in the

sense of departures from prescribed or ideal procedure, may occur in early phases of the interview without producing a discrepancy between the true response and the end-product answer recorded in the interview. The error in such instances is not "effective" error and not subsumed under the concept of "gross error."

2. On the legitimacy of certain interviewing norms as avenues to viewing valid data, see Chap. I.

3. In the Marks and Mauldin study, there is a clear demonstration, for given characteristics, of the way in which net effects can be much smaller than gross effects due to canceling of component errors. Eli S. Marks and W. Parker Mauldin, "Response Errors in Census Research," *Journal of the American Statistical Association*, XLV (1950), 424–38.

4. A vivid illustration of the difficulty surrounding such appraisals of the relative merits of the contrasted methods is presented in Chapter IV, in the discussion of the Lazarsfeld-Franzen study, which involved the comparison of two methods of enumeration.

5. See Ferber and Wales for the use of such an assumption in estimating and adjusting results for net effects. Robert Ferber and Hugh Wales, "Detection and Correction of Interviewer Bias," *Pub. Opin. Quart.*, XVI (1952), 107–27.

6. See, for example, the quality check procedures of the Census Bureau, in Marks and Mauldin, *op. cit.*, or the Katz study, where the subgroup of most experienced interviewers was taken as a criterion. Daniel Katz, "Do Interviewers Bias Polls?" *Pub. Opin. Quart.*, VI (1942), 248–68.

7. It should be noted that studies of this design can be intended simply to measure "inter-interviewer variation" (the class of measurement to be discussed in the next section), practically disregarding differential net interviewer effect. In many cases, it is not clear whether a study is intended to examine differential net effects, inter-interviewer variation, or both.

8. The studies that were examined are listed in Appendix C.

9. Hugh J. Parry and Helen M. Crossley, "Validity of Responses to Survey Questions," *Pub. Opin. Quart.*, XIV (1950), 61–80.

10. For a suggestive demonstration of the differential extent of gross effects among interviewers, the reader is referred to Marks and Mauldin, *op. cit.*, p. 434. Gross effects were determined by the criterion of a quality check interview. The experiment was replicated in several counties with different crews of interviewers. While respondent differences between counties are confounded with interviewer differences, nevertheless, it is interesting that the gross errors varied markedly between counties.

11. It is possible that given interviewers might obtain consistently invalid results in so far as invalidity is a generalized characteristic of respondents. While the interpenetrating sample design over the *long run* should operate to give different interviewers equivalent numbers of generally "honest" respondents, through the accident of sampling there might be a variation in the proportions of such respondents obtained. However, it is hard to imagine that this respondent factor alone through sampling variation would account for the moderately high intercorrelations in the validity of answers over interviewers.

12. For a fuller discussion of the Chi-squared tests, the inter-question

correlations over interviewers, and the influence of experience, see: J. J. Feldman, H. Hyman, and C. W. Hart, "A Field Study of Interviewer Effects on the Quality of Survey Data," *Pub. Opin. Quart.*, XV (1951), 734–61. For a fuller discussion of the relation between performance on the attitude-structure expectations test and the eliciting of invalid responses, see: H. L. Smith and H. Hyman, "The Biasing Effect of Interviewer Expectations on Survey Results," *Pub. Opin. Quart.*, XIV (1950), 491–506.

13. L. Guest, "A Study of Interviewer Competence," *Internat. Jour. Opin. Attit. Res.*, I, No. 4 (1947), 17–30.

14. Examples of types of "bad" probes were: offering respondent alternatives in the probe which should not be offered; asking a probe which was irrelevant to the objective of coding that particular reply, suggesting within the probe that the respondent's opinion fell closer to an end of the scale than respondent had previously indicated. Examples of "good" probes were: requests for elaboration of answer, repetition of the question, repetition of the alternative choices.

15. This canceling of gross effects is clearly demonstrated in the study by Marks and Mauldin, *op. cit.*

16. On the question of individual differences in error tendencies, the reader is also referred to Chapter VII.

17. American Jewish Committee, Department of Scientific Research (unpublished manuscript).

18. These twelve interviewers interviewed an average of twelve uncoached respondents each.

19. Frederick Mosteller, "The Reliability of Interviewers' Ratings," in H. Cantril, *Gauging Public Opinion* (Princeton: Princeton University Press, 1944), pp. 98–106.

20. This study was done in co-operation with the Bureau of Applied Social Research, Columbia University.

21. For the opinion data, we cannot regard the total unreliability as indicative of gross effect, since opinions may well change in time. However, this fact should not jeopardize the analysis of systematic effects over time, since whatever real change has occurred should be a constant in the comparison.

22. An alternative method would be to use the ratio of the number of respondents either mentioning "courageous" on both surveys or on neither survey to the total number of respondents. But the reliability percentage computed in this fashion is to some extent a function of the proportions of respondents mentioning the attribute on each of the surveys. As this proportion approaches 50 per cent, reliability computed in this fashion tends to diminish.

23. All the major studies in the literature that were examined are listed in Appendix C.

24. The two subsamples within a block were not random but geographically systematic samples. However, low correlation of responses for adjacent households, determined empirically, and some losses due to refusals and not-at-homes, probably make the sampling variances approximate those of random samples, so that the Chi-squared test should be a reasonably accurate test of significance.

25. Since we have used only the Chi-squareds cumulated over the ten blocks in this analysis, the Yates continuity correction has not been used on the assumption that the correction would overcompensate for the only minor discontinuity in the distribution of the cumulated statistic. See W. G. Cochran, "The Chi-squared Correction for Continuity," *Iowa State Journal of Science*, XVI (1942).

26. Feldman, Hyman, and Hart, *op. cit.*

27. Results on the field ratings and open-ended questions have already been discussed in chapter V.

28. Both of these findings are discussed at length in Chapter V of this monograph and in Feldman, Hyman, and Hart, *op. cit.*

29. H. Cantril, *op. cit.*, chap. 8, Parts 1, 3, 4a, and 5.

D. Cahalan, V. Tamulonis, and H. Verner, "Interviewer Bias Involved in Certain Types of Opinion Survey Questions," *Internat. Jour. Opin. Attit. Res.*, I, No. 1 (1947), 63–77.

30. Variation between clusters and between respondents can be ignored because the observed variance between interviewers already contains within it the cluster and respondent variance.

31. See, for instance, D. Katz, "Do Interviewers Bias Poll Results?" *Pub. Opin. Quart.*, VI (1942); H. Cantril, *op. cit.*, chap. 8, Parts 1, 3, 4a, 4b, 4c, 5; Cahalan, Tamulonis, and Verner, *op. cit.* Although from the published material it is not clear exactly how the analysis was made, Udow, "The Interviewer Effect in Public Opinion and Market Research Surveys," *Archives of Psychology*, No. 277 (1942), seems to have been properly analyzed.

In one study (H. Cantril, *op. cit.*, chap. 8, Part 2), where interviewers interviewed non-interpenetrating samples of respondents, only the respondents of matched pairs of interviewers, interviewers with differing opinions but working in the same general area, were used in the analysis. Here again, though, the analysis was made on the assumption that the aggregates of respondents interviewed by interviewers with given opinions were simple random samples. The factors previously discussed might tend to make the sampling variances derived from the assumption of simple random selection an underestimate, while the fact that only matched interviewers were used might lead to a positive correlation of the means of the response distributions obtained by the different groups of interviewers and thus tend to make the simple random sampling variances of the differences an overestimate.

32. J. S. Stock and J. Hochstim, "A Method of Measuring Interviewer Variability," *Pub. Opin. Quart.*, XV (1951), 322–34; Robert Ferber and Hugh Wales, "Detection and Correction of Interviewer Bias," *Pub. Opin. Quart.*, XVI (1952), 107–27.

33. See, for instance, Albert Blankenship, "The Effect of the Interviewer upon the Response in a Public Opinion Poll," *Jour. Cons. Psychol.*, IV (1940); Udow, *op. cit.*; Cantril, *op. cit.*; Cahalan, Tamulonis, and Verner, *op. cit.*; F. Mosteller et al., *The Pre-Election Polls of 1948* (New York: SSRC, 1949), chap. 7.

34. J. Durbin and A. Stuart, "Differences in Response Rates of Experienced and Inexperienced Interviewers," *Journal of the Royal Statistical Society*, Series A, 114 (1951). We are grateful to Messrs. Durbin and Stuart

and Professor M. G. Kendall for making these data available to us in advance of publication.

35. P. C. Mahalanobis, "Recent Experiments in Statistical Sampling in the Indian Statistical Institute," *Journal of the Royal Statistical Society,* CIX (1946).

36. This is probably somewhat of an overstatement of the prevalence of statistically significant inter-interviewer variation in this study, since it appears that the significance tests were not made properly. Apparently, for each question, the test was made on the difference between the two interviewers who differed the *most* on that question. Thus, the most extreme of the six possible differences was selected in each case.

37. This finding is also confirmed by an excellent study executed by Daniel Horvitz. He found great variation between different interviewers (and also between different types of interviewers) in the number of illnesses that were reported to them in a morbidity study. This was, of course, essentially an open-end question situation where the results were extremely dependent on the extent of probing by the interviewer. The sound design of the study makes the results conclusive. Daniel G. Horvitz, "Sampling and Field Procedures of the Pittsburgh Morbidity Survey," *Public Health Reports,* LXVII (1952).

38. Sam Shapiro and John Eberhart, "Interviewer Differences in an Intensive Interview Survey," *Internat. Jour. Opin. Attit. Res.,* I (1947).

39. Stock and Hochstim, *op. cit.*

40. This conclusion was reached on the basis of data not presented in the published article but kindly furnished us by the authors.

41. M. H. Hansen *et al.,* "Response Errors in Surveys," *Journal of the American Statistical Association,* XLVI (1951).

42. Durbin and Stuart, *op. cit.;* N. S. Booker and S. T. David, "Differences in Results Obtained by Experienced and Inexperienced Interviewers," *Journal of Royal Statistical Society,* Series A, 115 (1952).

43. Durbin, *op. cit.*

44. The detailed discussion appeared in Feldman, Hyman, and Hart, *op. cit.,* pp. 749–50.

45. Booker and David, *op. cit.*

46. This finding gives further support to the demonstration in Chapter V that factual questions, contrary to usual view, may be more susceptible to difficulty than many types of opinion questions.

47. See, for instance, the differences in responses obtained by white and Negro interviewers discussed in Chapter IV.

48. Mahalanobis, *op. cit.*

49. For an extended discussion of different manifestations of ideological bias, see Herbert Stember and Herbert Hyman, "How Interviewer Effects Operate through Question Form," *Internat. Jour. Opin. Attit. Res.,* III (1949).

50. Shapiro and Eberhart, *op. cit.,* pp. 4, 5.

51. *Ibid.,* pp. 16, 17.

52. Ferber and Wales report similar findings of an occasional interviewer deviating markedly from the mass. *Op. cit.*

NOTES TO CHAPTER VII

1. See Chap. VI for a description of each type of error and the manner of scoring errors.

2. Assuming that the correlations were based on the fifteen interviewers rather than the thirty-three interviews.

3. Paul B. Sheatsley, "An Analysis of Interviewer Characteristics and Their Relationship to Performance—Part III," *Internat. Jour. Opin. Attit. Res.*, V (1951), 193–97.

4. L. Guest and R. Nuckols, "A Laboratory Experiment in Recording in Public Opinion Interviewing," *Internat. Jour. Opin. Attit. Res.*, IV (1950), 346.

5. Duncan McRae, Jr., "Interviewer Performance in a Probability-Sampling Survey" (unpublished document on file at the National Research Council—Social Science Research Council sampling project).

6. Assuming that social skills and intelligence are uncorrelated—and that they have about the same variance—and assuming that the social skills and the kind of intelligence required in eliciting free-answers and in competently handling the clerical aspects are the same. This example is not intended as a realistic representation of the constituents of the two abilities, but merely to show that the possession of some common elements will result in a moderate degree of correlation.

7. L. Guest, "A Study of Interviewer Competence," *Internat. Jour. Opin. Attit. Res.*, I, No. 4 (1947), 26.

8. Guest and Nuckols, *op. cit.*

9. Dolores Anne Keyes, *A Study of Interviewer Effect and Interviewer Competence* (Master's thesis, University of Denver, 1949).

10. From data given in the A.J.C. report, we calculated the correlation between total *biasing* errors and the total *neutral* errors to be .19. The bias-neutral correlations for the various kinds of error would be even smaller.

11. Guest and Nuckols, *op. cit.*

12. This suggestion is supported also by the results of the Ferber study described later in this chapter. See Robert Ferber and Hugh Wales, "Detection and Correction of Interviewer Bias," *Pub. Opin. Quart.*, XVI (1952), 106–27. Some of the interviewers obtained answers significantly more unlike their own opinions, and this phenomenon is termed by the authors as "negative ideological bias." It seems more reasonable to explain such a phenomenon on the basis of a theory of bias as random error.

13. Some evidence on the association between different types of bias was presented in the article by Ferber and Wales. They compared the bias in selection of respondents on background characteristics using judgment sampling with the bias in responses obtained in the direction of the interviewer's own opinions for fourteen interviewers. Only a moderate positive correlation of .42, not statistically significant, was obtained, and owing to certain necessary crudities in the methods of *measuring* the bias, *this* finding probably overstates the degree of association. See *ibid.*

14. One minor bit of evidence on the relationship between expectational sources of bias and the routine skill of recording answers to simple pre-

coded questions was available in the Smith-Hyman study. Interviewers were classified into two groups on the basis of the number of errors they made in coding answers to innocuous questions and compared with respect to the errors they made on two questions testing "attitude-structure" expectations. No significant relationship was demonstrated, suggesting that such a simple mechanical skill is not correlated with expectational biases. H. Smith and H. Hyman, "The Biasing Effect of Interviewer Expectations on Survey Results," *Pub. Opin. Quart.*, XIV (1950), 491–506.

15. Selden Menefee, "Recruiting an Opinion Field Staff," *Pub. Opin. Quart.*, VIII (1944), 262–99.

16. Ruth Cavan, "Interviewing for Life History Material," *Amer. Jour. Sociol.*, XXXV (1929–30), 100–115.

17. It is interesting to note that the indeterminacy in the suggestions is so great on a trait most akin to "social orientation." In chapters II and IV, we showed by a lengthy theoretical discussion how complex is the influence of social orientation in the interview. This finding reveals quantitatively how much confusion has attended this theoretical complexity.

18. Guest, *op. cit.*

19. Guest and Nuckols, *op. cit.*

20. If one considers other aspects of interviewer performance besides error-proneness, such as dependability, Guest and Nuckols' caution against selecting the better educated takes on added significance. Sheatsley clearly demonstrates that turnover increases with formal education. See Sheatsley, *op. cit.*, p. 207.

21. Herbert Fisher, "Interviewer Bias in the Recording Operation," *Internat. Jour. Opin. Attit. Res.*, IV (1950), 394–411.

22. Sheatsley, *op. cit.*, Table 94.

23. Keyes, *op. cit.*

24. These values were derived from the Allport-Vernon study of values and are defined in the terms of the test.

25. Ronald Taft, *Some Correlates of the Ability to Make Accurate Social Judgments* (unpublished Ph.D. Dissertation, University of California, Berkeley, 1950).

26. E. L. Hartley, memorandum based on research conducted in Germany, for Columbia University Bureau of Applied Social Research, Project AFIRM, under the auspices of the Human Resources Research Institute, Air University, January, 1952.

This specific finding is supported by Vernon who, after examining the general literature on the appraisal of personality, states: "There is fairly good evidence that in the long run better judges are slightly superior in . . . introverted, asocial tendencies. This latter finding may indicate that the extraverted, sociable person is less capable of standing back and viewing others impartially." See P. E. Vernon, *The Assessment of Psychological Qualities by Verbal Methods*, Medical Research Council, Industrial Health Research Board, Report No. 83 (London: H. M. Stationery Office, 1938). Quoted by permission of the Controller of Her Britannic Majesty's Stationery Office.

27. See Chap. V, especially Table 55.

28. Smith and Hyman, *op. cit.*, 505–6.

29. H. Cantril, *Gauging Public Opinion* (Princeton: Princeton University Press, 1947), pp. 147–49.

30. In the study by Fisher alluded to earlier in the chapter, he reported a suggestive relationship between motor or clerical ability, as measured by a simple recording test, and selective or biased recording in the direction of the interviewer's ideology. However, in view of the statistical nonsignificance of the Fisher finding, plus the Guest-Nuckols finding on the lack of any correlation between clerical ability as revealed on the Minnesota test and ideological bias, it would seem that ideological bias is not predicted from simple motor or clerical ability.

31. Edwin Ghiselli, "The Validity of Commonly Employed Occupational Tests," *University of California Publications in Psychology*, V (1949), 267.

32. E. S. Marks and W. P. Mauldin, "Response Errors in Census Research," *Journal of the American Statistical Association*, XLV (1950), 435. Also see unpublished reports of the office of the Statistical Adviser to the Director, Bureau of the Census, Department of Commerce.

33. Personal communication from Louis Moss, Director, British Social Survey.

34. Page 99, ff.

35. The manuals that were examined included the following: "Interviewing for NORC," National Opinion Research Center; "Manual for Public Opinion Reporters," American Institute of Public Opinion (Gallup); "The Interviewers' Guide," Institute of Market Research; "Interviewers' Handbook," Elmo Roper; and "A Manual for Interviewers," Survey Research Center, University of Michigan.

36. The detailed information about NORC interviewers cited in this section is based on the previously cited articles by Sheatsley, and on the mail questionnaire administered to NORC's current staff, described in Chap. II and Appendix B.

37. H. Cantril, *Gauging Public Opinion* (Princeton: Princeton University Press, 1947), pp. 147–49.

38. Sheatsley, *op. cit.*

39. Stanley L. Payne, "Interviewer Memory Faults," *Pub. Opin. Quart.*, XIII (1949), 684–85.

40. Bernard J. Covner, "Studies in Phonographic Recordings of Verbal Material: IV. Written Reports of Interviewers," *Jour. App. Psychol.*, XXVIII (1944), 89–98.

41. Joseph C. Bevis, "Interviewing with Tape Recorders," *Pub. Opin. Quart.*, XIII (1949), 629–34.

42. Fay Terris reports 92 per cent of questions used by opinion survey agencies are too difficult for 12 per cent of the respondents, 73 per cent too difficult for 23 per cent, and 10 per cent too difficult for almost three-fourths (73 per cent) of respondents, "Are Poll Questions Too Difficult?" *Pub. Opin. Quart.*, XIII (1949), 314–19.

43. Cantril, *op. cit.*, pp. 118, 286–88.

44. In general, it can be shown that the average distortion under Case 1

is $B/4$, where B is the total bias, while for Case 2 it is $B/4 + B(p - .5)^2$, where p is the per cent of pro-interviewers, and hence the average is smaller for an equal distribution of interviewers.

Plus biases will occur in p per cent of the cases, will range from O to $B \times p$, and will average $(B/2)p$.

Minus biases will occur in $(1 - p)$ per cent of the cases, range from O to $B(1 - p)$, and will average $(B/2)(1 - p)$.

Average net bias

$$= p \times (B/2)p + (1 - p) \times (B/2)(1 - p)$$
$$= (B/2)[p^2 + (1 - p)^2] = (B/2)(2p^2 - 2p + 1)$$
$$= B(p^2 - p + .25 + .25) = B(p - .5)^2 + B/4$$

If $p = .5$, as for an equal distribution of interviewers, this reduces to $B/4$.

45. See P. C. Mahalanobis, "Recent Experiments in Statistical Sampling in the Indian Statistical Institute," *Journal of the Royal Statistical Society*, CIX (1946), 325–70.

46. L. J. O'Rourke, "Measuring Judgment and Resourcefulness: An Interview Technique," *Personnel Journal*, VII (1929), 428–40.

47. An instance in which training resulted in apparent interviewer improvement without reducing interviewer variability is cited by McClelland. Counseling interviewers were administered a test of attitudes toward counseling practices before and after training. Although the effect of instruction in changing counseling attitudes as shown by changes in mean score on the counselor attitude questionnaire is cited in the published article, a private communication from the author informs us that training did not appear to reduce the variability for the undergraduate group—F-tests of the variance before and after the counseling course did not give significant differences. On the other hand, it is true that the graduate students, a better-trained group, seemed to have less variability than the undergraduate group. See William A. McClelland, "An Investigation of a Counselor Attitude Questionnaire," *Educational and Psychological Measurement*, X (1950), 128–34.

48. As noted in chapter VI, "gross interviewer effect" is to be distinguished from the total error which may occur in a survey. Many procedural errors may occur which do not result in a deviation between the recorded response and the "true" response. An interviewer might erroneously alter the prescribed wording of a question and still obtain the same answer, or rather, the "true" response to the prescribed question, so that the error does not become effective error.

49. J. Stevens Stock and Joseph R. Hochstim, "A Method of Measuring Interviewer Variability," *Pub. Opin. Quart.*, XV (1951), 322–31.

50. *Ibid.*

51. The formulas used here are well known. The exact formulas, taking into account the variation in size of interviewer assignments, are:

$$\sigma_I^2 = \frac{(B - A)(k - 1)}{n - \frac{\Sigma n_i^2}{n}} = \frac{(.4861)(2)}{1015 - \frac{326^2 + 346^2 + 343^2}{1015}} = .00144$$

$$\sigma_p^2 = \frac{\sigma_I^2 \Sigma n_i^2}{n} + \frac{\sigma_R^2}{n} = .000479 + .000216 = .000695$$

where n_i is the number of respondents interviewed by the *i-th* interviewer. Thus the approximation which assumes equal size of interviewer assignments gives the same result as the more exact formula to 6 decimal places in this case.

52. P. C. Mahalanobis, *op. cit.*

53. This tendency for interviewer effect to locate within occasional aberrant interviewers was also noted in the Denver and Cleveland findings reported in chapter VI.

54. This statement does not seem completely justified, since we are only sure that error due to *inter-interviewer variability* was eliminated. Consistent bias over all interviewers may still have been present.

55. Morris H. Hansen *et al.*, "Response Errors in Surveys," *Journal of the American Statistical Association*, XLVI (1951), 147–90.

56. Ferber and Wales, *op. cit.*

57. Since the subsamples for interviewers were interpenetrating, the expectation is that differences between the two distributions could be accounted for by random sample fluctuations.

58. See *"Labor Force Memorandum No. 5" of the Current Population Reports, U.S. Bureau of the Census, November 8, 1950,* or *Estadistica, March 1948, Vol. VI, No. 18.*

59. Frederick Mosteller *et al., The Pre-Election Polls of 1948* (New York: SSRC, 1949), pp. 211–12.

60. See, for example, Phillip M. Hauser, "Some Aspects of Methodological Research in the 1950 Census," *Pub. Opin. Quart.*, XIV (1950), 5–13.

In addition to the use of the re-interview data as a basis for the adjustment, the Census also will check the enumeration data against independent records such as birth certificates and presumably derive additional empirical adjustments.

61. For a detailed discussion of scaling methods, the reader is referred to S. Stouffer *et al., Measurement and Prediction* (Princeton: Princeton University Press, 1950).

Index

Abramson, Gertrude, 151
Adorno, Theodor, 78 n., 178 n.
Agriculture Department, U.S., Program Surveys Division, 187 n.
Alden, P., 167 n.
Allport, Gordon, 15 n., 151 n., 292 n.
American Institute of Public Opinion, 35, 202, 304 n., 310; *see also* Gallup Poll
American Jewish Committee, Department of Scientific Research, 86 n., 151 n., 165 n., 177–78, 209, 238–43, 247, 277–78, 281, 283, 284
Anastasi, A., 192 n.
Animal experimentation, interviewer effects, 8
Anonymity, 182–85
Anthropology, social, interviewer effects, 4–6
Arapesh study, 5
Arensberg, C., 12 n.
Asch, S., 59–60, 87, 88, 89, 91 n., 92 n., 110 n., 121 n., 174 n.
Ash, P., 11
Attitude-structure expectations, 59, 94, 99, 105–8, 111, 222

Baker, K., 122–23
Baltimore study, 165, 247
Barker, Virginia, 167 n.
Bartlett, Frederic C., 6, 59, 66
Baughman, E., 13 n.
Beale, Howard K., 13 n.
Behavior, observation of, 17
Bengal Labour Enquiry, 264, 333, 335
Bennett, J. W., 4 n.
Benton, A., 167 n.
Bevis, Joseph C., 313
Bias: and independent variables, correlations of, 301; in selection of respondents, 262
Bias-producing cognitive factors within interviewer, 58
Bingham, W., 66 n.

Blankenship, Albert, 262 n.
Bobbitt, Joseph M., 9 n.
Bogardus, E. S., 34 n., 35
Booker, N. S., 267 n., 268
Breed, W., 18 n.
British Social Survey, 303
British studies, 10
Brody, E. B., 11 n.
Brown, Marshall, 70 n., 154
Bruner, J. S., 15 n.
Bureau of Agricultural Economics, 307
Bureau of Applied Social Research, Columbia University, 246 n., 247
Bureau of Labor Statistics study, 265
Burgess, Ernest W., 34, 63 n.

Cahalan, Don, 103 n., 164 n., 195 n., 217, 259, 260 n., 261 n., 262 n.
Cameron, Donald C., 9 n.
Campbell, D., 65, 123, 128, 135
Cantril, Hadley, 16 n., 35 n., 151 n., 154 n., 159 n., 173 n., 216, 219, 260 n., 261 n., 262 n., 300, 308 n., 314, 317, 344
Carlson, Robert O., 21 n.
Carmichael, H. T., 11
Cavan, Ruth Shonle, 27, 286
Census Bureau, U.S., 96, 97, 144, 230 n., 266, 303, 345
Chapman, P. J., 13 n.
Chapple, E., 12
Cheating errors, 241–42
Chicago study, 245
Child, Irvin, 151 n.
Christie, R., 8
Cincinnati study, 246, 247, 251
Cisin, Ira, 183
Clark, K. E., 65, 128
Cleveland study, 112–14, 116, 130, 131, 253–54, 256, 257, 258, 262, 263, 334 n.
Clinical psychology, interviewer effects, 12–13
Cochran, W. G., 253 n.
Cochrane, A. L., 13 n.

Recording: errors of, 240; and role expectations, 111
Redfield, Robert, 4
Redlich, F. C., 11 n.
Reorganization of expectations, 85, 86
Respondent orientation to social features of situation, 48
Respondent reaction: differential effects of group membership disparities between interviewers and respondents, 153; differential effects of personal interaction, 149; systematic effects of group membership disparities between interviewers and respondents, 150; systematic effects of personal interaction, 139
Rice, Stuart A., 34–35, 151 n.
Riesman, David, 48 n., 50 n., 51 n.
Riess, B., 162 n.
Riley, J. W., 26 n.
Robinson, D., 163
Roethlisberger, F. J., 2, 8 n., 29, 33
Rohde, S., 163
Rokeach, M., 68 n.
Role expectations, 61, 63, 76–77, 90–91, 97, 113, 221; and task difficulty, 117
Roles assumed by interviewers as function of cognitions, variations in, 79
Roper, Elmo, 103 n., 304 n.
Rorschach responses, 13, 167
Rose, A., 168 n.
Russell, Bertrand, 14

Scale scores, use of, to minimize bias, 346
Schwartz, E., 162 n.
Seashore, Robert, 103 n.
Secret ballots, 201–2
Seeman, Julius, 12
Self-administered questionnaires, 15, 139–45, 180–82, 186
Seward, G., 17 n.
Sex-linked role expectations, 97
Shaler, N. S., 63 n.
Shapiro, Sam, 198 n., 264, 265, 271–72
Sheatsley, Paul B., 26 n., 32 n., 69, 70, 71, 72 n., 75 n., 150, 151 n., 156 n., 168 n.,

184, 193, 194, 205, 207, 279, 280, 288, 289, 291, 295, 296, 297, 307 n., 308, 309, 361
Sherif, M., 219 n.
Sheriff, A., 57 n.
Simmel, Georg, 34
Sinaiko, H. W., 12
Situational determinants, 62, 176, 179; of cheating, 242; effects arising from specific situational factors, 190, from anonymity, 181, from increased opportunity for expectational processes, 110, 116, 221, from increased opportunity for respondent reaction, 201, from lack of structure in procedure, 190, from mechanical difficulties of the task, 205, from pressures which disrupt interviewer's role, 53, 54, 55, from psychological difficulties of the task, 208, from question form, 181, 211; nature of, 171; past literature on situational factors as a guide to refinement in theory and research, 180; tests of operation of total complex of, 172
Skills: and biasing behavior, correlation of, 283; and independent variables, correlations of, 286
Smith, H. L., 42 n., 58 n., 98 n., 99 n., 107, 135, 222, 235 n., 285 n., 299, 304
Smith, K., 145
Snyder, W. V., 12
Social anthropology, interviewer effects, 4–6
Social involvement, 75, 138–39
Social orientation, 67, 74; of respondents as function of personality of interviewers, 79
Social Science Research Council, 33; study of 1948 pre-election polls, 201
Sponsorship, 185, 187, 188
Spykman, Nicholas, 34 n.
Stanton, F., 122, 123 n.
Star, Shirley A., 9, 183, 187 n.
Stavrianos, B., 5
Stember, Herbert C., 64 n., 81 n., 130 n., 156 n., 158 n., 197 n., 214 n., 217 n., 271 n.
Stern, James, 42–43, 208
Stevens, S. S., 180 n.